PSYCHOLOGICAL INJURIES

American Psychology-Law Society Series

Series Editor

Ronald Roesch

Editorial Board

Gail S. Goodman

Thomas Grisso

Craig Haney

Kirk Heilbrun

John Monahan

Marlene Moretti

Edward P. Mulvey

J. Don Read

N. Dickon Reppucci

Gary L. Wells

Lawrence S. Wrightsman

Patricia A. Zapf

BOOKS IN THE SERIES

Death by Design: Capital Punishment as a Social Psychological System
Craig Haney

Trial Consulting
Amy J. Posey and Lawrence S. Wrightsman

Psychological Injuries: Forensic Assessment, Treatment, and Law
William J. Koch, Kevin S. Douglas, Tonia L. Nicholls, Melanie L. O'Neill

PSYCHOLOGICAL INJURIES

Forensic Assessment, Treatment, and Law

WILLIAM J. KOCH

KEVIN S. DOUGLAS

TONIA L. NICHOLLS

MELANIE L. O'NEILL

OXFORD
UNIVERSITY PRESS

2006

KH

OXFORD
UNIVERSITY PRESS

Oxford University Press, Inc., publishes works that further
Oxford University's objective of excellence
in research, scholarship, and education.

Oxford   New York
Auckland   Cape Town   Dar es Salaam   Hong Kong   Karachi
Kuala Lumpur   Madrid   Melbourne   Mexico City   Nairobi
New Delhi   Shanghai   Taipei   Toronto

With offices in
Argentina   Austria   Brazil   Chile   Czech Republic   France   Greece
Guatemala   Hungary   Italy   Japan   Poland   Portugal   Singapore
South Korea   Switzerland   Thailand   Turkey   Ukraine   Vietnam

Published by Oxford University Press, Inc.
198 Madison Avenue, New York, New York 10016

www.oup.com

Oxford is a registered trademark of Oxford University Press

Library of Congress Cataloging-in-Publication Data

Psychological injuries : forensic assessment, treatment, and law /
William J. Koch . . . [et al.].
p. cm.—(American Psychology–Law Society series)
Includes bibliographical references.
ISBN 10: 0–19–518828–4
ISBN 13: 978–0–19–518828–8
1. Liability for emotional distress—United States. 2. Personal
injuries—United States. 3. Forensic psychology—United States. 4.
Traumatic neuroses—Treatment—United States. I. Koch, William J.,
1951–II. Series.
KF1264.P79 2005
346.7303'23—dc22   200500387

1 3 5 7 9 8 6 4 2

Printed in the United States of America
on acid-free paper

6/23/06

Series Foreword

This book series is sponsored by the American Psychology-Law Society (APLS), an interdisciplinary organization devoted to scholarship, practice, and public service in psychology and law. Its goals include advancing the contributions of psychology to the understanding of law and legal institutions through basic and applied research; promoting the education of psychologists in matters of law and the education of legal personnel in matters of psychology; and informing the psychological and legal communities and the general public of current research, educational, and service activities in the field of psychology and law. APLS membership includes psychologists from the academic research and clinical practice communities, as well as members of the legal community. Research and practice is represented in both the civil and criminal legal arenas.

APLS has chosen Oxford University Press as a strategic partner because of its commitment to scholarship, quality, and the international dissemination of ideas. These strengths will help APLS reach its goal of educating the psychology and legal professions and the general public about important developments in the field of psychology and law. By including books on a broad range of topics, the focus of this series reflects the diversity of the field of psychology and law.

This is the third book in the American Psychology-Law Society series. The first book, by Craig Haney, focuses on the process of jury decision making in capital cases. The second, by Amy Posey and Larry Wrightsman, analyzes the practice of trial consulting. The present book by William Koch, Kevin Douglas, Tonia Nicholls, and Melanie O'Neill centers on the civil legal process and examines research and practice in cases in which some form of psychological injury may have taken place and the alleged injured party has initiated legal action to seek compensation. The authors provide a detailed review of legal issues and assessment approaches that will be of considerable value to psychologists involved in these evaluations. But the authors don't simply focus on clinical assessment practices; they provide a comprehensive discussion of prevention and rehabilitation of psychological injuries, and conclude with an analysis and critique of current practices and a blueprint for future research. This book is an exceptional contribution to both practitioners and researchers who are involved in these often-difficult civil cases.

Preface

This book arose from William J. Koch's perception that the field of forensic mental health assessment has been largely insulated from current knowledge of the epidemiology, psychopathology, and treatment of trauma survivors. The term psychological injuries refers primarily to traumatically precipitated emotional disturbances that impair functioning and well-being. Researchers, insurers, employers, and the courts increasingly recognize the negative economic and health impact of emotional disorders. Not surprisingly, psychological injuries, particularly that of posttraumatic stress disorder (PTSD), are increasingly the subject of compensation requests or legal actions. However, assessment and treatment practices in most clinicians' and forensic evaluators' offices compare poorly to the current scientific understanding of such conditions, resulting in less than optimal opinion evidence and rehabilitative efforts. This book is meant to bridge the gap between common practice and current scientific knowledge.

The following pages address the history of psychological injuries from mental health and legal perspectives and review relevant statutory and case law. Subsequently, several chapters discuss assessment issues, including such topics as empirically based assessment tools, vulnerabilities in psychological evidence, and the assessment of malingering. One chapter provides case examples illustrating different challenges for forensic assessment, and discusses in detail cultural and gender issues that influence survivors' responses to trauma. Additionally, our current knowledge of efforts at early intervention with trauma survivors is examined, as well as the results of clinical treatment trials of both a psychological and pharmaceutical nature. Finally, suggestions for further innovations and important research themes are provided.

This book is written for a variety of readers, including forensic mental health professionals, personal injury lawyers, clinicians who assess and treat trauma survivors, and graduate students in clinical and forensic psychology, as well as for researchers in this broad area.

A number of individuals deserve acknowledgement for their encouragement, understanding, and advice. William J. Koch's wife and daughters have tolerated his frequent disappearances into his home office on the weekends and evenings to work on this manuscript when he might have been otherwise helpful to family pursuits. He is grateful for their support and the joy they provide to him through their love and diverse accomplishments. Kevin S. Douglas is grateful to his wife for her endless support, for her willingness to move from one coast to the other, and for putting her own career on hold temporarily, and to his daughter, Julianna, who was born after the book was under way, just for being the little piece of joy that she is. Tonia L. Nicholls had a childhood filled with love, laughter, and books; for this, and so much more, she is grateful to her parents, Ed and Lucille Lamy. Her husband and daughters have been endlessly supportive and understanding of her professional pursuits. Numerous claimants and patients, through their attempts to obtain compensation, articulate their difficulties, and bravely recover their functioning, provided the stimulation for many of our ideas, as well as many cogent case examples. Melanie L. O'Neill is indebted to her husband, Dominic, who continues to be her pillar of support in all academic and professional pursuits. Lynn Alden, Charles Brasfield, and Margaret Kendrick all read parts of this book and made helpful suggestions. Ron Roesch, series editor, was understanding of some of the stresses and tribulations we suffered in putting this book together and tolerant of our delays.

Contents

PSYCHOLOGICAL INJURIES

1

Definition and History of the Concept of Psychological Injury

> It is rare to find a psychiatric diagnosis that anyone likes to have, but PTSD seems to be one of them.
>
> —Andreasen (1995)

Psychological injuries are referred to in the main title of this book, implying that a great deal is known about them. This is true in some ways, but not in others. For instance, a straightforward definition of psychological injury—damage of a psychological nature—would certainly include such conditions as posttraumatic stress disorder (PTSD), about which a fair amount indeed is known. On the other hand, psychological injury is not a term that appears in any official nosological system, nor is it a legal term of art (i.e., there is no tort of psychological injury). As such, its contours are ill-defined. Yet, it offers the advantage of not being tied to any particular psychiatric or legal principle, process, code, or classification system, but at the same time communicates a meaningful category of events and responses.

This chapter presents a coherent definition of psychological injury. Psychological injuries are stress-related emotional conditions resulting from real or imagined threats or injuries that may become the subjects of personal injury litigation, workers compensation claims, criminal injury compensation, other disability claims, or human rights tribunals. Such disorders include PTSD, acute stress disorder (ASD), major depressive episode (MDE), substance abuse disorders, and a myriad of other less-defined anxiety and depressive reactions. However, not all psychological states such as PTSD and MDE are legally compensable; there must be some mechanism that attaches liability to another party. Part of the definition

3

of psychological injury, then, includes *causation* by a third party, a legal concept that will be returned to several times.

The importance of this book is predicated on the economic impact of stress-related psychological conditions. While much remains to be done in the investigation of the economic impact of such conditions, accumulating data suggest that psychological injuries result in substantial economic costs. Because we have reviewed these data before (Samra & Koch, 2002), we will only highlight particular findings in this chapter.

The costs of mental health conditions have been extensively studied in the United States. Rice and Miller (1998) noted that the total economic cost of mental illness in the United States was estimated to be $147.8 billion in 1990. Anxiety disorders (such as PTSD) and affective disorders had total costs of $46.6 billion and $30.4 billion, respectively. Indirect costs of mental health problems (e.g., lost productivity) were estimated as higher than the direct costs. Economic correlates of the prototypical psychological injury, posttraumatic stress disorder (PTSD, American Psychiatric Association, 2000), have been studied primarily in veteran populations, but one community study has important implications. Amaya-Jackson et al. (1999) found that persons with posttraumatic stress symptoms (PTSS) are more likely to report that their income poorly meets their needs, to have spent more than seven days in bed in the preceding three months, to report increased general medical and mental health outpatient visits, and to use psychotropic drugs. They also found that individuals meeting diagnostic criteria for PTSD are more functionally impaired than are those who meet subthreshold levels of PTSS. Fairbank, Ebert, and Zarkin (1999) reviewed research on employment and income for trauma survivors and found that exposure to trauma was consistently associated with worse economic outcome. It should be recognized, however, that much of the literature reviewed by Fairbank et al. (1999) concerned combat veterans and may not be generalizable to survivors of other forms of traumatic experience.

Depression is another frequently cited psychological injury in torts litigation and disability claims. Greenberg et al. (1993) estimated total annual costs of depression in the United States to be more than $43 billion, with more than half of this related to reduced productivity. Among depressed patients, work absenteeism is predicted by severity of depressive symptoms, comorbid anxiety, and psychomotor retardation (Tollefson, Souetre, Thomander, & Potvin, 1993). Not only do depression, PTSD, and anxiety reduce sufferers' work attendance and income, they also increase health care costs for these individuals. Depressed and anxious individuals generate per capita health care costs almost five times that of nondistressed people (Simon, Ormel, VonKorff, & Barlow, 1995).

With the evidence that psychological distress has significant economic implications, and having stated the basic elements of psychological injury (legally compensable psychological damage), the bulk of this chapter traces the evolution of the concept of psychological injury and summarizes its contemporary meaning. Because psychological injury inherently involves both mental health and legal aspects, we attend to its development in both circles, which at times have overlapped. Specifically, we discuss the development of the concept of trauma in the intersection between the fields of mental health and law. In addition, the changes in the law's receptivity to the construct of psychological injuries are outlined.

The Roots of Psychological Injury as a Construct

One certainty is that recognition of psychological trauma as part of the human condition is not recent; in fact, this was discussed by the most venerable of ancient Greeks—Plato. Homer, too, in his *Iliad*, similarly included reference to the psychological sequelae of war (Shay, 1991). In the seventeenth century, writers such as Samuel Pepys noted the presence of sleep disturbance and intrusive thoughts in response to the "Great Fire" of 1666 in London (Daly, 1983). Pepys wrote, "it is strange to think how to this very day I cannot sleep a night without great terrors of the fire" (from Saigh & Bremner, 1999, p. 1).

Freud's early work considered early trauma, and a person's fixation to it, the source of hysteria. A number of terms have been used in the past 150 years to describe the reaction of people to extreme trauma, whether war-related or civilian-related. The concept of psychological injury has developed over these years in various contexts. For instance, in response to railway accidents that became very common in nineteenth-century England with the advent of mass railway travel, commentators developed the concept of *railway mind* (Harrington, 1996) to describe the apparent psychological effects (anxiety, chronic pain) of such accidents. Some commentators preferred the term *railway spine* because of the medical assumption that the psychological effects were in fact caused by physical injuries to the central nervous system. This medical assumption, which was common to nineteenth-century thinking, entrenched itself in the legal processing of such cases, with physical manifestation of injury being a necessary component of recoverable claims in some jurisdictions for many years. For this reason, the term *nervous shock* was sometimes applied in the nineteenth century in order to reflect the medical assumption that psychological effects of railway accidents typically stemmed from shock to the nervous system, such as subtle compression of the spine (Page, 1885). Some professionals, however, considered these claims to be fraudulent and termed them *compensation neurosis* (see Levy, 1992).

In the United States, the Civil War gave rise to terms such as *soldier's heart, irritable heart,* and *effort syndrome.* These referred to apparently biological conditions resulting from physical stress and manifesting as weakness and heart palpitations (Tomb, 1994). *Shell shock* was commonly used to describe the psychological condition, characterized by anxiety and fatigue, of some World War I soldiers (Mott, 1919). As with some other conditions, such as railway spine, the ultimate etiology of shell shock was presumed to be physical (i.e., brain damage from exploding shells). War neurosis made the link clear between the trauma of war and the associated effect on some soldiers (Grinker & Spiegel, 1945).

Mental Health Perspectives

This section traces the concept of psychological injury from a mental health perspective, focusing on the diagnoses of PTSD and ASD, to which it is closely aligned. As Stone (1993) noted, no other diagnosis comes close to PTSD in terms of impact on the legal system. Given its preeminence among psychological injuries, and spotlight in the law, described below is what we perceive to be the major controversies surrounding PTSD. We start, however, with a brief history of its development.

We return to the war theme, which unfortunately has given the mental health field much to learn about the effects of trauma. During the 1940s, some of the more influential psychiatrists actually served in the military—during and after World War II—hence directing the psychiatric spotlight onto stress reactions from combat (Kardiner, 1947). Consequently, Gross Stress Reaction appeared in the *Diagnostic and Statistical Manual of Mental Disorders* (DSM-I) in 1952 (American Psychiatric Association, 1952), described as a temporary state elicited by extreme environmental conditions. The DSM-II, published during the early to middle stages of the Vietnam War (American Psychiatric Association, 1968), dropped Gross Stress Reaction, and in fact had no other event-related disorder. As Scott (1990) noted, the primary psychiatrists behind the DSM-II did not have combat experience and hence did not witness firsthand the effects of war, as the generation of DSM psychiatrists before them had.

By the time the DSM-II was revised in 1980, it was clear that many Vietnam veterans experienced some form of severe psychological reaction to their combat experiences. Similarly, research and commentary on the effects of sexual assault were increasing, leading to the construct of *rape trauma syndrome* (Burgess & Holmstrom, 1979). As such, the political and social zeitgeist was conducive to the official entrenchment of an event-based trauma diagnosis in the DSM system.

As such, posttraumatic stress disorder, or PTSD, was born. It required the presence of a stressor that was outside the usual realm of experience of most people. As noted, the nature of the stressor has changed quite substantially between DSM-III, DSM-III-R (American Psychiatric Association, 1987), and DSM-IV (American Psychiatric Association, 1994), so that it no longer requires events to be outside the realm of normal human experience. Each iteration of the DSM since DSM-III has included the stressor criterion as well as three main substantive areas of symptoms (reexperiencing, avoidance, hyperarousal).

The current DSM-IV diagnostic criteria require the following symptoms:

At least one of: recurrent and intrusive recollections of the event, recurrent distressing dreams of the event, acting or feeling as if the traumatic event were recurring, intense physiological distress at exposure to internal or external reminders of the event, physiological reactivity on exposure to internal or external reminders.

At least three of: efforts to avoid thoughts, feelings, or conversations about the trauma; efforts to avoid activities, places, or people that are reminders of the event; inability to recall an important part of the event; markedly diminished interest or participation in significant activities; feelings of detachment or estrangement; restricted affect; sense of a foreshortened future.

At least two of: difficulty falling asleep or staying asleep, irritability or anger, difficulty concentrating, hypervigilance, exaggerated startle response.

History and Controversies in PTSD and ASD
Sociopolitical aspects of trauma-related diagnoses. Scott (1990) adopted a sociopolitical interpretation of events leading to the introduction of PTSD into the DSM system, challenging the traditional psychiatric position that the disorder's inclusion was based on scientific evidence. In Scott's view, the addition of PTSD to the DSM-III, and hence its "recognition," "was profoundly political, and displays the full range of negotiation, coalition formation, strategizing, solidarity affirmation, and struggle" (p. 295).

As described above, the seeming extrascientific factors that led to the inclusion of Gross Stress Reaction in the DSM-I included several leading psychiatrists who had seen firsthand the psychological correlates of war. This was not the case when DSM-II was published, but it certainly was when the American Psychiatric Association prepared to revise the DSM-II during the 1970s. Several factors contributed to the ultimate inclusion of PTSD in the DSM-III. For instance, the grassroots organization formed in 1967 called Vietnam Veterans against the War (VVAW), a pro–veterans' rights, antiwar organization, ultimately developed into a powerful lobbying voice (Scott, 1990).

There were also a number of antiwar psychiatrists, social workers, and other professionals (such as Robert Lifton, Sarah Haley, Arthur Blank, and Chaim Shatan) who had informal connections with groups like VVAW (hence, were "pro-rights") and/or a professional connection with the Veterans Affairs (VA) administration (hence, had large exposure to Vietnam vets), and ultimately would be influential mental health professionals who advocated in the form of work groups for PTSD to be included in the DSM-III (Scott, 1990). Robert Spitzer was subsequently persuaded to consider the merits of including a disorder in the DSM-III, and included himself and Nancy Andreasen, a now-prominent psychiatric researcher, along with "pro-inclusionists" Lifton, Shatan, and Jack Smith, on a DSM-III task force on reactive disorders. After years of collecting case histories and lobbying, these task force members persuaded Spitzer, Andreasen, and others, suggesting the disorder be called catastrophic stress disorder. The rest, as the saying goes, is history, and the disorder was ultimately approved under the name of posttraumatic stress disorder.

As Scott (1990) convincingly argued, "PTSD is in the DSM-III because a core of psychiatrists and veterans worked consciously and deliberately for years to put it there" (p. 308). Without these few dedicated and politically savvy psychiatrists, PTSD may not have come to be. The dramatic impact that event-based symptomatology, under the name PTSD, has had on the mental health field and the law would likely not have occurred. As we argue, the law's reticence to accept mental injury claims lessened once there was an official psychiatric diagnosis to that effect, especially one that required the injuries to stem from a specifiable event (i.e., something and someone to blame, a key legal issue).

Andreasen (1995), many years after being appointed to the DSM-III task force for reactive disorders in the 1970s, wrote that PTSD was created to meet the needs of Vietnam vets who were returning home and needed treatment, but had no diagnosis. Over time it was realized that the original stressor, required to be outside the range of usual human experience, actually excluded many traumatized persons (e.g., crime victims, accident victims). This is no longer a feature of PTSD in the DSM-IV, which, as others have noted (Tomb, 1994), tends to emphasize the *perception* of threat rather than threat itself. Hence, a relatively minor car accident could lead to PTSD under the DSM-IV, where this would not have been permissible under the DSM-III.

These debates still play out. An exchange between Summerfield (2001) and Mezey and Robbins (2001) in the *British Medical Journal* is testament to this. Summerfield noted the sociopolitical aspects of the disorder, as described above, whereas Mezey and Robbins countered by pointing out that *any* diagnostic system is a product of the times, recognizing that cultural factors do indeed influence thinking about psychopathology. Summerfield (2002) countered with the following indictment:

> Psychiatrists serve neither society nor patients with psychiatric difficulties when they uncritically endorse the medicalisation of life (though they may well serve the pharmaceutical industry, with its vested interest in the medicalisation of the human predicament . . .). It is academic shallowness and complacency that may permit sociocultural (and often political) values and expectations to be dressed up as medico-psychiatric facts. (p. 914)

Mezey and Robbins also attempted to downplay the importance of vulnerability factors for PTSD by stating in the same breath that schizophrenia and depression also have vulnerability factors without which some persons might not develop the disorder.

The nature of the disorder. Is PTSD biological or psychological? Andreasen (1995) noted that PTSD was once considered the quintessential psychological disorder, but has turned out to have quite strong biological underpinnings, or at least correlates. However, this is somewhat of a false dichotomy, a point made by Andreasen (1995). Yehuda and McFarlane (1995) concluded that the contemporary biological research, though supportive of a construct of PTSD, was actually inconsistent with the original theory and conceptualization of PTSD under psychosocial theory and stress research. That is, biological findings have emerged showing biological processes that are not the same as typical stress responses, contradicting the claim made in the DSM-III that PTSD is a normative stress response to an extreme environmental stressor.

This leads to another question—is PTSD normative or pathological? Originally, perhaps partially to normalize the suffering of Vietnam veterans, PTSD was construed as a normative response to an extreme event. As Yehuda and McFarlane (1995) described, its addition to the DSM-III satisfied political, social, and mental health needs. As noted above, however, the biological response to PTSD is *not* the same as a normal stress response, and PTSD is *not* the normative response (i.e., 50% plus one) to almost every trauma, with the possible exception of physical torture. Further, as described in more detail below, there is now quite convincing evidence that the event itself is not the most important predictor of PTSD, but rather individual characteristics and perceptions of the event (Bowman, 1999).

Are the memories that putatively sustain the disorder subject to distortion over time? Southwick, Morgan, Nicolaou, and Charney (1997) asked this question, and observed that the more severe the PTSD symptomatology among Gulf War vets, the more inaccurate and distorted were the memories of traumatic events. That is, approximately 70% of a sample of Gulf War vets reported events 2 years posttrauma that they had failed to report one month posttrauma. These findings have important implications for what the traumatology field holds as accepted knowledge, and question the wisdom of relying upon retrospective recall as a methodological feature of studies. Nemiah (1995) echoed this sentiment, remarking that such designs can confuse cause and effect. Retrospective designs can make disentangling the event and preexisting personality or emotional pathology difficult. One should note that the low reliability of retrospective memory is not unique to compensation seeking samples, but appears to be common in the general population (see chapter 7 for a full discussion).

DSM vs. ICD systems. Two main nosological systems for mental disorders exist—the *Diagnostic and Statistical Manual for Mental Disorders* published by the American Psychiatric Association (fourth edition published in 1994; Textual Revision, or TR, published in 2000, and the *International Classification of Diseases* [ICD], the 10th edition of which was published in 1992 by the World Health Organization). Although some attempt was made in recent revisions of both systems to promote their convergence, important differences exist that can result in different prevalence estimates of disorder. This has implications for the general scientific body of knowledge on disorders, since their identification and incidence is partially method-dependent.

For example, Peters, Slade, and Andrews (1999) observed that the ICD system tends to produce approximately twice as many PTSD diagnoses as does the DSM system (based on 1,300–1,500 interviews with a "disorder-enriched" population). In this study, the concordance between the systems was 35%. The DSM and ICD systems differ in two important respects that lead to such differences. First, the DSM system requires that distress or impairment be present, and the ICD does not. The DSM also requires numbing of general responsiveness as part of its symptomatology and the ICD does not (although the ICD does describe it as a frequent concurrent feature of the disorder). Peters et al. (1999) pointed out that concordance would rise to 56% if changes were made to bring these two differences closer together.

Some of the individuals involved in actually writing the DSM (First & Pincus, 1999) argued that Peters et al. (1999) overstated the problem. They pointed out that Peters et al. used an inappropriate version of ICD-10 (the research version rather than the version for general clinical use) because the ICD-10 clinical version actually includes the numbing symptom that is excluded from the research version. They further argued that the DSM simply rests on more solid scientific footing in terms of how diagnostic categories were defined, refined, and tested.

Other classification differences include the discouragement in ICD of multiple concurrent diagnoses, in contrast to the encouragement in DSM to do so (Shalev, 2001). This has implications for the degree of comorbidity observed with PTSD, and, generally, our understanding of the nature of the disorder. Most North American–based studies of PTSD observe high comorbidity with other anxiety disorders, mood disorders (especially major or unipolar depression), personality disorders, and substance-related disorders. In adolescents, PTSD is often comorbid with attention deficit hyperactivity disorder (ADHD) (Weinstein, Staffelbach, & Biaggio, 2000). This high degree of comorbidity has led some to question the necessity and integrity of PTSD as a distinct disorder, and propose rather that it is part of a larger construct such as negative affectivity (Bowman, 1999; Watson, 1999), a point we return to later. Watson (1999) described anxiety disorders generally within a hierarchical model, with negative affectivity common to each, and each involving a unique construct.

The nature of Criterion A—the stressor. Because PTSD and, later, ASD essentially codified what had been observed in humans for millennia—that mental and emotional functioning can be disturbed by dangerous or traumatic events—each iteration of the DSM that has included PTSD (since the DSM-III) has by necessity included a stressor that must be present in order to diagnose the disorder. Even the first DSM made reference to a stressor in the context of Gross Stress Reaction disorder, though PTSD had yet to be officially recognized. The nature of the stressor for PTSD has changed, quite substantially, in every iteration of the DSM since the DSM-III (when it was first introduced). It has done so not without some controversy, leading some commentators to question the integrity of the disorder when its criteria shift so rapidly.

Since the DSM-III, the stressor criterion arguably has broadened substantially. In the DSM-III, the stressor was required to be outside the realm of usual human experience. In the DSM-III-R (American Psychiatric Association, 1987), the stressor was required to cause significant distress in almost anyone. The DSM-IV (1994) changed yet again, so that there are now two stressor criteria, one detailing possible types of stressors, and the other requiring the subject's response to include fear, helplessness, or horror. This provides a subjective emphasis more so than an objective one. As Tomb (1994) described, the DSM-IV places almost as much emphasis on the perception of threat as it does on actual physical threat, perhaps leading to an increased risk of subjectivity in diagnosis, and confusion in applications such as the legal system. Further, the stressor no longer has to be outside the range of usual human experience. Breslau and Kessler (2001), based on a random sample of more than 2,000 people, estimated that the number of events qualifying under Criterion A has increased by 59% under the DSM-IV. Still, some argue that it is not broad enough, since it ostensibly omits *nonphysical* stressors such as psychological torture (Priebe & Bauer, 1995).

One of the most interesting implications of the stressor criterion has to do more with the variable response to stressors across people rather than the stressor criterion per se. That is, we know that vastly more people in the population experience Criterion A stressors than actually go on to develop PTSD. In summarizing this literature, Lee and Young (2001) reported that up to 93% of the population could be defined as having experienced a traumatic event, yet only 5–12% of the population ever develop PTSD. Some people might develop PTSD in response to a relatively minor traffic accident, whereas others could go through heavy combat, violent victimization, or even rape and not develop PTSD. This observation has led some to posit that "individual differences are significantly more powerful than event characteristics in predicting PTSD" (Bowman, 1999, p. 28). In fact, as Bowman asserted, event characteristics contribute "relatively little variance" to the development of PTSD (p. 28).

In addition, as Bowman (1999) explained, certain individual characteristics, such as beliefs about emotionality, are defined in part by group (i.e., culture) membership, leading to vastly different responses to similar events across cultures. Accordingly, Bowman noted that reports in the literature have observed seemingly discrepant outcomes; for instance, 0% of approximately 500 Israeli children showed a traumatic disorder after being locked into sealed rooms during SCUD missile attacks, whereas 100% of 23 American children demonstrated trauma after a bus hijacking. She suggested that cultural differences between Israelis and Americans accounted for this difference. As another example, there is epidemiological evidence that the prevalence of PTSD varies even across Western countries such as Australia and the United States, despite similar rates of trauma exposure (Creamer, Burgess, & McFarlane, 2001).

This possibility has interesting implications when PTSD enters the legal arena. If a greater proportion of the variance is accounted for by individual and cultural characteristics than by an event, should a wrongdoer be held responsible for the symptoms a "victim" experiences? This issue, discussed further below, often plays out legally in determinations of injury and damage causation.

PTSD across the lifespan. PTSD was developed with adults in mind. Most research focuses on trauma survivors between the ages of 18 and 50 years. Conceptually and empirically, people at both ends of the lifespan have generally been neglected. From a developmental perspective, this is problematic, since there are well-documented psychological differences across the lifespan. As alluded to above, and discussed in detail in chapter 4, numerous age-relevant psychological factors mediate the relationship between a traumatic event and PTSD; these include attributional style, cognitive processing, and emotionality. To the extent that these differ across developmental stages, the prevalence, course, and expression of PTSD might differ as well.

As an extreme example, some investigators have studied the effect of trauma in children younger than four, and whether the DSM system is appropriate and applicable to this age group (Scheeringa, Zeanah, Drell, & Larrieu, 1995). Scheeringa et al. first noted that nearly half of DSM-IV's symptoms are reliant on patient self-report, making such symptoms largely impossible to assess in very young children, a point also made by Davidson and Foa (1991). They had raters attempt to complete a DSM-IV PTSD checklist based on published case accounts of 20 traumatized children in the literature. None reached diagnostic threshold, despite obvious traumatic effects; only three children reached threshold for Cluster B (reexperiencing).

Scheeringa et al. (1995) found that the DSM-IV criteria were not sensitive enough to capture psychological distress in young children. They used empirical means to develop alternative criteria that purportedly were more age-appropriate than the DSM-IV criteria—more behaviorally based, less reliant on inner subjective experience that is difficult to access in very young children. These alternative criteria were more sensitive and more reliable than the DSM-IV criteria. Other research with 7- to 14-year-old children is consistent with the finding above. Carrion, Weems, Ray, and Reiss (2002) reported that there were no differences in terms of distress and impairment between subthreshold children and those who met all three clusters of DSM-IV's PTSD diagnosis. Interestingly, symptoms showed a greater tendency to cluster meaningfully in later stages of childhood (Carrion et al., 2002), suggesting again that the diagnosis is more appropriate for adults.

It is known that children and adults differ in their responses to trauma. Children, for instance, appear more likely to recollect traumatic experiences through daydreams and fantasies, and are more likely to have sleep disturbances (Benedek, 1985). Numbing is also considered less common in children compared to adults (Terr, 1985). As such, differing symptomatological phenomenology calls into question the appropriateness of the DSM system for assessing traumatic responses in children. This might be especially true for younger children whose memory, perceptual, emotional, and cognitive processes are still in development.

At the other end of the life spectrum, Averill and Beck (2000) reviewed research and theory on PTSD among older adults (aged 65+), and noted that few studies have focused on this age group, especially comparatively with other age groups. They concluded that PTSD does occur in older adults with similar symptom expression as younger adults; however, important differences emerged. For instance, some studies have reported that older adults show a more severe preoccupation, hyperarousal, intrusion, sleep disturbance, and cue-related distress, although there have not been enough systematic comparisons or longitudinal studies for definitive statements to be made. As with children, certain developmental differences between older adults and younger adults (e.g., declining memory) complicate the diagnostic process.

The role of dissociation. Dissociation has played a much more prominent role in the DSM system since the introduction of ASD in the DSM-IV. ASD requires three dissociative symptoms to be met, although critics assert that this emphasis on dissociation is not empirically warranted because it excludes a large proportion of people actually suffering from trauma (Marshall, Spitzer, & Liebowitz, 1999). That is, under the current DSM setup, many people will meet PTSD at one month posttrauma, but will not have met ASD criteria. Marshall et al. (1999) called for a return to the DSM-III feature that allowed PTSD to be diagnosed prior to one month; this, they argued, is more consistent with the extant data. Having ASD and PTSD as separate disorders arbitrarily dichotomizes a naturally occurring continuum.

Can PTSD and traumatic brain injury co-occur? A number of commentators have argued that traumatic brain injury (accompanied by loss of consciousness) precludes the possibility of PTSD, since one cannot perceive the event if one is not conscious (Price, 1994; Sbordone & Liter, 1995; Warden, Labbate, Salazar, & Nelson, 1997). Conversely, other writers have suggested that PTSD often occurs comorbidly with head injuries, as it might with any physical health condition. Thus, PTSD symptoms may follow from changes in the brain-injured person's self-concept (Wright & Telford, 1996), from a "nondeclarative memory" of the traumatic event (Layton & Wardi-Zonna, 1995), or when an "island" of memory for the trauma (e.g., hospital emergency room procedures) exists in head-injured persons (King, 1997). Alternatively, PTSD symptoms may occur in cases where the head-injured person subsequently appraises either the episode or his/her injuries as traumatic, despite no direct memory of the event (Davidoff, Kessler, Laibstain, & Mark, 1988). Consistent with the latter hypothesis, Bryant (1996) suggested that posttraumatic "pseudomemories" based on information given to head-injured subjects at a later date may behave in a similar manner to flashbacks and other intrusions, thus resulting in PTSD.

It is important in evaluating this debate to remember that a large part of PTSD involves fear and avoidance, and that not all phobias are acquired traumatically. Thus, it is possible that individuals without a memory of the specific traumatic event may learn something during their later experience that results in fear, avoidance, and other PTSD symptoms. As well, Parker (2002) has argued that the DSM-IV-TR does not adequately distinguish between PTSD and traumatic brain injury (TBI), despite symptom overlap, and hence may contribute toward diagnostic confusion. Ultimately, the critical question is the extent to which brain injury and PTSD occur together in representative samples. Some studies have examined the effects of loss of consciousness, whereas others have focused on head injuries specifically.

Studies of loss of consciousness. Ehlers et al. (1998) found that unconsciousness predicted PTSD only in univariate analyses at 3-month follow-up (it did not predict at a 1-year follow-up, or in any multivariate analyses, suggesting it had no independent predictive power). Hickling, Gillen, Blanchard, Buckley, and Taylor (1997) compared the rates of PTSD in motor vehicle collision (MVC) victims who either did or did not lose consciousness to determine whether rates of PTSD were lower among those who lost consciousness. They further tested the proposition that apparent PTSD symptoms in MVC victims who lost consciousness are actually the result of mild brain injury or concussion by comparing patients' functioning on neuropsychological tests. If what is being diagnosed as PTSD is actually the result of brain injury, then performance on these tests should be worse among MVC victims who had PTSD diagnoses compared to those who did not. Hickling, Gillen, et al. (1997) found that there was no difference in the rate of PTSD across persons who did or did not lose consciousness, or who did or did not strike one's head or suffer whiplash in the MVC. There also were no differences on the neuropsychological tests between those who met the diagnostic criteria for PTSD and those who did not.

However, Bryant and Harvey (1996) found that *lack* of loss of consciousness (LOC) did predict intrusion, but not avoidance, as measured by the Impact of Events Scale (IES). These findings are reconcilable with those of Hickling et al. (1997). In principle, persons can develop PTSD with relatively fewer intrusion symptoms (only 1 of 5 possible reexperiencing symptoms is necessary for diagnosis) relative to other types of symptoms (3 of 7 avoidance/numbing and 2 of 5 hyperarousal symptoms).

Studies of head-injured MVC victims. Ohry, Rattok, and Solomon (1996) reported that 33% of 24 TBI patients met criteria for PTSD. Parker (1996) found that more than 90% of 33 Minor (MTBI) patients had other psychiatric disorders, while Powell, Collin, and Sutton (1996) assessed that one-third of their 62 MTBI patients suffered from some anxiety or stress-related condition 3 months post-injury. On the other hand, Sbordone and Liter (1995), when comparing PTSD and MTBI patients, found that MTBI subjects did not report intrusions, hyper-vigilance, or phobic avoidance to the same extent as did PTSD patients. In larger-scale research, Bryant and Harvey (1999a, b), in a sample of 63 MTBI and 71 non-TBI patients, hypothesized that intrusions would be less common among MVC victims who also suffered MTBI. There were very few differences (2 of 17 symptoms) between those with and without MTBI—fear and helplessness during the MVC were less prevalent for the MTBI group. Importantly, these symptoms are not among those that must be present at least one month posttrauma in order for a diagnosis of PTSD to be given (i.e., they are part of Criterion A). Friedland and Dawson (2001) found that MTBI patients had *more* posttraumatic stress (PTS) symptoms on the IES at nine-month follow-up than did non-TBI patients. Bryant, Marosszeky, Crooks, and Gurka (2000) extended their research to *severe* TBI MVC victims, reporting that while only a minority (19%) of comorbid TBI/PTSD patients had intrusive memories of the trauma, 96% reported cued emotional reactivity to reminders of the trauma. Taken together, these studies are incompatible with the notion that LOC or TBI protects the victim from development of PTS symptoms.

Evidence from child samples is mixed. In one study, children with severe TBI had more PTS symptoms than children without TBI (Levi, Drotar, Yeates, & Taylor, 1999), a finding consistent with those reported above. However, Max et al. (1998) reported that fewer than 5% of their TBI participants received a diagnosis of PTSD, although 68% of them experienced at least one PTSD symptom at 3 months post-injury.

There appear to be three general conclusions from this body of research. First, the presence of TBI or amnesia for the traumatic event does not render persons immune to PTSD. Second, the majority of studies show some substantial comorbidity of TBI and PTSD (e.g., 25–26%, Bryant & Harvey, 1999a, b; Bryant, Marosszeky, et al., 2000). Third, the symptom picture, particularly in the short term, may consist of relatively fewer intrusive symptoms for MTBI than for non-MTBI persons. Further, although it appears that PTSD symptom profiles do not differ between MTBI and non-TBI MVC victims, it is likely that those with MTBI suffer additional, non-PTSD symptoms such as cognitive deficits and postconcussive symptoms (e.g., headaches), and that PTSD symptoms may potentiate both postconcussive symptoms and functional impairment. The effects of these non-PTSD symptoms on the longer-term course, remission, and treatment of PTSD remain unclear, pending empirical investigation.

Legal Perspectives

It was not until the nineteenth century that the law became responsive to psychological injuries. This development appears related in commonwealth countries to the advent of railway travel, in the same way that the mental health field started to pay attention to psychological injuries at this time. In fact, the legal history of psychological injury is closely intertwined with its mental health history. Just as psychiatrists were struggling with new concepts of event-based psychological effects, so too was the law defining a new frontier of justiciable issues and compensable injuries. In fact, the construct of psychological injury truly had a medicolegal nature to it in the mid-1800s. Not only were the medical and legal fields both trying to come to terms with the phenomenon, but also the medical field was often called upon to help evaluate the claims made by persons against railway companies.

Most of the same concepts discussed earlier, such as railway spine, are therefore relevant here as well. Chapter 2 covers the details of case and statutory law dealing with psychological injuries. In this chapter, we communicate more generally the evolution of the legal system's receptivity to, conception of, and mechanisms for addressing psychological injuries. The legal history surrounding psychological injuries (more often called mental injury in legal discourse), unfolds primarily in the context of the law of tort, and specifically in the law of negligence. For this reason, our discussion focuses mainly on tort law, but outlines other relevant areas such as workers' compensation law.

Courts historically have been skeptical of claims for psychological injury or emotional distress, for a variety of reasons. They overtly fear that such claims may be easily fabricated since there are no clear, objective markers for whether a psychological injury exists. Courts have also had difficulty determining the proper degree of compensation. As Shuman and Daley (1996) discussed, it is fairly easy to gauge the damage to a car in an accident, but how does one determine the value of the emotional suffering of parents whose child died in that car? Further, how does one prove causation of psychological injury, which is the penultimate legal question in negligence, especially when there are usually so many other putative causes at play (e.g., psychological vulnerability factors)?

Courts have had fewer problems providing compensation for emotional injuries that stemmed from traditional intentional torts, such as battery, in part as punishment for the tortfeasor. Torts such as battery have existed for centuries. A more recent intentional tort, however, is the deliberate infliction of emotional distress, in which a person can be held liable for extreme behavior designed specifically to inflict serious emotional damage. Although this intentional tort is now accepted by most jurisdictions, it was not recognized in the United States until the 1948 Restatement of Torts.

A murkier area is that of negligent infliction of emotional distress. This, in fact, was not an independent tort in the United States until 1970 (*Rodrigues v. State*, 1970). In the past, again for fear of opening the floodgates, courts in the United States and in Commonwealth countries required some sort of physical injury or impact in order to allow a claim for negligently inflicted emotional distress. Over time, the rule was broadened to include persons within the so-called *zone of danger*, or within close enough proximity to fear for their safety (e.g., standing next to the person who was hit by a car that runs off the road). Some jurisdictions allow recovery to persons who witness the death or mutilation of others—if they are closely connected to the victim (i.e., mother, father, child, sibling)—even if they were not themselves in physical jeopardy. Some jurisdictions no longer rely on the zone-of-danger concept, but have reverted to the traditional negligence principle of *foreseeability*. In other words, the law asks, was psychological or emotional injury or harm to the victim reasonably foreseeable by the tortfeasor? If so, then liability attaches to the behavior; if not, it does not. The California case of *Dillon v. Legg* (1968) spearheaded this approach when it awarded compensation to a mother who witnessed her daughter's death in a motor vehicle collision, though she was far enough away that her own physical safety was not at risk. Again, chapter 2 covers these concepts in more detail.

The "creation" of PTSD in 1980 did much to further persuade the law to compensate persons for emotional injuries. PTSD became an official, medically sanctioned disorder with a name on which the law could rest its judgments. Although the torts of intentional and negligent infliction of emotional distress both existed prior to the appearance of PTSD in 1980, its emergence was influential in shaping court decisions. As Stone (1993) wrote, "By giving diagnostic credence and specificity to the concept of psychic harm, PTSD has become the lightning rod for a wide variety of claims of stress-related psychopathology in the civil arena" (p. 29). He also argued, "no diagnosis in the history of American psychiatry has had a more dramatic and pervasive impact on law and social justice than post-traumatic stress disorder" (p. 23).

Generally, then, PTSD facilitated an already shifting legal philosophy that was increasingly recognizing the legitimacy of psychological injuries. However, one issue that the law has always struggled with, and still does, is the determination of actual causation of psychological injuries. As we discuss in chapter 2, it is not necessary to prove that an event (e.g., MVC) is the *sole* cause of psychological injury; it does, however, have to be a *contributing* cause. Because of the complicating nature of vulnerability factors for psychological injuries—which, again, some argue are more important than actual stressors in causing conditions such as PTSD (Bowman, 1999)—we spend some time on how the law has handled this challenging task.

Thin skulls, crumbling skulls, and eggshell psyches. The legal constructs of *thin skulls*, *crumbling skulls*, and *eggshell psyches* all have implications for the concept of psychological injury and the determination of causation in tort law. As described above, vulnerability factors likely account for a greater proportion of the explanatory PTSD variance than the event itself. In legalese, these vulnerability factors in essence represent the concept of eggshell psyches, a cousin of thin skulls and crumbling skulls, which refer to physical conditions. These issues arise when a preexisting condition of the plaintiff is material to the event-related injuries. Where a plaintiff was predisposed to develop some particular injury, but was asymptomatic prior to the event, the thin skull doctrine applies. In short, tortfeasors take their victims as they find them (*Athey v. Leonati*, 1996). This doctrine, applied to mental injuries, is known by the unflattering term of *eggshell personality* (*Janiak v. Ippolito*, 1985). The key legal question is the extent to which the preexisting condition, versus the event of contention, caused the subsequent ailments.

Not surprisingly, there is a fair degree of variance between jurisdictions in the United States over the degree to which preexisting sensitivity to emotional injuries bars a successful claim for negligent infliction of emotional distress. Texas appears to allow compensation of persons with eggshell psyches (*Padget v. Gray*, Tex. Ct. App., 1987). Other jurisdictions are less sanguine about compensating persons who are more than ordinarily sensitive (*Theriault v. Swan*, Maine Sup. Jud. Ct., 1989).

To be distinguished from the thin skull (or eggshell psyche) is the crumbling skull doctrine. Thin skulls pertain to preexisting, though asymptomatic, sensitivities (though in psychological terms, this is highly suspect, given that often these sensitivities or vulnerabilities will be personality-based and hence relatively invariant). Crumbling skull doctrine comes into play when a plaintiff was already experiencing symptoms that were *worsened* or *aggravated* by an accident. The tortfeasor, though still liable for causing the aggravation to the injuries, will likely secure a reduction in the award to be made. Tort theory espouses the principle that plaintiffs ought to be returned to their pre-tort positions (Waddams, 1997), and hence that defendants ought not to be required to compensate them as if they were in perfect health.

The Louisiana Court of Appeal case *Miramon v. Bradley* (1997) illustrates concepts dealing with preexisting conditions and multiple causal factors. This case involved an MVC, but was complicated by an earlier MVC as well as the plaintiff's preexisting psychological problems. After the first accident, the plaintiff was described as having difficulties with an eating disorder, as well as difficulty managing stress. She sought mental health treatment for problems related to her first MVC. The second, and less objectively severe, accident occurred while she was receiving this treatment. The treatment team agreed that the second accident led to depression, increased anxiety, fear of driving, and setbacks in treatment progress. Further complicating matters, there were additional stressful events occurring in the plaintiff's life that also affected her psychological health. About a year after the second accident (the one being contested), the plaintiff was diagnosed with PTSD stemming from her involvement in both accidents.

Issues at trial and on appeal included: (a) whether the second accident caused an aggravation of the plaintiff's preexisting psychological problems; (b) whether the second accident was, or was required to be, the sole cause of the plaintiff's injuries; and (c) the damages that the plaintiff was entitled to. The experts were unable to attribute the plaintiff's psychological problems to one or the other accident. The trial judge held that the plaintiff could not recover compensation; however, the appeal court disagreed, holding that "if a defendant's tortious conduct aggravates a pre-existing condition, the defendant is liable to the extent of the aggravation" (*Miramon v. Bradley*, 1997, p. 478). The event need not be the *sole* cause of the aggravation, and the presence of preexisting psychological vulnerabilities does not preclude recovery for the aggravation (we detail both of these topics in chapter 2).

Other cases have struggled with the issues of preexisting conditions and multiple causes that manifest themselves in somewhat different form. In *Koury v. Lanier Express, Inc.* (1988), for example, the court held that the plaintiff's PTSD was caused by the MVC she had suffered, despite the fact that she had experienced a great many traumas in her life, including physical abuse, repeated sexual abuse, rape, the witness of a murder, and a miscarriage-inducing beating at the hands of her partner. In a different vein (and country), the court in *West v. Zehir* (1997) accepted expert evidence that the plaintiff did not have PTSD, but rather had antisocial personality disorder (APD), and that this preexisting psychological condition was consistent with the defense's argument that the plaintiff was exaggerating his difficulties. Finally, in a Canadian case (*Strain v. Donesky*, 1991), the judge accepted the psychological thin skull principle, but also believed that the plaintiff's preexisting anxious personality led him to embellish his psychological difficulties (including PTSD). Although the MVC caused the PTSD, the preexisting personality condition decreased damages.

Generally, then, the law in the United States and in most Commonwealth countries has evolved from a skeptical system that disallowed claims in which there was not a physical injury, to a system quite accepting of psychological injuries, even in the presence of preexisting vulnerability factors that might have partially caused the event-related psychological disturbance. As long as the event was a *contributing*, *material*, or *proximate* cause (all concepts we return to in chapter 2), then it *legally* caused the injuries. The amount of damages may be reduced proportionally to the extent to which nonevent factors were deemed to cause the injuries. Also, if preexisting vulnerabilities led to embellishment or exaggeration, rather than true symptom expression, courts will either reduce damages further or deny the claim altogether.

Other Areas of Law

Over the years, the concept of compensation neurosis has arisen in the context of litigation for mental injuries. As the name implies, it is a nervous condition that occurs in the presence of possible payoff. Typically, compensation neurosis is raised by those who generally are skeptical of the claims made by "injured" parties for compensation. British neurologist Henry Miller (1961), for instance, has adopted rigidly skeptical positions on the legitimacy of claims for mental injury that have affected the opinions of legal players, despite being less than credible.

Workers' Compensation

Unlike the law of negligence, there is no need under worker compensation schemes to prove that the third party's behavior failed to meet some standard of care. This is sometimes called "no-fault" law. That is, it matters only that the injury was caused at the workplace while the employee was engaged in work activities—it matters not who or what caused the injury. Unlike tort law, workers' compensation law was a creature of the legislature (i.e., statute), developed, in fact, in response to the near-impossibility under common law tort laws for injured employees to recover from injuries sustained at work. Most of these statutes became active in the latter part of the nineteenth century. As discussed in chapter 2, most have provisions for mental injuries, though their strictness varies by jurisdiction.

Criminal Law

Legal commentators also have discussed the potential role of PTSD in criminal law, providing the basis for defenses of insanity, automatism, diminished capacity, or unconsciousness (Daniels, 1984; Higgins, 1991; Stone, 1993), as well as for procedural issues such as competence to stand trial. Although this is not our focus for this book, most of the assessment principles we discuss apply to forensic assessment of PTSD and other conditions in these contexts as well as in civil litigation.

Conclusions

What then, *are* psychological injuries? Well, they are railway mind, shell shock, war neuroses, hysteria, PTSD, ASD, depression, other anxiety disorders (e.g., panic disorder), as well as less-defined states of anxiety, fear, or dysphoria that are inflicted upon a person by a third party, and for which the injured party is legally entitled to compensation. It is a concept that requires *harm*, though harm of a primarily nonphysical nature (acknowledging that many psychological conditions have biophysical correlates). There is also a threshold implicit in this definition that should be made explicit. The concept requires not only harm, but *enough harm* to be protected by legal mechanisms. There must be interests protected; for example, the interest protected by the tort of battery is physical integrity, and the interest protected by the torts of intentional or negligent infliction of emotional distress is *emotional tranquility*.

There is an analogy that can be made to physical injuries concerning the degree of harm required. If you lightly brush your finger along an inch of your neighbor's arm, this technically is the tort of battery (intentional, nonconsensual contact). However, no court would award damages to your neighbor because there is no meaningful injury caused by your behavior. The "victim" was not put in a meaningfully worse position or state by the activity, and hence does not need to be restored to their pre-tort physical status. Similarly, the psychological equivalent of the (lack of) injury caused by the finger brushing (say, fleeting mild embarrassment) would not qualify as psychological injury. The challenge is to find the dividing line for what is, and what is not, compensable or *protected* psychological functioning.

It should be noted that this is an inherently *psycholegal* definition. Both psychological and legal factors must be present. We pointed out, with a tort-related example, that a third party must be responsible and that the victim is entitled to compensation; however, we must stress that the definitional components of *third party* and *responsible* can be met in a variety of ways. This is dealt with more fully in chapter 2, but third parties can include private individuals, companies, employers, governments, or other agents, and responsibility may or may not require proof, by some legal standard, of causation, negligence, intention, or mere status (e.g., as an employer in workers' compensation frameworks). The legal framework could be tort (intentional or negligence), nuisance, criminal compensation, workers' compensation, government compensation, or disability insurance. We also note that if a psychological injury is deemed noncompensable, technically for our purposes it is not a psychological injury, although it may be so from a purely mental health perspective.

2

Legal Contexts and Law Related to Psychological Injuries

> mental pain or anxiety the law cannot value, and does not pretend to redress . . .
>
> —*Lynch v. Knight* (1861)

> I am having a flashback . . . all the way to the bank.
>
> —Eden (2001)

The law has treated psychological injuries with reactions ranging from outright rejection to skeptical acceptance. Despite the controversies described in chapter 1, the concept of psychological injury has become and remains firmly entrenched in many areas of law. Mental health professionals inevitably come into contact with the construct of psychological injury within various legal contexts. This chapter is devoted to explicating the primary areas of law in which psychological injury is likely to be material and relevant, and in which mental health professionals are likely to find themselves practicing.

In particular, we discuss tort law (both intentional and negligent), workers' compensation law, antidiscrimination law (sexual harassment, employment discrimination, housing discrimination), and laws governing airline accidents. These areas cover a majority of incidents that might give rise to litigation about psychological injuries, such as motor vehicle and other accidents, criminal victimization, harassment, discrimination, workplace injuries, and a host of other circumstances that might give rise to actions in negligence (e.g., medical malpractice, mishandling of dead bodies, consumer liability).

There are numerous other legal contexts that may permit recovery for psychological injury in certain circumstances in some jurisdictions, such as breach of contract, breach of statutorily imposed duty, insurance, violations of bankruptcy stays, disability compensation (e.g., stemming from military duty), and the torts of nuisance and trespass (as well as the psychological injury that can stem from other torts in a parasitic fashion, such as battery or unlawful confinement). Although psychological injuries can sometimes be relevant in these areas, space precludes full coverage of these topics, and dictates that we devote greater space to the contexts that are most likely to be encountered by mental health professionals.

Some of these areas (e.g., tort) command greater attention than others (e.g., airline conventions or treaties), in a manner roughly proportionate to the frequency with which psychological injury surfaces as a material issue. For each area of law, we describe the salient legal issues, the legal tests that are used to determine causation, and the law's construal of psychological injury. A thorough review of case law is not feasible, although its principles and important cases are discussed.

Tort

A tort is a civil (opposed to criminal) wrong that the law deems worthy of compensation in order to restore people to their previous (pre-tort) status. The word tort stems from the Latin *tortus* (crooked), and the French word *tort* (wrong) (Klar, 1996). Essentially, a tort is a wrong caused by one party to another for which the former party is deemed legally at fault and responsible for compensation. There are two primary categories of tort—*intentional torts* and *negligence*. The defining difference lies in the intent requirement—for intentional torts (e.g., battery), the wrongdoer must be found to have intended the harm that was produced by his or her actions. In negligence, intention is not required—the tortfeasor (i.e., the negligent party) can be liable for acts she or he reasonably ought to have known would cause harm. This area of law is the genesis of the so-called reasonable man or reasonable person test—if a reasonable person would have foreseen the harm that an action might cause, then liability may attach to a person's behavior. Although the majority of tort actions are for negligence, we first discuss intentional tort.

Intentional Tort
To illustrate intentional tort, we examine the tort of battery. A battery is simply contact made by one person on another to which the second person did not consent. In practical terms, the contact has to be nontrivial. Clearly, acts that the criminal law would define as assault or sexual assault would potentially qualify for the tort of battery. As mentioned above, a person has to intend the harm that results from their action. There are two primary ways in which psychological injuries are relevant here. First, the *intentional infliction of mental or emotional distress or shock* is a stand-alone tort in most, if not all, jurisdictions. That is, if a tortfeasor intends to cause emotional shock or harm, he or she can be held liable

for it. The second way in which psychological injury can be considered under intentional tort is as a *parasitic tort*. That is, a person can be held responsible for the psychological injury they cause in the context of performing another (typically more traditional) intentional tort, such as battery. In fact, until the 1948 supplement to the Restatement (Second) of Torts, recovery for psychological injury was *only* possible through parasitic means.

Section 46 of the current Restatement (Second) of Torts states: "One who by extreme and outrageous conduct intentionally or recklessly causes severe emotional distress to another is subject to liability for such emotional distress, and if bodily harm to the other results from it, for such bodily harm." Of course, case law has attempted to discern exactly what the terms *extreme and outrageous* mean with respect to the tortfeasor's behavior, and *severe emotional distress* in terms of the effect on the plaintiff. Fox (2003) argued that the law has made the concept of extreme and outrageous, notwithstanding its subjectivity, the gatekeeper to successful actions under this tort. That is, if the conduct is proven to be extreme and outrageous, it will generally be assumed that it caused severe emotional distress. Contrarily, if it is apparent that severe emotional distress is present, but it is not proven that the conduct was extreme and outrageous, often the claim will not succeed.

With respect to the severe emotional distress component of this tort, comment j in section 46 of the Restatement (Second) of Torts describes it as including "all highly unpleasant mental reactions, such as fright, horror, grief, shame, humiliation, embarrassment, anger, chagrin, disappointment, worry, and nausea." It also states that the intensity and duration of these mental reactions is germane to severity. As such, it is clear that severe emotional distress is not limited to cases in which the presence of a psychiatric disorder is confirmed, suggesting the importance of evaluating subsyndromal psychological reactions to tortious conduct in these cases. It also implies that when a disorder, such as posttraumatic stress disorder (PTSD), is actually present, it will likely satisfy the "extreme emotional distress" component of this tort. Some of the mental reactions listed in comment j actually overlap with symptoms of several mental disorders, particularly PTSD and other anxiety disorders.

As with negligent infliction of emotional distress, the law allows a claim for third-party intentional infliction of emotional distress, as specified in section 46(2) of the Restatement (Second) of Torts: "Where such conduct is directed at a third person, the actor is subjected to liability if he intentionally or recklessly causes severe emotional distress (a) to a member of such person's immediate family who is present at the time, whether or not such distress results in bodily harm, or (b) to any other person who is present at the time, if such distress results in bodily harm."

Third-party intentional infliction of emotional distress has been applied successfully in the context of domestic violence. In *Bevan v. Fix* (2002), the Wyoming

Supreme Court, in overturning a lower court's decision to summarily dismiss the claim, held that children exposed to domestic violence could have a claim of third-party intentional infliction of emotional distress. In this case, two children visually witnessed part of an attack on their mother by her boyfriend, and heard other parts of it. Mental health professionals noted that both children suffered distress related to the event. One child was diagnosed with PTSD, and the other with dysthymia (the latter suggesting that disorders other than PTSD or major depression may constitute the "severe emotional distress" component of the law), which the Supreme Court held constituted sufficient evidence for emotional distress to preclude summary dismissal on this point. In *Bevan*, being "present" was not deemed to require visual observation of an entire incident, but rather allowance was made for contemporaneously experiencing an event through senses other than vision.

It is likely that intentional torts more likely stem from behavior that is clearly criminal in nature, such as the tort of battery arising from a criminal assault or sexual offense, or the tort of unlawful confinement arising from the crime of kidnapping. For this reason, these tortious acts in principle could also form the basis for compensation under many jurisdictions' criminal compensation laws.

Negligence

Psychological injury cases more commonly find themselves in the legal framework of negligence. The vast majority of accidental injuries (e.g., motor vehicle accidents, "slip and fall" accidents, medical accidents) give rise to causes of action in negligence, not intentional torts.

Several elements must be proved by the plaintiff in any negligence case: (1) that a duty of care was owed to the plaintiff; (2) the standard of care in the given context; (3) that the defendant's behavior fell below, or breached, the duty of care; (4) that the plaintiff was injured in some legally relevant way; (5) that the defendant's behavior caused the injury; and (6) that the plaintiff suffered damages (Restatement (Second) of Torts, s. 281–282). For mental health professionals acting within a civil lawsuit, issues 4, 5, and 6 are most germane to their role. Duty of care, standard of care, and breach of duty are more in the realm of legal decision makers (although mental health professionals might be asked to comment on the standard of care for a given issue). Readers are referred to landmark cases and sources of law (*Brown v. Kendall*, 1850; *Donoghue v. Stevenson*, 1932).

This book is most concerned with regard to the injury or damages suffered by a plaintiff. Here, we are concerned about psychological injuries, of which PTSD is just one example. Legally, psychological injuries such as PTSD, or mental anguish more broadly, have been termed, variously, *emotional shock*, *nervous shock*, *psychiatric damage*, or *emotional injury* (Linden, 1997; Melton, Petrila, Poythress, & Slobogin, 1997). In chapter 1, we reviewed the history of this concept, and the reticence with which it has historically been received by the law. In essence, courts in both the United States and Canada were hesitant to award damages for such "psychic injuries." As Linden (1997; see also Romeo, 1997), a justice of the federal court of Canada, explained, "tort law was slow to grant protection to the interest of mental tranquility" (p. 385). Yet, this interest of mental tranquility—that is, the legally protected interest against disturbance of our mental tranquility by others—has come to be recognized by courts within the context of tort and other areas of law. The only issue, then, is what constitutes a legally recognized disturbance to mental tranquility?

As with intentional torts, psychological injuries were first recognized in a parasitic fashion—typically accompanying physical injuries sustained, for instance, in a negligence action resulting from a car accident (Levit, 1992). Now, in both Canada and the United States, there is a range of restrictions, varying by jurisdiction, placed on whether plaintiffs can recover for psychological injuries. Some American jurisdictions require that plaintiffs suffer a physical injury, or at least a physical impact, in order to recover for emotional injuries; others require that plaintiffs be in a "zone of danger," meaning that they were at least in danger of suffering physical impact or injury by reason of proximity to the incident (American Jurisprudence, 1968/1997a).

In both the United States and Canada, psychological injuries have been increasingly recognized as distinct injury claims. In Canada, courts tend to require either a physical manifestation of psychiatric damage, or a recognizable psychiatric disorder, in addition to reasonable foresight of the psychiatric damage by the defendant (Linden, 1997). Diagnoses such as depression or PTSD fit the requirements of Canadian law, and case law supports this assertion.

Similarly, in the United States, since the mid-twentieth century, restrictions on recovery for psychological injuries (i.e., physical impact, physical injury) have been eroding. In many jurisdictions, recovery for psychological damages is allowed independent of physical injuries (Brown, 1996). In some American jurisdictions (e.g., Alabama), negligent infliction of emotional distress has not been adopted as an independent tort but, rather, psychological injuries are given consideration in the damages stage of a traditional negligence action (Huffaker, 2001). Other than these rare exceptions, the entrenchment of PTSD as a sanctioned diagnostic entity certainly has facilitated this legal movement toward the recognition of the negligent infliction of emotional distress as an independent tort (Newman & Yehuda, 1997).

Causation in Negligence Cases
Causation in Canada (*Athey v. Leonati*, 1996) and the United States (*Chaney v. Smithkline Beckman Corp.*, 1985) is tested with the "but for" test, which asks, "*but for* the negligent act, would the injuries have resulted?" If, on a balance of probabilities, a judge or jury decides that the injury would not have occurred but for the negligent behavior of the defendant, then causation is proved. In some

contexts, especially if competing causal factors are at play, courts also apply a *material contribution* test. If the defendant's tortious conduct can be viewed as a material contribution to the plaintiff's psychological injury, then, despite the presence of other causal factors, causation may be found.

To illustrate, in *Miramon v. Bradley* (1997), a trial court rejected the plaintiff's claim stemming from a car accident because she had been in another car accident some two years earlier, and the second accident could not be isolated as the sole cause of the aggravation of psychological problems. The appellate court deemed this decision to be in error, ruling that tortious conduct need not be the sole causal factor of a plaintiff's injury, as long as it is a "significant contributing factor" (p. 478).

Within the context of applying the "but for" or material contribution tests, courts rely upon the interrelated concepts of proximity, remoteness, and foreseeability. If a putative cause is considered to be too remotely connected to the injury, then it is not considered to be a proximate cause, and causation will not be made out (Epstein, 1995). If an injury is deemed not to have been foreseeable by the defendant, then causation may not be made out. However, there is some controversy over this point, especially in regard to cases involving emotional injuries, with some authorities opining that in psychological damage cases, the injury need not be foreseeable to the defendant, as long as the negligent act remains the proximate cause of the injury (American Jurisprudence, 1968/1997a). The establishment of proximate cause entails an examination of how far the defendant's liability should extend for the consequences of the negligent act (Epstein, 1995).

In *Pokrifchak v. Weinstein* (1998), the plaintiff experienced serious emotional reactions to a car accident, including anxiety and nightmares (although it was not specified whether PTSD was diagnosed). In treatment, she claimed to have recalled that she was sexually abused as a child, and attempted to receive damages not only for the injuries that stemmed from the accident, but also for the trauma that arose from her recollection of sexual abuse (which, she argued, only arose because she was in treatment for the accident caused by the defendant). Under the "but for" test, causation for the physical and emotional injuries stemming from the accident was conceded. The judge, however, held that the accident was not a proximate cause of the trauma stemming from the recalled abuse; this injury was considered too remote or far-removed from the putative cause (the accident).

However, this issue is not treated consistently across jurisdictions—the North Carolina Supreme Court indeed held that a plaintiff could legitimately recover damages for the trauma caused by childhood sexual abuse that was apparently recalled only because of the defendant's tortious sexual harassment conduct (*Poole v. Copland, Inc.*, 1998). Note that this is an application of the thin skull doctrine applied to psychological injuries (discussed in chapter 1). In this case, the plaintiff was diagnosed with PTSD as well as dissociative disorder. She had flashbacks of the sexual abuse that were deemed to have stemmed from the defendant's conduct. It could be that this claim was accepted in *Poole* because the sexual harassment was more substantively similar to the previous trauma, whereas in *Pokrifchak*, the second trauma was a car accident.

Often, there are multiple possible causes of a plaintiff's injuries, which is not only a relevant issue legally, but also in terms of a mental health professional's assessment (i.e., to determine which of several possible causes actually led to the psychological injuries). This situation may arise in cases involving a preexisting condition (e.g., an anxiety disorder), or in cases where other traumas may have caused the psychological injury (e.g., a different accident or assault, etc.). The presence of multiple possible causes of PTSD will be a major focus of litigation, for it represents to the defense an opportunity to negate liability. As Brown (1996) states, "causation must be attacked" (p. 57).

Finally, we remind the reader of our discussion in chapter 1 concerning *eggshell psyches* or personalities, the psychological equivalent of the more traditional concept of the *thin skull* and *crumbling skull* doctrines. We do not repeat that discussion here, but summarize its importance to the issue of legal causation in psychological injury cases. The colorful term *eggshell personality* (*Janiak v. Ippolito*, 1985) applies when a person has a predisposition to suffer psychologically, and hence might be more easily harmed by behavior that would not typically have harmed a person not so predisposed. This reflects the more general principle that tortfeasors take their victims as they find them. An applied example might be the greater ease with which PTSD develops in a person who has several risk factors (high neuroticism, previous anxiety disorder, tendency to ruminate) than it would in a person without such risk factors (see *Poole*, above). The *crumbling skull* doctrine applies when a person was already symptomatic at the time of the tortious conduct, and his or her symptoms were worsened by the defendant's behavior. In these cases, the defendant will still be liable for the harm he or she caused, but monetary damages will tend to be reduced to reflect the fact that there was already a certain degree of injury present at the time of the tortious conduct. Not surprisingly, jurisdictions vary in the degree to which they are receptive to psychological thin and crumbling skulls (see chapter 1 for greater detail), with some limiting liability for psychological injury to people who are "normally constituted." Some commentators, of course, fear that allowing the application of the thin and crumbling skull doctrines to psychological injuries will result in the inevitable (though never verified) flood of frivolous and dubious claims (Eden, 2001).

The existence of the eggshell personality doctrine, at least in some jurisdictions, suggests that mental health evaluators should consider pre-tort mental health functioning and trauma history of plaintiffs (a recommendation that is expanded upon in chapter 3). Note that this process is also necessary to understand the potential role of competing causes and preexisting conditions. In some circumstances, competing causes will preclude recovery in a tort action if they reduce the causal contribution of the defendant's actions. Similarly, if a mental health condition was preexisting, the plaintiff might not recover damages if defense can demonstrate that the defendant's behavior was not at least a material cause to its existence or aggravation. In yet other circumstances, depending on jurisdiction, defendants might be liable for worsening a preexisting mental health condition. In any event, it is important for mental health professionals to attempt to document how the plaintiff's mental health condition differs from pre-tort status.

Who can recover? As mentioned, there have been several restrictions placed on recovery in psychological injury cases, such as the requirement of physical impact, injury, or a physical manifestation of the psychological injury. The earliest restriction was simply to refuse recovery for purely psychological injuries for fear of frivolous claims. However, in many jurisdictions, these restrictions have been lessened (Marrs, 1992), perhaps because of increased recognition by some courts of a heightened sophistication of medical and psychological science and research, hence making proof of emotional injury more objective and reliable than in the past (e.g., *James v. Lieb*, Neb. S. Ct., 1985).

The law restricts recovery for psychological injuries in various ways. To understand this, it is important to distinguish between negligent infliction of emotional distress cases that involve a *direct* victim versus a *bystander*, or *percipient*, victim. First, concerning direct victims, courts historically required that there be a physical impact as part of the claim, although this no longer tends to be the case (Dobbs, Keeton, Owen, & Keeton, 1984). There are only approximately five states that still require a physical impact component in negligent infliction of emotional distress cases (see *Consolidated Rail Corp. v. Gottshall*, 1994). Most courts now require that a plaintiff suffer a physical injury or illness or manifestation of the psychological injury (Koopman, 2003; Dobbs et al., 1984). This is in keeping with the law's desire to limit fraudulent or frivolous claims. However, a groundbreaking California case has further abrogated the physical injury or manifestation requirement in direct victim cases (see *Molien v. Kaiser Found. Hosps.*, 1980). Some jurisdictions have followed suit, not requiring physical manifestation in direct victim cases, whereas others still require it. To some extent, this is case specific, and depends on the court's judgment with respect to the circumstances that would be expected to yield serious emotional harm without physical injury or manifestation present to "verify" it.

Second, one of the more contentious areas in which negligent infliction of emotional distress plays out is in so-called *bystander* cases. The landmark supreme court of California case of *Dillon v. Legg* (1968) illustrates this situation, and has set a precedent that many other jurisdictions have followed, albeit often with loosening or tightening modifications. In *Dillon*, a mother observed her daughter being run over and killed by a car. The car did not impact the mother, nor was she in any real danger. The mother sued the defendant for psychological injuries, and the court agreed with her. In its ruling, the court held that bystander witnesses could recover for emotional or psychological injuries, but limited recovery to those who were near the incident, observed it (rather than those who learned about it later), and were closely related to the primary accident victim (these are the requirements for proving foreseeability in these cases). They also required a physical injury or manifestation (though not impact), as with direct victim cases.

Approximately half of all states have followed *Dillon* in abandoning this zone-of-danger requirement (*Gottshall*). For instance, the supreme court of Iowa followed California's lead in abandoning the physical zone-of-danger requirement, reasoning that genuine emotional distress could still follow the observation of a loved one being injured or killed, and that to require presence in a zone of danger results in "harshness and artificiality" (*Barnhill v. Davis*, 1981); however, the court retained the physical injury or manifestation requirement.

Yet, subsequent case law suggests that this physical injury or manifestation requirement is also eroding in bystander cases. *Rodrigues v. State* (1970) is often heralded as the first case to fully recognize negligent infliction of emotional distress as a stand-alone tort without a physical injury or manifestation requirement (Dobbs et al., 1984). Now, more than a dozen jurisdictions no longer require physical impact or manifestation (see also *Molien* for direct-victim cases). Whereas physical injury or manifestation was included as part of the legal test as an attempt to ensure the veracity of the claim, courts that currently accept the "no physical injury" rule instead have adopted a more general test that the psychological injury or emotional distress be "serious" (e.g., *Molien*) and/or "genuine" (e.g., *Rodrigues*, above, and *Potter*, below). (*"What psychological injuries are recoverable?"* expands on these concepts, below.)

In bystander cases, many jurisdictions have followed the recommendation within the Restatement (Second) of Torts that bystanders be within a *zone of physical danger*. This principle essentially holds that a person can only recover for purely psychological damages within a bystander context if they *could have been* physically injured by the defendant's actions. *Dillon* rejected the *zone-of-danger* rule (as have approximately half of all jurisdictions), although it does apply in some state jurisdictions.

In addition to the zone-of-danger rule (where it applies), plaintiffs in various jurisdictions also have to meet other requirements first delineated in *Dillon*, such as (a) how close they were to the accident in question, (b) how they learned of the injury to the primary victim (i.e., whether they contemporaneously observed the accident), and (c) how closely related they were to the primary victim (the foreseeability component of these cases—as in closely related family members, who might predictably suffer more mental shock from the traumatic injury/death than would strangers or mere acquaintances). These components of bystander cases differ by state (American Jurisprudence, 1968/1997a). Perhaps surprisingly, in California, subsequent case law has restricted the "closely related" prong of the test. In *Elden v. Sheldon* (1988), the California Supreme Court ruled that recovery in a bystander case was precluded because the plaintiff was not actually married to the primary victim, but only cohabited in a marital-like relationship. In *Thing v. La Chusa* (1989), the same court ruled that, in the absence of physical impact or injury to the plaintiff, recovery for negligent infliction of emotional distress should be limited to close relatives living together, or to parents, children, grandparents, or siblings. Interestingly, the California legislature has seemingly trumped this line of cases by enacting section 1714.01 of the California Civil Code in 2002, which reads: "Domestic partners shall be entitled to recover damages for negligent infliction of emotional distress to the same extent that spouses are entitled to do so under California law." It remains to be seen what impact this change will have beyond California.

Some jurisdictions have retained a mixture of the physical impact or manifestation rules in bystander cases. Florida has explicitly retained a physical impact requirement, but carves out limited exceptions on a case-by-case basis. For instance, in *Champion v. Gray* (1985), a mother who did not suffer a physical impact upon *hearing* her daughter being killed by a car was successful at trial because she did sustain physical manifestations of the distress. The court did not abandon the physical impact rule, but held that in certain circumstances it essentially could be suspended or waived. In this case, the rule was suspended because the emotional distress (and physical manifestation thereof) was the direct result of a physical injury to another person. Another context in which Florida has suspended the physical impact rule is when it simply seems not to reasonably apply to the fact pattern—such as wrongful birth cases. In *Kush v. Lloyd* (1992), the plaintiffs had one child with a disorder that the physician diagnosed as nongenetic, and hence did not indicate elevated risk for the same disorder in subsequent children. However, the physician was wrong, and the plaintiffs' next child also had the same genetic disorder. They ultimately were successful in court, which held that the impact rule did not apply in such circumstances where emotional suffering is a natural consequence of the circumstances.

Clearly, given the various possible tests (and modifications, combinations, and iterations thereof) for causation that exist across jurisdictions, mental health professionals should query the attorneys with whom they work about what tests will be applied in their given jurisdiction, depending on the type of tort action. While the question of whether causation is proved ultimately will be decided by legal players, knowledge of the relevant test will inform the forensic assessor in terms of how previous conditions, traumas, physical concomitants of psychological injury, and experiences of the plaintiff may be treated by the courts.

What psychological injuries are recoverable? As another way to limit recovery for psychological injury, most jurisdictions require that such injury is "serious" and "genuine." Severity has in some jurisdictions been defined by example, whereby psychosis, neurosis, phobias, and chronic depression were enumerated as meeting the seriousness test (*Shultz v. Barberton Glass Co.*, 1983). In other jurisdictions, it has been defined by broader principles—that the emotional distress is "medically diagnosable and must be of sufficient severity so as to be medically significant" (*Bass v. Nooney Co.*, 1983). Others still have attempted to provide behavioral markers for when emotional distress may be considered serious—the supreme court of Montana listed, for example, being "on the verge of tears," "animated," "agitated," and "disoriented" as such markers (*Johnson v. Supersave Mkts., Inc.*, 1984, p. 212). In determining genuineness, courts will be interested in whether the psychological injuries can be corroborated by medical or mental health evidence, bringing the reliability and validity of such evidence into the spotlight (see *Potter*; also *Rodrigues*). These restrictions of seriousness and genuineness—in conjunction with the court's increasing recognition of the reliability and utility of behavioral science and practice regarding psychological injuries (*James v. Lieb*, 1985), and the emergence of official diagnostic entities such as PTSD—help to accomplish what the historical outright rejection of psychological injury cases also did—to protect against trivial or frivolous actions.

Moreover, the U.S. Supreme Court has stated that emotional injuries are distinct from the tort law concept of pain and suffering, which are conceptualized as stemming from physical injuries (*Consolidated Rail Corp. v. Gottshall*, 1994). Rather, emotional or psychological injury refers to "mental or emotional harm (such as fright or anxiety) that is . . . not directly brought about by a physical injury, but that may manifest itself in physical symptoms" (p. 544). Some courts have provided legal definitions of when "psychological disorders" might be said to exist. For instance, psychological disorder has been defined to occur when any medically determined nonpermanent injury endures for 90 days or more and substantially limits the performance of daily activities (*Granowitz v. Vanvickle*, 1993). In *Molien v. Kaiser Found. Hosps.* (1980), the court held that serious emotional injury occurs when "a reasonable man, normally constituted, would be unable to adequately cope with mental stress engendered by the circumstances of the case" (p. 928). This implies a functional aspect to recovery—that is, the injury must impair a person's ability to cope—and that a thorough functional analysis of any psychological distress should be conducted in psychological injury cases. While functional analysis of psychological distress is theoretically an important part of diagnosis, the court decisions discussed above underscore the importance of such functional assessment.

Some courts have specifically recognized PTSD as satisfying the "serious" requirement for psychological injury. In the New York case of *Quaglio v. Tomaselli* (1984), PTSD and other psychiatric ailments were accepted as sufficient evidence to conclude that the plaintiff sustained a serious psychiatric injury. Appeal courts have overturned trial courts that have rejected expert testimony demonstrating PTSD (e.g., *Koury v. Lanier Express, Inc.*, 1988). In *Johnson v. May*

(1992), the court rejected an expert's position that PTSD was a "malingerer's disorder," and asserted that the validity of PTSD as a disorder is not open to serious question. Other cases reviewed in this chapter have upheld damages on the basis of diagnoses of dysthymia and dissociative disorders.

As noted earlier, the Restatement (Second) of Torts has defined "severe emotional injury" as "all highly unpleasant mental reactions, such as fright, horror, grief, shame, humiliation, embarrassment, anger, chagrin, disappointment, worry, and nausea." Numerous jurisdictions have incorporated this definition into their case law with respect to emotional injury cases (whether intentional or negligent). For instance, the Texas case of *Trevino v. Southwestern Bell Tel. Co.* (1979) defined emotional injury as follows: "The term 'mental anguish' implies a relatively high degree of mental pain and distress. It is more than mere disappointment, anger, resentment, or embarrassment, although it may include all of these. It includes a mental sensation of pain resulting from such painful emotions as grief, severe disappointment, indignation, wounded pride, shame, despair and/or public humiliation" (p. 584).

Clearly, this definition is broader than any one diagnostic category, suggesting that mental health professionals, in addition to assessing for a variety of disorders, must evaluate numerous areas of mental and emotional functioning that are either subsyndromal, or do not happen to cluster into actual diagnoses (e.g., severe and persistent anger, or embarrassment). Further, given the Restatement's inclusion of effects such as "nausea," in conjunction with the requirement (in some jurisdictions) that psychological injuries be accompanied by physical injury or manifestation, it would seem important for mental health professionals to evaluate possible physical manifestations of the psychological phenomena they are assessing.

No-Fault Insurance Jurisdictions

Some jurisdictions, such as New York, have adopted no-fault motor vehicle policies, reducing the role of negligence actions. In New York, plaintiffs have to first demonstrate that their injuries are "serious," as defined by New York's Insurance Law, section 5102, in order to pursue a third-party lawsuit. A serious injury includes death, dismemberment, serious disfigurement, fractures, and other physical injuries, as well as "a medically determined injury or impairment of a nonpermanent nature which prevents the injured person from performing substantially all of the material acts which constitute such person's usual and customary daily activities for not less than 90 days during the 180 days immediately following the occurrence of the injury or impairment." Although this provision has tended to be interpreted fairly strictly, the New York Appellate Division, Third Department held that PTSD could indeed satisfy the statutory requirement of "serious injury" (*Chapman v. Capoccia*, 2001).

Toxic Torts

A *toxic tort* is simply a pithy way of describing the situation in which persons are exposed to toxic agents through the failure of the tortfeasor (often a company) to meet the standard of care in preventing the release of such agents. A common example would be the exposure of people to asbestos; another would be exposure to chemical agents from an industrial site. Most often, the harm that is litigated in these cases is the physical effects of such exposure (e.g., cancer, birth defects, radiation damage). However, as described by Tuohey and Gonzalez (2001), courts, at least in California, are willing to compensate the often-accompanying psychological distress.

Although a toxic tort is often evaluated under the general rules of negligence, it is discussed separately because claims can also be made under nuisance, trespass, battery, strict liability, and other legal mechanisms (see Tuohey & Gonzalez, 2001). When framed as negligence, there are some practical differences to traditional negligence actions that have implications for recovery for psychological injury. That is, in toxic tort cases, the physical injuries suffered tend to be more insidious, more slowly emerging, and less easily attributed to the putative tortious conduct. As such, in the toxic tort arena, many cases have rejected negligence claims for psychological injury without physical injury (*Metro-North Commuter R.R. Co. v. Buckey*, 1997; though see *Lilley v. Bd. of Supervisors of La. State Univ.*, 1999).

In California, however, cases such as *Cottle v. Superior Court* (1992) and *Potter v. Firestone Tire & Rubber Co.* (1993) "are quite clear that in toxic cases, neither physical impact nor physical injury is required for emotional distress . . . claims" (Tuohey & Gonzalez, 2001, p. 673). Tuohey and Gonzalez, however, were commenting about recovery options within the law broadly, and not limiting their comments to negligence cases, which may not necessarily be so liberal. It might help that the California Civil Code (section 3333) states that tort defendants are liable for all detriment caused, which includes fear, anxiety, and other emotional distress (Tuohey & Gonzalez, 2001). Tuohey and Gonzalez go on to state, however, that recovery for emotional distress may be more likely (when the only injury claimed is emotional or psychological in nature) when the action is formulated as nuisance rather than as intentional or negligent infliction of emotional distress, because the focus is more on the harm suffered by the plaintiff than on the conduct of the defendant.

Certain types of toxic tort cases have enjoyed some success for psychological injury—fear cases; that is, exposure to carcinogens understandably gives rise to the fear that cancer will develop. The physical injury in this context—cancer—might never develop, or could take years to do so, and courts tend not to require its presence (Heinzerling, 2001; Tuohey & Gonzalez, 2001). However, courts in these cases (depending on jurisdiction) are inclined to require a physical manifestation of the fear itself, which some criticize as inviting dishonesty and dramatics on the part of plaintiffs—where certain legitimate cases are rejected and others, though less legitimate on their merits, are rewarded because the plaintiff is a capable actor (Heinzerling, 2001).

Attempts to claim PTSD in the context of toxic tort cases have not typically been successful (Heinzerling, 2001). Courts have balked at the notion that a prolonged exposure to a toxic element could meet the intent of the American Psychiatric Association's (1994) definition of trauma in the *Diagnostic and Statistical Manual of Mental Disorders* (DSM) system. As the court stated in *Sterling v. Velsicol* (1987), "drinking or otherwise using contaminated water . . . does not constitute the type of recognizable stressor identified either by professional medical associations or courts" (p. 1210).

Heinzerling (2001) has described the current system of toxic torts as being "confused and ignorant, even backward" (p. 77), arguing that the knowledge of the *risk* caused by exposure to toxins causes enough psychological distress—even dread—to warrant being considered a legally compensable injury. She asserted that "if courts took seriously the psychological and sociological literature" (p. 90) on the psychological effects of exposure to potentially deadly agents, they would be more likely to compensate them.

The point of this section is to illustrate that in toxic exposure cases, the legal frameworks that might be used are numerous, and the type of emotional injury will tend to take on a different hue than in more traditional tort contexts, such as motor vehicle accidents. The psychological injury might be more chronic, persistent, and colored with fear over the unknown, rather than a reaction to an acute physical event such as a motor vehicle accident. Mental health professionals should be prepared to address these types of psychological injuries, and to inquire of lawyers the type of action being framed with the resultant implications for causation.

Damages in Tort

While it is beyond the scope of this chapter to fully discuss the rules governing the quantum of monetary damages awarded in various tort claims involving psychological injuries (other sources that do so include Douglas, Huss, Murdoch, Washington, & Koch, 1999; Louisiana Personal Injury Awards, 2002), we do briefly discuss why damages are important to the mental health professional's evaluation. Generally, monetary damages are intended to return the plaintiff to pre-tort status. Although this function sounds retrospective in nature, it also includes a forward-looking estimation procedure that surrounds issues such as ability to work, time required to recover, treatment needs, and so forth.

Much of the law of damages for tort comprises various forms of compensatory damages (as opposed to punitive damages, which are intended to "punish" the tortfeasor for outrageous behavior). In the United States, *special damages* arise from the injury in a manner that is peculiar or special to the case; they include natural and actual, though not necessary, results of the case, as well as past and future economic losses stemming from the incident (Restatement (Second) of Torts, 1979, section 671). *General damages* are more immediate, direct, and prox- imate results of the incident; they might comprise any form of direct economic loss such as medical bills, lost wages, or property damage (Rest. 2d, 1979, section 670). *Pecuniary damages* (which can be either general or special) are losses that are financially estimable and compensated with money. Plaintiffs can recover *future damages* for the future effects of the wrongdoing (e.g., loss of capacity to work, future pain and suffering, future medical expenses). Future pain and suf- fering damages must be based on solid evidence. In addition, injured parties can recover damages that are said to be inherent to the injury itself, such as pain and suffering, disabilities, or disfigurements.

In Canada, the heads, or categories, of damage use the same terminology, although it refers to different concepts than in the United States. *General damages* in Canadian law refer to *nonpecuniary damages* (damages that are not quantifi- able), including pain and suffering (which itself subsumes "lost expectation of life" and "lost enjoyment of life"). *Special damages* (also called *pecuniary dam- ages*) can be quantified, and basically include out-of-pocket expenses up to the time of trial (e.g., medical expenses, loss of earning capacity and past wages). Other heads of damage in Canadian law include *cost of future care* and *loss of future earning capacity*.

Therefore, the mental health professional's evaluation can, in principle, inform decisions about damages in terms of specifying the past and current severity of the psychological injury, and the likely course of the injury in the future. This includes the nature and severity of future pain and suffering, as well as its likely impact on functioning in major life domains, whether it will preclude or diminish the plaintiff's capacity to work, what the most probable course of treatment will be, and its expense.

Workers' Compensation

Workers' compensation laws, in the form of state statutes, evolved in the late nineteenth century, in response to tort law that, at the time, essentially precluded employees from being compensated under tort for injuries sustained on the job (Shuman & Daley, 1996). While tort law and workers' compensation share the objectives of compensating injured parties, they also are significantly different. First, the scope of injury that is compensable is much more limited in workers' compensation, with the majority of reimbursement devoted to loss of earnings. How, then, are psychological injuries relevant to workers' compensation? While a person is not compensated for the violation to the personal interest of mental tranquility, as in tort law, a person's earnings may be reimbursed as a function of having suffered a psychological injury that prevents him or her from working.

Another significant difference between the systems relates to causation and fault. In tort, causation is always relevant, whether the tort is one of intention or negligence—it is one of the primary elements that must be proved. So too is fault relevant in tort, in which tortfeasors must either have intended or ought to have foreseen the harm that flowed from their actions. Causation in workers' compensation is more limited—it must be proven, essentially, that the employment setting caused the injury, even if by accident (e.g., getting one's hand caught in heavy machinery). Fault, however, is irrelevant—injuries can arise entirely by accident and still be compensable.

Further, workers' compensation law is governed primarily by statute, rather than common law (depending on jurisdiction), meaning that what is compensable, and to what degree, is restricted by legislation. Certain types of injuries, or benefits, can simply be written out of the recovery matrix. For many injuries, workers' compensation acts are the exclusive remedy available—employees essentially waive their rights to sue in tort for injuries suffered at work. There are exceptions, however (again, depending on jurisdiction), if the harmful behavior, despite happening at work, was not related to employment (e.g., a sexual assault of one employee by another) (Jordan, 2000).

It should be noted that in some jurisdictions, the exclusivity criterion of workers' compensation acts, coupled with disallowance of certain types of injuries, has resulted in situations in which employees are in a bind that does not permit recovery *either* under workers' compensation law *or* under tort. This was recently the case in Ohio, where persons, under the workers' compensation statute, could not recover for purely psychological injuries unaccompanied by physical impact. Yet, they were also barred from suing under negligence. *Bunger v. Lawson Co.* (2001) removed this particular bind in Ohio, when the court decided that such persons could be allowed to sue in negligence.

As with tort law, psychological injuries historically were rejected in workers' compensation settings, or at least were less likely to be compensated than physical injuries, for many of the same reasons (Melton, Petrila, Poythress, & Slobogin, 1997). Today, they are recognized in most jurisdictions, although this depends on their category. Three categories of workers' compensation claims have usually been identified with respect to psychological injury: (a) physical events or traumas that cause mental/psychological injury ("physical-mental" claims), (b) mental/psychological events that cause physical injuries ("mental-physical" claims), and (c) mental/psychological events that cause mental/psychological injuries ("mental-mental" claims). Not surprisingly, this latter category of claim has received the most skepticism and is most likely to be rejected by decision makers (usually administrative tribunals).

Physical-Mental Claims

Tribunals and courts have few problems with this category of claim, in which a physical impact gives rise either directly to a mental injury, or to a physical injury that then develops into mental or psychological injuries. Courts and administrative tribunals tend to recognize these claims because the physical element provides an ostensible safety net against frivolous or fraudulent claims—similar to the rationale underlying the physical injury or manifestation rule in tort law. The types of physical events that can substantiate a claim are numerous and varied (e.g., being criminally victimized at work, or accidental physical injury or maiming), as are the descriptions of psychological injury (various anxiety conditions and disorders, sometimes developing years after the event) (see Melton et al., 1997).

These cases may most resemble negligence cases, at least superficially, in that the psychological injury in question often stems from an accident that causes physical injury. Courts have been willing to uphold claims in which mood disorders (commonly depression) or anxiety disorders accompanied some physical accident (*Chamberlain Mfg. Corp. v. Workmen's Compensation Appeal Board*, 1979; *Gilchrist v. Trail King Industries*, 2000)

Causation in these claims contains two aspects—that a psychological injury exists, and that it was caused by a physical injury or event that occurred in the context of work (*Chamberlain*). As with tort law, the physical event or injury need not be the sole causal factor, so long as it is a contributing factor (*Gilchrist*). Courts in some jurisdictions also seem to permit a lengthy period between the physical event and the psychological injury—perhaps even years (*Getsinger vs. Owens Corning Fiberglass Corp.*, 1999), although this is likely to vary by jurisdiction.

Mental-Physical Claims

Courts and tribunals also tend to accept claims that assert physical injury (e.g., heart attack, stroke) that can be linked to mental or psychological phenomena (e.g., shock, fright, accumulated stress) (Melton et al., 1997). Often, the psychological injury that precipitates the physical injury takes the form of prolonged job stress and pressure. This suggests that mental health professionals should be prepared to evaluate these forms of chronic, long-lasting psychological states, as opposed to the acute psychological distress that often is the substance of tort cases.

Causation in these cases will typically be supported if it is proven that the injury happened in the context of employment, and that the mental/psychological condition in some way caused the physical injury (e.g., *Borough of Media and PMA v. Workmen's Compensation Appeal Bd.*, 1990). How restrictive this second causal element is depends on jurisdiction, with some requiring more of a direct causal link than others.

Mental-Mental Claims

As Melton et al. (1997) explained, although a majority of American jurisdictions do allow these claims, a substantial minority do not. Jurisdictions that do permit recovery for these claims, including Canadian jurisdictions, tend to place restrictions on them that are not placed on the other two categories. For instance, some permit recovery only under circumstances of unusual stress, while others require that additional evidence be adduced that employment, and not other factors, primarily caused the injury. The mental cause of the injury is often limited to those precipitants that are sudden and/or unexpected. The routine stresses of employment tend to be ruled out as accepted causes of psychological injury in these cases.

Psychological injuries that have been compensated under this category include schizophrenia that was deemed to arise from occupational stress (*Leo v. Workmen's Compensation Appeal Bd.*, 1998), panic disorder arising from harassment at work (*McDonough v. Workmen's Compensation Appeal Bd.*, 1984), and PTSD resulting from inappropriate sexual acts (*Everingim v. Good Samaritan Center of New Underwood*, 1996—in this case, the employee had been sexually assaulted as a child, suggesting increased psychological vulnerability to subsequent untoward sexual behavior).

Causation is more difficult in these cases. A psychological injury must be proven, and it also must typically be established that the specific work-related "unusual circumstances" referred to above were a proximate cause of the psychological injury (Larsen, 1993). Further, as mentioned above, in some jurisdictions, the causal agent must be sudden or unexpected. Further limiting these claims, most jurisdictions impose an objective, rather than subjective, burden of proof, meaning that the suddenness or unusualness of the relevant events are to be decided based on the reasonable person's viewpoint, not from the employee's perspective (*Joseph v. Jefferson Parish Fire Department*, 2000).

Thin and Crumbling Skulls, Revisited

As with tort law, the presence of preexisting psychological conditions is a relevant consideration in workers' compensation claims. If a preexisting disorder or condition is made worse by an employment-related event or condition, then compensation may follow (Melton et al., 1997). Courts may be willing to allow recovery for psychological injuries that were deemed to lay "dormant" until a subsequent trauma, even if not work-related (*Ryan v. Workmen's Compensation Appeal Bd.*, 1998). However, proving the causal link between employment and psychological injury is muddied when preexisting psychological conditions are present.

Sexual Harassment

Legislation and case law in the United States and Canada define sexual harassment in two ways: (1) *quid pro quo* harassment, which refers to situations in which the employment of persons is made contingent upon their complying with sexual demands, remarks, gestures, or behaviors; and (2) *hostile environment* harassment, which describes circumstances in which sexual demands, remarks, or behaviors make the work environment intolerable. In both the United States and Canada, sexual harassment is illegal under antidiscrimination legislation, such as the Canadian Human Rights Act (1985) and Title VII, section 703(2) of the American Civil Rights Act (1964/1991). The Equal Employment Opportunity Commission (EEOC, 1980) defines sexual harassment as illegal under the Civil Rights Act (1964/1991) as follows:

> Unwelcome sexual advances, requests for sexual favors, and other verbal or physical conduct of a sexual nature constitute sexual harassment when (1) submission to such conduct is made either explicitly or implicitly a term or condition of an individual's employment, (2) submission to or rejection of such conduct by an individual is used as the basis for employment decisions affecting such individual, or (3) such conduct has the purpose or effect of unreasonably interfering with an individual's work performance or creating an intimidating, hostile, or offensive working environment.

Case law in both countries has supported the proposition that sexual harassment is prohibited under antidiscrimination statutes. For instance, in *Meritor Savings Bank v. Vinson* (1986), the U.S. Supreme Court proclaimed that victims of sexual harassment must show that, based on their gender, they received unwanted sexual behavior that created a hostile working environment. More specifically, *Meritor* stated that Title VII is violated when the workplace is permeated with "discriminatory intimidation, ridicule, and insult" (p. 65) "that is sufficiently severe or pervasive to alter the conditions of [the victims'] employment and create an abusive working environment" (p. 67). Severity and pervasiveness must be proven both subjectively and objectively. That is, there must be consideration of whether the victim in question found the behavior hostile or abusive (i.e., it caused psychological harm—fear, anxiety, humiliation—to the particular victim) and whether the reasonable person would have agreed.

In *Harris v. Forklift Systems, Inc.* (1993), the U.S. Supreme Court overruled a lower court that had held that the harassing behavior must cause serious (or, as the court also termed it, tangible or concrete) psychological harm in order to be actionable. *Harris* held that, while serious psychological harm is certainly one consideration, Title VII cases do not require its presence to be successful. If it is present, however, it will likely contribute to a finding of discrimination under Title VII. The court stated that the totality of circumstances must be taken into account to determine if a work environment has been made hostile or abusive, and psychological harm is one of the considerations. As the court stated in *Harris*, "Title VII comes into play before the harassing conduct leads to a nervous breakdown" (p. 22). Courts will be concerned with both the severity and frequency of the behavior. Isolated mere utterances or stray remarks typically will not be actionable (*Meritor*), although if coupled with threats of physical harm, or if such utterances cause psychological harm, they may well be actionable (*Harris*). Courts often will pay particular attention to whether the behavior caused humiliation (*Harris*). Despite these pronouncements by the U.S. Supreme Court, commentators have criticized some lower courts, and some circuit courts, of attempting to retain the "serious psychological injury" component of sexual harassment law by, for instance, finding exceptions to the general rule that dismisses its necessity (Schnapper, 1999).

In Canada, sexual harassment is illegal under civil rights legislation on the ground of gender discrimination. Such was the ruling of the Supreme Court of Canada in *Janzen and Governeau v. Platy Enterprises Ltd.* (1989). Two waitresses successfully argued that their treatment by another employee constituted discrimination based on sex under the Manitoba Human Rights Act (1974). After two appeals, the Supreme Court agreed, and defined sexual harassment as a subtype of sexual discrimination, and therefore as illegal. An earlier Supreme Court of Canada case, *Robichaud v. Canada (Treasury Board)* (1987), established that employers are responsible for the actions of their employees in terms of sexual harassment, meaning that an employee may take legal action against a company if a coworker sexually harasses her or him, as happened in *Janzen*.

There has been an interesting expansion of Title VII sexual harassment claims fairly recently, which has been termed *bystander sexual harassment*. Some courts have held that sexual harassment need not be directed at an individual in order for him or her to recover, if it nonetheless altered the work conditions and caused a hostile environment. In *Leibovitz v. New York City Transit Auth.* (1998), a worker observed a supervisor sexually harassing her colleagues, and when she complained to him about it, she was informed that doing so would have an adverse effect on her career. She complained of severe emotional distress, was diagnosed with depression, and was described as suffering weight gain, sleep problems, and anxiety.

What seems clear from the sexual harassment/Title VII jurisprudence, and is reflected more generally in employment discrimination jurisprudence, of which sexual harassment/Title VII is one species, is that the degree of emotional harm necessary for a claim to be actionable seems lower than in tort cases. While psychological injuries in tort law are broader than diagnostic categories, they must nevertheless be "serious." In sexual harassment litigation (and employment discrimination law more broadly), psychological injuries need not be "serious, tangible, or concrete" to support a claim. It clearly does not need to be accompanied or caused by a physical injury or manifestation (or, at least, minimally so), as in tort or airline convention law. It also will often include a focus on humiliation, anger, resentment, and other psychological reactions following offensive behavior, many times in public. This means that the mental health professional will need to be prepared to evaluate these psychological states even in the absence of a diagnosable mental disorder. Clearly, when a mental disorder is present, it would seem likely to satisfy the law's demands in these cases (depending somewhat on jurisdiction).

Employment Discrimination

Employment discrimination is actually a broader category that encompasses sexual harassment. It can draw from a variety of state and federal antidiscrimination and civil rights laws that bar discrimination on the basis of age, race, sex, disability, and so forth. Depending on the particular statute, plaintiffs will be entitled to back pay, front pay, reinstatement, compensatory damages, and perhaps punitive damages. It is notable that, under Title VII, compensatory damages were not available for emotional distress until the Civil Rights Act of 1991 permitted them. This Act now permits compensatory damages for "emotional pain, suffering, inconvenience, mental anguish, loss of enjoyment of life" (s. 1981a(b)(3)). Some commentators have suggested that emotional injuries need not be terribly serious, or even supported by very strong evidence, to support a successful claim of employment discrimination. Cucuzza (1999), for instance, stated that, at least in the Second Circuit, "as long as a plaintiff's testimony is not limited to his or her subjective feelings and describes some physical manifestations of emotional distress, however slight or transient, the defendant will not be able to reverse or vacate the jury's verdict" (p. 398). She went on to catalog a number of successful cases in which the following types of psychological injuries were present: feeling angry, upset, hurt, or shocked; feeling inadequate; loss of self-esteem; concern over the future; short temper; and strained family relations. In addition, the following physical manifestations have been reported in successful cases: sleep problems, appetite problems, upset stomach, headaches, crying, shortness of breath, and chest pains. Less commonly, Cucuzza posits, plaintiffs have more serious emotional and physical conditions.

In *Carrero v. New York City Housing Authority* (1989), the Second Circuit upheld an award on the basis of the plaintiff having experienced substantial humiliation, discomfort, stress, anxiety, and crying, as well as having obtained a prescription for valium and suffering strained family relations. In *Annis v. County of Westchester* (1998), the same court dismissed a claim because there was no evidence short of the plaintiff's subjective testimony (i.e., affidavits) and no report of any physical manifestations (even just crying). In employment discrimination cases, it is common for plaintiffs to be successful based solely on their testimony—that is, without medical or psychological experts (Cucuzza, 1999)—suggesting that there is a much lower evidentiary burden on such plaintiffs than in tort cases, as well as a much lower level of emotional distress that is required. Commentators have read such cases as suggesting that even slight physical manifestations—such as crying or stomach pains—will be enough to support claims of emotional distress (Cucuzza, 1999). If other corroborating evidence is introduced, or if the emotional distress is very serious, it seems most likely that a claim would have little problem succeeding. Having said this, it is also the case that the quantum of awards will likely differ as a function of the severity of emotional harm. Hagood (1999) has commented that while expert testimony typically is not required to establish a claim, damages tend to be smaller without it.

As with other areas of law, "emotionally sensitive" plaintiffs are entitled to recover so long as the discriminatory behavior also passes the objective ("reasonable person") test (Hagood, 1999). Similarly, persons with psychological "crumbling skulls" also can recover if their condition was made worse by the discriminatory behavior, although damages might be reduced to return the plaintiff only to their prediscrimination level of functioning. Further, as with other areas of law, it must be proven that the discriminatory behavior caused the emotional distress.

Housing Discrimination

The Fair Housing Act, which is part of the Civil Rights Act of 1968, prohibits discrimination in the selling, buying, leasing, or renting of real property on the basis of race, color, religion, sex, national origin, and familial status. It shares similarities with other types of discrimination law (employment, sexual harassment) as well as with tort law. Because there was no specific provision in the law to compensate emotional injuries, courts had to look to other sources of law for guidance. The U.S. Supreme Court interpreted this law in *Curtis v. Loether* (1974), reasoning that the purpose of the law was to "make whole" persons who have been subjected to this type of discrimination—a purpose akin to the role of tort law in restoring plaintiffs to their pre-tort status. The court stated, "an action to redress racial discrimination may also be likened to an action for defamation or intentional infliction of mental distress. . . . [R]acial discrimination might be treated as a dignitary tort" (pp. 195–196, note 10).

In other words, the court's interpretation was that the law sought to redress the indignity of being denied the basic need of fair housing, or housing at all, on the basis of race (or other personal attribute). Because of its reliance on tort law, there has been a perhaps more conservative judicial approach to psychological injuries within this area of discrimination law as opposed to other areas such as employment or sexual harassment. While courts have recognized emotional distress as a compensable injury in housing discrimination cases, commentators have noted that such injuries tend to be undervalued, and that the inconsistency of recognition is greater among federal courts compared to the administrative tribunals that often hear such actions (Goode & Johnson, 2003; Hale, 1999). However, because this area is not simply a specific instantiation of intentional infliction of emotional distress, courts have taken some leeway as well. For instance, as with other areas of discrimination, expert testimony is not required to succeed at trial (courts have held that judges or juries are well suited to infer whether psychological harm is present based on the circumstances of the case), although some commentators have described such expert evidence as an "invaluable tool" in these cases (Hale, 1999). Further, the defendant's conduct need not be characterized as "outrageous," as in traditional torts, likely because discrimination is often subtle, covert, and insidious (Goode & Johnson, 2003).

The role of humiliation and embarrassment, as in other areas of discrimination law, as well as indignancy, will often be relevant in housing discrimination cases (Goode & Johnson, 2003). The injury must be more than the transient and expected trivial irritation involved with looking for housing (*Steele v. Title Realty Co.*, 1973). It also will be important to take individual plaintiff's circumstances into account—for instance, denial of housing on the basis of race, though always offensive, may understandably cause even greater anger and anxiety when that person is, for example, a single parent. Psychiatric evidence from victims of housing discrimination suggests that the effects thereof often consist of "feelings of numbness, withdrawal, difficulty in concentrating and focusing, depression, anxiety, and the diminished quality of care given to children" (Goode & Johnson, 2003, p. 1157, note 72, citing psychiatric evidence given in a housing discrimination hearing). Goode and Johnson devised a 32-item "Emotional Harm Checklist" for use in these cases. Although it is best considered an aide-mémoire for lawyers to interview their clients, and not a psychometric instrument, it does represent a potentially useful source for asking questions that will be relevant to the legal issues at hand.

As with other areas of discrimination law, as well as additional areas such as tort, the causal link between the discrimination and pursuant psychological injury must be proven. In addition, as with other areas of law, defendants take their victims as they find them, meaning that psychologically vulnerable plaintiffs, and plaintiffs with preexisting psychological problems are not barred from recovery (although some courts are criticized for not recognizing this legal principle—see Goode & Johnson, 2003).

Convention (Airline Accidents)

Airline accidents might represent the ultimate in terms of potential for catastrophic injury, damage, and death. One of the legal differences between airline crashes and other accidents (say, motor vehicle collisions) is that airlines and air travel are governed partially by international law, meaning that a straightforward application of domestic law is not possible.

The Convention for the Unification of Certain Rules Relating to International Transportation by Air (1929), also called the Warsaw Convention, was created in order to protect airlines by limiting their liability for injuries caused to passengers, yet also allow recovery for injured passengers in certain circumstances. The United States ratified the Convention in 1934, and signed an "update" in 1966 that served to increase the amount of damages that injured parties could recover (Chester, 2000).

There has been a fairly extensive history of litigation surrounding emotional injuries suffered on flights under the auspices of the Warsaw Convention. In summarizing these, Chester (2000) concluded that lower courts have split over whether psychological injuries are compensable, even if accompanied by physical injuries. The U.S. Supreme Court has held that purely psychological injuries are not recoverable in the context of air accidents if there are no physical injuries suffered (*Eastern Airlines, Inc. v. Floyd*, 1991). They did not, however, state that such psychological injuries are, indeed, recoverable if there is an accompanying physical injury. Some lower courts have, however, allowed recovery for emotional damages that are either caused by, or simply accompany, a physical injury.

Despite pleas from some commentators to allow recovery for psychological injury accompanied by physical injuries because this has been claimed to reflect the intent of the treaty framers (Chester, 2000), it appears that more recent jurisprudence is heading in the opposite direction. The U.S. Court of Appeals, Second Circuit, has recently interpreted the Warsaw Convention as not permitting recovery for psychological injuries that are accompanied by, *but not caused by*, physical injuries (*Ehrlich v. American Airlines, Inc.*, 2004). The court ruled, after a comprehensive examination of various primary and secondary sources of law, that the Warsaw Convention only permits recovery for psychological damages if they are caused by, not merely accompanied by, physical injuries.

It is noteworthy that, while this case was being litigated and later appealed, some 50 countries, including the United States and Canada, ultimately ratified and put into force a new treaty designed to essentially replace—though not disturb the jurisprudence developed under—the Warsaw Convention. This new, so-called Montreal Convention was preceded during negotiations by substantial discussion over whether to allow recovery for emotional damages unaccompanied by physical injury, although no consensus could be reached, and the relevant provisions are little changed from its predecessor (see *Ehrlich* for a discussion).

The implications for mental health professionals are that, in such evaluations, which admittedly will be rarer than other psychological injury cases, there must be a clear demonstration that any psychological injuries were caused by the sustained physical injuries (e.g., depression and grief over loss of a limb rather than fear and anxiety stemming from the accident itself).

Tests of Admissibility

We refer readers to fuller accounts of admissibility than the present chapter allows (Dixon & Gill, 2002; Garcia-Rill & Beecher-Monas, 2001). Between the United States and Canada, there are three admissibility tests by which potential expert evidence will be adjudicated. First, in *Daubert v. Merrell Dow Pharmaceuticals* (1993), the U.S. Supreme Court ruled on the admissibility of expert evidence in jurisdictions that are governed by the Federal Rules of Evidence (FRE). The basic elements of the *Daubert* test are reliability, relevance, and legal sufficiency of evidence. Together, these elements focus legal attention on the quality of scientific evidence (e.g., testable theoretical basis, peer-reviewed publication of data, and acceptability of the assessment or research procedure in the field), the relevance of testimony (e.g., will admission of the evidence make a fact in issue more or less probable?), and the legal sufficiency of expert evidence (e.g., is the evidence more probative than prejudicial, as per FRE 403?).

Although binding only in federal jurisdictions, many states have adopted *Daubert* (or highly similar language) into their evidentiary codes (Goodman-Delahunty, 1997). The *Daubert* test has important implications for experts who testify about PTSD and other psychological injuries. In *Miramon v. Bradley* (1997), citing *Daubert*, the court noted that the "trial judge serves a 'gatekeeping' function to screen and exclude 'invalid' and irrelevant material" (pp. 478–479). *Daubert* applied to scientific experts; subsequent U.S. Supreme Court case law (*Kumho Tire Co., Ltd. v. Carmichael*, 1999) has extended it to essentially all expert evidence (including psychology and mental health testimony, which is not typically always "scientific" by the law).

Some legal commentators have argued that PTSD easily meets the *Daubert* criteria, unlike so-called syndrome evidence (e.g., battered woman syndrome), although it is often excluded by judges who are misinformed or uneducated about such evidence (which is really the fault of attorneys who seek to introduce it) (Garcia-Rill & Beecher-Monas, 2001). The introduction of the *Daubert* test for the admissibility of expert evidence may have the effect of introducing more objectivity into testimony on PTSD and other psychological injuries (Newman & Yehuda, 1997). Indeed, surveys of case law suggest that expert evidence is given more scrutiny by judges than prior to *Daubert* (Krafka, Dunn, Johnson, Cecil, & Miletich, 2002). Such increased scrutiny arguably results in an increased quality of expert evidence. Further, neurochemical and psychophysiological indicators of PTSD may be welcomed in court as providing objective evidence for the existence of the disorder, as well as evidence that symptoms are not malingered. The presence of neurochemical changes associated with PTSD also may satisfy the physical impact or injury tort requirements of some jurisdictions, if such changes could be proved with respect to the individual plaintiff (Pitman, Saunders, & Orr, 1994).

The second test, in place in many U.S. jurisdictions, stems from the 1923 U.S. Supreme Court decision of *Frye v. United States*. This test, known as the "general acceptance" test, requires that scientific evidence or testimony be generally accepted in the particular field. This test has sometimes excluded evidence on PTSD (Goodman-Delahunty, 1997), and, frankly, is a poor indicator of whether psychological science is necessarily valid and reliable. Finally, the Supreme Court of Canada recently enumerated the criteria for the admissibility of expert evidence in *R. v. Mohan* (1994): (1) relevance, (2) qualification of the expert, and (3) necessity of the evidence. Under *Mohan*, expert testimony is admissible only when it makes the proof of some fact more or less probable, when the testimony is more probative than prejudicial, when the proposed expert has advanced or specialized knowledge in the field, and his or her testimony rests on an established body of knowledge. The testimony must also be necessary to assist the trier of fact, in that it must relate to issues that are beyond the understanding of the average layperson.

Conclusion

Psychological injuries have a tumultuous history in the law. They have been outright rejected, begrudgingly accepted, and are still met with skepticism and additional burdens in terms of proof. Nevertheless, they have found their way into many areas of law, the four main areas of which have been outlined above: tort (intentional and negligent), workers' compensation, airline convention, and discrimination (sexual harassment, employment, and housing). There are certainly similarities among these areas, although clear differences emerge as well in terms of the nature of the psychological injury that will be actionable, the level of proof required to establish a claim, whether expert testimony is required, and so forth. Even within categories, such as negligent infliction of emotional distress, substantial variability exists across jurisdictions in terms of whether physical injuries or manifestations are required to accompany the psychological injury.

While serious mental disorders will surpass whatever threshold the law has crafted, it is also the case that a much broader range of psychological phenomena will possibly satisfy the law's demands. These psychological phenomena may understandably take on different hues across the different legal areas. For instance, humiliation and feeling as if one's dignity has been violated might be a more salient psychological injury in the various discrimination contexts, whereas PTSD, depression, or other diagnosed anxiety disorders might be more common in tort. In all contexts, issues of causation and preexisting psychological disturbance will be important. Mental health professionals have to be prepared to respond to the law's varying needs depending on which context and jurisdiction they find themselves practicing. Consulting with attorneys about these various issues should enhance the quality, relevance, and, in turn, helpfulness of the mental health professionals' psychological injury evaluations. The remainder of this book is devoted to explicating just how mental health professionals might go about conducting optimally informative and valid evaluations in these various legal contexts.

3

General Assessment Issues with Psychological Injuries

> If a little knowledge is dangerous, where is the man who has so much as to be out of danger?
> —T. H. Huxley *On Elementary Instruction in Physiology* (1877)

It might be fairly said that forensic assessors know sufficient information about psychological injuries to be dangerous—to claimants, to insurers, to the courts, and to themselves. The aim of this chapter is to increase the knowledge base of forensic assessors and consumers of such assessments, perhaps reducing such danger. Discussions below include what is known about the frequency of traumatic and nontraumatic stressors, the all-too-commonly missing trauma histories in many assessments, and the prevalence of posttraumatic stress disorder (PTSD) and comorbidity-related issues. We describe the limitations on our knowledge of the conditional prevalence of PTSD; and finally, we examine some commonly used evidence-based assessment instruments, including both clinician interviews and self-administered tests.

Frequency and Assessment of Traumatic Stressors

At one time, traumatic events sufficient to cause PTSD were thought to be rare. For example, "The essential feature of (PTSD) is the development of characteristic symptoms following a psychologically distressing *event that is outside the range of usual human experience.* . . . The stressor producing this syndrome would be markedly distressing to almost anyone" (American Psychiatric Association, 1987,

49

p. 247). Contrary to the statement above, research during the past decade has shown that traumatic stressors are all too common in everyday life, and that many such ordinary events have a relatively high association with PTSD.

Perhaps the first study reflecting the ubiquity of trauma exposure was that of Norris (1992), who sampled 1,000 adults in four separate southeastern U.S. cities following Hurricane Hugo. Twenty-five percent of Norris's sample had been exposed to robbery, 15% physical assault, 4% sexual assault, 30% tragic death, 23% motor vehicle accidents (MVAs), 9% combat, and 69% any trauma. Resnick, Kilpatrick, Dansky, Saunders, and Best (1993) randomly sampled 4,008 women in the United States by telephone for prevalence of criminal and noncriminal traumas. Replicating the findings of Norris (1992), 69% of the sample had been exposed to at least one trauma.

Because of the results of studies such as these, the criterion for determining the presence of a traumatic stressor changed in the fourth edition of the *Diagnostic and Statistical Manual of Mental Disorders* (DSM-IV) to "both of the following were present [during the event]: (1) the person experienced, witnessed, or was confronted with an event or events that involved actual or threatened death or serious injury, or a threat to the physical integrity of self or others [or] (2) the person's response involved intense fear, helplessness, or horror" (American Psychiatric Association, 1994, pp. 427–428). The latter inclusion of an individual's appraisal of the event was a watershed event in the conceptualization of PTSD and resulted in controversy in some circles.

Since the advent of DSM-IV, sophisticated prevalence studies have continued to demonstrate the ubiquity of traumatic stress. For example, in a U.S. national random sample of 505 adults, Elliott (1997) found that 72% of respondents had experienced at least one Criterion A stressor, including 27% MVA, 23% child sexual abuse, 20% child physical abuse, 23% adult physical assault, 25% witnessing domestic violence as a child, and 21% witnessing nondomestic violent crime. Therefore, within the general population or selected nonclinical populations, the lifetime prevalence of exposure to at least one Criterion A traumatic stressor approximates 70% of the general public! The average subject of either a clinical or forensic mental health assessment is more likely than not to have experienced a traumatic stressor in his/her lifetime.

Missing Trauma Histories in Clinical Assessment

If trauma exposure is so common, it behooves clinicians and forensic assessors to obtain a detailed trauma history from a patient or plaintiff. However, various sources suggest that many trauma victims do not freely present for mental health assessment and treatment. For example, Kimerling and Calhoun (1994) found that only 19% of rape survivors initially seen in a hospital emergency room later sought mental health care of any kind.

There are a number of strategies for eliciting more accurate trauma histories, including: (a) adding a preface about others' experiences of trauma prior to the inquiry, (b) avoiding legal descriptions in favor of behaviorally specific language to describe acts of sexual victimization, and (c) allowing for reports of multiple traumatic experiences (Resnick, Falsetti, Kilpatrick, & Freedy, 1996). In a move to improve the detection of traumatic events, general prefatory statements about trauma exposure are now more commonly used in structured interviews for PTSD. However, Weaver (1998), in a sample of 43 women, found that behaviorally specific inquiries (e.g., about childhood physical and sexual abuse or adult sexual assault) markedly increased the endorsement rate for such events when compared to the preface used in the Structured Clinical Interview for DSM-III-R (SCID): "Have you ever had an experience that was really frightening or traumatic, like having your life threatened, seeing someone dead or badly hurt, or having your house burn down?" Close examination of this particular prefatory remark suggests that respondents might understandably not mention exposure to date rape, motor vehicle accidents, sexual harassment, or life-threatening medical illness, among other potentially threatening events. In Weaver's sample of battered women, having a behaviorally specific question about childhood sexual abuse increased the endorsement rate for such experiences from 7% to 53% of respondents. Failure to inquire in a behaviorally specific manner about previous traumas will lead to the underdetection of such traumas.

Assessing Traumatic Experiences

Because the first criterion for diagnosing PTSD (American Psychiatric Association, 1994, 2000) is the determination that the claimant suffered a particular event with accompanying adverse emotion, some debate has revolved around how an assessor determines whether a specific event was, in fact, "traumatic." Some authors advocate focusing on the objective severity of the traumatic event (e.g., physical injury, amount of property damage; see Malmquist, 1996), and there appears to be a general fear in some circles (e.g., the insurance industry) that considering the subjective response during trauma exposure will markedly increase claims for psychological distress. This stems both from natural skepticism and from admonitions coming out of the DSM Task Force—"The major question in defining posttraumatic stress is whether or not to include reactions to the numerous stressors that are upsetting or not life threatening" (Frances, First, & Pincus, 1995, p. 259). However, Kilpatrick et al. (1998), in the DSM-IV field trials, found that restrictions on the definition of Criterion A stressors had only modest effects on PTSD prevalence.

Despite the findings of Kilpatrick et al. (1998), we believe that a thorough forensic assessment of PTSD or other emotional consequences of trauma should include a detailed evaluation of the subject trauma and the claimant's initial emotional response. Our preferred strategy for such evaluation is reviewed briefly. First, did the claimant suffer a life-threatening injury during or because of the traumatic event? Severe orthopedic injuries or loss of blood from lacerations, head injuries, or gunshots would obviously qualify as life threatening. Second, did the claimant suffer a physically disabling injury that could conceivably limit his/her employment or accomplishment of important life goals (e.g., spinal cord injury)? Third, did the claimant witness a death or severe injury, such as death via homicide, vehicular accidents, or within medical settings (e.g., hospital emergency departments)? Fourth, did the claimant have a realistic fear that his/her life was in danger despite no obvious traumatic injury (e.g., HIV-infected blood splash or needle puncture, stalking by stranger or ex-romantic partner)? Fifth, did the claimant suffer some threat to his/her physical integrity (e.g., threatened or actual coercive sexual contact)?

If the answer is yes to one or more of these types of events, the examiner must ask for a description of the claimant's emotional state at the time of the traumatic event. DSM-IV specifies intense fear, helplessness, or horror as the requisite emotional states. However, the examiner must use his/her clinical judgment to ascertain whether the claimant was in one or more of these states or some similar form of negative emotional arousal. Thus, the assessor should probe to determine if the claimant feared for his/her life, or that something worse than the actual physical outcome might occur (e.g., "What did you think the stalker would do to you?"). Also relevant are descriptions of intense emotional reactions. There is evidence (e.g., Nixon & Bryant, 2003) that panic attacks during the subject trauma predict PTSD status.

There is considerable debate about the role of dissociation at the time of the trauma (termed "peritraumatic dissociation") in the development of PTSD. Supporting the role of peritraumatic dissociation in the prediction of PTSD are results from several different trauma populations (e.g., Mellman, David, Bustamante, Fins, & Esposito, 2001). On the other hand, Holeva & Tarrier (2001) found that peritraumatic dissociation did not independently predict PTSD status 4 to 6 months post-MVA, when measures of personality (e.g., neuroticism) were included in the regression equation.

Sometimes, objective data concerning heightened emotional arousal such as emergency room vital signs (e.g., heart rate) will be available. However, empirical investigation of heart rate obtained during vital signs assessment within emergency departments has had mixed results with respect to predicting PTSD (e.g., Blanchard, Hickling, Galovski, & Veazey, 2002; Shalev et al., 1998).

Thus, a careful forensic assessment of PTSD following exposure to trauma will evaluate systematically the objective and subjective threat experienced by the claimant during the trauma, as well as the presence of negative emotional arousal. Beyond DSM-recommended emotional states such as fear, helplessness, and horror, the careful assessor will ask the claimant what he/she anticipated happening to him/her during the trauma (e.g., loss of life, life-altering injury, or threat to personal well-being) and assess for the presence of panic, peritraumatic dissociation and physiological hyperarousal.

Another issue with respect to assessing Criterion A stressors involves the topographic and temporal boundaries of the traumatic event. It may not be the fender-to-fender impact of two vehicles that engenders a sense of threat, but the comment by the paramedic afterward that "you're lucky to be alive" or the disabling and unexplained pain on the subsequent day. Thus, forensic assessors must carefully delineate what the claimant perceived as threatening about the event.

Prevalence of PTSD

Studies of PTSD prevalence in the general population suggest that approximately 8% to 9% of members of Western society will suffer from PTSD in their lifetime (e.g., Breslau, Davis, Andreski, & Peterson, 1991). However, knowing the lifetime prevalence of PTSD within the general population is of little utility in a psycho-legal context. Rather, it is more important to know the conditional prevalence, that is, the percentage of trauma-exposed persons who develop PTSD following a given traumatic stressor. Perhaps the first studies to address this issue were epidemiological studies conducted by Breslau, Davis, Andreski, and Peterson (1991), Norris (1992). Breslau et al. (1991), using a sample of 1,000 young adults, found a 9% lifetime prevalence of PTSD, based on a traumatic event exposure prevalence of 39% and a conditional PTSD prevalence of 24%. The publication of this particular study was important because previous studies (e.g., Breslau, Davis, Andrewski, & Peterson, 1991) suggested lifetime prevalence for PTSD in the general public of approximately 1%. Kilpatrick and Resnick (1993) sampled 1,500 women and found lifetime conditional rates of PTSD to vary from 10% to 39%, with higher rates among rape and assault victims.

Norris (1992), in an attempt to improve on these previous studies, used a more open-ended inquiry about potentially traumatic events and stratified her random sample by ethnicity (50% White, 50% Black), gender, and age (young, middle-aged, and older adults). This study resulted in a current PTSD prevalence of 6.2%. The lowest rate of current PTSD was associated with a history of combat exposure (2%), the highest with sexual assault (14%), physical assault (13%), and MVA (12%). Resnick, Kilpatrick, Dansky, Saunders, and Best (1993) sampled 4,008 randomly selected women and found lifetime and current PTSD prevalence as follows: completed rape (32% lifetime, 12% current); other sexual assault (31%, 13%); physical assault (39%, 18%); noncrime trauma, for example, disaster or accident (9%, 7%).

More recently, Shercliffe (2001) conducted a statistical meta-analysis of PTSD prevalence rates among civilian samples. He further limited data sets used in this study by excluding any acute samples (e.g., less than six months posttrauma). In this meta-analysis, the author clustered trauma types into three groups: interpersonal (e.g., crime), technological (e.g., MVA), and life-threatening illness (e.g., cancer). Current (mean one year posttrauma) PTSD rates were, respectively, 25%, 15%, and 7% for interpersonal, technological, and illness traumas.

In summary, it appears that PTSD is most common following criminal victimization, with the incidence of chronic PTSD (greater than six months in duration) being between 13% and 39% of victims. Technological traumas such as MVAs, other transportation accidents, and workplace accidents have an arguably lower prevalence of PTSD, between 9% and 15% of victims. Less is known about the conditional prevalence of PTSD for other specific traumatic stressors. However, it is apparent that estimates of PTSD prevalence can be influenced markedly by the method of inquiry. Assessment methods that closely approximate those utilized in the best epidemiological and clinical research studies will increase the reliability and validity of forensic assessments of PTSD.

While the PTSD prevalence data above reflect our best current understanding, there are problems with even the best of these epidemiological studies. Some complications in accurately estimating PTSD prevalence from MVA and industrial trauma arise from the clinical contexts in which such patients are seen and comorbid problems common to injury survivors. First, some of the associated features of severe physical injuries may result in hyperarousal (Criterion D) symptoms such as sleep disturbance, concentration deficits, and irritability through the effects of acute physical pain (see review by O'Donnell, Creamer, Bryant, Schnyder, & Shalev, 2003). Behavioral avoidance of reminders (e.g., driving a vehicle) may be difficult to reliably assess in MVA survivors if (a) their opportunities for driving are limited by their physical injuries (e.g., patients who are still confined to inpatient medical wards), or (b) they are not driving because of physical limitations (e.g., broken leg). As well, interviewers/assessors must differentiate intrusive memories of a nonvoluntary nature from voluntary ruminative thought content concerning the MVA. The latter would not fulfill Criterion B (reexperiencing symptoms), but it is not clear that all research studies successfully differentiate these two classes of thought content.

Prevalence of Nontraumatic Stress and its Consequences

While the focus of litigation may revolve around specific traumatic stressors (e.g., MVAs, assaults, or harassment), such events and their emotional consequences occur in a fluid social and environmental context, in which people are exposed to a high rate of distressing nontraumatic stressors as an ongoing part of their personal and work life. It is important for professionals who conduct forensic assessments to have some basic understanding of the incidence of nontraumatic stressors and their relationship to emotional distress. In recent years, studies of daily stress and distress have benefited from the development of diary-based assessments (e.g., Bolger, DeLongis, Kessler, & Schilling, 1989). Bolger et al. (1989) have collected data on interpersonal stressors (e.g., marital arguments), role overload (work, home, demands from others), as well as transportation and financial problems. All of these nontraumatic stressors are at least as likely to affect personal injury claimants as other members of the general population, and therefore exert some influence on their well-being independent of that arising from traumatic stressors.

Daily stressors, particularly interpersonal conflict, have robust effects on mood within members of the general population (e.g., Bolger et al., 1989). Interpersonal conflict appears to occur frequently in the general population, with the married couples in Bolger et al. (1989) averaging 0.9 marital conflicts per month. Combining both interpersonal and other stressors, Bolger et al. found that one quarter of their (nonclinical) sample's diary days contained at least two concurrent stressors. Interestingly, most individuals appear to "bounce back" rather quickly from short-lasting daily stressors with mood returning to usual levels on the day following such stressors (Bolger et al., 1989), but socially isolated or chronically stressed individuals experience more persistent distress (Caspi, Bolger, & Eckenrode, 1987). Therefore, it appears that interpersonal conflict is a relatively frequent occurrence in the general population and results in significant psychological distress that may be more persistent in vulnerable individuals.

Few data exist concerning the prevalence of PTSD symptoms in the absence of a traumatic stressor (partially because reexperiencing and some avoidance symptoms are tied to specific trauma experiences—how do you ask someone if they have distressing memories of a nonexistent trauma?). However, information on other stress-related symptoms in the general population comes from the literature on postconcussive symptoms (PCS). This is relevant to our topic because the research diagnostic criteria for postconcussional disorder include a 3-month history of concentration or other cognitive difficulties, fatigue, sleep disturbance, headache, dizziness, irritability, anxiety or depression, changes in personality, and apathy (American Psychiatric Association, 1994). All of these symptoms but headaches overlap with symptoms of PTSD or depression. It should be recognized that chronic pain is often comorbid with PTSD (e.g., Sharp & Harvey, 2001). Of note for the current discussion, this list of postconcussive symptoms includes 3 of the 5 PTSD Criterion D (hyperarousal) symptoms (anger/irritability, concentration problems, and sleep disturbance).

How common are such symptoms in the general public? Fox, Lees-Haley, Earnest, and Dolezal-Wood (1995) assessed the presence of PCS in 1,116 patients. Four hundred of these subjects were seeking psychotherapy, 104 were neurology patients, 124 were family practice patients, 192 were internal medicine patients, and 296 had just enrolled in the health maintenance organization (HMO) and were undergoing an initial evaluation. The authors asked patients to indicate whether they had experienced any postconcussive symptoms in the last two years. For our purposes, the important results involve the percentage of endorsements for complaints of dizziness, concentration difficulties, fatigue, and irritability in the family practice and initial evaluation samples, both of whom would be expected to have a low rate of psychiatric disturbance or cognitive symptoms in comparison to the psychotherapy or neurology samples. Within the family practice sample, 27%, 40%, 59%, and 44% of subjects endorsed symptoms of dizziness, concentration, fatigue, and irritability, respectively, within the previous two years. Within the evaluation sample, 24%, 19%, 34%, and 33% complained of the same symptoms. Therefore, these symptoms (common to both PCS and PTSD) occur at least intermittently in a large percentage of general medical patients without known psychiatric diagnoses. What, then, does it mean when 59% of a nonpsychiatric, nonlitigating sample of general medical patients endorse feeling fatigued at some time? What are the implications of such a high complaint base rate within the general population for forensic assessment of individuals with mental health claims? Clearly, careful delineation of the frequency, intensity, and associated interference should be a critical part of forensic assessments.

Comorbidity

While PTSD is the psychological condition most often litigated in personal injury claims, injured claimants' mental and physical health concerns are rarely limited to symptoms of PTSD alone. First, diagnoses are not synonymous with psychological injuries. Individuals can suffer psychological injuries in forms of psychological distress (e.g., shame, humiliation, apprehension, or anger) that do not conform to any known diagnostic nomenclature such as that found in DSM-IV. Nonetheless, such injuries may be severe, disabling, and compensated by courts of law. Second, as a principal diagnosis, PTSD has a much higher rate of comorbidity with other anxiety and mood diagnoses than any other anxiety disorder. Comorbidity refers to the joint occurrence of two or more diagnoses or clinical problems in the same person. While the term comorbidity reflects its origins in a medical or disease model of mental health problems, we prefer to use this term to refer to the co-occurrence of different forms of disabling or distressing life problems independent of whether these problems conform to specific diagnostic nomenclature. Within this section, we review comorbidity of problems across mental health diagnoses, pain, other medical complaints and health perceptions, as well as more specific emotional difficulties.

Brown, Campbell, Lehman, Grisham, and Mancill (2001), in a sample of 1,217 treatment-seeking outpatients, found that 92% of individuals with principal PTSD diagnoses had another current mental health diagnosis, while 100% of PTSD cases had a lifetime history of at least one other mental health diagnosis. Within a community sample of 391 women, Boudreaux, Kilpatrick, Resnick, Best, and Saunders (1998) found that women with PTSD were more likely to have any Axis I disorder (64% vs. 25%), major depressive episode (32% vs. 4%), panic disorder (14% vs. 1%), agoraphobia (18% vs. 1%), obsessive-compulsive disorder (27% vs. 3%), and social phobia (18% vs. 4%) than were women in general. Logistic regression analyses using demographic and crime factors as well as PTSD as predictor variables for other non-PTSD disorders showed PTSD status to be an important mediator of major depressive episode, panic disorder, agoraphobia, and obsessive-compulsive disorder. In another treatment-seeking sample of 310 outpatients, Zayfert, Becker, Unger, and Shearer (2002) found that 74% of principal PTSD patients had at least one other anxiety disorder diagnosis, while 50% of principal PTSD patients had at least two comorbid anxiety disorder diagnoses. When depression was included, 86% of principal PTSD cases had at least one other disorder. Feeny, O'Neill, and Foa (under review) examined comorbidity of clinical and personality disorders in 222 female victims of sexual and nonsexual assault. Women with current PTSD were more likely to be diagnosed with another (both lifetime and current) Axis I disorder than those without PTSD. Women with PTSD were more likely to meet criteria for major depression and adjustment disorder than those without PTSD. Women who met symptom criteria for PTSD were also more likely to have personality disorder diagnoses (39.1%) than women who did not meet symptom criteria for PTSD (19.6%). Women with PTSD reported higher rates of self-defeating and borderline personality disorders.

PTSD and Depression

An important question has been raised about the meaning of the substantial comorbidity between PTSD and depression following trauma exposure. As mentioned above, Boudreaux et al. (1998) found that 32% of women with PTSD had concurrent depression, while Blanchard and Hickling (1997) found that more than 50% of MVA-PTSD cases suffered from a major depression. What accounts for this very high degree of comorbidity? Are PTSD and depression following exposure to trauma separate clinical phenomena, or is their high level of comorbidity an artifact of shared symptoms?

Blanchard, Buckley, Hickling, and Taylor (1998) addressed this question in a creative manner using a sample of 158 MVA survivors, 62 of whom met full criteria for PTSD and 45 of whom met criteria for subsyndromal PTSD (i.e., failing to meet criteria on either the avoidance/numbing or hyperarousal clusters). Within these two sets of patients, 33 and 3, respectively, met criteria for a major depressive episode. The authors then analyzed the goodness of fit of two separate hypothetical factor solutions for subjects' responses on PTSD and depression-related tests/interviews. The two-factor solution was a better fit than a single-

factor solution, although substantial shared variance existed between the two underlying latent variables (r = .88). Thus, PTSD and depression appear to have
some statistical independence, at least within a sample of MVA survivors. The
authors then divided the 62 full PTSD sufferers into four groups: (a) PTSD w/
MDE (5 to 6 depressive symptoms), (b) PTSD w/MDE (7 to 9 depressive symptoms), (c) PTSD with preexisting MDE, and (d) PTSD without MDE. In short,
those subjects with PTSD and MDE showed greater global distress and worse
functioning than those subjects with PTSD alone, and there were no functional
differences between the two PTSD/MDE groups based on number of depressive
symptoms. Finally, when reexamining 55 of the PTSD subjects six months later,
the authors found different rates of spontaneous remission among these four
groups. Specifically, those PTSD sufferers who were depressed at initial assessment were less likely to have spontaneously remitted 6 months later than PTSD
cases without comorbid depression. Thus, MVA survivors with both PTSD and
depression have a worse outcome than those MVA survivors with PTSD alone,
suggesting that there are important functional implications of depression independent of PTSD.

In short, the diagnosis of PTSD appears to be associated with substantially
higher rates of depression as well as higher rates of other anxiety disorders (e.g.,
panic disorder, obsessive compulsive disorder). Suffice it to say, psychological
assessment of a plaintiff in a personal injury claim should not be limited to determining the presence or absence of PTSD, but should include assessment of
these other apparently interrelated diagnoses of major depression, panic disorder,
and obsessive-compulsive disorder, among the wider range of anxiety disorders.
Decisions about appropriate treatments for such patients also need to take into
account such comorbidity.

PTSD and Substance Abuse

Yet another important mental health condition that frequently co-occurs with
PTSD is substance abuse. In a recent review, Stewart (1996) concluded that trauma
exposure is associated with increased risk of alcohol problems and that a diagnosis
of PTSD following trauma exposure increases such risk. The relationship between
PTSD and alcohol problems has been most extensively studied in combat veterans, assault victims, and disaster victims. We know relatively less about the prevalence of alcohol and other substance abuse problems in survivors of transportation or work-related traumas.

Some recent research explicates the mechanisms behind this relationship between PTSD and substance use problems. In a study that appears to be representative of other findings, Stewart, Conrod, Pihl, and Dongier (1999) factor analyzed
PTSD symptom scores in 295 non–treatment-seeking substance-abusing women
and found a four-factor solution (intrusions, arousal, numbing, and avoidance).
Forty-six percent of this sample met criteria for PTSD. Alcohol dependence was

significantly but modestly correlated with the PTSD arousal symptom factor; anxiolytic dependence correlated with both arousal and numbing factors; and analgesic dependence correlated with arousal, intrusions, and numbing factors. While these data are correlational and thus weak indicators of causality, they do suggest that maladaptive substance (e.g., alcohol, anxiolytic) use may be motivated by PTSD sufferers' motivation to reduce negative emotion.

In summary, both alcohol abuse/dependence and other forms of substance abuse appear to occur concurrently with PTSD, possibly motivated by the emotional discomfort of PTSD symptoms.

PTSD and Pain

Sharp and Harvey (2001) reviewed research concerning the comorbidity between PTSD and chronic pain, as well as suggested several potential avenues by which these two conditions may maintain each other. These authors concluded that the rates of pain complaints in PTSD samples range from 25% to 80%. Second, there appears to be a higher than expected prevalence of PTSD in chronic pain populations.

Sharp and Harvey described seven different mechanisms by which PTSD and chronic pain experience may exacerbate each other. First, because of their threat-related attentional biases, PTSD patients may excessively attend to, and thus amplify, their pain sensations. Second, high levels of anxiety sensitivity (fear of the sensations of autonomic arousal) in PTSD sufferers may aggravate fear of pain among chronic pain patients who also suffer from PTSD. Third, chronic pain sensation may serve as a reminder of the traumatic event in which both the PTSD and physical injury were acquired, thus motivating avoidance of both such anxiety provoking reminders and activities that may increase pain experience. Fourth, avoidant coping, a common characteristic of both disorders, may account for the relationship. Fifth, the connection between PTSD and pain may be a result of the high rate of depressive symptoms associated with both these disorders. The fatigue and lethargy common to depression may result in reduced activity levels that serve to maintain low levels of activity and exposure to trauma-related stimuli, as well as reduce involvement in physical rehabilitation, thus impeding recovery on both these dimensions. Sixth, the high levels of anxiety common in PTSD may directly increase pain perception. Finally, effective pain coping may be adversely affected by the high level of negative cognitive activity (e.g., catastrophic thinking, cognitive intrusions of the trauma) because of a finite supply of attentional resources. Obviously, a great deal of research is needed with regard to the complex relationship between PTSD and pain.

A better understanding of the interplay between PTSD and pain is important for forensic assessors, rehabilitation professionals, and lawyers. The task for forensic assessors is to ascertain how an individual PTSD claimant's symptoms from these two domains may be related and mutually maintaining each other. The rehabilitation counselor needs to coordinate the simultaneous treatment of both conditions so that the existence of one condition does not preclude successful treatment of the other. Legal counsel must better understand the interplay between these two conditions so as to interpret forensic assessments more meaningfully and understand the complex nature of claimants' disabilities.

PTSD and General Physical Health

Pain is but one facet of physical health. During the past decade, different research groups have investigated the relationships among trauma exposure, PTSD symptoms, general psychological distress, and physical health. Epidemiological studies (e.g., Golding, 1994) consistently find that trauma-exposed persons report a much larger number of physical illnesses and related symptoms.

In an enlightening prospective study, Kimerling and Calhoun (1994) followed 115 recent sexual assault victims for one year. These victims were compared to 87 nonassaulted, demographically matched women. The assessment included information about social network, mental health problems, medical utilization and physical symptoms (excluding those directly related to the assault), and mental health service utilization. Victims had more mental health problems than nonvictims throughout the year postassault, and initially higher physical symptoms than the nonvictim group. This latter difference declined by the end of the first year, but general medical utilization (not mental health care) remained higher than for nonvictims at one year postassault. Social support appeared to buffer victims against the negative physical health effects of sexual assault and led to reduced medical utilization. Later empirical work and reviews (e.g., Schnurr & Green, 2004) suggest that PTSD status serves as a mediating variable between trauma exposure and subsequent worsening physical health.

There is substantial evidence that trauma exposure leads to a decline in individuals' perception of their physical health and increased general medical utilization. Any of PTSD symptoms, depressive symptoms, or more global psychological distress may mediate this relationship between trauma and complaints of physical illness. Ultimately, it appears that mental health symptoms mediate some proportion of physical health complaints in trauma survivors.

PTSD and Anger

The relationship between PTSD and anger has been studied primarily in combat veterans (e.g., Novaco & Chemtob, 2002) and crime victims (e.g., Feeny, Zoellner, & Foa, 2000). First, we address the issue of anger arousal and its implications for PTSD in assault victims. The initial study, to our knowledge, that investigated the intersection of PTSD and anger in noncombat samples was that of Riggs, Dancu, Gershuny, Greenberg, and Foa (1992). These authors compared 116 adult female assault victims with 50 adult women matched on demographic variables. Those victims who met criteria for PTSD one month later were angrier than non-

PTSD victims. A regression analysis found that one-month PTSD severity was predicted by guilt, life threat, and state anger at one week. Thus, anger appeared to contribute to the development of PTSD at one month postassault. Feeny, Zoellner, and Foa (2000) investigated the relationships among anger, dissociation, and PTSD symptoms at 2, 4, and 12 weeks postassault in a sample of 104 female assault victims. Regression analyses revealed that anger expression but not dissociation contributed to the prediction of PTSD symptoms at four weeks. Dissociation, but not anger expression, predicted worse social functioning at three months. Therefore, it appears likely that anger potentiates PTSD. Ehlers, Mayou, and Bryant (1998) assessed via questionnaires a large sample of consecutive hospital admissions at both 3 and 12 months post-MVA. Anger about the accident was one of several variables that predicted later PTSD. In multivariate analyses, angry thought content was one of several variables that predicted PTSD at both 3 and 12 months. Clearly, anger is an important psychological variable that predicts new cases of PTSD and requires careful assessment within both forensic assessment and routine clinical care.

Evidence-Based Assessment

Given the history of underdetection of traumatic stressors described earlier, it is heartening to know that some researchers have developed psychometrically sound tests for assessing the occurrence of traumatic events. Self-report and interview tools for traumatic event screening have been developed by a number of authors (e.g., Goodman, Corcoran, Turner, Yuan, & Green, 1998). While there are several such measures, we limit our current discussion to Goodman et al. to illustrate specific screening issues.

The Stressful Life Events Screening Questionnaire (SLESQ, Goodman et al., 1998) is a 13-item self-report measure. It was specifically developed to assess the lifetime prevalence among subjects of DSM-IV PTSD Criterion A stressors. The SLESQ consists of 11 specific types of trauma: (a) life-threatening illness, (b) life-threatening accident, (c) robbery or mugging, (d) traumatic death of family member or friend, (e) forced vaginal, oral, or anal intercourse, (f) attempted forced intercourse, (g) nonconsensual sexual touching, (h) physical child abuse, (i) physical assault as an adult, (j) threatened with weapon, and (k) present during another's death, injury, or assault. Two "other" items are included, which if the subject endorses, he/she is asked to describe. Goodman et al. (1998) reported data from the SLESQ from 202 university undergraduates. One hundred forty respondents completed a follow-up assessment two weeks after their initial assessment. Seventy-two percent of respondents reported at least one traumatic event (mean = 1.83 events, SD = 1.96). Independent ratings by the first three authors of a randomly selected sample of 46 protocols found that 85% of reported events met the authors' severity threshold for a Criterion A traumatic stressor. According to the authors, the false positive responses in these surveys primarily involved peer fights as children, spanking by parents, and non–life-threatening illnesses. Reliability was good (two-week test-retest reliability for total number of events, r = .89; and individual kappas ranged from .31 to 1.00, median k = .73). Attempted sexual assault and witnessing a traumatic event were the only items having kappas below .60. Comparison of the SLESQ with interview suggested that the interview increased trauma reporting because it tapped events that were below DSM thresholds for Criterion A traumatic stressors. We learn a few things from these data. First, a self-report asking about exposure to traumatic events with sufficiently descriptive categories is reliable. Second, interviews (as opposed to self-report measures) may increase the rate of trauma reporting by eliciting endorsements from subjects of relatively low-threat events. Third, overendorsement appears to be largely a consequence of subjects setting the threshold too low for defining a traumatic event. It is apparent that trauma-screening measures with adequate psychometric quality are available and should comprise part of a forensic assessment battery.

Reliability of PTSD, Anxiety, and Mood Diagnoses

The clinical assessment of mental disorders has a checkered record. Approximately 40 years ago, Ward, Beck, Mendelson, Mock, and Erbaugh (1962) discovered that disagreements between clinical assessors had been disproportionately accounted for due to the use of different standards for clinically relevant symptoms or complaints and to variations in the nature of questions, observations, and the organization of such information by examiners. The implicit message from this study was that mental disorders could be more reliably assessed if examiners used standardized inquiries and agreed on the threshold at which a complaint or emotional experience becomes clinically severe. More recently, Steiner, Tebes, Sledge, and Walker (1995) studied the agreement between clinical interview and the Structured Clinical Interview for DSM-III-R (SCID) in 100 admissions to a community mental health center. While kappas for schizophrenia and bipolar disorder (.55 and .47, respectively) were fair, kappas for other conditions were much worse (e.g., major depression [.34], panic disorder [0], and adjustment disorder [.10]). These studies and others gave rise to the opinion of Rogers (2001) that regular use of structured diagnostic interviews would help clinical diagnosis by reducing idiosyncratic questions, variable coverage of mental disorders, and idiosyncratic sequencing of questions, as well as systematizing ratings of symptom severity.

We briefly mention some of the more commonly used and empirically supported measures of PTSD symptoms. The proliferation of PTSD measures over the past decade precludes an exhaustive review. We begin with semistructured diagnostic interviews that canvas a broader range of disorders, followed by discussions of more narrowly focused diagnostic interviews, and subsequently by an examination of self-report inventories.

Structured Clinical Interview for the DSM-III-R or DSM-IV (SCID)

The SCID is a comprehensive, semistructured interview for diagnosing psychopathology according to DSM-III-R or DSM-IV. The SCID is often used as the "gold standard" of diagnosis. The original purpose of the SCID was to standardize DSM-III (American Psychiatric Association, 1980) diagnoses. It is a hierarchical interview with branching instructions and great breadth so that it captures a wide range of psychopathology. Nonetheless, the SCID does not cover certain areas (e.g., dissociative disorders, sleep disorders, factitious disorders). Inter-rater reliability for specific diagnoses ranges from moderate (kappas $> .75$) to very good (kappas $> .85$) (reviewed in Rogers, 2001). The SCID appears to have moderate test-retest reliability, although Williams et al. (1992), with a large sample of clinical and nonclinical subjects, found moderate reliabilities for individual current diagnoses (mean kappa $= .61$ for clinical subjects), but great variability across research sites in test-retest reliability of individual diagnoses (e.g., kappas ranged from .37 to .82 for depression). Of note to our emphasis on forensic assessment, two factors were thought to explain the variable test-retest reliability: (a) interviewers were transferred from research site to research site so that they had variable pre-interview experience with the individual patients being assessed, and (b) the study was conducted across countries (the United States and Germany) and languages. This bodes ill for the reliability of SCID evaluations in forensic assessments, given that forensic assessors often have less pre-interview experience with the subject of their evaluation than do treating clinicians. However, its reliability within samples of motor vehicle accident victims, common personal injury claimants, is excellent (kappa $> .95$) (Ursano et al., 1999).

Because the SCID corresponds to DSM criteria, little research has focused on concurrent validity. In a comparison of the SCID and the computerized Diagnostic Interview Schedule (DIS) in a sample of substance abusing patients, Ross, Swinson, Larkin, and Doumani (1994) found overall percent agreement on individual diagnoses to be high (median $= 84\%$), but poor agreement was reached for mood and anxiety disorders (median kappa $= .22$). This would suggest that if two separate forensic examiners were to assess the same patient, one using the SCID and the other the DIS, they would be unlikely to agree on mood or anxiety disorder diagnoses.

Diagnostic Interview Schedule (DIS)

The DIS was developed by the U.S. National Institute of Mental Health to aid in assessing DSM-III mental disorders. Early data showed variable inter-rater agreement between psychiatrists and lay interviewers using this schedule, with sensitivity for diagnoses ranging from 41% to 100%, and specificity ranging from 84% to 100% (Robins, Helzer, Croughan, & Ratcliff, 1981). Kappas between lay interviewers' DIS diagnoses and psychiatric chart diagnoses ranged from .39 to .03, with better agreement for affective, obsessive-compulsive, and schizophrenic disorders; it was poorest for phobias (Erdman, Klein, Greist, & Bass, 1987). In a larger study than that of Wittchen, Kessler, Zhao, and Abelson (1995) however, Vandiver and Sher (1991) found the DIS to be moderately reliable for assessing lifetime psychopathology. In general, the DIS may be of less utility for the diagnosis of anxiety disorders than other interview schedules.

Composite International Diagnostic Interview (CIDI)

The CIDI is a structured diagnostic interview for mental health conditions developed by the World Health Organization. It is capable of providing data for either DSM-IV or International Classification of Diseases (ICD) diagnoses (Andrews & Peters, 1998). Inter-rater reliability for diagnosis of anxiety disorders with the CIDI has been described as excellent (Andrews, Peters, Guzman, & Bird, 1995), and test-retest reliabilities are generally good, with the only anxiety disorder exception being generalized anxiety disorder (Wittchen, Lachner, Wunderlich, & Pfister, 1998).

Anxiety Disorders Interview Schedule (ADIS)

DiNardo, O'Brien, Barlow, Waddell, and Blanchard (1982) developed the ADIS for three purposes: (a) differential diagnosis of anxiety disorders, (b) ruling out other disorders (e.g., substance abuse, mood disorders), and (c) providing treatment-relevant clinical data. Thus, the ADIS has a more limited scope of target disorders/problems than do the SCID, DIS, or CIDI. As its name suggests, the ADIS has modules for PTSD, generalized anxiety disorder (GAD), acute stress disorder (ASD), panic disorder (PD), agoraphobia, specific and social phobias, and obsessive-compulsive disorder (OCD), as well as other modules for mood and substance abuse/dependence disorders. The ADIS is relevant to our discussion of psychological injuries because (a) PTSD is considered an anxiety disorder in DSM-IV, (b) PTSD has a high rate of comorbidity with other anxiety disorders and depression (see discussion above), and (c) personal injury and disability claimants may have psychological losses that are not necessarily best conceptualized as PTSD.

Rogers (2001) has described the ADIS as moderately reliable with respect to diagnosing anxiety disorders. Of relevance to our discussion, Blanchard, Gerardi, Kolb, and Barlow (1986) found high agreement (percent agreement on diagnosis = 93%, kappa = .86) for combat-related PTSD and clinician diagnosis. More recently, Brown, DiNardo, Lehman, and Campbell (2001) reported on the reliability of ADIS assessments in 362 treatment-seeking subjects. Inter-rater reliability kappas for DSM-IV current diagnoses ranged from .22 (dysthymia) to .86 (specific phobia), with relatively good to modest kappas for other disorders (e.g., OCD = .85, PD = .72, GAD = .67, major depressive disorder—MDD = .67, PTSD = .59). For our discussion, it is worth noting that despite the large overall sample size (n = 362), these authors had only 14 PTSD subjects. The latter small sample size may account for the poorer reliability of PTSD diagnoses. The authors also reviewed the sources of disagreement between raters with the ADIS and noted that the majority of disagreements were accounted for by either differences in patient report (i.e., gave different answers to the same question to two different interviewers) or diagnostic threshold (interviewers disagreeing on whether a problem was severe enough to merit a diagnosis). In brief, the ADIS-IV is moderately reliable in diagnosing anxiety disorders, although it may have lower levels of agreement for PTSD than for some other anxiety disorders. There are limited data for its concurrent validity with clinicians' diagnoses.

Clinician-Administered PTSD Scale (CAPS)
The CAPS, originally developed by Blake et al. (1998), is a structured assessment guide administered by clinicians within a diagnostic interview. Clinicians rate the frequency from 0 to 4 of 17 PTSD symptoms within the previous month: 0 (not present), 1 (once or twice, or less than 10% of the time), 2 (once or twice per week, 20–30%), 3 (several times per week, 50–60%), 4 (daily or almost daily, more than 80%). The severity of symptoms also is rated from 0 to 4. Thus, each symptom receives a rating from 0 to 8. In order for a symptom to be counted toward a diagnosis, the traditional scoring rule is that it must have a combined score of 3, comprised of a rating of at least 1 on either the frequency or severity scale (i.e., 1-2 or 2-1). Inter-rater reliability for CAPS ratings of symptoms is very good, with correlations between raters ranging from .82 to .99, and averaging .975 (e.g., see Blanchard, Hickling, Taylor, Forneris, Loos, & Jaccard, 1995). Diagnostic agreement is also very good (kappa = .81) (Blanchard, Hickling, Taylor, & Loos, 1995).

The use of different scoring rules for the CAPS has been investigated by a number of authors; for example, Blanchard, Hickling, Taylor, Forneris, Loos, and Jaccard (1995) found that PTSD prevalence among MVA victims varied from 27% to 44% dependent on the stringency of the CAPS scoring rule and that those who met the more stringent CAPS criteria were significantly more distressed on psychological tests. Weathers, Ruscio, and Keane (1999) evaluated the sensitivity, specificity, and optimal discrimination of multiple rules in several samples of U.S. veterans. In brief, the traditional rule of 3 originally advocated by Blake et al. (1990) resulted in the highest rates of PTSD (48% to 82%), while a combination rule of 3 plus total symptom severity score of 65 was an easily scored rule that resulted in relatively equal false negatives and false positives, and a PTSD rate of 34% to 59%. This research suggests that the rules clinicians use to define a symptom as present or absent and the cutoff they use for total symptom severity have a significant impact on PTSD prevalence.

PTSD Checklist (PCL)

While the CAPS, SCID, DIS, CIDI, and ADIS are interviews, researchers have developed numerous self-report measures of PTSD or related constructs. Based on a small sample of 27 MVA victims and 13 sexual assault victims, Blanchard, Jones-Alexander, Buckley, and Forneris (1996) evaluated the validity of the PTSD Checklist (PCL), a 17-item self-report PTSD measure, by correlating it with the CAPS. The PCL requires persons to rate the 17 PTSD symptoms according to the degree to which they were bothered by the symptoms in the previous month. Internal consistency for the PCL total score was .94; for Criterion B items, it was .94; for Criterion C, .82; and Criterion D, .84. These values are very good, and suggest that the PCL consists mainly of "true-score" variance rather than "error variance." Validity coefficients also were good; the overall correlation between the PCL and CAPS was .93. Thus, the PCL shows good concurrent validity with an interview measure of PTSD. However, we must caution that this was a small sample study, and its participants were mostly female (92%).

More recently, Ruggiero, Del Ben, Scotti, and Rabalais (2003) examined the psychometric properties of the PTSD Checklist—Civilian Version (PCL-C) with 392 university students. Of note, their sample reported a very high prevalence of traumatic event exposure (96.7%). The PCL correlated highly with both the Impact of Event Scale (IES) and Mississippi Scale for PTSD (r = .77 and .82 between the PCL and the IES and Mississippi total scores, respectively). These correlations between measures of the same construct were significantly if marginally greater than the correlations between the PCL and measures of different constructs such as depression (r = .67), trait anxiety (r = .60), and general distress (r = .70). Small subsamples of this group of subjects completed the PCL either on the same day, one week later, or two weeks later. Test-retest correlations for the PCL over these intervals were .92 (same day), .88 (one week), and .68 (two weeks), suggesting reasonable temporal stability of scores on this measure.

Impact of Events Scale (IES)

The IES (Horowitz, Wilner, & Alvarez, 1979) is a self-report measure that assesses avoidance and intrusion symptoms. It consists of 15 items, split into subscales of intrusion (7 items) and avoidance (8 items). Split half reliability of the total scale is high (r = 0.86), and internal consistency measured by Cronbach's alpha is high for both intrusion (0.78) and avoidance (0.82) items. Test-retest reliability over a one-week interval is 0.87 for total score, 0.89 for the intrusion subscale, and 0.79 for the avoidance subscale. Scores on the total scale, as well as the two subscales, differentiated a sample of patients with exposure to traumatic experiences from a sample of medical students responding shortly after witnessing their first cadaver. More recent commentary has expressed some concerns about the utility of some of the items and psychometric qualities of the scale (e.g., Briere & Elliott, 1998). Joseph (2000) reviewed research on this scale, and noted that internal consistency and test-retest reliability are adequate for the IES, although relatively few studies have reported such data. With respect to validity, there is some debate about whether all IES items can be considered measures of psychological distress ("I had dreams about it."). While many clinicians treat the IES as a measure of posttraumatic stress symptoms, it does not contain any items tapping Criterion D (hyperarousal symptoms). As well, the IES does not sample some Criterion C symptoms traditionally considered related to the emotional numbing aspects of posttraumatic response (detachment, diminished interest). Given that Criterion C is the "gatekeeper" criterion for diagnosing PTSD, such an omission would lead to overestimation of PTSD prevalence if clinicians were to use the IES as a proxy for formal diagnosis of PTSD. Despite such poor content validity, the IES differentiates between those who receive a diagnosis of PTSD and those who do not (e.g., Bryant & Harvey, 1996). In summary, the IES has some utility in the discrimination of distressed versus nondistressed trauma survivors, but it should not be used as a proxy for measures, whether self-report or interview-based, that can reliably diagnose PTSD and that provide a fuller coverage of the range of PTSD symptoms.

Posttraumatic Symptoms Scale-Self-Report (PSS-SR) and
Posttraumatic Stress Diagnostic Scale (PDS)

PDS (Foa, Cashman, Jaycox, & Perry, 1997) and PSS-SR (Foa, Riggs, Dancu, & Rothbaum, 1993) are both self-report measures of PTSD symptoms. The symptom severity score of this newer test has good test-retest reliability over 10 to 22 days (kappa = .74, diagnostic agreement between the two administrations of 87%). The test is also internally consistent (Cronbach's alpha of .92). Using the SCID as the diagnostic gold standard, the PDS had a sensitivity of 82% and specificity of 77%, with overall agreement of 79%, and a kappa of .59. In Foa's normative sample (n = 230), the symptom severity score correlated highly with all of the Beck Depression Inventory—BDI (r = .79), (State Trait Anxiety Inventory—State Version) STAI-S (r = .73), (State Trait Anxiety Inventory—Trait Version) STAI-T (r = .74), (Intrusion scale of the IES) IES-I (r = .80), and (Avoidance scale of the IES) IES-A (r = .66).

Mississippi Scale for PTSD (Civilian and
Combat-Related Versions)

The Mississippi Scale for PTSD is a 35-item scale with a five-point Likert response scale for each item. Items cover PTSD symptoms such as intrusions, avoidance, emotional numbing, and hyperarousal (all DSM-IV criterion symptom domains), as well as depression, suicidal ideation, and guilt. Eleven of the 35 items are worded differently in the civilian version than in the combat version in order to avoid combat references. The possible range of scores is 35 to 175, with a higher score indicating greater distress.

Vreven, Gudanowski, King, and King (1995) studied the responses of 668 nonveterans from the National Vietnam Veterans Readjustment Study. Their results suggested caution in the use of the Civilian Mississippi. While the distribution of scores on this instrument was similar to that of the Combat Mississippi, the item structure appeared less homogenous for the civilian version with lower item-total score correlations, and its factor structure appeared to suggest a multifactor solution rather than a single higher order PTSD factor shown by the combat version. Thus, these authors found substantial psychometric differences between the civilian and combat versions of the Mississippi scale. More damaging however, were their findings that the Civilian Mississippi had limited evidence of criterion validity. While scores on the Civilian Mississippi were more highly related to subjects' reports of frequency of lifetime traumatic stressors than they were to concurrent nontraumatic stressors (e.g., job loss, divorce, serious illness), the Civilian Mississippi shared only a small amount of variance with the DIS-PTSD module score. The authors concluded "the [Civilian Mississippi] should be used with caution in both research and diagnostic decision-making pending additional, more favorable, and definitive validational research" (Vreven et al., 1995, p. 106).

In a further evaluation of the Civilian Mississippi, Inkelas, Loux, Bourque, Widawski, and Nguyen (2000) randomly sampled 656 adults residing in the San Francisco Bay area approximately six months following the 1989 Loma Prieta earthquake. Cronbach's α for the whole scale was .74, but the internal consistency was higher for the 25 nonreverse scored items (α = .86, item-total r's ranged from .29 to .57) than for the 10 reverse-scored items (α = .73, item-total r's ranged from .19 to .50). While the 25 nonreverse scored items formed a single factor, the 10 reversed-score items did not load on that single factor. While the Civilian Mississippi correlated moderately with other measures of psychological distress, it was minimally related to important characteristics of trauma exposure.

In brief, while the Civilian Mississippi appears to be a reliable measure of psychological distress, with total score meaningfully related to trauma exposure, it has limited utility with respect to the assessment of PTSD, per se.

Beck Depression Inventory-II (BDI-II)

BDI-II (Beck, Steer, & Brown, 1996) is a 21-item, self-report questionnaire that assesses symptoms of depression. The BDI, and its successor the BDI-II, are the most commonly used self-report measures of depressive symptoms and are part of most self-report assessment batteries for forensic and clinical assessors. Items are scored on a four-point scale. Psychometric characteristics of the BDI-II are satisfactory, with internal consistency high for both the psychiatric outpatients and university student samples reported in the manual (alphas = .92 and .93, respectively (Beck et al., 1996). Limited data on test-retest reliability reported in the manual suggest that BDI-II scores are stable over one week. One issue with respect to using the BDI-II with psychological injury claimants involves the substantial variance associated with somatic and cognitive symptoms. Factor analyses of this instrument suggest that the items on this test form two discrete factors: one reflecting negative affect and physical concerns, the other reflecting cognitive concerns. Dozois, Dobson, and Ahnberg (1998), in a recent article examining the psychometric characteristics of the BDI-II and the BDI, found that somatic and vegetative symptoms appeared to load on a separate factor to the emotional symptoms. Given the high prevalence of orthopedic injuries and significant prevalence of mild head injuries in MVA survivors, the BDI-II may overestimate the extent of depressive symptoms through oversampling symptoms like sleep disturbance and fatigue.

Depression Anxiety Stress Scales (DASS)

A relatively new measure, the DASS (Lovibond & Lovibond, 1995) was developed in order to better differentiate the emotional constructs of depression, anxiety, and stress. While this instrument has not been studied as extensively as the BDI and BDI-II, it has the advantages of providing somewhat more specific measures of depressed affect, as well as of the different dimensions of anxiety and stress. Antony, Bieling, Cox, Enns, and Swinson (1998) factor analyzed the DASS in a sample of clinical patients with diagnoses of major depression, panic disorder, obsessive-compulsive disorder, social phobia, and specific phobia. A 3-factor solution was found corresponding to the individual subscales. These scales differentiated clinical cases from a nonclinical control group. More significantly, the major depression sample was higher on the DASS depression and stress subscales than other clinical groups, while the panic disorder group was higher on the anxiety subscale than the other groups. Thus, this inventory has some potential for differentiating those distressed claimants who suffer depression from those who have more anxiety-related distress.

Minnesota Multiphasic Personality Inventory-2 (MMPI-2)

No discussion of the assessment of psychological injuries would be complete without at least mentioning the MMPI-2. There are two scales on this commonly used multiscale inventory that merit discussion here. Scale 2 has 57 items and is developed to measure the construct of depression. Unfortunately, this scale has relatively low internal consistency and appears not to be unidimensional; rather the scale appears to reflect both somatic and affective problems (see review by Nezu, Ronan, Meadows, & McClure, 2000). While a multiscale inventory such as the MMPI-2 has the advantage in forensic assessments of providing a broad screen for a variety of mental health problems, as well as tests of response bias (see chapter 4), Scale 2 itself is likely of limited utility with respect to assessing depressed mood.

Many clinicians have also used the MMPI and MMPI-2 to aid in the diagnosis of PTSD. In particular, Scale PK (MMPI scale developed by Terrence Keane) (Keane, Malloy, & Fairbank, 1984) has been studied extensively with combat veterans, as well as with civilian PTSD patients. Despite the frequent use of the MMPI-2 and PK in forensic assessments, there are significant problems in its use for the assessment of PTSD. Several studies have examined the utility of PK in differentiating PTSD sufferers from controls within nonmilitary contexts (e.g., Gaston, Brunet, Koszycki, & Bradwejn, 1996). While these studies superficially suggest that PK can differentiate PTSD from non-PTSD patients, the earlier of these studies fell prey to some serious methodological problems. For example, Gaston et al. (1996) compared their PTSD sample to patients who had not experienced a traumatic stressor. This begs the question of whether PK reflects PTSD status or merely trauma exposure and diffuse psychological distress. Other studies have not necessarily controlled for severity of distress or impairment, leaving open the possibility that PK measures the severity of general psychological distress rather than PTSD. More recent studies have examined the latter hypothesis. Scheibe, Bagby, Miller, and Dorian (2001) compared 28 Workers Compensation Boards (WCB) claimants who had been independently diagnosed with PTSD and 22 WCB claimants with no diagnosis (36%), depression (32%), pain disorder (18%), other anxiety disorders (14%), or adjustment disorder (14%). Regression analyses looking at comparative predictive power found that PK lagged behind independently assessed functional impairment GAF (Global Assessment of Functioning)), and the MMPI-2 content scales of anxiety and anger in differentiating PTSD from non-PTSD claimants. In short, PK may be no more than a measure of general emotional distress.

Behavioral Assessment

From our perspective, behavioral assessment is a frequently neglected aspect of forensic assessments. Behavioral assessment, as apparent from its name, refers to the observation or quantification of some overt behavior. Within the assessor's office, behavioral assessment is of limited utility for the assessment of PTSD, depression, or related anxiety disorders. However, it is useful for the examiner to compare the claimant's verbal endorsements of symptoms (e.g., hypervigilance, easy startle response, fatigue, and emotional upset when reminded of the trauma) with observations of his/her overt behavior during the interview. Marked discrepancies between the claimant's reports and presentation during assessment should make the examiner search for independent information about the claimant's functioning.

However, more ecologically valid information is best obtained outside the interview room. Forensic mental health professionals must remember that it is the claimant's disability outside the mental health professional's office that constitutes the true loss, not his/her presentation within the examining room. For example, individuals who complain of PTSD or acquired driving phobias post-MVA should (given the importance of fear and avoidance in the diagnosis of PTSD) show some overt signs of phobic vigilance and avoidance of vehicular travel. Our clinical observations suggest that legitimately fearful MVA claimants consistently show some combination of heightened tension (e.g., grasping door handles or dashboard when a passenger, vigilant scanning or shoulder checking) or overtly excessive safety behavior (e.g., "backseat driving," stepping on nonexistent brakes on the passenger side) when in a vehicle or when confronted with increased traffic density. They may also show heightened physiological arousal (e.g., perspiration, increased heart rate or respiration) during such exposure. Taking claimants for a short drive while recording their self-reported fear/anxiety and observing them for signs of excessive vigilance, tension, or excessive safety behavior can be a useful adjunct to forensic assessment of driving-related fear that is a common corollary of PTSD following MVAs. Similar types of behavioral observation may be useful for individuals who claim PTSD or related phobias following different types of trauma (e.g., pedestrian accidents, industrial accidents, dog attacks), where correlates of disabling fear (e.g., avoidance behavior, hypervigilance) should, if present, be observable during close exposure to thematically related stimuli.

Behavioral assessment poses some unique ethical issues. First, if it involves observations outside the mental health professional's office, appropriate consent should be obtained. Probably all forensic assessors have had the experience of engaging a stranger in their office parking lot, lobby, or elevator before realizing that this person is the subject of their next assessment. During that casual encounter, the claimant may behave in a manner consistent with some emotional condition (e.g., appear overly cautious while driving in a parking lot, appear agitated and stressed in the lobby); on the other hand, the claimant may show no such signs of distress during casual observation. Independent of whether such observations might support or discredit the claimant's case, there is a serious ethical problem with such encounters because they precede formal introductions and an appropriate warning of the nature of the forensic assessment. Without informed consent, inclusion of such observations within a forensic assessment would constitute an ethical violation.

When taking claimants out of the office for behavioral assessment, consent for this specific procedure should be obtained, even if consent has already been given for the interview and other assessment methods. There are two reasons for this: First, the claimant may be exposed to other overt dangers outside the examining office. For example, if he/she is taken for a drive as part of a behavioral assessment of driving fear, there is some chance of a collision. Second, because more of the weight in behavioral assessments is based on observations of motor behavior and involuntary reactions, the claimant should be informed that he/she is being observed. Common sense dictates that forensic assessors who conduct such behavioral assessments in motor vehicles have appropriate insurance. We believe that behavioral assessment of fear as part of a condition like PTSD enhances the quality of forensic assessments.

Collateral Information

The discussion of behavioral observations above underscores our belief that the use of multiple methods of obtaining information about claimant functioning enhances our understanding of the claimant's difficulties. The latter multitrait, multimethod model for psychological assessment has been around for a long time (Campbell & Fiske, 1959), but it is still useful and perhaps critical in understanding complex presentations of psychological distress and disability as they present in personal injury or compensation claims. Meyer (2002) summarized this point of view cogently, "If we wish to accurately describe or classify patients, we must synthesize information from multiple independent methods and multiple independent sources. This is not just a good idea. Rather, it is a necessity if we wish to have a refined, empirically grounded taxonomy of psychological health and illness" (p. 97).

To that end, information from collateral sources is also beneficial in forensic assessment. Some authors (e.g., Melton, Petrila, Poythress, & Slobogin, 1997) state strongly that within forensic assessments, independent information about the claimant's functioning will play a larger role and self-reported information a lesser role than in clinical assessment because of concerns about the validity of self-report during forensic assessment. Beyond concerns about the reliability of claimant's self-report, it is clear that multiple sources of information provide a richer description of claimant's difficulties.

Sources of collateral information can vary on a number of dimensions. For example, forensic and clinical assessors can review other health professionals' reports and integrate these into their own diagnostic or forensic formulation. While an important source of collateral information, it is notable that many of these assessments will rely on claimant self-report alone and may use similar enough assessment methods to not provide substantial additional information to that of the forensic assessor's interview.

Treatment notes by family physicians or mental health professionals, when viewed chronologically, offer a longitudinal perspective on the claimant's health concerns. However, such records have the following problems for forensic assessment: First, most notes in family physician records are driven by a complaint presented by the patient, not by a systematic mental health review by the family physician. Thus, the absence of a note about depression or other mental health symptoms tells the reader only that mental health symptoms were likely not discussed during that appointment. The absence of evidence about mental health complaints is not synonymous with evidence of the absence of mental health problems. Therefore, if mental health complaints of a particular nature are documented clearly in a family physician record for a particular period of time, the forensic assessor can feel more comfortable that such issues were of concern to the claimant at that time. However, the absence of such documentation is not especially strong evidence for the absence of problems.

Family members are another important source of collateral information. While they may also have some motivation to misrepresent the claimant's mental health problems (because of sympathy with the claimant or related motivation for financial compensation), they have the unique perspective of seeing the claimant over time in his/her daily activities. Such collateral information can be collected in either unstructured interviews (e.g., "Have you seen any changes in your wife's emotional state over the years? How so? When did this begin? What stressors or life events do you think cause her difficulties?"), or via some structured interview or questionnaire. For example, during his assessments of MVA-related trauma, the first author utilizes a family member report questionnaire that asks the claimant's relatives to rate the extent of his/her difficulty with respect to a variety of PTSD, depression, and other anxiety disorder symptoms; the extent of interference the claimant experiences across different life areas; and open-ended questions about the nature of the claimant's emotional/physical concerns; as well as a third-party form of the Accident Fear Questionnaire (AFQ) (Kuch, Cox, & Direnfeld, 1995).

In short, forensic assessments of psychological injury claimants can be enhanced through the use of assessment data collected via different sources (claimant interview, psychological tests, behavioral observations, preexisting health records, and collateral data from family members).

Future Directions

While much has been accomplished, even more remains to be done in the scientific development of reliable and valid measures of psychological injuries. It is clear that epidemiological research with respect to PTSD, in particular, needs to become more sophisticated so that putative PTSD symptoms (e.g., sleep disturbance, behavioral avoidance) are evaluated more carefully within these research interviews. Such increased sophistication may very likely reduce the prevalence estimates of PTSD. It is also important that we learn more about the differential prevalence of a wider range of psychological problems in different claims settings (e.g., MVAs, industrial accidents, white collar work settings, health care settings). It is likely that certain occupations pose specific risks for specific mental health conditions and that the functional impact of any one mental health condition may vary markedly dependent on the individual's occupational context. For example, professional drivers will likely suffer more occupational impairment from MVA-PTSD, while white collar professionals may suffer more functional impairment if their interpersonal behavior is negatively affected. These are areas that have not been systematically explored and deserve attention by researchers.

Additionally, while we are learning more about the spontaneous remission of PTSD within the first year posttrauma, future research must extend longitudinal research in the following ways: We need to know more about longer term (e.g., five or more years) prognosis in order to better inform insurers and the courts. It appears likely that the average PTSD claimant in everyday forensic practice is assessed well past the temporal point for which we have well-established scientific knowledge about spontaneous remission and so longitudinal research that follows trauma survivors for five years or more is critical. Also, we need to know more about the predictors of remission versus chronicity. While some research has been done with the predictors of developing PTSD, less has been conducted with respect to remission from PTSD (see review by Douglas & Koch, 2001), and these studies have dealt with varying samples (e.g., MVA survivors, assault survivors) so that they are not always generally applicable across other types of trauma.

Furthermore, many of the empirically based measures of PTSD, in particular, have been developed on samples of convenience and may not generalize to other PTSD samples. For example, while the AFQ (Kuch et al., 1995) is a good measure for determining behavioral avoidance with MVA survivors, it is irrelevant to sexual-assault PTSD patients. A measure that captures functional impairment in crime victims would help us to understand the behavioral consequences of criminal victimization in a manner that can aid in the determination of losses. On a similar vein, psychological injuries such as PTSD, depression, and other anxiety disorders are thought to be maintained by different underlying concerns, psychological coping mechanisms, or beliefs. For example, the Posttraumatic Cognitions Inventory (PTCI) (Foa, Ehlers, Clark, Tolin, & Orsillo, 1999) measures constructs such as negative beliefs about oneself, negative beliefs about the safety of the world or trustworthiness of others, and self-blame. It is likely that the experiences of survivors of different types of trauma (e.g., MVA vs. sexual assault) may differ substantially on such measures. Such differential responding may have implications for both treatment and prognosis. However, measures of such mediating variables for PTSD, depression, and the like have not been systematically investigated across samples involved in insurance or other disability claims as well as nonclaiming or non–treatment-seeking samples. For example, if behavioral avoidance of driving or riding as a passenger is part of MVA-PTSD or posttraumatic driving phobia, it would be interesting to see (a) how a large general sample of accident-free licensed drivers responds to the AFQ, and (b) how beliefs about traffic safety differ between MVA-PTSD/driving phobics and such a general population sample. Similar questions can be posed about different measures of PTSD phenomena and different sources of trauma. For example, how does the sensible, adult woman who has not suffered a sexual assault differ from an assaulted woman with PTSD with respect to her beliefs about sexual safety and her avoidance of interpersonal intimacy?

Finally, many of the tests commonly used in forensic or clinical assessments have not necessarily been evaluated scientifically in an ecologically valid manner for the populations usually seen in psychological injury evaluations. Future research in this area needs to address questions such as the effect of chronic physical pain, narcotic analgesics, or litigation status on responses to a self-report test (e.g., PCL-C) used to assess the severity of a psychological condition such as PTSD.

While we know a great deal about the epidemiology and assessment methods for a number of psychological conditions that may arise from trauma, there are large scientific gaps between this research and the application of such knowledge to specific claimants. It is all the more important, therefore, that forensic assessors be aware of the available research and limit their assessment methods and conclusions according to up-to-date scientific evidence.

4

Detecting Exaggeration and Malingering in Psychological Injury Claims

Grant L. Iverson
Rael T. Lange

Careful assessment for exaggeration and malingering is an essential component of every civil forensic psychological and neuropsychological evaluation. Researchers have developed sophisticated assessment techniques for identifying exaggerated psychological problems and poor effort during cognitive testing. Psychologists who conduct evaluations for court are expected to be familiar with research relating to the specific instruments they use, as well as the literature in general. Fortunately, excellent reviews are available for this enormous literature in both clinical psychology (e.g., Resnick, 1997a, b; Rogers, 1997) and neuropsychology (e.g., Hayes, Hilsabeck, & Gouvier, 1999; Iverson, 2003; Iverson & Binder, 2000; Reynolds, 1998; Rogers, 1997; Sweet, 1999; Vickery, Berry, Hanlon Inman, Harris, & Orey, 2001).

Researchers repeatedly have demonstrated that specialized assessment techniques can assist with the detection of exaggeration and malingering in criminal forensic evaluations, such as those involving competency to stand trial or criminal responsibility, where the detection of faked insanity is essential (Berry, Baer, & Harris, 1991; Rogers, Sewell, & Salekin, 1994; Rothke et al., 2000). To this end, there have been many studies using the Minnesota Multiphasic Personality Inventory-Second Edition (MMPI-2) (Greene, 2000; Iverson, Franzen, & Hammond, 1995; Lees-Haley, Iverson, Lange, Fox, & Allen, 2002; Rogers, Sewell, Martin, & Vitacco, 2003; Rothke et al., 2000) and a few using the Structured

Interview of Reported Symptoms (SIRS) (McCusker, Moran, Serfass, & Peterson, 2003; Poythress, Edens, & Watkins, 2001; Rogers, Kropp, Bagby, & Dickens, 1992).

The purpose of this chapter is to review the methods for identifying exaggeration and malingering in civil forensic evaluations involving posttraumatic stress disorder. The discussion is divided into four sections: (a) overview of malingering, (b) exaggerated injury claims, (c) specialized assessment techniques, and (d) conclusions. Our goal is to provide detailed information to assist clinicians with conceptualizing, evaluating, and reporting information relating to whether a plaintiff appears to be exaggerating his or her psychological problems or disability.

Overview of Malingering

Malingering is the intentional production of false or greatly exaggerated symptoms for the purpose of attaining some identifiable external reward (American Psychiatric Association, 1994). Within the context of a psychological evaluation, an individual who is malingering may exaggerate subjective symptoms that are difficult to define or to measure precisely, such as depression, anxiety, pain, stiffness, dizziness, sleep disturbance, memory problems, poor concentration, or personality change. A person may decide to malinger to (a) receive more money than he/she is entitled to in a personal injury lawsuit, (b) receive workers' compensation or disability benefits, (c) obtain prescription medications, (d) avoid prosecution for criminal activities (vis-à-vis a determination of incompetency to stand trial), or (e) avoid criminal responsibility (i.e., not guilty by reason of insanity).

From a social psychological perspective, malingering occurs on a spectrum of severity. Many people have engaged in this behavior from time to time. Some obvious examples include pretending to be sick or exaggerating minor illness to avoid school or work, or pretending to be ill to avoid a social engagement (so as not to hurt a friend's feelings). These examples generally are considered benign. In fact, malingering may not be considered "wrong" unless the underlying motivation for the behavior is much more serious. Examples include the person accused of murder who malingers mental illness to be deemed incompetent to stand trial, or the accident victim who fakes chronic pain, depression, and disability from whiplash to get an insurance settlement.

There are, of course, different types of malingering in civil and criminal forensic settings, described by Resnick (1997a) as "pure malingering" (a complete fabrication of symptoms), "partial malingering" (exaggerating actual symptoms or reporting past symptoms as if they are continuing), and "false imputation" (the deliberate misattribution of actual symptoms to the compensable event). Recognition of these types is important because mental health and legal professionals might have a simplistic view of malingering (i.e., only pure malingering is considered malingering). To assume that a person with a real condition, such as PTSD, depression, or the lingering effects of a traumatic brain injury could not malinger would be extraordinarily naïve and tantamount to concluding that people with these conditions are not capable of engaging in goal-directed behavior (i.e., exaggeration of symptoms to influence their litigation).

To diagnose malingering in a personal injury litigation case, the clinician must make an inference regarding the plaintiff's underlying motivation or reasons for exaggerating or fabricating problems. There are, in essence, three underlying reasons for presumed deliberate exaggeration that are typically considered in personal injury cases. First, and most commonly, the clinician might conclude that the plaintiff has exaggerated as a "cry for help." This euphemism implies that the person has serious psychological or psychiatric problems and he or she is desperately seeking recognition of, and attention for, these problems. There is a long history of conceptualizing exaggeration as a cry for help in psychology, whereas in psychiatry and general medicine, clinicians are inclined to attribute exaggeration to "psychological factors" or "psychiatric problems." Second, a plaintiff might deliberately exaggerate because he or she has a deep-seated psychological need to be perceived as sick and disabled. The motivation is not the litigation per se, but to be seen and treated as a sick and disabled person. Under these circumstances, the person would be diagnosed with a factitious disorder. Finally, a person might deliberately exaggerate because he is trying to influence the outcome of his psychological and medical evaluations in order to manipulate the results of his litigation. This latter behavior is what we consider malingering.

Some clinicians are reluctant to diagnose malingering because they say it is not possible for them to determine if the exaggeration was "conscious" or "unconscious." The conscious-unconscious dichotomy has its roots in psychoanalytic theory and can be used by those whose orientation is not psychodynamic as a convenient way of avoiding attributing cause to the plaintiff's behavior. However, if a clinician suspects an unconscious or subconscious underlying motivation for current symptoms or problems that appear to be exaggerated, then the clinician should be considering a diagnosis of one of the somatoform disorders (e.g., conversion disorder, hypochondriasis, somatization disorder, or somatoform disorder NOS).

Some clinicians emphasize that they cannot provide an opinion as to whether someone is malingering because they cannot determine whether the underlying motivation for the presumed exaggeration was a desire to influence the outcome of the litigation. This is a reasonable position; however, clinicians who adopt this thinking should be equally cautious and circumspect when attributing exaggeration to other causes, such as a "cry for help." The attribution of an underlying cause for exaggeration requires careful consideration. Clinicians should not simply jump to one conclusion or another in the absence of thoroughly considering reasonable explanations. The clinician who infers an underlying cause for exaggeration should state clearly the foundations for that opinion. All too often, unfortunately, when a person exaggerates problems during a psychological or medical evaluation, plaintiff experts simply attribute the cause to a cry for help or psychological factors, and defense experts conclude malingering, without providing the foundations for their opinions. Either extreme is an example of bias (as discussed in chapter 5).

In reality, very little is known about a personal injury litigant's underlying motivation to engage in deliberate exaggeration of symptoms or problems. There is no doubt that litigation can be very stressful; the plaintiff typically undergoes multiple independent evaluations from physicians and psychologists retained by the respective parties in the action. Some examiners, usually retained on behalf of the plaintiff, might be warm and sympathetic, whereas others, usually retained by the defendant, might be distant and even hostile. The repeated rehearsal of symptoms and problems to a variety of parties, some sympathetic and others skeptical, might lead to different behaviors, symptoms, and problems being emphasized to different examiners. Over time, the plaintiff might not even be sure of the true nature and extent of his reported symptoms.[1] In addition, family members, lawyers, treating professionals, and expert witnesses often have competing vested interests in the assessment, treatment, and rehabilitation of the plaintiff. In fact, there might even be pressures to avoid effective treatments and to remain out of work in order to illustrate the damages resulting from the tort. Undoubtedly, protracted litigation can be associated with a variety of direct and indirect stressors, and a plaintiff who was once significantly injured, but who has largely recovered, might feel entitled to the compensation anticipated by his lawyer, thus feeling justified in his decision to grossly exaggerate his current disability.

Exaggerated Psychological Injury or Disability Claims

Clinicians who examine patients within the context of personal injury litigation or disability claims must carefully consider whether the claimant is exaggerating or malingering. It is easy to exaggerate symptoms and problems associated with PTSD, anxiety, depression, chronic pain, and the persistent postconcussion syndrome. Therefore, Resnick's (1997a) "partial malingering" or "false imputation" can be very difficult to detect. In this section, we discuss factors specific to PTSD that can help the clinician identify exaggeration or malingering.

---

1. In this regard, the reader should consider the literature on biased retrospective memory, as discussed in chapter 5.

Posttraumatic Stress Disorder

Exaggeration and malingering in people with alleged posttraumatic stress disorder (PTSD) has been a concern for clinicians, researchers, insurance companies, and the U.S. Veterans Administration for many years. The Veterans Administration authorized compensation and other benefits for delayed-onset PTSD in 1980, the same year this disorder was officially recognized by the American Psychiatric Association in its *Diagnostic and Statistical Manual of Mental Disorders, Third Edition* (DSM-III). From the beginning, there were concerns about veterans exaggerating past combat details and current symptoms and problems. Within a few years, case reports appeared in the literature describing factitious and fraudulent claims, including PTSD claims in veterans who did not serve in Vietnam (Lynn & Belza, 1984; Sparr & Pankratz, 1983). "Simulation is easy, since the symptoms described by DSM-III mostly reflect private phenomenology and since by definition the symptoms are caused by events now past. Patients may manufacture or exaggerate symptoms and misidentify their origin. It is not always easy to determine if distortions are outright lies or subtle misperceptions" (Sparr & Pankratz, 1983, p. 1018).

For more than 20 years, research relating to exaggeration and malingering in PTSD (e.g., Fairbank, McCaffrey, & Keane, 1985) has occurred in tandem with research designed to better understand the predictors, nature, diagnosis, and treatment of this psychiatric illness. Researchers have demonstrated convincingly that naïve healthy subjects can easily and accurately falsify symptoms of PTSD, sufficient to meet diagnostic criteria, when given a symptom checklist. This was first demonstrated with naïve undergraduates: 86% met diagnostic criteria for PTSD (Lees-Haley & Dunn, 1994). Burges and McMillan (2001) reported that 94% of naïve subjects successfully simulated PTSD using a standard symptom checklist. Clearly, it is not difficult to self-report symptoms and problems associated with PTSD, making this an easy disorder to fake, if desired.

When considering the diagnosis of PTSD, or malingered PTSD, it is important to consider carefully the type and severity of the traumatic stressor. Developing PTSD following a car accident is uncommon. Some estimates of the rate of this disorder in accident victims have been 9% (Blanchard & Hickling, 1997), 12% (Breslau, Davis, Andreski, & Petersen, 1991), and 6.3% and 8.8% for men and women, respectively (Kessler, Sonnega, Bromet, Hughes, & Nelson, 1995). Essentially, 90% of people in car accidents do not develop PTSD. Less than 5% of individuals develop PTSD after a natural disaster (Kessler et al., 1995). In a sample of survivors of the September 11, 2001, terrorist attack on the Pentagon, 14% had PTSD seven months after the event (Grieger, Fullerton, & Ursano, 2003). Rape is associated with the highest incidence of PTSD, with estimates ranging from 46% to 80% (Breslau et al., 1991; Kessler et al., 1995). Therefore, when examining a plaintiff in a motor vehicle accident, it is appropriate to ask oneself:

"Is this person likely to be in the group of 90% of accident victims who do not have PTSD or in the 10% who do?"

The first step in diagnosing PTSD, or malingered PTSD, is to determine if the plaintiff experienced an extreme traumatic stressor sufficient to meet Criterion A for a diagnosis. Minor motor vehicle accidents, such as rear-end collisions, do not meet this criterion. Having an unpleasant disagreement with a supervisor or coworker does not meet this criterion. Any combination of symptoms and problems reported by the patient at some point after the event are not sufficient for a diagnosis in the absence of a qualifying traumatic stressor, such as rape or a motor vehicle accident involving the death of a family member. In a forensic evaluation, it is possible to either over- or underemphasize the importance of the traumatic event. Therefore, it is also important to assess Criterion A2, the individual's initial response to the traumatic event (e.g., see the discussion in chapters 3 and 5), and not simply use the nature of the specific event as a superficial heuristic.

Veterans have been known to fabricate the traumatic stressor, such as a male solider providing vivid combat details when he didn't actually serve in Vietnam. Misrepresentation appears to be quite common. For example, Burkett and Whitley (1998) obtained the military records of the members of the American Ex-Prisoner of War Association and discovered that nearly 30% were never prisoners of war. Accident victims often do not have to exaggerate or fabricate the traumatic stressor; however, they might simply exaggerate their *reaction* to the stressor. In some cases, it is not necessary for a plaintiff to exaggerate his reaction to a stressor if he or she is evaluated by a "sympathetic" expert who (a) assumes the accident must have been traumatic, (b) applies very liberal criteria for Category B, such as having some mildly distressing thoughts about the accident, and then (c) documents the largely nonspecific Category C symptoms reported by the plaintiff. Thus, it is possible for a plaintiff expert to misdiagnose PTSD, which might contribute to a defense expert misdiagnosing malingered PTSD. The former misdiagnosis could occur because the plaintiff clearly did not meet Criterion A (the traumatic event). The latter misdiagnosis could occur because the defense expert assumed that the diagnosis of PTSD is emanating from the plaintiff, when in fact the plaintiff expert has misdiagnosed PTSD. Thus, the plaintiff might be endorsing (perhaps exaggerating) nonspecific symptoms that the plaintiff expert attributes to PTSD.

Greiffenstein, Baker, Axelrod, Peck, and Gervais quantified a number of atypical factors in several well-defined clinical groups. There are no definitive data on the usefulness of these factors, singly or in combination, for identifying exaggerated or malingered PTSD. However, these factors are related to PTSD and, as more data emerges, they might be increasingly useful as "red flags" for implausible PTSD claims. Several of the atypical factors have considerable support in the literature, whereas other factors are derived from clinical judgment and common sense (Greiffenstein et al., 2004).

One atypical factor is delayed onset of symptoms. Symptoms following exposure to a traumatic event typically occur in the initial days and weeks. The onset of PTSD symptoms in the survivors of the Oklahoma City bombing was swift, with 76% reporting symptoms on the day of the event (North et al., 1999). Delayed symptom onset is uncommon; for example, there were no cases of delayed onset PTSD associated with the Oklahoma City bombing (North, 2001). If delayed onset PTSD is reliably diagnosed, it might better reflect an individual who was distressed, but undetected or merely subsyndromal shortly following the trauma. Buckley, Blanchard, and Hickling (1996) compared seven MVA survivors who did not meet PTSD criteria at initial assessment (1 to 4 months post-MVA) with a larger sample of MVA survivors with acute onset PTSD. Delayed onset subjects differed from acute onset patients by having lower perceived social support, greater avoidance (but without meeting sufficient PTSD Criterion C avoidance and numbing symptoms), greater physical injury severity during follow-up assessment, and more negative life events during the follow-up interval. This particular study and others (e.g., Ehlers, Mayou, & Bryant, 1998) emphasize the relative infrequency of delayed onset PTSD, but suggest that the delayed onset phenomena may be a joint product of (a) insensitive diagnostic criteria and methods, (b) individual differences in avoidance behavior that masks other PTSD symptoms, and (c) posttrauma stressors that exacerbate psychological distress, as well as (d) delayed compensation motivation.

Patients with PTSD frequently have comorbid diagnoses (e.g., borderline personality disorder—Zlotnick, Franklin, & Zimmerman, 2002; psychotic disorders—Seedat, Stein, Oosthuizen, Emsley, & Stein, 2003; substance dependence—Vaidya & Garfield, 2003; major depression—Kilpatrick et al., 2003), but they tend not to have multiple comorbid diagnoses. A controversial comorbid diagnosis is traumatic brain injury. Logically, it should be difficult to have a traumatic brain injury and PTSD because patients with significant traumatic brain injuries are often densely amnestic for the circumstances of the traumatic event, making it difficult to (a) be horrified [criterion A] and (b) reexperience the event [criterion B]. There are data to support the position that traumatic brain injury and PTSD typically are mutually exclusive (Sbordone & Liter, 1995), although researchers have put forward a compelling rationale for how, under certain circumstances, PTSD could emerge in a patient with a brain injury (Bryant & Harvey, 1999; Harvey, Brewin, Jones, & Kopelman, 2003; see also chapter 1 of this book). Other atypical factors relate to the severity of the symptoms, the course of the disorder, and the extent of the reported disability. In particular, readers need to be aware that a large percentage of PTSD sufferers spontaneously remit within the first 12 months.

Greiffenstein et al. (2004) formed groups for an MMPI-2 study based partly on these atypical factors. The first group consisted of 57 compensation-seeking patients with improbable posttraumatic stress claims. These individuals clearly did not meet Criterion A for exposure to a traumatic event, they had prolonged work disability claims, they were in litigation, and they had at least two atypical factors. The percentages of these patient subjects with each atypical factor was as follows: three or more comorbid diagnoses = 93.5%; delayed symptom onset of one or more months = 87.5%; dual claims of mild traumatic brain injury and PTSD = 81.8%; symptoms not responsive to any psychotropic medication = 78.6%; unchanged or progressive symptom course = 76.7%; able to participate normally in enjoyable activities, incapacity in work only = 67.9; nonadherence to treatment = 64.7%; externalizes all blame, no guilt experienced at any point = 58.6%; hallucinations of trauma = 6.3%. The second group was comprised of 32 individuals involved in litigation who clearly met Criterion A for exposure to a traumatic event. The third group consisted of 40 patients seen for initial psychological evaluations following a relatively recent exposure to a qualifying traumatic event (mean of 4.6 months post, *SD* = 8.4). None of the patients in the third group were involved in litigation.

As seen in figure 4.1, there was a fairly dramatic relationship between the total number of atypical factors and group membership. These factors were very uncommon in nonlitigating clinical patients who had been exposed to traumatic stressors. They were more common in the litigating groups, with the highest rates in those with implausible traumatic stressor exposure. The authors illustrated that patients involved in litigation scored considerably higher on the MMPI-2 Fake Bad Scale, with the highest scores occurring in litigants with implausible post-

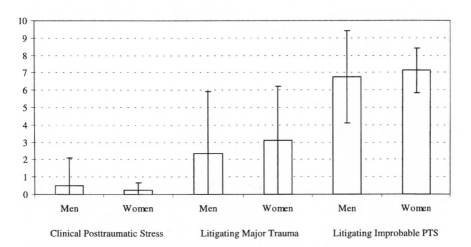

Figure 4.1. Total number of atypical factors by gender and group membership. *Source*: Derived from Greiffenstein, Baker, Axelrod, Peck, and Gervais (2004).

traumatic stress claims. These data are illustrated in figure 4.2. In addition, we have added several known groups from the literature to illustrate that the Fake Bad Scale appears to be useful for identifying exaggeration in patients with post-traumatic stress claims.

The clinician must consider carefully the nature, course, and severity of the symptoms and problems reported by litigating patients with posttraumatic stress claims. When patients present with a number of atypical features of PTSD, this obviously should raise the clinician's index of suspicion for exaggeration, alternative diagnoses, or both. Resnick (1997a) encouraged clinicians to consider the following factors as suspicion indices for malingered posttraumatic stress disorder: (a) poor work record, (b) prior "incapacitating" injuries, (c) markedly discrepant capacity from work and recreation, (d) unvarying, repetitive dreams, (e) antisocial personality traits, (f) overly idealized functioning before the trauma, (g) evasiveness, and (h) inconsistency in symptom presentation.

Specialized psychological tests also can be used to identify exaggeration. The MMPI-2 is most commonly relied on for inferences regarding exaggeration and malingering in patients with alleged PTSD. This test has been used in numerous studies, most of which have focused on combat veterans. Several analog malingering studies have been conducted with university students who have been instructed to malinger PTSD.

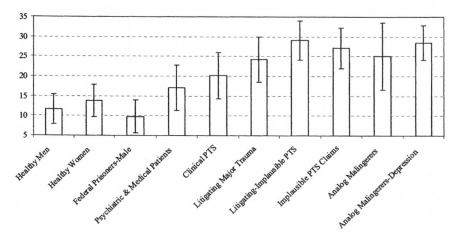

Figure 4.2. Fake Bad Scale scores in known groups. *Source*: Healthy men and women (Greene, 1997); federal prisoners (Iverson et al., 1995); psychiatric and medical patients (Tsushima & Tsushima, 2001); clinical posttraumatic stress (PTS), litigating major trauma, and litigating implausible posttraumatic stress (Greiffenstein et al., 2004); implausible PTS claims (Lees-Haley, 1992); analog malingerers (Lees-Haley et al., 1991); and analog malingerers faking depression (Bagby et al., 2000).

Malingered PTSD on the MMPI-2

There have been several analog studies of malingered PTSD that utilized similar methodologies. Only two are described in detail, to illustrate the general methodology of this research. A more comprehensive review of the MMPI-2 validity scales are provided later in the chapter; the performances of subjects with presumed genuine PTSD and experimental malingers are described in that section.

Elhai, Gold, Sellers, and Dorfman (2001) examined the ability of the MMPI-2 validity scales to discriminate 64 adult outpatients from a child sexual abuse survivor treatment program from 85 psychology university students instructed to fake PTSD. The clinical sample was diagnosed with PTSD according to DSM-III-R or DSM-IV criteria. The simulation group was provided with training materials consisting of information on PTSD, including common symptoms of the disorder and several case studies. On average, individuals instructed to feign PTSD scored significantly higher on all validity scales evaluated, with the exception of the F-F$_B$ (F scale minus the FB scale) index. A stepwise discriminant function analysis, using the MMPI-2 validity scales as the predictor variables, revealed that F(p), F-K, and O-S were the best validity scales for differentiating between individuals with presumed genuine PTSD and those instructed to fake the disorder. Examination of classification rates, by gender, using a range of cutoff scores for F(p), F-K, and O-S revealed that a cutoff score of 5 for F(p) produced the best classification rates for both men and women. For the F-K index, a cutoff score of 12 for men and 12 or 13 for women was considered optimal. A cutoff score of 150 for men and 180 for women on the Obvious-Subtle index produced the highest classification rates.

Wetter, Baer, Berry, Robison, and Sumpter (1993) examined the usefulness of the MMPI-2 validity scales for differentiating patients with genuine PTSD ($n = 20$) or paranoid schizophrenia ($n = 20$) from individuals instructed to fake these two disorders separately (feign PTSD group, $n = 20$; feign paranoid schizophrenia group, $n = 22$). Both simulator groups were provided with specific information regarding their assigned disorder and were instructed that they would be required to pass a quiz prior to participation. Significant differences were found on all validity scales, with the exception of L and VRIN, when comparing each faking group to their corresponding genuine patient group. For both comparisons, the faked disorder group scored lower on L and higher on F, F$_B$, F-K, and Ds (Dissimulation Scale) compared to their respective patient samples (effect size range = 0.79 to 2.47). The best classification rates for PTSD were found using the following cutoff scores: F ≥ 96T (85% simulators, 70% patients), F$_B$ ≥ 98T (80% and 65%), F-K ≥ 15 (75% and 85%), and Ds ≥ 35 (75% and 85%).

Most MMPI-2 studies of patients with PTSD have used combat veterans from Veterans Administration (VA) hospitals (e.g., Elhai, Gold, Frueh, & Gold, 2000; Elhai et al., 2002; Franklin, Repasky, Thompson, Shelton, & Uddo, 2002; Frueh, Gold, & de Arellano, 1997; Smith & Frueh, 1996). A relatively consistent finding is that a subset of these patients has frankly elevated validity scales, such as F and F(p). Researchers have struggled to understand whether these elevations represent true psychological distress associated with PTSD, exaggeration, or some combination of factors (Frueh, Hamner, Cahill, Gold, & Hamlin, 2000). Studies attempting to elucidate this tend to be methodologically limited and sometimes circular in reasoning.

In an innovative study of the MMPI-2 for assessing exaggerated PTSD symptoms, Elhai et al. (2002) developed the Infrequency-Posttraumatic Stress Disorder Scale (Fptsd), designed to assess exaggeration of symptoms in individuals seeking disability for PTSD. This new 32-item scale shares 20 items with F(p) and includes infrequently endorsed items within the MMPI-2 normative sample and a sample of male combat veterans diagnosed with PTSD. An obvious limitation with this new scale is the implicit assumption that none of the veterans ($n = 940$) used in its development were actually frankly exaggerating or malingering. Additional research on this scale might help clarify its clinical usefulness.

Malingering PTSD on the Personality Assessment Inventory
The Personality Assessment Inventory (PAI) (Morey, 1991) is a 344-item objective personality inventory designed to measure psychological functioning across multiple domains. Unlike the MMPI-2, there is no item overlap on the scales. In addition, items are answered on a four-point Likert scale as opposed to a true/false format. In addition to the clinical scales, the PAI has four validity scales: (1) the Inconsistency Scale is comprised of 10 highly correlated items, (2) the Infrequency Scale contains eight items that are rarely endorsed by healthy adults and are believed to be minimally related to psychopathology, (3) the Positive Impression Management Scale is designed to evaluate fake good responding, and (4) the Negative Impression Management Scale (NIM) contains nine items that are rarely endorsed by persons in the general population and are considered to reflect exaggerated psychological problems. Morey (1996) described eight score patterns that comprise a "Malingering Index" on the PAI. If the patient demonstrates three or more of these score patterns, malingering is suspected; five or more and malingering is likely. Rogers, Sewell, Morey, and Ustad (1996) conducted an extensive study of the PAI validity scales, using undergraduates and psychology graduate students as simulators. A discriminant function analysis provided better classification accuracy than the single validity scales (Rogers, Sewell, Morey, & Ustad, 1996). This discriminant function is now included in the computerized scoring program for the PAI.

Two studies have examined the performances of experimental malingerers on the Personality Assessment Inventory. Liljequist, Kinder, and Schinka (1998) conducted an analog malingering study in which participants included four groups: 29 men with a diagnosis of PTSD and alcohol dependence, 30 men with a diagnosis of alcohol dependence, 27 undergraduate psychology students instructed to fake PTSD, and 30 undergraduate psychology student controls. Simulators were asked to "imagine that they were attempting to convince a team of health-care professionals that they were suffering from a combat-related mental health disorder that was manifested in the symptoms listed on the paper given to them. These symptoms were read aloud, and a copy was provided for their review during the remainder of the test completion" (p. 327). On average, individuals instructed to fake PTSD produced PAI profiles that were significantly different from both the student control group and the veterans with PTSD. Simulators tended to report more psychopathology and consequently had higher T scores. When compared to controls, simulators had higher scores on the Negative Impression Management (NIM) Scale and multiple clinical scales (e.g., anxiety, depression, schizophrenia, and borderline). Similarly, when compared to the PTSD group, simulators had higher scores on the NIM validity scale and several of the clinical scales (e.g., anxiety, schizophrenia, and paranoia). Simulators also scored higher on Morey's (1996) eight-item Malingering Index than either group of veterans and controls. A cutoff score of ≥3 resulted in only 44.4% simulators being correctly classified as faking PTSD, with low false positive error rates in the alcohol dependence group (3.4%). The accuracy of NIM was not evaluated in this study.

Calhoun, Earnst, Tucker, Kirby, and Beckham (2000) examined the ability of the NIM Scale and the Malingering Index to identify individuals instructed to fake PTSD. Twenty-three undergraduate men instructed to fake PTSD, 23 male veterans diagnosed with combat-related PTSD, and 23 men randomly selected from the PAI standardization sample were included in this study. Simulators were provided with information regarding DSM-IV criteria for PTSD. Participants were given 10 minutes to read the diagnostic criteria for PTSD and then they completed the PAI and the Mississippi Scale for Combat-Related PTSD. Nearly all of the individuals instructed to fake PTSD (91%) were able to achieve scores on the Mississippi Scale above the suggested cutoff score for PTSD. No signifi-cant differences were found between mean scores on the Mississippi Scale in this group when compared to the actual combat veterans. Using the PTSD LOGIT function for considering a diagnosis of PTSD on the PAI as described by Morey (1991, 1996), 83% of the combat veterans were correctly identified as having the disorder, none of the control subjects were identified as having PTSD, and 70% of the individuals who were faking PTSD produced PAI profiles that were con-sidered reflective of the disorder. Using only those individuals from the faking group who received a diagnosis of PTSD based on their PAI profile, 75% of this subgroup was detected as simulating using a NIM raw score cutoff of ≥8. Using the recommended cutoff score for clinical populations for the Malingering Index (i.e., ≥3) and NIM (i.e., ≥13), only 43.8% of the group was detected as simu-lating using each of these scores separately. The false positive error rate in the PTSD sample was high, with 65% of combat veterans incorrectly identified as faking using a NIM cutoff score of ≥8, 57% using a cutoff score of >11, and

35% using a cutoff score of ≥13. The authors concluded that the PAI is susceptible to the faking of PTSD.

The literature to date suggests that PTSD can be successfully faked on the PAI. The Negative Impression Management Scale is reasonably sensitive to more extreme forms of malingered mental illness such as schizophrenia (e.g., Rogers, Ornduff, & Sewell, 1993; Rogers, Sewell, Morey, & Ustad, 1996), but it is relatively insensitive to malingered PTSD. Additional research is needed to more clearly delineate the classification accuracy of NIM in patients with genuine versus malingered PTSD.

Conclusions—Malingered PTSD

There is no doubt that the symptoms and problems experienced by people with PTSD can be exaggerated or fabricated. Using symptom checklists makes it particularly easy to appear as if you have the condition. The PAI has limited clinical usefulness for detecting exaggerated or malingered PTSD because it fails to identify the majority of experimental malingerers. The Atypical Responses Scale from the TSI (Trauma Symptom Inventory) also fails to identify a large percentage of experimental malingers. The items comprising this scale are unusual or frankly bizarre, and the suggested cutoff for suspecting exaggeration or malingering is much too high. The MMPI-2 holds the most promise for detecting exaggeration and malingering; however, the literature is complicated and dominated by studies with combat veterans. A careful review of the MMPI-2 validity scales and indices is provided in the next section.

Specialized Assessment Techniques

This section reviews several specialized assessment methods for identifying exaggeration and malingering. Most of the discussion is devoted to summarizing the various validity scales and indices for the MMPI-2. Brief summaries are provided of the Structured Inventory of Malingered Symptomatology and the Malingering Probability Scales because they have been utilized in relatively few studies. Selected specialized tests designed to detect poor effort during cognitive testing are also reviewed.

Minnesota Multiphasic Personality Inventory- Second Edition

There is an enormous literature relating to exaggeration on the MMPI-2. The validity scales and indices that are most often referred to in the literature are summarized, and data from known clinical groups are provided for many of them. Many of these scales and indices are described in detail elsewhere (e.g., Greene, 2000; Guriel & Fremouw, 2003; Lees-Haley, Iverson, Lange, Fox, &

Allen, 2002; Meyers, Millis, & Volkert, 2002; Rogers, Sewell, Martin, & Vitacco, 2003).

L and the F Family [F, F-K, F$_B$, and F(p)]

The L (Lie) Scale, consisting of 15 items, is one of the standard validity scales. Elevated scores are believed to reflect defensiveness or a desire to portray oneself as overly virtuous. In contrast, very low scores on L might reflect exaggeration. Greene (2000) noted that low scoring clients (e.g., raw score 0–2), "may be attempting to create an extremely pathological picture of themselves" (p. 94). There has not, however, been systematic research demonstrating that the L Scale can reliably detect exaggeration in personal injury litigation.

The F (Infrequency) Scale is also one of the standard validity scales, and consists of 60 items that are infrequently answered by healthy adults. Fewer than 10% of the MMPI-2 normative population answered these items in the scored direction (Greene, 1991, 2000). Butcher (1990) noted that, "The F scale was devised as a measure of the tendency to admit to a wide range of psychological problems or to fake bad. An individual who scores high on the F scale is admitting to a wide range of complaints that are infrequently endorsed by the general population and reflect a tendency to exaggerate problems" (pp. 28–29).

In the MMPI-2 manual (Butcher et al., 2001), exaggeration is listed as one of the potential explanations for F scale scores that exceed 70T. However, Butcher (1998) recommended that T scores of 90–99 are "Exaggerated", T = 100–109 are "Highly Exaggerated", and T ≥ 110 (with VRIN < 79) are "Likely Malingering." Certainly, F scale T scores in excess of 100 are frequently seen in community volunteers, federal inmates, and psychiatric patients instructed to malinger severe psychiatric illness (Bagby, Rogers, Buis, & Kalemba, 1994; Graham, Watts, & Timbrook, 1991; Iverson, Franzen, & Hammond, 1995; Rogers, Sewell, & Ustad, 1995; Wetter, Baer, Berry, Robison, & Sumpter, 1993). Greene (2000) reported that elevations of T = 81–110 are associated with a readily apparent level of psychological distress or exaggeration. Therefore, mental status observations of the patient can help clarify the more likely hypothesis. Greene further noted that an elevation of T > 110, if based on accurate responses by the patient, suggest a severely disorganized, floridly psychotic patient. Such a presentation is highly unusual among personal injury plaintiffs, and more likely a product of gross exaggeration.

The F-K (F minus K) Index, developed by Gough (1947, 1950), is sometimes referred to as the Gough Dissimulation Index. The average F-K score in the MMPI-2 normative sample is negative 11 (−11). Approximately 95% of the normal population score below zero on this index. Various cutoff scores have been proposed, such as ≥ 0, ≥ 5, ≥ 6 and ≥ 8, although no score is universally accepted. Clinicians need to examine the literature carefully to identify the most appropriate cutoff scores for specific populations (e.g., Bagby et al., 1997; Bagby,

Nicholson, Buis, & Bacchiochi, 2000; Elhai, Gold, Frueh, & Gold, 2000; Elhai, Gold, Sellers, & Dorfman, 2001; Fox, Gerson & Lees-Haley, 1995; Frueh, Gold, & de Arellano, 1997; Lees-Haley, 1992; Rothke et al., 1994; Sivec, Lynn, & Garske, 1994; Walters & Clopton, 2000; Wetter et al., 1993; Wetter & Deitsch, 1996).

The Back Infrequency Scale [F_B] consists of 40 items, and was developed similarly to the F scale (i.e., these items were answered in the scored direction by fewer than 10% of the MMPI-2 normative sample; Greene, 1991). The items for the standard F scale all appear within the first 370 items of the test; the items for F_B are all found in the second half of the test, beginning with item 281. The F_B is routinely reported in studies relating to exaggeration and malingering; similar to the F scale, it is typically elevated in these samples. The F_B Scale is useful for identifying faked depression (Bagby et al., 1997, 2000; Walters & Clopton, 2000). Greene (1991, 2000) suggested that the same interpretive statements be used for both F and F_B.

The Infrequency-Psychopathology [F(p)] Scale contains 27 items that are usually not endorsed by psychiatric inpatients (Arbisi & Ben-Porath, 1995). No more than 20% of psychiatric patients ($N = 1,129$) or the MMPI-2 normative sample endorsed each item on this scale in the deviant direction (Greene, 2000). The scale taps a number of content areas, including severe psychotic symptoms, very unusual habits, highly amoral attitudes, and identity confusion (Greene, 2000). Researchers have suggested that the F(p) scale is less sensitive to real psychiatric illness than the F or F_B scales (e.g., Arbisi & Ben-Porath, 1997; Rothke et al., 2000; Strong, Greene, & Schinka, 2000). Greene (2000) noted that F(p) raw scores ranging from 4 to 8 indicate "these clients either are experiencing and reporting a significant level of emotional distress or they may be embellishing the severity and extent of their psychopathology" (p. 76). In one study, F(p) was superior to F in identifying malingered PTSD (Elhai et al., 2001).

Researchers have suggested that the F(p) scale can be used to refine interpretation of the F scale (e.g., was the elevation on the F scale due to real psychopathology?). The following sequence has been proposed: (a) rule out random responding and an acquiescence response set by eliminating profiles with elevated VRIN (T = 100) or TRIN (T = 80) scores, (b) rule out malingering or exaggeration by considering whether the F(p) scale is elevated (and whether F-K is elevated), and (c) if steps a and b are negative, then a high F scale might be due to psychopathology (Arbisi & Ben-Porath, 1995; Rothke et al., 2000).

Consistency Scales

The Variable Response Inconsistency Scale (VRIN) consists of 67 pairs of items with similar or opposite content (Graham, 1993). Each inconsistent answer counts as one point on the raw score for VRIN. Elevations on VRIN render the MMPI-

2 protocol meaningless for interpretation because it is assumed that the respondent is not endorsing items consistently, which might reflect a careless or random response style. Therefore, it is recommended that VRIN be one of the first scales evaluated. Wetter, Baer, Berry, Smith, and Larson (1992) found that VRIN was elevated with random responding, but not with malingering. Thus, in the case where a protocol has a high F or F_B, VRIN can help clarify whether these scores are elevated due to inconsistent responding (i.e., high VRIN, high F) or due to exaggeration (i.e., normal VRIN, high F).

The True Response Inconsistency Scale (TRIN) consists of 23 pairs of items with opposite or contradictory content, and is designed to assess for the consistency of item responding. If the subject responds true to both items in the contradictory pair, for example, he or she is responding inconsistently. The scale can be helpful for identifying indiscriminate true (i.e., yea-saying) or false (i.e., nay-saying) responding.

Obvious Minus Subtle Scales

Wiener and Harmon (1946; Wiener, 1948) sorted questions on the MMPI into two categories that they called "obvious" and "subtle." The original concept was that the differential ability of laypeople to fake obvious and subtle items provided measures of exaggeration on specific scales. In a meta-analytic review of 24 studies using the original MMPI to detect malingering, Berry, Baer, and Harris (1991) cautioned the use of the Obvious/Subtle scales because they had smaller effect sizes compared to other validity scales (i.e., F, Ds, & F-K Index). In contrast, Rogers, Sewell, and Salekin (1994) conducted a meta-analysis of the MMPI-2 validity scales and found that Total Obvious minus Subtle (O-S) scores had a very strong effect size that was maintained across both nonclinical controls and psychiatric groups. They recommended using the Total Obvious minus Subtle score, F, and K when evaluating malingered MMPI-2 profiles. Greene (2000) reported that these scales show promise for detection of overreporting of symptoms on the MMPI-2, and he included these scales in his computerized interpretation program for the MMPI-2 (Greene, Brown, & Kovan, 1998).

Hedlund and Won Cho (1979) reported data from 8,646 male and 3,743 female psychiatric patients that showed a mean score of 56.5 ($SD = 85.1$) for Total T score difference between Obvious-Subtle scales on the original MMPI. Only 28% to 29% of adults who were so disturbed that they required psychiatric hospitalization exceeded the cutoff of 100T. With regard to the MMPI-2, Lees-Haley and Fox (1990) found that only 16% of inpatients with psychosis would be misclassified using a T difference of 100. In other words, high scores are not expected from outpatients and they are improbable. Rogers et al. (1994) recommended using Total O-S > 81 as a screening measure for suspecting exaggeration.

We have extracted information from numerous studies relating to the Obvious

Table 4.1. Obvious-Subtle Index (O-S) T Score Performances in Known Groups

GROUP	N	M	SD
Normal Control Subjects			
University Students[1]	40	35.1	59.9
University Students[2]	58	80.8	47.4
University Students[3]	95	47.7	64.7
University Students[4]	90	61.0	74.7
University Students (Male)[5]	58	53.4	69.1
University Students (Female)[5]	140	51.3	71.3
University Students (Male)[6]	56	9.0	59.9
University Students (Female)[6]	49	28.0	61.7
Psychiatric Patients			
Inpatients (Major Depression)[1]	40	79.1	60.8
Inpatients (Schizophrenia)[1]	40	78.8	78.8
Inpatients (Mixed Diagnoses)[4]	95	90.4	87.6
Nonforensic Inpatients (Mixed Diagnoses—Male)[5]	64	90.0	94.8
Nonforensic Inpatients (Mixed Diagnoses—Female)[5]	65	88.2	83.3
Forensic Inpatients (Mixed Diagnoses—Male)[5]	131	73.7	101.3
Forensic Inpatients (Mixed Diagnoses—Female)[5]	28	93.4	82.4
Inpatients (Mixed Diagnoses—Male)[6]	29	50.1	98.7
Inpatients (Mixed Diagnoses—Female)[6]	20	81.3	96.5
Outpatients (Mixed Diagnoses)[7]	42	140.1	87.9
PTSD and Chronic Pain			
Child Sexual Abuse Outpatients with PTSD[8]	64	155.3	66.5
Combat War Veterans with PTSD[9]	124	196.1	74.3
Non–Compensation-Seeking Combat Veterans[10]	38	128.2	71.8
Mixed Neurological/Chronic Pain—Not in Litigation[11]	100	27.7	61.8
Compensation-Seeking			
Mixed Neurological/Chronic Pain Litigants[11]	100	91.1	89.0
Personal Injury Claimants (PS/PK scores < 61)[12]	64	−2.1	46.4
Compensation-Seeking Combat Veterans[10]	87	219.4	65.1
Work Comp./Personal Injury Claimants (Mixed Psych)[13]	289	65.6	88.9
Implausible PTSD Litigants[12]	55	150.7	54.6
Analog Malingerers			
Fake PTSD (University Students)[8]	85	220.2	81.5
Fake PTSD (University Students)[9]	84	221.8	80.7
Fake Depression (University Students)[1]	20	213.9	71.8
Fake Depression (University Students—Depression & Validity Info)[3]	112	162.2	58.7
Fake Depression (University Students—Depression Info Only)[3]	80	196.9	66.8
Fake Depression (University Students—Validity Info Only)[3]	89	171.8	66.0
Fake Depression (University Students—No Training)[3]	89	228.1	49.1
Fake Depression (University Students—Successful Mals)[3]	111	130.3	46.3
Fake Depression (University Students—Unsuccessful Mals)[3]	259	212.5	56.2
Fake Schizophrenia (University Students)[1]	20	224.1	75.2

GROUP	N	M	SD
Fake Somatoform Disorder (University Students)[2]	58	172.9	83.1
Fake Paranoid Psychosis (University Students)[2]	58	295.5	57.4
Fake Psychiatric Problems (Psychiatric Outpatients)[7]	42	193.8	82.7
Fake Bad (University Students)[4]	58	204.8	69.2
Fake Bad (University Students)[2]	58	288.4	67.9
Fake Bad (Male University Students)[5]	29	189.8	69.1
Fake Bad (Female University Students)[5]	45	198.8	59.9
Fake Bad (Male University Students)[6]	29	254.8	48.8
Fake Bad (Female University Students)[6]	20	260.4	47.7
Students Instructed to "Fake Good"			
Fake Good (University Students)[4]	67	−40.0	51.4
Fake Good (Male University Students)[5]	14	−36.2	47.2
Fake Good (Female University Students)[5]	56	−36.4	54.9
Fake Good (Male University Students)[6]	27	−60.1	58.2
Fake Good (Female University Students)[6]	29	−53.8	70.5

Note: All values have been rounded to one decimal.

Source: [1]Bagby et al. (1997), [2]Sivec et al. (1994), [3]Walters & Clopton (2000), [4]Bagby et al. (1994), [5]Bagby et al. (1995), [6]Timbrook, Graham, Keiller, & Watts (1993), [7]Rogers et al. (1995), [8]Elhai et al. (2001), [9]Elhai et al. (2000), [10]Frueh et al. (1997), [11]Meyers et al. (2002), [12]Lees-Haley (1992), [13]Fox et al. (1995).

and Subtle scales. These tables can be used to compare the scores from an individual patient to a number of known experimental and clinical groups (See tables 4.1 to 4.3).

Ego Strength (Es)

The Ego Strength (Es) Scale consists of 52 items. It was originally developed as a measure of prognosis for psychotherapy (Barron, 1956). Other researchers have reported that low Es scores might reflect severe psychiatric illness. For example, Caldwell (1988), referring to the original MMPI, noted that patients with a T score of 20 or lower have a "usually urgent if not critical" need to be hospitalized in a mental ward (p. 37). He also noted that patients with a T score of 30 and below "consistently need extensive care and support from others and very possibly hospitalization." Graham (1993) and Greene (2000), in reference to the MMPI-2, noted that low Es Scale scores can be associated with exaggeration or over-reporting of psychological problems. Thus, in clinical practice, it can be useful to compare a person's Es score to their actual level of functioning. Extremely low scores, in the absence of obvious, independently verifiable psychiatric problems, should be considered suspicious for exaggeration.

Table 4.2. Total Obvious T Score Performances in Known Groups

GROUP	N	M	SD
Normal Control Subjects			
University Students[1]	40	276.3	50.7
University Students (Male)[2]	58	240.1	44.2
University Students (Female)[2]	140	240.9	48.8
University Students (Male)[3]	56	268.7	43.9
University Students (Female)[3]	49	285.4	53.8
PTSD			
Child Sexual Abuse Outpatients with PTSD[4]	64	395.4	54.7
Combat War Veterans with PTSD[5]	124	434.1	63.1
Psychiatric Patients			
Nonforensic Inpatients (Mixed Diagnoses—Male)[2]	64	281.8	66.9
Nonforensic Inpatients (Mixed Diagnoses—Female)[2]	65	287.5	52.8
Forensic Inpatients (Mixed Diagnoses—Male)[2]	131	263.4	62.3
Forensic Inpatients (Mixed Diagnoses—Female)[2]	28	270.7	55.3
Inpatients (Major Depression)[5]	48	359.4	56.8
Inpatients (Major Depression)[1]	40	341.9	48.3
Inpatients (Schizophrenia)[1]	40	331.4	63.2
Inpatients (Mixed Diagnoses—Male)[3]	29	320.2	76.0
Inpatients (Mixed Diagnoses—Female)[3]	20	341.8	72.0
Inpatients (Mixed Diagnoses)[6]	50	331.7	60.0
Analog Malingerers			
Fake PTSD (University Students)[4]	85	452.6	71.3
Fake PTSD (University Students)[3]	84	454.3	70.2
Fake Depression (University Students)[1]	20	446.9	57.7
Fake Depression (Mental Health Professionals)[6]	23	428.1	42.7
Fake Schizophrenia (University Students)[1]	20	462.1	60.2
Fake Bad (Male University Students)[2]	29	338.8	48.6
Fake Bad (Female University Students)[2]	45	341.9	44.9
Fake Bad (Male University Students)[3]	29	510.9	50.2
Fake Bad (Female University Students)[3]	20	506.8	39.2
Students Instructed to "Fake Good"			
Fake Good (Male University Students)[2]	14	183.9	24.7
Fake Good (Female University Students)[2]	56	183.6	36.4
Fake Good (Male University Students)[3]	27	224.4	31.0
Fake Good (Female University Students)[3]	29	229.5	49.7

Note: All values have been rounded to one decimal.

Source: [1]Bagby et al. (1997), [2]Bagby et al. (1995), [3]Timbrook et al. (1993), [4]Elhai et al. (2001), [5]Elhai et al. (2000), [6]Bagby et al. (2000).

Table 4.3. Total Subtle T Score Performances in Known Groups

GROUP	N	M	SD
Normal Control Subjects			
University Students (Male)[1]	58	241.9	24.3
University Students (Female)[1]	140	244.1	26.5
University Students (Male)[2]	56	259.7	25.9
University Students (Female)[2]	49	257.4	25.9
Psychiatric Patients			
Nonforensic Inpatients (Mixed Diagnoses—Male)[1]	64	255.1	31.7
Nonforensic Inpatients (Mixed Diagnoses—Female)[1]	65	259.7	32.0
Forensic Inpatients (Mixed Diagnoses—Male)[1]	131	256.9	33.2
Forensic Inpatients (Mixed Diagnoses—Female)[1]	28	244.5	27.1
Inpatients (Mixed Diagnoses—Male)[2]	29	270.0	33.2
Inpatients (Mixed Diagnoses—Female)[2]	20	260.6	31.8
Analog Malingerers			
Fake Bad (Male University Students)[1]	29	232.9	20.5
Fake Bad (Female University Students)[1]	45	231.4	18.4
Fake Bad (Male University Students)[2]	29	256.1	17.5
Fake Bad (Female University Students)[2]	20	246.4	12.7
Students Instructed to "Fake Good"			
Fake Good (Male University Students)[1]	14	266.0	26.2
Fake Good (Female University Students)[1]	56	264.5	24.1
Fake Good (Male University Students)[2]	27	284.6	31.9
Fake Good (Female University Students)[2]	29	283.4	26.9

Note: All values have been rounded to one decimal.

Source: [1]Bagby et al. (1995), [2]Timbrook et al. (1993).

Dissimulation Scale (Ds/Dsr)

The original Dissimulation Scale (Ds), consisting of 70 items, was created by Gough (1954). In 1957, Gough created the revised, 40-item scale by asking normal persons to pretend to be neurotically disturbed. Those items that differentiated normal people faking disturbance from genuinely disturbed patients were then identified. During the conversion from MMPI to MMPI-2, a number of items were dropped or changed. The MMPI-2 Ds scale has 58 items and the Dsr scale has 34 items. Berry, Baer, and Harris (1991) conducted a meta-analysis of the original MMPI and reported that the Ds scale had one of the largest effect sizes of the malingering scales. Researchers examining the clinical utility of the MMPI-2 Ds or Dsr validity scales have repeatedly demonstrated that individuals instructed to fake a psychiatric or neurological condition (e.g., PTSD, paranoid schizophrenia, depression, or traumatic brain injury) perform significantly higher on the Ds and Dsr scales compared to either healthy subjects (e.g., Bagby et al.,

Table 4.4. Dissimulation Index (Ds) Raw Score* Performances in Known Groups

GROUP	N	M	SD
Normal Control Subjects			
University Students[1]	40	14.2	5.0
University Students[2]	95	58.2T	12.2
University Students[3]	58	14.2	6.3
University Students[4]	36	12.9	5.8
University Students (Baseline)[5]	32	14.7	6.4
University Students (Retest)[5]	32	14.7	6.6
Job Applicants[6]	43	5.6	3.8
Psychiatric Patients			
Inpatients (Borderline Personality Disorder)[7]	36	22.6	9.7
Inpatients (Schizophrenia)[1]	40	19.0	9.2
Inpatients (Paranoid Schizophrenia)[7]	20	18.6	8.9
Inpatients (Major Depression)[8]	48	17.9	8.2
Inpatients (Major Depression)[1]	40	17.7	7.9
Inpatients (Mixed Diagnoses)[8]	50	17.3	8.6
Outpatients (Mixed Diagnoses)[9]	42	24.9	10.4
Outpatients (Mixed Diagnoses)[10]	30	65.5T	14.1
Psychiatric and Medical Patients[6]	208	13.2	8.0
PTSD and Chronic Pain			
Psychiatric Inpatients (PTSD)[7]	20	24.4	9.7
Combat War Veterans (PTSD)[11]	124	87.1T	13.1
Child Sexual Abuse Outpatients (PTSD)[12]	64	82.2T	15.8
Combat Veterans (Eval. for PTSD—Noncompensation)[13]	38	26.6	6.5
Compensation-Seeking			
Personal Injury Litigants[6]	120	13.0	7.5
Combat Veterans (Eval. for PTSD—Compensation-Seeking)[13]	87	32.2	6.3
Analog Malingerers			
Fake PTSD (University Students)[7]	20	42.3	11.1
Fake PTSD (Baseline)—University Students[5]	30	38.8	12.2
Fake PTSD (Retest)—University Students[5]	30	34.1	13.9
Fake PTSD (University Students)[11]	84	100.4T	18.0
Fake PTSD (University Students)[12]	85	100.0T	18.3
Fake Depression (Mental Health Professionals)[8]	23	34.7	7.8
Fake Depression (University Students)[1]	20	37.5	8.6
Fake Depression (University Students—Depression & Validity Info)[2]	112	86.3T	14.8
Fake Depression (University Students—Depression Info Only)[2]	80	92.6T	16.3
Fake Depression (University Students—Validity Info Only)[2]	89	87.3T	17.3
Fake Depression (University Students—No Training)[2]	89	101.8T	15.0
Fake Depression (University Students—Successful Mal)[2]	111	75.9T	9.8
Fake Depression (University Students—Unsuccessful Mal)[2]	259	98.6T	14.6
Fake Borderline Personality Disorder (University Students)[4]	23	37.5	9.3
Fake Psychiatric Disability (University Students)[4]	23	32.5	9.9
Fake Psychiatric Problems (Psychiatric Outpatients)[9]	42	39.4	10.9
Fake Somatoform Disorder (University Students)[3]	58	27.3	10.2

GROUP	N	M	SD
Fake Paranoid Psychotic (University Students)[3]	58	43.4	9.2
Fake Paranoid Schizophrenia (University Students)[7]	22	45.4	9.5
Fake Schizophrenia (University Students)[1]	20	41.4	9.9
Fake Cry for Help (Psychiatric Outpatients)[10]	30	106.9T	16.4
Fake Bad (University Students)[3]	58	42.4	10.0
Fake CHI (Baseline)—University Students[5]	34	28.7	11.4
Fake CHI (Retest)—University Students[5]	34	27.2	10.1

*All values are raw scores with the exception of the denoted values that are T scores. All values have been rounded to one decimal.

Source: [1]Bagby et al. (1997), [2]Walters & Clopton (2000), [3]Sivec et al. (1994), [4]Wetter et al. (1994), [5]Wetter & Deitsch (1996), [6]Tsushima & Tsushima (2001), [7]Wetter et al. (1993), [8]Bagby et al. (2000), [9]Rogers et al. (1995), [10]Berry et al. (1996), [11]Elhai et al. (2000), [12]Elhai et al. (2001), [13]Frueh et al. (1997).

1994; Rogers et al., 1995; Sivec et al., 1994; Walters & Clopton, 2000; Wetter & Deitsch, 1996) or psychiatric patient controls (e.g., Bagby, Buis, & Nicholson, 1995; Bagby et al., 1994, 2000; Berry et al., 1996; Elhai et al., 2000; Storm & Graham, 2000; Wetter, Baer, Berry, & Reynolds, 1994; Wetter et al., 1993). In regard to the MMPI-2, Greene (2000) noted that, "it clearly needs to be used in evaluating whether the person is overreporting psychopathology" (p. 78). Rogers et al. (2003) also strongly recommended interpreting this scale. We have extracted the Ds and Dsr scores from numerous studies and presented them in tables 4.4and 4.5. The reader should note that these tables contain a mix of raw scores and T scores.

Fake Bad Scale (FBS)

The Fake Bad Scale (FBS) is not one of the standard validity scales. It was developed in 1991, two years after the MMPI-2 was published, to measure exaggeration in personal injury litigation evaluations. According to Lees-Haley, English, and Glenn (1991), personal injury malingerers may present with a blended fake good/fake bad response set. They portray themselves as premorbidly well adjusted, high functioning, honest, conscientious, and hard working, yet currently psychologically traumatized or disabled. These researchers developed the FBS (Lees-Haley et al., 1991) to assess this response set. The scale consists of 43 questions. In the original study, medical outpatients were instructed to simulate emotional distress under a variety of circumstances, such as in relation to a motor vehicle accident, toxic exposure, or on-the-job stress (Lees-Haley et al., 1991). For these three combined groups of experimental malingerers ($N = 67$), their average score on the FBS was 25 ($SD = 8.5$).

Table 4.5. Dissimulation Index Revised (Ds-R) Raw Score* Performances in Known Groups

GROUP	N	M	SD
Normal Control Subjects			
Hospital Patients[1]	192	11.0	6.6
University Students[2]	95	57.2T	12.1
University Students[3]	90	11.7	4.6
University Students (Male)[4]	58	10.0	5.7
Psychiatric Patients			
Outpatients (Mixed Diagnoses)[5]	42	16.4	7.2
Inpatients (Mixed Diagnoses)[3]	95	12.7	5.6
Nonforensic Inpatients (Mixed Diagnoses—Male)[4]	64	11.3	6.7
Nonforensic Inpatients (Mixed Diagnoses—Female)[4]	65	12.1	6.3
Forensic Inpatients (Mixed Diagnoses—Male)[4]	131	10.0	6.2
Forensic Inpatients (Mixed Diagnoses—Female)[4]	28	12.0	6.5
PTSD and Chronic Pain			
Mixed Neurological/Chronic Pain (Nonlitigation)[6]	100	54.2T	10.1
Combat Veterans (Eval. for PTSD—Noncompensation)[7]	38	14.3	4.4
Compensation-Seeking			
Mixed Neurological/Chronic Pain (Litigation)[6]	100	66.9T	17.2
Work Comp./Personal Injury Claimants—Psych Disorders[8]	289	63.8T	15.9
Combat Veterans (Eval. for PTSD—Compensation-Seeking)[7]	87	19.7	4.6
Analog Malingerers			
Fake Psychiatric Problems (Psychiatric Outpatients)[5]	42	24.7	7.0
Fake Depression (University Students—Depression & Validity Info)[2]	112	83.2T	13.2
Fake Depression (University students—Depression Info Only)[2]	80	87.7T	14.6
Fake Depression (University Students—Validity Info Only)[2]	89	84.2T	15.7
Fake Depression (University Students—No Training)[2]	89	96.2T	12.5
Fake Psychiatric Problems (Uncoached)[1]	67	23.3	6.9
Fake Psychiatric Problems (Coached)[1]	93	16.4	5.6
Fake Depression (University Students—Successful Mal)[2]	111	75.4T	9.9
Fake Depression (University Students—Unsuccessful Mal)[2]	259	93.0T	13.4
Fake Bad (University Students)[3]	58	20.8	5.0
Students Instructed to "Fake Good"			
Fake Bad (Male University Students)[4]	29	19.7	5.9
Fake Bad (Female University Students)[4]	45	21.0	4.5
Fake Good (Male University Students)[4]	14	12.4	5.4
Fake Good (Female University Students)[4]	56	13.7	4.7
Fake Good (University Students)[3]	67	6.3	3.2

*All values are raw scores with the exception of the denoted values that are T scores. All values have been rounded to one decimal.

Source: [1]Storm & Graham (2000), [2]Walters & Clopton (2000), [3]Bagby et al. (1994), [4]Bagby et al. (1995), [5]Rogers et al. (1995), [6]Meyers et al. (2002), [7]Frueh et al. (1997), [8]Fox et al. (1995).

Lees-Haley (1992) identified a sample of personal injury litigants with "pseudo-PTSD." Pseudo-PTSD patients were those who (a) claimed to be suffering a psychological injury, (b) maintained that the injury was so severe that it was disabling, (c) said it was due to an experience that was entirely implausible as a candidate for PTSD Criterion A in DSM-III-R, and (d) scored T = 65 or higher on both PK and PS, the posttraumatic stress disorder subscales of the MMPI-2. On average, litigants with pseudo-PTSD scored 27.1 (*SD* = 5.2) on the FBS. For comparison, as reported by Greene (1997), the average score for men in the MMPI-2 normative sample on the FBS was 11.7 (*SD* = 3.8) and for women 13.8 (*SD* = 4.1). Greiffenstein, Baker, Axelrod, Peck, and Gervais (2004) also reported high FBS scores in personal injury litigants with improbable posttraumatic stress claims (*M* = 29.1, *SD* = 5.0).

Although the FBS was originally oriented toward emotional distress injuries, researchers have shown that it is useful for detecting "somatic malingering" (Larrabee, 1997, 1998). Somatic malingering is characterized by major exaggeration of both physical and psychological problems. It appears most likely to occur in patients with chronic pain and/or mild traumatic brain injuries (and an alleged persistent postconcussion syndrome). Larrabee (1997) suggested that "somatic malingering should be considered whenever elevations on scales 1 and 3 exceed T = 80, accompanied by a significant elevation on the FBS" (p. 203).

The FBS has been used successfully in numerous studies involving litigating patients with mild traumatic brain injuries or other conditions believed to at least mildly affect their cognitive and psychological functioning. The FBS has been shown to be more accurate for identifying exaggeration than the traditional MMPI-2 validity scales in several studies (Greiffenstein, Baker, Gola, Donders, & Miller, 2002; Larrabee, 2003a; Ross, Millis, Krukowski, Putnam, & Adams, 2004). Larrabee (2003b) combined the FBS with atypical performance patterns on standard neuropsychological tests to successfully identify malingering. In a recent study involving MTBI litigants, ROC curve analysis revealed that a cutoff score of 21 had a sensitivity of 90%, specificity of 90%, and an overall correct classificatory rate of 90% (Ross et al., 2004).

Tsushima and Tsushima (2001) found that the FBS was the only validity scale that differentiated a large sample of personal injury litigants from a sample of clinical patients. They concluded that high FBS scores could be affected by litigation stress and exaggeration, and further noted that their data were consistent with the growing evidence that personal injury litigants tend to demonstrate somatic preoccupation and symptom overreporting on the MMPI-2.

It should be noted that, based on available cutoff scores and a large data set, the majority of personal injury litigants do not appear to frankly exaggerate on the FBS (Lees-Haley, 1997). Therefore, elevations, when they occur, likely are clinically meaningful. Greene (2000) recommended additional research with the FBS based on its low correlation with the infrequency scales (thus, its unique

Table 4.6. Fake Bad Scale Scores in Known Groups

GROUP	N	MEAN	SD
Normal Control Subjects			
MMPI-2 Normative Sample Males[1]	1,138	11.7	3.8
MMPI-2 Normative Sample Females[1]	1,462	13.8	4.1
Federal Prison Inmates Minimum Security Males[2]	25	9.8	4.1
Medical Patients			
Traumatic Brain Injury[3]	59	14.6	4.7
Severe Traumatic Brain Injury[4]	15	15.4	5.2
Moderate Traumatic Brain Injury[4]	12	16.6	7.0
Mixed Neurological Group[4]	13	15.8	3.2
Moderate-to-Severe Traumatic Brain Injury[5]	29	15.7	6.0
Medical Outpatients Transplant Candidates Males[2]	20	15.3	7.6
Chronic Pain[6]	100	19.0	5.5
Psychiatric Patients			
MMPI-2 Psychiatric Sample Estimated Scores for Males[7]	—	16.9	—
MMPI-2 Psychiatric Sample Estimated Scores for Females[7]	—	19.1	—
Patients with Chronic Psychiatric Problems[8]	42	22.1	5.8
Male Veterans Inpatient Substance Abuse Unit[2]	25	15.6	6.4
Psychiatric and Medical Patients[9]	208	17.1	5.7
Patients with Depression[10]	48	22.0	5.5
Psychiatric Patients[10]	50	18.5	6.6
Psychiatric Patients[4]	14	18.2	5.0
Posttraumatic Stress[11]	48	20.2	5.9
Child Custody Litigants[12]			
No Alleged Abuse Males	—	13.8	3.0
No Alleged Abuse Females	—	13.8	3.0
Alleged Physical Abuse Males	—	13.6	3.1
Alleged Physical Abuse Females	—	15.1	3.6
Alleged Sexual Abuse Males	—	13.5	3.1
Alleged Sexual Abuse Females	—	16.0	3.5
Personal Injury Litigants			
Head Trauma, Chronic Pain, or Both[12]	95	22.3	6.9
Unselected, Consecutive Litigants[13]	492	20.8	6.7
Personal Injury Litigants[9]	120	20.7	6.2
Atypical Mild Traumatic Brain Injury[14]	159	24.8	6.2
Moderate-to-Severe Traumatic Brain Injury[14]	68	17.6	6.5
Chronic Pain[6]	100	22.7	6.3
Improbable Posttraumatic Stress[11]	57	29.1	5.0
Major Trauma Posttraumatic Stress[11]	32	24.3	5.7
Personal Injury Litigants[7]	25	27.6	4.7
Litigants with Presumed Spurious PTSD Claims[15]	55	27.1	5.2
Analog Malingerers			
Medical Outpatients: Simulate Emotional Distress from MVA[7]	16	26	6.7

GROUP	N	MEAN	SD
Medical Outpatients: Simulate Emotional Distress from Toxic Exposure[7]	15	21	9.6
Medical Outpatients: Simulate Emotional Distress from Job Stress[7]	36	27	8.0
Medical Outpatients: Total Analog Malingerers[7]	67	25	8.5
Patients with Psychiatric Problems: Malinger Severe Psychiatric Problems[8]	42	24.8	5.7
Federal Inmates: Malinger Severe Psychiatric Problems[2]	25	21.6	5.8
Sophisticated Malingerers Faking Depression[10]	23	28.4	4.4
Suspected Malingerers			
Suspected Malingerers (MTBI and Neurotoxic Exposure Litigants)[16]	33	25.6	4.6
Mild Head Injury Litigants[3]	59	28.6	5.1
Mild Head Injury and Other Litigants[5]	24	26.4	5.2
Mild Head Injury and Other Litigants[5]	17	26.7	5.7

Note: In Posthuma & Harper (1998), there were 188 individuals involved in custody evaluations.

Source: [1]Greene (1997), [2]Iverson, Henrichs, Barton, & Allen (2002), [3]Ross et al. (2004), [4]Larrabee (2003b), [5]Larrabee (2003c), [6]Meyers et al. (2002), [7]Lees-Haley et al. (1991), [8]Rogers et al. (1995), [9]Tsushima & Tsushima (2001), [10]Bagby et al. (2000), [11]Greiffenstein et al. (2004), [12]Posthuma & Harper (1998), [13]Lees-Haley (1997), [14]Greiffenstein et al. (2004), [15]Lees-Haley (1992.) [16]Larrabee (2003a).

contribution to the assessment of validity). The performances of subjects in known groups on the Fake Bad Scale are presented in table 4.6

Rogers et al. (1995) included the FBS in an analog malingering study using psychiatric outpatients in a within-subjects design. This study found low sensitivity of the FBS to the extreme exaggeration response set (mean F scale score was 109.6) of chronically mentally ill outpatients and a problematic rate of false positive classifications (19%) in the psychiatric patient sample. This, of course, is not surprising because the FBS was not designed to detect malingered psychosis.

Butcher, Arbisi, Atlis, and McNulty (2003) have recently questioned the use of the FBS for the purpose of detecting malingering. They completed a large-scale study examining the psychometric characteristics of the FBS scale in more than 20,000 MMPI-2 protocols that included 6,731 psychiatric outpatients, 2,897 individuals from a correctional facility, 4,408 patients from a chronic pain program, 5,090 general medical patients, 901 Veterans Administration (VA) Hospital inpatients, and 157 personal injury litigants. All protocols were obtained from the National Computer Systems MMPI-2 archival data files. These authors present malingering classification rates by group using four different cutoff scores: FBS >20, >22, >24, and >26. Using a cutoff score of 26, malingering classification rates ranged from 2.3% to 23.9% for males, and 2.5% to 37.9% for females. The lowest classification rates were for the correctional facility group for both men and women, while the highest classification rates were for the VA inpatient sample for men, and personal injury sample for women. The authors concluded that:

> the results indicate that the FBS is more likely to measure general maladjustment and somatic complaints rather than malingering. The rate of false positives produced by the scale is unacceptably high, especially in psychiatric settings. The scale is likely to classify an unacceptably large number of individuals who are experiencing genuine psychological distress as malingerers. It is recommended that the FBS not be used in clinical settings nor should it be used during disability evaluations to determine malingering. (Butcher et al., 2003, pp. 473–474)

This study by Butcher et al. has been criticized on theoretical and methodological grounds (e.g., Greiffenstein et al., 2004; Greve & Bianchini, 2004; Larrabee, 2003a; Lees-Haley & Fox, 2004). We believe the literature, as a whole, supports the use of the Fake Bad Scale as an indicator of exaggeration in personal injury cases (see table 4.6).

MMPI-2 Validity Index

Meyers, Millis, and Volkert (2002) developed the MMPI-2 Validity Index. The Validity Index combines seven validity scales from the MMPI-2 (i.e., F-K, F, FBS, F(p), Dsr, Es, and O-S). Each validity index is assigned a weighting of one or two points based on an arbitrarily defined score range on each validity scale. Scores on the Validity Index can range from 0 to 14. A cutoff score of 5 or higher was recommended as a preliminary criterion for exaggeration based on the Validity Index scores of 100 nonlitigant chronic pain patients, 100 litigating chronic pain patients, and 30 sophisticated simulators instructed to feign the emotional and cognitive difficulties demonstrated by chronic pain patients. Using a cutoff score of 5 or above, 100% of nonlitigant chronic pain patients were successfully classified as honest responders, and 86% of the simulators were correctly identified as exaggerating symptomatology. In the litigating chronic pain patients sample, 33% scored 5 points or higher on this index. These authors conclude that the MMPI-2 Validity Index appears to be superior to any single validity scale; however, replication of these findings was recommended.

In a recently presented Australian MMPI-2 study, Senior, Lange, and Douglas (2003) examined base rates of MMPI-2 Validity Index scores in 1,038 personal injury litigants referred for psychiatric evaluation and/or neuropsychological assessment, 310 community controls, and 25 confirmed malingerers. Using the recommended cutoff score of =5, 76% of the confirmed malingerers were correctly classified using the Validity Index. The presumed false positive error rate in community controls was 7.1%. Several large subsamples of litigants were evaluated. The breakdown of litigants by diagnostic group who scored 5 or higher was as follows: depression ($n = 136$) = 33.1%, PTSD ($n = 116$) = 39.7%, chronic pain

(n = 248) = 22.2%, and alleged traumatic brain injury (n = 156) = 25.6%. These results suggest that the recommended cutoff score of 5 or higher on the Validity Index might be too low. Of course, it is not possible to know what percentage of these litigating patients might be exaggerating or frankly malingering.

Conclusions—MMPI-2

There is a tremendous body of literature relating to exaggeration and malingering on the MMPI-2. There are several recent summaries of this literature (e.g., Guriel & Fremouw, 2003; Lees-Haley et al., 2002; Rogers et al., 2003). There is clear and compelling evidence that experimental malingerers produce elevations on multiple validity scales and indices. Thus, various MMPI-2 scales and indices are sensitive to exaggeration and malingering.

Clinicians are rightfully concerned about falsely labeling someone as exaggerating or malingering. We think that some clinicians are too conservative and others are too liberal when they interpret the MMPI-2 validity scales and indices. We hope that the data provided in tables 4.1 to 4.6 are useful for better understanding individuals' scores in relation to known groups.

Cutoff T scores for five MMPI-2 validity scales are provided in table 4.7. These cutoffs were derived from the recent meta-analysis by Rogers et al. (2003). Ag-

Table 4.7. Cutoff T Scores for Five MMPI-2 Validity Scales and Indices for Patients with Depression, PTSD, or Heterogeneous Diagnoses

GROUP	F	F_b	F(P)	OBVIOUS-SUBTLE	DS
Depression	71.7	82.0	59.9	79.1	64.4
	(21.6)	(24.2)	(17.4)	(61.6)	(15.0)
90th Percentile	99	113	82	158	84
PTSD	86.3	92.3	69.0	182.2	68.4
	(21.6)	(24.6)	(21.0)	(71.8)	(14.6)
90th Percentile	114	124	96	274	87
Schizophrenia	80.1	79.4	66.7	58.6	65.7
	(23.2)	(24.3)	(20.1)	(91.6)	(16.2)
90th Percentile	110	110	92	176	86.4
Mixed Diagnoses	75.6	79.2	60.0	73.8	54.8
	(23.7)	(24.8)	(19.0)	(91.1)	(14.2)
90th Percentile	106	111	84	190.4	73

Note: The 90th percentile was calculated by multiplying the standard deviation by 1.28 and adding it to the mean.

Source: The means and standard deviations (in parentheses) are derived from table 4 in Rogers et al. (2003) meta-analysis.

Table 4.8. Cutoff Scores for Various MMPI-2 Validity Scales and Indices

| SCALE / INDEX | 99.9% GENERAL POPULATION | Rogers et al. (2003) Meta-Analysis | | Caldwell Data (Greene, 2000) | |
		AVERAGE CUTOFF	NORMATIVE CUTOFF	93RD PERCENTILE PSYCHIATRIC PATIENTS	98TH PERCENTILE PSYCHIATRIC PATIENTS
F	17	20	105T	17	24
F-K	11	12	18	7	15
F_B	14	18	117T	14	20
F(p)	8	7	98T	4	7
Obvious-Subtle	197	156	256	186	240
Ds	32	35	91T	28	35
Lachar-Wrobel	62	74	80	60	73

Note: Obvious minus Subtle (O-S) scores are T-difference scores. All scores are raw scores unless followed by a "T." The cutoff scores for the MMPI-2 normative sample (i.e., "general population") were derived from Greene (2000). The Caldwell clinical dataset consists of 52,543 psychiatric in-patients and outpatients. The cutoff scores for the 93rd and 98th percentiles are derived from Greene (2000). The "average cutoff" is the mean cutoff score reported in table 5 of the Rogers et al. (2003) meta-analysis. The "normative cutoff" score represents the 98th percentile for the entire patient sample in the meta-analysis.

gregated means and standard deviations for four patient groups are provided. The T score corresponding to the 90th percentile for each patient group was calculated. For example, 90% of patients with depression are expected to have T scores less than or equal to 99 on F, 113 on Fb, 82 on F(p), 158 on O-S, and 84 on Ds. Patients scoring above these cutoffs have unusually high scores. Note that the data from the PTSD group is heavily influenced by the fact that most studies have been conducted with combat veterans. When patients score above these cutoffs, they are endorsing symptoms in an atypical manner, which might reflect exaggeration or malingering.

Table 4.8 also is useful for evaluating several validity scales. The cutoff scores for the 99.9th percentile in the general population are provided. Notice that the average cutoff scores across studies reviewed in the Rogers et al. (2003) meta-analysis are quite similar to the scores corresponding to the 99.9th percentile for healthy adults. The final three columns represent T scores and raw scores that are unusual or rare in presumed genuine psychiatric patients.

Structured Inventory of Malingered Symptomatology (SIMS)

The Structured Inventory of Malingered Symptomatology (Smith & Burger, 1997) is a brief paper-and-pencil screening measure designed to detect exaggerated psychological and subjective cognitive complaints. The SIMS consists of 75 true/false items grouped into five subscales, with 15 items in each subscale. The five subscales consist of five different conditions commonly feigned by individuals: low intelligence, affective disorders, neurological impairment, psychosis, and amnestic disorders. Many items were generated based on characteristics of malingerers reported in the literature, and other items were selected and modified based on questions appearing in other tests. The detection of deviant or malingered response patterns is based on three strategies: (a) endorsement of bizarre experiences (e.g., "Sometimes my muscles go limp for no apparent reason so that my arms and legs feel as though they weigh a ton"), (b) highly atypical symptoms (e.g., "At times, I am so depressed I welcome going to bed early to 'sleep it off' "), and (c) approximate answers (e.g., If you have $1.50 and I take fifty cents away, you will have 75 cents left"; Merckelback & Smith, 2003).

A few analog malingering studies have been conducted with the SIMS. In the initial development, Smith and Burger (1997) reported high sensitivity (95.6%) and specificity (87.9%) for total SIMS scores (using a cutoff score of 14) to differentiate honest responders versus those instructed to simulate a specific psychological disorder corresponding to one of the SIMS subscales. Moderate to high sensitivity (i.e., 74.6% to 88.3%) and specificity (51.5% to 90.69%) values were reported when using the subscales alone. In a similar study, Edens, Otto, and Dwyer (1999) examined the ability of the SIMS to detect individuals instructed to fake depression, psychosis, or cognitive impairment. High sensitivity and specificity values were found for the SIMS affective disorders subscale (81.5% and 100%, respectively), psychosis subscale (93.2% and 91.5%), and the neurological impairment subscale (93.1% and 94.4%) to detect their corresponding experimental malingering group. The SIMS total score also showed high sensitivity and specificity values to differentiate honest responders from all malingering groups regardless of their feigned disorder (96.4% and 91.3%, respectively).

Rogers, Hinds, and Sewell (1996) conducted an analog malingering study using adolescent offenders. Participants completed the SIMS on two occasions, once under honest conditions, and again under instructions to fake major depression, generalized anxiety disorder, or schizophrenia. Predictive power values were calculated for the total score and each of the five subscales. Using a cutoff score of 16, the SIMS total score demonstrated high positive predictive power (PPP = .87) but only moderate negative predictive power value (NPP = .62) for differentiating honest responders from experimental malingerers. The highest PPP was reported for the affective disorders scale (PPP = .91) and the highest NPP for the low intelligence Scale (NPP = .81). The best overall SIMS score was the Low Intelligence Scale (PPP = .91 and NPP = .70).

Lewis, Simcox, and Berry (2002) examined the clinical usefulness of the SIMS and selected MMPI-2 validity scales (F, F-K, F_B, F(p)) to differentiate faking from honest responding in 55 federal prison inmates undergoing pretrial psychological evaluations for competency to stand trial or criminal responsibility. Of this group, 31 were classified as honest responders and 24 as feigning, based on Structured Interview of Reported Symptoms (SIRS) scores. Using a cutoff score of 16, SIMS total scores demonstrated high sensitivity (1.00) and negative predictive power (1.00) values, and moderate specificity (.61) and positive predictive power (.54) values for identifying suspected malingerers from honest responders. Compared to the SIMS total scores, MMPI-2 validity scales had lower sensitivity (.50 to .83) and negative predictive power (.81 to .91) values, but higher specificity (.94 to 1.00) and positive predictive power (.86 to 1.00). These authors concluded that both tests have potential as a screen for malingering. However, these results suggest that the MMPI-2 validity scales were more useful than SIMS total scores at identifying suspected exaggerators, while SIMS total scores were more useful than MMPI-2 validity scales at identifying individuals who were honest responders.

In the most recent study, Merckelbach and Smith (2003) examined the ability of a Dutch translation of the SIMS to differentiate 241 honest responders (231 university students, 10 patients) from 57 university students instructed to feign amnesia, schizophrenia, or neurological disease. Using the recommended cutoff score of 16 for the total score on the SIMS, high sensitivity (.93), specificity (.98), positive predictive power (.90), and negative predictive power (.98) values were demonstrated for the SIMS to differentiate individuals instructed to feign a disorder from honest responders. These authors conclude that these results "provide a basis for cautious optimism regarding the usefulness of the SIMS as a screening tool for malingering" (p. 152).

Malingering Probability Scale (MPS)

The MPS (Silverton & Gruber, 1998) is a 139-item true/false self-report inventory designed to "assess whether an individual is attempting to produce false evidence of psychological distress" (p. 1). These statements are similar in appearance to MMPI-2 items. The test contains two validity scales: (1) the Inconsistency Scale measures consistency of responding to items, and (2) the Malingering Scale is comprised of statements that describe spurious yet seemingly authentic symptoms of psychological distress. Spurious psychological distress items parallel symptoms associated with depression and anxiety, dissociative disorders, posttraumatic stress disorder, and schizophrenia. Although the MPS was designed primarily as a tool to assess exaggeration of psychological distress, as a secondary purpose, the MPS also provides four clinical scales that assess the presence of bona fide psychological distress in the four areas above. These items were included to provide a context in which the foil items for the Malingering Scale could be included. The distinction between real (e.g., "I hear voices") and false (e.g., "I am bothered by voices in my head") symptoms was designed to be subtle and difficult for individuals who have not experienced such symptomatology to differentiate without sufficient understanding of the relevant scientific literature.

The two validity and four clinical scales can be interpreted using T scores. For the clinical scales, when the inconsistency and malingering results indicate that the responses to the MPS are meaningful, scores of 60T or higher on depression, dissociative disorder, and posttraumatic stress, and 65T or higher on schizophrenia are considered to be elevated. For the validity scales, inconsistency scores of 70T or higher indicate inconsistent responding. For the Malingering Scale, "if the INC score is not elevated, a MAL score of 70T or higher can be considered an initial strong indicator of an effort to exaggerate or simulate psychological distress" (Silverton & Gruber, 1998, p. 6). However, a more sophisticated interpretation of the Malingering Scale is offered in the test manual, and the authors suggest that the interpretation of the T score for the Malingering Scale should only be considered preliminary. Rather, they propose that the conclusion of whether a person is exaggerating or malingering be coined in terms of a probability score (e.g., 80% probability of malingering) rather than using a cutoff score to render a dichotomous classification. In addition, the probability score varies depending on the *a priori* expectation of malingering base rates in a certain population or setting (e.g., personal injury litigants vs. hospital patients). For example, for a score of 80T on the malingering scale, the probability of malingering will be either 97%, 88%, and 76%, depending on whether the expected base rate of malingering in that particular setting is assumed to be 50%, 20%, or 10%, respectively.

The majority of the research using the MPS has been undertaken as part of the test development, with Silverton and Gruber (1998) reporting high sensitivity (i.e., 80% to 90%) and specificity (94% to 96%) of the MPS validity scales to differentiate honest responding from feigned psychological symptoms in a sample of university students and prison inmates. Higher base rates of invalid MPS protocols were also reported in forensic/workers' compensation settings versus clinical outpatients. To our knowledge, the only other study using the MPS is by Leark, Charlton, Allen, and Gruber (2000). In an unpublished analog malingering study, they examined the ability of the MPS to detect faked symptoms in 54 individuals instructed to feign psychological distress under "simple faking" (i.e., feign distress instructions), "motivated faking" (i.e., financial incentive), and "honest responding" conditions. Statistically significant differences were found between the honest responding condition and both the simple faking and motivated faking conditions, while no differences were found between the two faking conditions.

Effort Tests in Neuropsychology

Some of the most sophisticated tests and procedures for detecting exaggeration have been developed in clinical and forensic neuropsychology. Essentially, these tests measure exaggeration by inference; they actually measure poor effort (a.k.a. suboptimal effort, nonoptimal effort, incomplete effort, or negative response bias). Specifically, there are numerous empirically validated procedures for determining whether a patient, or plaintiff, is underperforming during neuropsychological testing. One explanation for poor effort is a deliberate attempt to make oneself look cognitively compromised due to an alleged neurological or psychological injury.

There are two approaches to detecting poor effort in neuropsychology. First, researchers have examined performance patterns on specific neuropsychological tests or test batteries that (a) are uncommon in healthy people, (b) are uncommon in patients with psychiatric conditions, brain injuries, or brain diseases, yet (c) are relatively common in people known or suspected to be exaggerating and/or malingering. Second, researchers have developed specialized tests designed specifically to detect poor effort. The potential use of a specialized test in civil forensic psychological evaluations is illustrated in the following section.

Test of Memory Malingering

The Test of Memory Malingering (TOMM) (Tombaugh, 1997) is a traditional symptom validity test. Fifty target line drawings are presented to the patient and then a two-alternative forced-choice recognition task is administered (Trial 1). The procedure is repeated for Trial 2. After approximately 10–15 minutes, a retention test is given in which the original 50 items are paired with distracters.

The TOMM appears difficult, but is actually quite easy. For example, Tombaugh (1997) administered the test to a sample of 70 community dwelling adults. On average, these subjects correctly recalled 47.8 pictures on Trial 1, 49.9 pictures on Trial 2, and 49.9 pictures on the retention trial. Moreover, Tombaugh reported scores from several groups of patients with brain injuries and diseases. In general, these patients performed well on the TOMM, indicating that the test is not very sensitive to the effects of acquired brain damage, but instead measures effort.

Tombaugh recommends that a cutoff score of 45 for either Trial 2 or the retention trial be used as an index for poor effort. This cutoff score has repeatedly been supported in the literature. A significant proportion of patients with dementia score below the cutoff (Teichner & Wagner, 2004; Tombaugh, 1997). However, no other patient group reported in the literature is likely to fail the test.

Therefore, if a litigant with alleged depression, PTSD, chronic pain, a persistent postconcussion syndrome, or some combination of diagnoses scores below the cutoff, the most probable explanation is poor effort. People don't fail the test because of concentration problems, depression, anxiety, or pain. Rees, Tombaugh, and Boulay (2001) administered the test to 26 patients with such severe depression that they were admitted to a psychiatric unit; no patient failed the test. Ashendorf, Constantinou, and McCaffrey (2004) administered the test to 197 older community dwelling adults (average age = 64.6, SD = 5.5). They identified subgroups with at least mild depression, mild anxiety on the day of testing, and mild anxiety in general. Not a single older adult, regardless of psychological state, failed the TOMM. LePage, Iverson, Koehler, Shojania, and Badii (2004) gave the test to 56 community dwelling patients with fibromyalgia. This group reported considerable pain, symptoms of depression, and functional problems associated with their condition; however, no patient failed the test. The TOMM is a very simple test, passed easily by children (Constantinou & McCaffrey, 2003). Even patients with aphasia or traumatic brain injuries pass the test without difficulty (Rees, Tombaugh, Gansler, & Moczynski, 1998; Tombaugh, 1997).

We believe the TOMM is useful in civil forensic psychological evaluations as a measure of effort. By inference, it can be used in some cases as a measure of exaggerated cognitive impairment associated with depression or another psychological condition. It should not, however, be considered a *direct* measure of exaggerated symptoms. Weinborn, Orr, Woods, Conover, and Feix (2003) reported that the test is useful in criminal forensic psychological evaluations involving competency to stand trial. They reported a very high failure rate, for example, in patients with pending murder charges. It is essential to appreciate, however, that the TOMM is highly *specific* to exaggeration, but its *sensitivity* varies; that is, it will fail to identify a subset of people who are exaggerating. Researchers have shown that the TOMM is less accurate for identifying exaggeration than some of the other effort tests (Gervais, Rohling, Green, & Ford, 2004; Tan, Slick, Strauss, & Hultsch, 2002). Therefore, it would be a mistake to conclude definitively that someone who passes the TOMM (or any single effort test, for that matter) has given full and complete effort throughout the entire evaluation. This is simply one test performance. The proper conclusion is that the person passed the TOMM; thus, there wasn't obvious evidence of poor effort as measured by this test. To be clear, the TOMM is useful for identifying poor effort (although it will miss some cases), but it cannot be used to make definitive statements about good effort.

Conclusions

Every civil forensic psychological evaluation should include careful assessment for exaggeration and malingering. To determine if someone is malingering, the psychologist must establish that the patient is deliberately exaggerating or fabricating symptoms or intentionally performing poorly on testing. By definition, this must be judged to be goal-directed behavior designed to achieve a readily identifiable external incentive (American Psychiatric Association, 1994; Slick, Sherman, & Iverson, 1999). The identification of malingering requires careful consideration of multiple sources of data and the systematic ruling out of several differential diagnoses. It is much easier to determine if a person is exaggerating problems or providing poor effort during testing than it is to determine if he or she is malingering.

Some clinicians rather naïvely propose that because a person has, or had, a clearly identifiable psychiatric condition, he or she couldn't be malingering. Obviously, it is possible to malinger within the course of depression or PTSD, or to malinger in the presence of observed structural brain damage following a traumatic brain injury. To say otherwise is tantamount to suggesting that the person could not engage in goal-directed behavior. The systematic process of considering multiple differential diagnoses and factors is needed to determine if one or more of these can completely account for the observed exaggeration of symptoms or poor effort on tests. Important differential diagnoses to consider are factitious disorder, somatization disorder, somatoform disorder NOS, hypochondriasis, and conversion disorder.

Detecting Exaggeration on Specific Tests

There is a tremendous amount of research relating to detecting exaggeration on the MMPI-2. Much of the analog malingering research has suggested that the traditional and supplemental infrequency validity scales, such as F, F_B, and F(p) are effective for identifying exaggeration. There is no doubt that some personal injury litigants will substantially elevate these scales. This often represents frank and somewhat unsophisticated exaggeration. It is important to note, however, that these scales are more appropriate for identifying exaggeration of severe mental illness, such as in criminal forensic evaluations involving competency to stand trial. Validity scales and indices that can be particularly useful for identifying exaggeration in civil forensic evaluations include the Fake Bad Scale, Obvious-Subtle Scales, and the Dissimulation Scale. Cutoff scores that are highly improbable in the healthy population and in psychiatric patients are provided in tables 4.7 and 4.8. Essentially, this is a form of "psychological severity indexing." Scores that fall in such an extreme range require thoughtful and objective comment, and it would be inappropriate for a psychologist to ignore or dismiss them.

The Personality Assessment Inventory is a well-designed and validated measure for identifying psychological, behavioral, and personality problems. The healthy normative sample and the clinical comparison sample are impressive. One method of screening for exaggeration is to determine whether the person's symptom reporting seems extreme relative to the clinical sample. If so, do the assessment results converge to suggest that this is reflective of the person's true condition? That is, when considering interview findings, behavioral observation, medical records, and other collateral information, does it make sense that the person could be experiencing the extreme symptoms and problems? Psychologists should be cautious about overrelying on the Negative Impression Management (NIM) or the Malingering Index. These measures are more likely to detect extreme and bizarre symptom reporting, such as that seen in a criminal forensic evaluation of someone who is faking insanity. These measures are considerably less sensitive to exaggeration in civil forensic evaluations.

The Malingering Probability Scale and the Structured Inventory of Malingered Symptomatology have solid empirical support as useful measures for detecting exaggeration. We recommend that psychologists use these measures cautiously, however, as one source of information regarding whether a person might be exaggerating. More research is needed to (a) better understand how people exaggerate, and (b) document the performances of nonexaggerating clinical groups (in order to create tables such as those for the MMPI-2).

We believe that effort tests (i.e., the so-called malingering tests) are useful in civil forensic psychological evaluations. By inference, poor effort might reflect exaggerated memory or cognitive problems. As a general rule, most of the effort tests are not adversely affected by anxiety, depression, pain, or other psychological factors. Essentially, they should be considered *effortless tests of effort.* Therefore, when a person frankly fails one of the well-validated effort tests, such as the TOMM, it is inappropriate to conclude that the failure was due to depression, anxiety, or both unless there is compelling evidence to support this inference (such as the patient had profound psychomotor retardation and seemed to provide a number of random responses on the test). This is because researchers have demonstrated repeatedly that patients with psychiatric conditions do not fail these simple effort tests. When failure occurs, the most likely conclusion is that the person was underperforming; if the poor effort was an attempt to appear cognitively impaired and to influence the outcome of personal injury litigation, then this would be malingering. Some clinicians mistakenly assume that if a person passes an effort test, this means he or she gave full and complete effort throughout the evaluation and there is no evidence of exaggeration or malingering. It is reasonable to conclude that there was no obvious evidence of poor effort (if this is supported by the rest of the test data), but it is not reasonable to infer good effort throughout the evaluation based on this single test result.

Approach to Assessment

Malingering should not be inferred from a single test; rather, this conclusion is derived from converging evidence that the person was deliberately exaggerating symptoms and/or performing poorly on testing to increase the probability of obtaining an obvious external incentive. It is possible that a person scoring below an empirically derived cutoff score on a single test designed to detect poor effort could (a) be a false positive, or (b) could have performed poorly, even deliberately, for reasons other than those associated with malingering (e.g., general uncooperativeness or severe psychiatric disturbance). It is possible that a person might deliberately exaggerate or fabricate symptoms, yet not be malingering. The best example would be someone with a factitious disorder. It is also possible that a person could exaggerate symptoms out of desperation to be taken seriously (e.g., the so-called cry for help), or to be manipulative for interpersonal reasons (e.g., borderline personality disorder).

To sort out the complexities of differential explanations and diagnoses, it is often important to consider (a) behavioral observations, (b) interview data, (c) collateral records, (d) collateral interviews, and (e) psychological test results. Before concluding that a person is malingering, the clinician should systematically rule out alternative explanations for the behavior. Psychologists have an ethical responsibility to report assessment results fairly, accurately, and objectively. When there is clear evidence of exaggeration, this should be stated plainly in one's report; it should not be dismissed or obfuscated. The failure to accurately report presumed exaggeration would be tantamount to inaccurately reporting symptoms of depression. Exaggeration, of course, does not equal malingering, so it would be irresponsible and unethical for a clinician to conclude that a person is malingering simply because he or she appeared to be exaggerating. We should be very cautious in our assumptions regarding malingering; the clinician should have persuasive converging evidence before reaching this conclusion.

5

Common Vulnerabilities in Psychological Evidence

> The truth is rarely pure, and never simple.
> —Oscar Wilde *The Importance of Being Earnest* (1895)

Oscar Wilde, as quoted above, could easily have been writing about expert testimony in the modern day courtroom. Expert opinions about the existence and causality of psychological injuries are complex reconstructions of the nature and history of a litigant's mental health problems and the environmental and social stresses that influence his/her well-being. These opinions are constructed from sometimes questionable assumptions and potentially unreliable information. Unfortunately, expert witnesses all too frequently portray the nature of plaintiff injuries in an overly definitive and simplistic manner, leading to poor—and sometimes unethical—practices. Current ethical standards in forensic psychology require psychologists to be both fair and accurate in their written and oral opinions (e.g., Committee on Ethical Guidelines for Forensic Psychologists, 1991).

Differences Between Forensic and Therapeutic Assessment

Forensic assessment of psychological injuries differs from standard clinical assessment on a number of dimensions. As noted by Melton, Petrila, Poythress, and Slobogin, (1997), the individual claimant's perspective is less important in a forensic assessment than it would be in a clinical assessment. While a clinician solicits the client's perspective on his/her problems both to facilitate treatment planning and rapport, a forensic assessor solicits the claimant's perspective as one of several sources of information about the nature, severity, and history of the claimant's problems. The clinician's concern is in his patient's best interest. The forensic assessor's goal is to provide a coherent and accurate description of the claimant. Thus, forensic assessments of psychological injuries require a broader range of information than the claimant's self-report.

Claimants should be warned of the differences between forensic and clinical assessments. Most psychological injury claimants are participating in the assessment reluctantly, either because of their fear of an untoward result ("the insurer won't pay my claim") or because of the apparent intrusiveness and loss of confidentiality. In the case of psychological trauma, claimants may resist the assessment process because they fear bringing up old memories that have been partially suppressed, or because they feel that the defendant (e.g., an alleged sexual harasser) will have inappropriate access to their personal history.

Given the potential for financial compensation to alter the claimant's self-description, forensic assessors must be vigilant to threats that may affect the validity of the assessment process. Such threats come from the claimants themselves (e.g., motivation for compensation, defensiveness about self-disclosure), attorneys (e.g., coaching), family members (e.g., through motivation to see their loved one compensated), and representatives of the defense (e.g., through adversarial actions that contribute to the claimant's distress). What Melton et al. (1997, p. 45) call the "pace and setting" differences between clinical and forensic assessments refers to the fact that forensic assessments are typically arranged on a one-time-only basis. Thus, the forensic assessment is a "snapshot" of the claimant without the opportunity of observing waxing and waning of symptoms over time, albeit forensic assessments are more often supplemented with historical records, collateral sources, and more sophisticated assessment tools than are clinical assessments.

Heilbrun (2001, table 1.2 particularly) has provided a useful analysis of the differences between forensic and therapeutic assessment. Some of the main areas of difference that he noted include: (a) the purpose of the assessment (diagnose/ treat vs. assist legal decisions), (b) relationship between assessor and assessed (helping vs. independent roles), (c) identity of client (subject of assessment vs. the court or lawyer), (d) standard of care (psychological/medical vs. legal), (e) response style (honesty assumed vs. honesty not assumed), (f) clarification of reasoning and limits of knowledge (not typically done formally vs. typically done formally), and (g) written report (brief vs. lengthy). Practitioners must be acutely aware of these differences in order to competently provide forensic assessments.

Evaluators also need to be familiar with ethical and professional guidelines that specifically apply to forensic work, such as the American Psychological

Association's *Ethical Principles of Psychologists and Code of Conduct* (2002c, especially section 9.01), and the *Specialty Guidelines for Forensic Psychologists* (Committee on Ethical Guidelines for Forensic Psychologists, 1991). It would also be advisable for clinicians involved in forensic work to be familiar with forensic commentators' published counsel on ethics and standards of care in forensic assessment (e.g., Ogloff & Douglas, 2003).

Based on our previous discussions, we assume that mental health conditions like posttraumatic stress disorder (PTSD) and depression are valid constructs and are relevant to the legal arena of psychological injuries. In this chapter, we review vulnerabilities in psychological evidence from a conceptual perspective. First, we describe how biases and decision-making heuristics may affect forensic assessments, followed by a discussion of the implications of assumed base rates of mental health conditions for forensic assessment. We then discuss the differential reliability of structured versus clinical interviews. Problems in the assessment of psychological injuries are reviewed from a hypothesis testing perspective, discussing the following topics—identifying a psychological injury, attributing causality, determination of functional disability, and estimation of prognosis. In addition, the limitations of psychological tests with ethnic minorities are reviewed. Finally, suggestions for cross-examination of expert evidence and promising areas for research are presented. We also provide in tabular form suggestions for limiting these vulnerabilities within forensic assessments. Specific case examples of vulnerabilities in psychological evidence are provided in chapter 9.

Validity of Mental Health Diagnoses and Psychological Injuries

The valid assessment of psychological injuries requires several elements: (a) a valid mental health condition that is the focus of assessment; (b) structured, reliable, and valid assessment methods that are directly relevant to the legal questions at hand; (c) the systematic application of such valid assessment methods to the individual case; and (d) the application of scientific knowledge about the clinical course of such injuries to the individual case.

The Focus of Assessment Should Be a Valid Mental Health Condition

While psychological injuries are not constrained to specific medical diagnoses (e.g., PTSD, American Psychiatric Association, 2000), it is worthwhile using the validity of medical diagnoses as a starting point in discussing validity issues in forensic assessment. According to Syndeham (1753, cited in Rogers, 2001), a medical disorder is composed of three necessary elements: (a) inclusion criteria or the core characteristics of a disorder, (b) exclusion criteria or the characteristics of the disorder that set it apart from other disorders, and (c) outcome criteria, that is, the expected clinical course of the disorder. These elements still apply today.

With respect to PTSD for instance, we have a reasonably good understanding of its core inclusion criteria. According to DSM-IV and DSM-IV-TR (American Psychiatric Association, 1994, 2000), these are: reexperiencing symptoms (e.g., nightmares, intrusive memories), hyperarousal symptoms (e.g., sleep disturbance, irritability), effortful avoidance, and emotional numbing symptoms. Factor analytic research has been somewhat inconsistent in supporting the three sets of criterion symptoms model of DSM. Some research (e.g., Taylor, Kuch, Koch, Crockett, & Passey, 1998) has suggested that PTSD symptoms fit best within a two-factor solution in which reexperiencing symptoms and effortful avoidance vary together and hyperarousal and emotional numbing symptoms vary together, while other research (e.g., Foa, Riggs, & Gershuny, 1995) suggests that three factors (arousal and avoidance, emotional numbing, and reexperiencing symptoms) best described PTSD.

One comment stemming from the work on the factorial and construct validity of PTSD requires statement here. Some symptoms appear to be more important than others. Maes et al. (1998) reported that only Criterion C symptoms were able to differentiate trauma victims with and without PTSD. Yet, the prevalence of these symptoms was substantially lower than for Criteria B and D. This led the researchers to argue that Criterion C, while largely responsible for PTSD, is also too restrictive (or that B and D are too sensitive). For example, Schützwohl and Maercker (1999) reported that certain subthreshold PTSD cases (people who did not meet Criterion C) were more distressed on psychological measures than were some people who met criteria for PTSD. They proposed that "partial PTSD" be recognized as a legitimate classification option for persons who do not meet criteria for PTSD but who clearly are traumatized. Although the clinical characteristics of PTSD appear stable across different victim groups, giving credence to PTSD's status as a coherent construct and diagnosis, composed of reliable and distinct, yet interrelated factors, the original tripartite conceptualization of PTSD symptoms does not appear to be valid and avoidance/numbing symptoms appear to largely control the differentiation of PTSD from non-PTSD cases under current diagnostic guidelines.

A related issue is exposure to a traumatic stressor (Criterion A), in particular the individual's initial emotional response. The American Psychiatric Association (2000) criteria require that "the person's response involved intense fear, help-lessness, or horror" (p. 467). The trauma survivor's emotional response was first included as part of the diagnostic criteria in DSM-IV (American Psychiatric Association, 1994). However, it is likely that this will be revised in the future to include other forms of adverse emotional responses. Recent research (e.g., Brewin, Andrews, & Rose, 2000) suggests that intense emotions such as shame or anger may mediate the development of PTSD. This has implications for both the validity of the diagnosis (i.e., the precipitating emotional responses may be more variable than the current DSM suggests) and for the forensic assessment of PTSD claimants because it appears likely that shame and anger at perpetrators may be important emotions that mediate between the traumatic event and subsequent emotional disability.

True exclusionary criteria do not really exist for PTSD, as is evident by its high degree of comorbidity with other anxiety, mood, and substance use disorders (see chapter 3). The reader should note, therefore, that a forensic examiner cannot logically rule out PTSD based on exclusion criteria, but rather must rule out the disorder based on (a) the absence of criterion-required symptoms, (b) atypical course characteristics (e.g., onset of symptoms temporally unrelated to trauma exposure), or (c) alternative explanations (e.g., malingering). This means that the task of diagnosing PTSD in a personal injury case requires close systematic attention to diagnostic criteria, the temporal course of symptoms as they relate to the subject trauma, and alternative explanations. Valid diagnoses also require the assessor to be guided by formal, structured, and scientifically accepted procedures.

Also, according to Syndeham, a condition should have a known clinical course. In the case of PTSD, we know that not all trauma survivors develop PTSD (see review by Bowman, 1999). Of those who do develop acute stress disorder (ASD) or PTSD within the first few months posttrauma, as many as 50% remit from clinical status within the first one to two years posttrauma (e.g., Blanchard & Hickling, 1997). Unfortunately, somewhere in the vicinity of 10% of trauma survivors remain symptomatic for several years posttrauma (e.g., Mayou, Ehlers, & Bryant, 2002). The safest conclusions about course characteristics of PTSD at this time include: (a) a sizeable proportion of trauma-exposed survivors will experience substantial PTSD symptoms within the first month posttrauma; (b) of those who do evidence distress, as many as 50% will spontaneously remit within months of the trauma; and (c) upwards of 10% of survivors will develop a course of PTSD in excess of one year.

Structured, Reliable, and Valid Assessment Methods

In chapter 3, we reviewed a variety of interview- and test-based assessment tools for both PTSD and depression. According to Heilbrun (1992), psychological tests used in forensic assessment should be of adequate reliability. It is clear that reasonably reliable and valid assessment methods exist for the assessment of specific mental health conditions, including those most likely to be a source of psychological injury claims. The use of established assessment instruments increases the reliability, and hence validity, of clinical diagnoses and decisions. However, Heilbrun (1992) also stated that tests should be applicable to the population and purpose for which they are used. Major gaps still exist in the research base concerning the reliability and validity of many of these instruments in compensation-seeking samples, as well as in ethnocultural minority groups. Beyond this important gap in the research, our observations suggest that few forensic assessors routinely use the majority of the tests reviewed above.

Systematic Application of Valid Assessment Methods to Individual Cases

This section discusses biases and heuristics, as well as their impact on diagnostic decision making. Subsequently, the implications of base rates for diagnosing mental health conditions and the differences between semistructured and clinical interviews are examined. Different ways in which evidence gathering can fail within the context of forensic assessments are described, followed by a discussion of issues with respect to the use of psychological tests with minority group members.

Biases and Heuristics

Clinicians and forensic assessors exhibit a number of biases and diagnostic heuristics that negatively affect the validity of their assessments. While an exhaustive review of types of biases is beyond the scope of this chapter, it is worthwhile describing the following: illusory correlations, confirmatory bias, and confirmatory information-seeking bias, as well as ethnic and gender biases.

Illusory Correlation

Illusory correlation refers to the phenomenon in which clinicians observe that two events co-occur within a limited sample and draw the conclusion that these two events co-occur more commonly than they would in a more representative sample. According to Garb (1998, p. 24), "Research on illusory correlations indicates that clinicians frequently report correlations between test indicators and personality traits or psychiatric symptoms when in fact no relations exist." Readers of forensic opinions should be alerted to the potential for illusory correlations whenever they read the phrase "in my experience."

Confirmatory Bias

Confirmatory bias refers to a cognitive process in which "clinicians knowingly or unknowingly review patient information in such a way that they seek and attend to information that can support but not counter their initial hypotheses" (Garb & Boyle, 2003, p. 25). Thus, confirmatory bias affects the subsequent interpretation of information gathered by the assessor in support of a favored hypothesis. Readers of forensic assessments can detect such bias through the absence of discussion of assessment results that would appear not to be consistent with the ultimate conclusion given by the assessor.

Confirmatory Information-Seeking Bias

Confirmatory information-seeking bias refers to clinicians' unbalanced search for information that confirms their prior hypothesis about the patient while simultaneously neglecting to look for facts that might conflict with that initial diagnosis. The difference between confirmatory bias and information-seeking bias is that the prior reflects an interpretive bias, while the latter reflects the investigative behavior of the clinician. For example, assessors may limit their inquiries in such a way as to preclude finding evidence for either preexisting pathology (through neglect of historical inquiry) or a breadth of other mental disorders (through restriction of inquiry about current symptoms or problems). It is important to note in this regard the findings of Ward, Beck, Mendelson, Mock, and Erbaugh (1962) that almost one-third of the variability in diagnoses given by clinicians arises from variations in what questions are asked by the examiner.

Perhaps the most common information-seeking bias shown by forensic assessors is abandoning systematic symptom inquiry too early, presuming that patient endorsement of prototypical symptoms of a disorder (e.g., nightmares for PTSD) means that no further inquiry is necessary. In fact, empirical evidence suggests that the avoidance and emotional numbing symptoms (e.g., thought suppression, emotional distancing from others, and loss of interest in usual activities) are more predictive of full PTSD than other symptoms (e.g., Maes et al., 1998). An exclusive focus on reexperiencing symptoms will lead to overdiagnosis of PTSD.

Heuristics

Heuristics are simple rules clinicians use to make judgments or diagnoses. Clinicians may develop a heuristic based on their clinical experience that allows them to efficiently eliminate particular diagnoses from investigation without undue interview time. In fact, structured and semistructured diagnostic interviews have heuristics built into them by design. All such interviews for PTSD, for example, begin with a limited survey of the patient's exposure to traumatic life events. The limited number of such events routinely surveyed in such interviews is itself a problem, as discussed in chapter 3. Next, interviewers for PTSD question the patient about initial emotional responses such as fear of bodily injury, death, or other serious outcome, as well as reactions to such threat with extreme fear, horror, and feelings of helplessness (i.e. the peritraumatic response). Subsequently, all structured interviews ask the patient about the presence of intrusive thought content related to the traumatic event (e.g., flashbacks, nightmares). Each of these formal heuristics within structured interviews serves a gatekeeping purpose. That is, one cannot earn a PTSD diagnosis if one has not: (a) had a traumatic event, to which one (b) subsequently had an initial severe emotional response, and then (c) suffered a significant number of intrusive thoughts, *even if one were to meet all other symptomatic criteria for PTSD.*

Similarly, structured diagnostic methods utilize heuristics for the diagnosis of depression. According to the *Diagnostic and Statistical Manual of Mental Disorders* (DSM) (American Psychiatric Association, 2000), "The essential feature of a Major Depressive Episode is a period of at least 2 weeks during which there is either depressed mood or the loss of interest or pleasure in nearly all activities . . . The symptoms must persist for most of the day, nearly every day" (p. 349). It should be apparent to the reader that the restrictions above (at least two weeks, nearly all activities, most of the day, nearly every day) are meant to create a threshold of severity for determining clinically severe cases.

How do interview heuristics affect the determination of a major depressive episode? Typically, the interviewer initially asks the subject whether he/she has been feeling depressed, sad, empty, or whether he/she has lost interest or pleasure in almost all usual activities. If the subject of the assessment denies experiencing these symptoms, as well as responds negatively to a follow-up question intended to determine whether family or friends have commented on his/her depression/ loss of interest, the inquiry about a potential major depression ends at that point. This heuristic presumes that a sufficiently depressed subject of the assessment will recognize his/her depressive affect or loss of interests or that someone in his/ her social environment will have brought this to his/her attention. This is likely a safe bet for many who suffer a major depressive episode, but may not be the case for those claimants who suffer disabling subclinical depressive symptoms or who are lacking in insight about their distress. If the subject of the assessment endorses depression or reduced interests, the interviewer then inquires whether feelings of depression and lost interest have been present nearly every day over the past two weeks, and then reviews the severity and presence (nearly every day) of symptoms of altered appetite/weight, sleep disturbance, psychomotor retardation/agitation, fatigue, excessive guilt, impaired concentration and suicidal ideation. To meet criteria for a major depression, the subject must have five symptoms of sufficient severity and pervasiveness (nearly every day).

These heuristics generally are agreed upon by researchers in the area and are encoded in the DSM-IV (American Psychiatric Association, 1994, 2000). However, clinicians often devise their own idiosyncratic heuristics that may have significant effects on the frequency and accuracy of their diagnoses of PTSD or any other disorder. For example, some forensic assessors may not follow up on PTSD symptom inquiries if the subject trauma is not objectively severe (e.g., a motor vehicle accident not requiring hospital attendance), or if the claimant does not endorse specific reexperiencing symptoms such as nightmares or flashbacks. Such idiosyncratic heuristics ignore the fact that subjective appraisals of traumas are more predictive of PTSD than objective measures of injury, and that nightmares and flashbacks are only two of the five potential reexperiencing symptoms noted in DSM-IV (American Psychiatric Association, 1994, 2000). Alternatively, an optimistic examiner may diagnosis PTSD on the basis of reexperiencing symptoms without sufficient inquiry about avoidance/numbing symptoms. Individual assessors may also devise idiosyncratic heuristics for inquiries about depression (e.g., overemphasize vegetative symptoms such as reduced appetite, weight loss, sleep disturbance over affective symptoms) that vary from formal diagnostic rules. Sample cases illustrating idiosyncratic diagnostic heuristics that may hamper the validity of forensic assessments are provided in chapter 9.

Two other sources of bias merit discussion here. First, it is clear that the patient's ethnicity contributes significantly to clinician diagnoses independent of the clinical presentation. For example, African Americans have been found to receive more severe mental health diagnoses relative to Caucasians (Loring & Powell, 1988), while Caucasian counselors gave less-severe diagnoses to patients described in vignettes as Native American than they did to patients described as Caucasian (Allen, 1992). While it is not clear that ethnic minority status leads to consistent over- or underdiagnosis of mental health problems, it appears that ethnic status can contribute inappropriately to clinicians' diagnoses when clinical data from patients may not differ at all (e.g., Allen, 1992). Such diagnostic bias is particularly problematic given the absence of psychological tests with appropriate normative data for ethnic minority groups. We do not yet know whether ethnic minority group members receive different diagnoses in psychological injury evaluations. Given the increasingly multicultural nature of Western society, this is an important area of future research.

Second, gender bias has been shown to occur in clinicians with respect to the diagnosis of mental health conditions. Becker and Lamb (1994) surveyed 311 psychologists, psychiatrists, and social workers (from a total of 1,080 mail-outs for a 32% response rate), asking these professionals to rate goodness of fit of case vignettes that contained both borderline personality disorder (BPD) and PTSD symptoms and were otherwise identical, with the exception of the patients' genders. Female cases were more likely to be given BPD diagnoses than were male cases. Thus, forensic assessors must be aware of the potential for this form of gender bias to affect their own opinions.

How Biases and Heuristics Influence Diagnoses

The process of forming a forensic conclusion concerning a psychological injury requires several steps. When a forensic assessor receives a referral, the first task is to formulate potential hypotheses to investigate. Each of these hypotheses must be formulated in a manner that is subject to refutation. To clarify, the hypothesis must be worded in such a fashion that it is possible to support or refute the hypothesis via detailed assessment. For example: "Is this person suffering from PTSD?" or "Is this person exaggerating or otherwise overreporting symptoms?"

One obvious source of diagnostic bias arises in the lawyer-assessor relationship. Those forensic assessors who derive a disproportionate share of their referrals from either defense or plaintiff counsel may be prone to diagnostic bias for reasons described by Garb and Boyle (2003). That is, any assessor's perception of a particular clinical phenomenon such as PTSD is colored by the assessor's prior experience, by the preferred assessment methods, and by the unfortunate absence of any feedback about prior diagnostic accuracy. In effect, plaintiff and defense lawyers refer only partially overlapping samples of patients for assessment. Defense lawyers initiate a forensic assessment because of their suspicions that something is illegitimate about the claimant's presentation, while plaintiff lawyers refer a wider range of claimants. Thus, claimants referred by defense counsel are a particular subset of a larger population of claimants. Consequently, defense-hired experts may behave differently toward such claimants, and these claimants may behave differently during examination than they would in the office of a similar professional who is perceived to have a helping relationship with the claimant (Melton et al., 1997).

If defense experts see such a unique subsample, they may alter their expectations and thus their assessment methods (e.g., greater use of malingering assessment tools, more critical evaluation of complaints). Because very few personal injury cases go to court for critical examination of assessment findings and because longitudinal assessment of personal injury claimants is virtually nonexistent, forensic assessors do not obtain any feedback about the accuracy of their diagnoses. This is why there is little opportunity for assessors to learn from experience, and why their idiosyncratic biases may not change over time (Garb & Boyle, 2003).

Assessors who primarily consult to plaintiff counsel are no less prone to bias. They typically see a broader sample of claimants so that "suspicious" cases comprise a smaller percentage of their practices. Their selection of assessment tools thus varies from that of individuals who conduct primarily defense-initiated assessments (e.g., fewer tests of malingering, less-critical acceptance of claimants' self-descriptions). Plaintiff experts also suffer from the absence of feedback about their diagnostic accuracy.

A critical and scientifically based assessor must formulate hypotheses in a nonbiased fashion, so that all alternative hypotheses are given equal attention. We use PTSD as an example, but the same process of hypothesis generation and testing can be applied to psychological injuries more generally, even if they do not conform strictly to DSM-IV (American Psychiatric Association, 2000) diagnoses. One way to combat biases is simply to be aware of them. More concretely, evaluators are advised to incorporate some degree of structure into their evaluations (i.e., structured interviews and tests), in order to attenuate subjectivity. Later in this chapter, we review critical hypotheses that the forensic assessor must test and the limits to reliable assessments with respect to each hypothesis.

Implications of Base Rates on Accurate Diagnosis

Bias within forensic assessments frequently occurs within the hypothesis generation phase of the assessment. For example, a forensic examiner may markedly over- or underestimate the prevalence of PTSD to specific Criterion A traumatic stressors. Such bias in hypothesis generation can then result in biased selection of assessment tools. There are, for example, forensic assessments of PTSD claimants in which the assessors have applied dated lifetime prevalence rates of PTSD to suggest that only 1% of motor vehicle accident (MVA) victims develop PTSD. This is a classic example of the misapplication of base rates, which can then lead to underdetection of PTSD in claimants. The lifetime prevalence of PTSD within the general population is not comparable to the conditional prevalence of PTSD following an MVA or sexual assault.

There are three base rate scenarios of interest to this discussion. The *lifetime prevalence* of a condition refers to the percentage of the general population who will develop a condition during their lives; as reviewed in chapter 3, the lifetime prevalence of PTSD in the general population is approximately 8%. The *conditional prevalence* of PTSD refers to the percentage of trauma-exposed persons who develop the disorder. According to the meta-analysis of Shercliffe (2001), approximately 25% of crime victims, 15% of transportation or other technological disaster victims, and 7% of life-threatening illness victims develop PTSD. Finally, the *treatment-seeking prevalence* of a condition refers to the percentage of individuals who have a given condition and present for evaluation by specialists. This percentage will arguably be much higher than the conditional prevalence because the latter subjects have defined themselves prior to assessment as having some psychological disturbance; the same might be said of individuals involved in litigation.

While conditional prevalence is relevant to the assessment of individuals claiming psychological injuries following some tortious act (e.g., MVA, assault), point prevalence is more relevant to assessments of disorders that arise outside the context of a tortious act (e.g., employment disability claims related to depression). In such cases, lifetime prevalence of depression results in a higher prevalence estimate than point prevalence, the prevalence of a condition within the general population at any specific point in time. For example, lifetime risk for major depressive disorder ranges from 10% to 22% for women and 5% to 12% for men, while point prevalence estimates of depression for women is 5% to 9% and 2% to 3% for men (American Psychiatric Association, 1994). From this discussion, we might conclude that a forensic assessor in an employment disability case involving a claim of depression should be using the point prevalence figures rather than the lifetime prevalence figures in formulating hypotheses. That is, the lifetime risk of developing depression is less relevant to an individual forensic assessment of depression-related disability than is the point prevalence of depression (i.e., the probability that a randomly chosen person from the general population would suffer from depression). However, the use of point prevalence has its limitations. For example, point prevalence estimates of a condition may underestimate the occurrence of this condition across the general population (as the difference between lifetime and point prevalence of depression illustrates). In addition, the use of point prevalence in research studies may produce an inaccurate picture of the characteristics of individuals with that condition (e.g., comorbid personality disorders) because more persistent cases of a condition are more likely to be detected in a point prevalence sampling study than in a lifetime prevalence sample (see discussion by Phelan & Link, 1999). Certainly, future research concerning psychological injuries such as PTSD and depression will have to sort out differential characteristics of persistently symptomatic and disabled sufferers from episodically distressed individuals.

Both forensic and clinical assessments are conducted under an implicit assumption; that the acquisition of more information about a plaintiff or patient will result in more reliable and valid conclusions. However, such assessments and predictions are valuable only to the extent that they improve upon predictions made from base rate information. Finn and Kamphuis (1995) noted that "decisions based on more information may actually be less accurate than those based on less information." This is because the lower the base rate of a given phenomenon (i.e., the percentage of cases showing the relevant characteristic or diagnosis), the harder it is for any assessment method to improve on predictions made solely on base rates.

Let us use an example relevant to this text—PTSD following MVAs. For the reader unfamiliar with diagnostic decision-making tables, we present table 5.1 to illustrate these issues. Keep in mind that the purpose of forensic assessment is to correctly identify four types of claimants. First, one wishes to correctly identify those who have PTSD (*true positives*) as well as to correctly identify those *without* PTSD (*true negatives*). Second, one wishes to minimize the number of legitimate cases of PTSD that one overlooks (*false negatives*) and the number of non-PTSD cases that one diagnoses as having PTSD (*false positives*).

If one presumes a base rate of 15% from MVA or similar traumas (Shercliffe, 2001), we can construct decision-making table 5.2 for 100 consecutive MVA survivors who have suffered some physical injury.

If one randomly diagnoses 15% of claimants with PTSD, on average 72 of the 85 people who do not suffer from PTSD (85% true negatives) and only 2 of the 15 legitimate PTSD claimants (13% true positives) will be correctly classified. While only 13 healthy people would be diagnosed with PTSD (15% false positives), fully 13 of the legitimate PTSD cases would not be diagnosed accurately (87% false negatives). Two points should arouse the reader's interest. First, under this base rate scenario, almost 75% of 100 MVA survivors, overall, will be *cor-*

Table 5.1. Accuracy Indices for Diagnostic Decision Making

		Outcome	
		PTSD	NO PTSD
Prediction	PTSD	A	B
	NO PTSD	C	D

ACCURACY INDEXES	FORMULAE
Base Rate	(A+C)/(A+B+C+D)
False Positive	Cell B
False Negative	Cell C
True Positive	Cell A
True Negative	Cell D
Specificity (True Negative Rate)	D/(D+B)
Sensitivity (True Positive Rate)	A/(A+C)
False Positive Rate	B/(B+D)
Positive Predictive Power	A/(A+B) × 100%
Negative Predictive Power	D/(D+C) × 100%
Odds Ratio	(A×D)/(B×C)

rectly classified without the expense and time of a formal assessment. Therefore, any legitimate assessment must guarantee some improvement over a 75% percent overall correct classification rate. Because rules of legal fairness barring arbitrariness would preclude the random assignment of diagnoses to cases, an individually tailored assessment procedure would still be required, even if *overall accuracy* could not be improved by a particular diagnostic procedure. Second, for a low base rate phenomenon like PTSD, actuarial prediction would do a disservice to most of the legitimate claimants because only 2 of 15 legitimate claimants would be accurately identified.

Formal assessment procedures are intended to improve upon this 75% overall classification rate. In particular, the objective is to reduce the false negatives and

Table 5.2. Base Rate Prediction of MVA-PTSD Presuming a 15% Conditional Prevalence

	ACTUAL PTSD	ACTUAL NO PTSD
Predicted PTSD	2 (13%) True Positive	13 (15%) False Positive
Predicted No PTSD	13 (87%) False Negative	72 (85%) True Negative

false positives. To demonstrate, let us consider what might happen if one were to use one of the tests reviewed in chapter 3. Blanchard, Jones-Alexander, Buckley, and Forneris (1996) evaluated the PTSD Checklist's (PCL—Ruggiero, Del Ben, Scotti, & Rabalais, 2003) agreement with the Clinician's Assessment of PTSD (CAPS—Blake et al., 1990) interview and found a markedly increased true positive rate (amounting to 80% vs. 13% in the actuarial example above), while still correctly identifying 86% of non-PTSD subjects (true negatives). Using the PCL within a PTSD claim should therefore correctly classify more plaintiffs than would an actuarial estimation based purely on base rates. This is an example of a psychological test improving diagnostic accuracy.

The discussion above has several purposes. First, all forensic assessors have either implicit or explicit base rate expectations for whatever conditions they are assessing, based variably on: (a) relevant and up-to-date epidemiological research, (b) summary statements from diagnostic manuals, (c) dated or less-relevant epidemiological research, or (d) clinical lore. Therefore, base rate expectations may vary widely among forensic assessors and are of variable validity for the purposes of forensic assessment. Second, base rate expectations have a significant impact on the ultimate diagnosis given by the forensic assessor. Unfounded expectations of a high base rate of a condition may lead to overdiagnosis if actual base rates are lower, while unfounded expectations of a low base rate may lead to underdiagnosis. Assessors should be aware of their own vulnerability to base rate assumptions and ensure that such assumptions are corrected by updated familiarity with the relevant forensic and epidemiological research. As well, consumers of forensic assessments need to question the base rate assumption of the assessor. Third, forensic assessors can improve on their diagnostic accuracy by using reliable and valid assessment tools. Forensic assessments that do not include either a validated diagnostic interview or procedure, or psychological tests with adequate validity data for the condition of interest are unlikely to improve upon the accuracy of base rate predictions. It is further important that the instrument chosen was either designed for use with the claimant's clinical population or that it has been validated in the population of interest.

Differences between Clinical and Semistructured Interviews

The forensic assessment process is intended to reveal facts about the claimant with respect to his/her psychological status. To achieve this goal, however, variability associated with different examiners must be reduced as much as possible. Remember Oscar Wilde's statement that "truth is rarely pure." Ward, Beck, Mendelson, Mock, and Erbaugh, (1962) analyzed the sources of diagnostic disagreement between psychiatrists assessing the same patients. Only 5% of disagreement was related to variations within patients (i.e., changes in their behavior between two different assessments), while 62.5% and 32.5%, respectively, were attributable to different examiners holding different standards for diagnoses or asking different questions of the patients. More recently, Steiner, Tebes, Sledge, and Walker (1995) compared Structured Clinical Interview for DSM-IV (SCID)-based diagnoses with those attained by psychiatric clinical interviews for 100 patients. Inter-rater agreement for major depression (a frequent subject of psychological injury claims) was very low. Thus, SCID interviews and unstructured clinical interviews have unacceptably low levels of agreement with each other for this common condition.

In lay language, the disagreements between assessors in the Ward et al. study (1962) had to do more with the behavior of the assessors than they did with the behavior of the patient. Findings such as those of Ward et al. (1962) led to the development of structured diagnostic interviews. According to Rogers (2001), structured interviews improve the diagnostic process by reducing unnecessary variance between clinicians. Unstructured clinical interviews are more likely to result in diagnostic variability from such sources as (a) idiosyncratic questions, (b) variable coverage of problems/diagnostic criteria, (c) different sequencing of questions, (d) variable recording of information given by patients, and (e) variability in rating the severity or frequency of symptoms. It is not hard to understand why forensic assessors frequently disagree on claimants' diagnoses if they are using their own idiosyncratic assessment methods.

Thus, one of the purposes of structured or semistructured diagnostic interviews is to establish an objective measurement system with respect to assessing and recording the patient's self-reported symptoms, so that clinically significant thresholds for given diagnoses can be scientifically determined and clinicians can improve the reliability and validity of their diagnoses. This is why the CAPS, for example, requires the examiner to ask the patient about the frequency of unwanted memories from 0 (never) to 4 (daily or almost every day) and the intensity of such memories from 0 (none) to 4 (extreme). Without such an explicit symptom-rating system, an individual who occasionally experiences unwanted memories with mild distress may be treated as equivalent to an individual who experiences unwanted memories on a daily basis and with incapacitating distress.

While one cannot expect forensic assessors to use precisely the same assessment tools all the time (to do so would make the role of the psychologist redundant with his/her tests), it is clear that assessors who use only unstructured clinical interviews will have a difficult time agreeing with other such assessors independent of claimant status. On the other hand, two assessors who use structured diagnostic interviews for the same problem will have a greater probability of agreeing on a diagnosis. Greater use of semistructured diagnostic interviews within forensic assessments, coupled with judicious clinical judgment, will improve the quality of such assessments. We note also, however, that professionals are responsible for choosing appropriate measures, for deciding when they are applicable and when they are not, and when it is appropriate to stray from the dictates of a strict, structured approach. Despite our enthusiasm for structured methods of assessment, ultimately, tests and measures are just tools for clinicians to use as part of a general assessment strategy.

Failures in Evidence Gathering

One of the tenets of evidence-based practice is that once one has formed a hypothesis, one must set up an experimental test of the hypothesis from which both confirming and disconfirming results are possible. Many forensic assessors do not clearly specify the alternative hypotheses (see above) available to them in an individual assessment. If an individual is exposed to some traumatic event and makes a claim for a psychological injury, the forensic assessor should explicitly test the following hypotheses: (1) Is a psychological injury present? (2) Did the tortious event contribute substantially to psychological injury? (3) Was the problem present immediately preceding the tortious event? (4) Are there credible alternative causes for the plaintiff's problems(s)? (5) Does the injury cause functional disability? and (6) What is the prognosis of the injury? Each of these hypotheses must be tested in a manner that allows for disconfirmation. Consumers of forensic assessments must be alert to cases in which the assessor has gathered inadequate data to offer a valid opinion about a particular hypothesis.

Is a Psychological Injury Present?

This question may be stated as, "Does this person meet diagnostic criteria for PTSD, depression, or otherwise suffer from some significant emotional problem?" Therefore, the forensic assessor must address the following specific questions: (a) what assessment results will convince me that PTSD or some other condition is present, and (b) what assessment results will convince me that no emotional problem is present?

Psychological injury claimants often arrive in the forensic assessor's office some years following the index trauma. At the time of referral, the assessor is typically asked whether the claimant suffers from one or more psychological conditions. The assessor is testing for the presence of PTSD and other anxiety disorders, depression and other mood disorders, and substance use disorders, as well as subclinical states of anxiety, depression, or other aversive emotional states. This assessment must test for the presence of injury both at the time of assessment (current status) and the period between the index trauma and the current period (past status). Even at this simplest level of hypotheses testing, many forensic assessments appear inadequate. First, assessors must use reliable assessment methods for the range of potential conditions from which a claimant might suffer.

As mentioned above, it is still uncommon to see forensic assessments that include structured or semistructured interviews. This reduces the reliability and thus validity of such assessments and begs the question of "how" the assessor knows whether the claimant does or does not have the claimed condition. It is just as important to rule out certain conditions by use of structured assessment as it is to rule others in.

Second, it is common to see forensic assessments that apparently touched on the criteria for only one type of psychological injury; the most common of these is PTSD. Given that PTSD has very high rates of comorbidity (see chapter 3), any assessment of a psychological injury claimant that is focused solely on PTSD without investigating for the presence of other anxiety disorders or depression is inadequate in scope.

One alternative hypothesis to the presence of one or more psychological injuries is that the complaints of the claimant are of such a limited severity and nondisabling nature that they do not qualify as injuries; although the expert should focus on describing the claimant's condition and leave the decision of whether an injury occurred to the law. Such a judgment on the part of a forensic expert requires measurement on a numerical scale that has more gradations than simple presence versus absence of a disorder. Following such measurement, forensic assessors must define severity thresholds above which they consider an injury substantially greater than the moment-to-moment unhappiness common in daily existence, and communicate their opinion that an injury is present while being able to defend this opinion based on objective data. Some assessors may utilize DSM-IV diagnoses as their threshold; however, the law does not limit compensable psychological injuries to DSM-IV diagnoses, and the astute forensic assessor or lawyer will develop systematic means for assessing, litigating, or defending against less well-defined injuries.

For example, a concept called subsyndromal PTSD (SS-PTSD) has recently arisen in the research literature (Blanchard, Hickling, Taylor, & Loos, 1995). SS-PTSD is defined as any case meeting Criterion A (exposure to a threatening event and an immediate reaction of extreme fear, helplessness, or horror), and Criterion B (at least one reexperiencing symptom), but only one of Criterion C (three or more avoidant/numbing symptoms) or D (two or more hyperarousal symptoms). In practice, patients typically fall short on Criterion C because of the DSM-IV requirement for at least three symptoms from this cluster. Blanchard and Hickling (1997) described their sample of patients in the Albany MVA Project with respect to diagnostic status, breaking out the SS-PTSD patients. They had, respectively, 61 PTSD, 44 SS-PTSD, 50 MVA survivors without PTSD, and 95 non-MVA control subjects. Using the Beck Depression Inventory (BDI—Beck & Steer, 1987, range of scores 0–63) as a continuous measure of general psychological distress; 77% of PTSD cases had BDI scores above the minimal depression range (0–9), 32% of SS-PTSD cases had BDI scores of clinical significance, and 18%

of non-PTSD cases had clinically significant BDI, while only 13% of non-MVA controls had BDI scores this high. Therefore, the SS-PTSD subjects were more likely (32% vs. 13%) than non-MVA victims to show significant depressed mood, suggesting that use of this category will capture additional cases of psychological injury, albeit cases that may be less severely distressed than those meeting full criteria for PTSD.

Did the Tortious Event Contribute Substantially to Psychological Injury?

Forensic assessors also are asked about the causal relationship between particular events and the claimant's psychological state. Given the law's preference for temporal relationships between causes and effects, a prerequisite for the expert speaking to causality is to answer the following alternative hypotheses: Did the claimant suffer one or more psychological problems temporally following the traumatic event? or Did the problems first appear at a time or in a manner that would not suggest a causal relationship to the traumatic event?

Given the high prevalence of potentially traumatic events (PTE) in the general population and the much lower prevalence of PTSD, assessors must resist the impulse to automatically connect a trauma history with psychological distress. As cogently argued by O'Brien (2003), personal histories of trauma and of mental health problems may coexist without being causally related.

A controversial issue in this regard involves the concept of delayed-onset PTSD. Bear in mind also that causing the exacerbation of preexisting problems (as in the crumbling skull doctrine reviewed in chapter 1) typically constitutes legally compensable injury. We pointed out earlier in this chapter that in the absence of other exclusionary diagnostic criteria for PTSD, atypical temporal relationships between the traumatic event and the onset of PTSD symptoms is a potential exclusionary criterion. That is, if plaintiff A is in an MVA in February 2003, sues for physical injuries in March 2003, and then experiences his/her first onset of PTSD symptoms in February 2004, the skeptical lawyer will have a hard time accepting the relationship of the claimant's PTSD symptoms to the February 2003 MVA. Therefore, the concept of delayed-onset PTSD is problematic as a diagnostic entity and for arguing PTSD in personal injury claims. Nonetheless, a number of well-controlled longitudinal prospective studies have documented the occurrence of what are called "delayed-onset" PTSD cases, with onset starting several months or more following the traumatic stressor. For example, Ehlers, Mayou, and Bryant (1998) assessed via questionnaire 967 consecutively admitted MVA survivors 3 and 12 months postadmission. Six percent of their participants, none of whom met criteria for PTSD at 3 months, subsequently met PTSD criteria at 12 months. Predictors of delayed-onset PTSD included physical injury severity, rumination, anger cognitions, and history of pre-MVA mental health problems. While this was a large sample, replication of studies finding a high prevalence of delayed-onset PTSD is needed (that is, the 6% who developed delayed-onset PTSD in this sample possibly could be accounted for by measurement error on the instruments).

Why might cases of PTSD arise in such a delayed manner? It is possible that some survivors of trauma acquire further information at a later date that alters their perception of the danger they faced during the trauma and thus their current feelings of safety. This information may not necessarily be traumatic (e.g., yet another MVA or assault), but may simply be information that makes them feel less safe (e.g., comments in emergency room or ambulance records about the life-threatening nature of their injuries, slow recovery from trauma-induced injuries).

Moreover, additional life stressors may aggravate the effects of a prior trauma or may account by themselves for a newly developed PTSD status (e.g., a subsequent trauma precipitating an unrelated PTSD). Because of the inadequacy of trauma screening in many studies and in usual clinical care, this hypothesis has some serious merit. Note that attributing causality to such subsequent life stressors will weaken the connection between the trauma being litigated and the claimant's damages.

Additionally, symptom endorsement biases among trauma survivors may change in valence over time. Thus, some trauma survivors may minimize PTSD symptom endorsement shortly after the index trauma for varied reasons (e.g., embarrassment, extreme avoidance behavior), while others may become increasingly distressed over time with their dawning realization of the severity of their physical injuries or other losses. Finally, there is evidence (reviewed in chapter 1) that memories of the traumatic event may change over time, particularly among those with more serious symptomatology (Southwick et al., 1997).

Adequate forensic assessments will carefully evaluate and document the dates of onset for different psychological injuries in relationship to the index trauma, as well as to other stressors or negative life events. Given the multiple scenarios under which PTSD can arise in a delayed manner and the epidemiological evidence showing such delayed onset to be relatively common; delayed onset itself does not appear to be a valid reason for presuming the absence of a causal relationship between a traumatic event and subsequent PTSD.

Was the Problem Present Immediately Preceding the Tortious Event?

As much care should be given to the diagnostic interview for psychological disturbance *preceding* the index trauma as to interviewing for disturbance *following* the trauma, so as to rule out a preexisting condition as the explanation for the posttrauma condition. This is a difficult area of forensic assessment for several reasons. First, few assessors use structured diagnostic interviews and thus find it hard to precisely replicate their symptomatic inquiries across different temporal points in the patient's history. Given the low reliability of unstructured clinical interviews, it is very difficult to place any faith in forensic assessors' judgments about the absence or presence of preexisting conditions. Second, such a historical assessment process is made more difficult by the relatively low reliability of humans' autobiographical memory. In particular, social psychological research suggests that individuals "reconstruct" their memories of subjective experiences (e.g., aches, pains, emotional distress) based at least partially on personal models they use to explain their experiences. Ross (1989) theorized that when individuals attempt to remember their personal characteristics in the past, they engage in a two-step process. The first step involves self-assessment of their current status on the dimension of interest, under the presumption that present status will be related to past status. Step two involves the application of whatever implicit theory the person has about the personal characteristic (e.g., is this characteristic likely to be stable over time or to vary in a particular manner?).

Arising from this theory, McFarland, Ross, and DeCourville (1989) constructed a very creative study that has significant implications for the assessment of psychological injuries. These authors based their study on the theory above and on the common belief that women suffer significantly more physical and emotional distress during their menstrual period. They demonstrated that young university women retrospectively recalled more pain and depressive symptoms during their period than they reported when self-monitoring on a daily basis. Of particular note here, subjects substantially overestimated the negative affect and pain occurring during their menstrual period when asked to retrospectively estimate the same symptoms, but significantly underestimated their negative affect and pain on days outside their menstrual period. Thus, retrospective recall of subjective symptoms of negative affect and physical discomfort appears to be controlled by stereotypical beliefs about causal factors for such distress.

Does this phenomenon apply to trauma survivors? Unfortunately for forensic assessors, it applies quite well. Harvey and Bryant (2000b) interviewed 56 accident victims about their ASD symptoms one month and two years postaccident. In the follow-up interview, they asked the patients when their symptoms had begun. PTSD symptom severity at two-year follow-up predicted inaccurate recollection of more symptoms during the first month after the accident than the patients had reported at the one-month assessment. Less symptomatic individuals at the two-year follow-up tended to underreport ASD symptoms compared to their reports at one month.

These results can be applied to a forensic assessment of psychological injuries in the following way. First, the plaintiff, through making a claim, has already asserted a personal theory that he or she has suffered a loss of functioning related to a particular traumatic event. Second, the forensic assessment takes place some months or years following the tortious event to which the plaintiff attributes his/her losses. Third, the assessor queries the plaintiff about his/her current status with respect to symptoms of PTSD, depression, or related subjective emotional or physical symptoms. Fourth, the assessor conducts a historical inquiry about the plaintiff's experience of these same symptoms prior and subsequent to the tortious event. One would predict, based on Ross's (1989) theory, and without interviewing the patient, that the claimant would retrospectively recall fewer symptoms pretrauma. Similarly, the claimant is likely to remember being more symptomatic shortly after the trauma than he/she was at that time. Therefore, the forensic assessor who understands this phenomenon of retrospective recall will use assessment methods (e.g., review of past health records, interviewing of collateral informants) that will reduce a reliance on the claimant's retrospective recall and adjust for the bias described above.

Are There Credible Alternative Causes for the Plaintiff's Problems?

The law requires that a claimant's complaints not be better explained by alternative explanations (e.g., malingering or other stressors). Although there can be more than one cause to a person's injuries while still allowing compensation, a credible forensic assessment will systematically search for alternative stressors or life events that may account for part or all of the claimant's psychological distress. Such assessment will include systematic evaluation of previous traumatic stressors, as well as assessment of daily hassles and other life events (e.g., divorce, death of family members, job loss) that may contribute to the claimant's psychological distress. Assessments that do not investigate a broad range of potential traumatic stressors in the claimant's history and potential ongoing life stressors or hassles, or alternatively do not carefully evaluate the claimant's psychological responses to such traumatic or nontraumatic stressors are at greater risk of misidentifying variables contributing to the claimant's distress. Also, many forensic assessors apparently neglect to investigate potential causal relations between substance abuse/dependence and psychological symptoms, which is unfortunate given the known negative effects of such abuse. For example, regular and excessive cannabis use has been shown to be strongly associated with depression (e.g., Troisi, Pasini, Saracco, & Spalletta, 1998). Many forensic assessments also neglect formal assessments of symptom over endorsement, and clinical assessments by therapists, psychiatrists, and family physicians almost never use such methods. In summary, adequate forensic assessments must screen for the alternative explanations for heightened psychological distress; presence of other traumatic and nontraumatic stressors, psychoactive substance use that is known to adversely affect psychological well-being, and symptom over endorsement or exaggeration.

Does the Injury Cause Functional Disability?

The forensic assessor must consider what evidence is needed to relate the patient's clinical status to employment or other functional deficits, and what evidence is required to conclude that the patient has no functional deficits related to his/her clinical status. Forensic assessors must investigate whether identified psychological problems lead in a logical fashion to deficits in the claimant's occupational, educational, social, or recreational functioning. From our experience in reviewing forensic and clinical assessments, this is yet another area in which many forensic assessments may be inadequate. Neither has psychological science systematically addressed the pathway between psychological distress and functional disability other than to note that many mental health conditions are associated with worse economic outcome.

Dillman (2003) proposed the following domains of psychological functioning that may have implications for employment functioning: (a) understanding and memory (e.g., understanding and remembering instructions), (b) sustained concentration and persistence (e.g., maintaining attention and concentration for extended periods), (c) social interaction (e.g., interacting appropriately with the general public), and (d) adaptation (e.g., responding appropriately to changes in the work setting). From our own perspective, most psychological injuries (e.g., PTSD, depression, traumatically acquired phobias, anxiety symptoms) *appear* to influence individuals' daily lives through impairment in one or more of the following dimensions: (a) deficits in attention and concentration, (b) problematic interpersonal relations, (c) decreased motivation and energy, (d) decreased stress tolerance, and/or (e) phobic avoidance (e.g., driving to work, working by oneself or in particular settings). While it is clear that mental health conditions such as PTSD, depression and other anxiety or affective disorders have demonstrable effects on employment and income at the population level, not all clinical cases of PTSD or depression will suffer substantial employment disability. Expert opinions with respect to disability may be more credible and valid for individual cases if the expert can trace individual claimant's symptoms and behaviors to important functional deficits that hinder employment or other duties. The reader of forensic opinions about disability must be careful to ensure that a logical pathway has been demonstrated between observed deficits of the claimant and the interaction of such deficits with specific occupational demands.

What is the Prognosis of the Injury?

To provide prognostic opinions, forensic assessors must ask themselves if and when the PTSD or other emotional problem is likely to remit (get better), and if it will improve with or without treatment. The expert must thus address those characteristics of the patient (history, personality, coping style, comorbid conditions, and clinical status) that the research literature suggests will lead to a slower or faster remission. With respect to PTSD, known predictors of negative prognosis include chronic pain or other physical disability and financial stress, as well as anger and rumination (see review by Douglas & Koch, 2000).

Misuses of Psychological Tests

Psychological tests can increase diagnostic accuracy and add rich information about subjects' psychological states. Above, we gave the example of how the PCL (a 17-item test of PTSD symptoms) increases predictive accuracy over base rate. "Mechanical" prediction (i.e., that prediction using automated judgments from test or other objective data) is generally more accurate than "clinical" prediction, that is, a prediction hinging on clinician judgment beyond test data (Grove, Zald, Lebow, Snitz, & Nelson, 2000). In Grove et al.'s statistical meta-analysis, clinical interviews were actually associated with a worsening of performance in comparison to mechanical prediction. Thus, psychological tests or other standardized methods of gathering data about the person can be beneficial to the forensic assessment process.

However, psychological tests can be applied in inappropriate clinical or forensic assessment situations, or misused to the detriment of a search for truth. It appears from Boccaccini and Brodsky's (1999) survey of forensic assessors that there is little consistency among experienced forensic assessors about a standard test battery for the assessment of psychological injuries. In fact, of the self-report instruments reviewed in chapter 4, only the Minnesota Multiphasic Personality Inventory-Second Edition (MMPI-2) and BDI are frequently used by forensic assessors in psychological injury cases (Boccaccini & Brodsky, 1999). Therefore, readers of such assessments should critically examine the appropriateness of individual psychological tests used in individual cases.

Cross-Examining Psychological Injury Evidence

Any cross-examination of a forensic assessor with respect to a psychological injury should start with questions about the assessor's perception of the base rate of the relevant injuries in a context relevant to the subject litigation. Such cross-examination also should inquire about the scientific support for such base rate assumptions, and should focus on the reliability and validity of the assessor's evaluation methods. We appreciate that the term *reliability* is sometimes used within the law to refer to issues of validity from a social scientific perspective (i.e., Does the instrument measure what it claims to?). Reliability of measurement in this context refers either to the extent of agreement between different assessors for a given condition via a specific method, (i.e., inter-rater agreement) or to the stability of findings by a measurement instrument over time (i.e., test-retest reliability). A measurement strategy with low levels of inter-rater agreement is problematic because the consumer cannot be confident that the assessment findings reflect the subject of the assessment more than they do the idiosyncratic characteristics of the assessor. A measurement strategy with low levels of test-retest reliability is problematic because the purpose of such assessments is to determine enduring characteristics of the claimant. Because such methods are theoretically intended to improve upon base rate assumptions, assessors must be able to justify the relevance and reliability of their methods under cross-examination. For example, expert witnesses in this area must be able to address questions about how their interview findings could be reasonably replicated by another trained professional, which would be exceedingly problematic unless they use some variant of a structured diagnostic interview during their assessment. As another example, experts should be able to defend their use of specific tests by referring to scientific studies showing this test to reliably measure a variable of interest in the psychological injury claim (e.g., PTSD or depression severity) with the population of interest (i.e., that the test is reliable and valid for use with people of the individual claimant's ethnic and cultural background).

In terms of validity, experts (and the lawyers who examine or cross-examine them) should be intimately familiar with the scientific research on the validity of the measures in question. That is, they should be able to defend (or attack) the instruments used in terms of how well they measure the constructs in question (i.e., PTSD, anxiety, depression), and any limitations in the research base.

As mentioned in one example above, some assessors conduct assessments that are too narrow in focus. A potentially fruitful line of cross-examination in such a case would be to question the assessor about methods used to rule out one or more of the following disorders/problems from consideration: PTSD, subsyndromal PTSD, depression, distressing but subclinical depressive symptoms, generalized anxiety disorder, panic disorder, and/or disabling phobias and avoidance behavior. For example, an expert who concludes that the subject of an evaluation does not meet criteria for any mental disorder should be cross-examined to determine how he or she ruled out each of the DSM-IV anxiety and mood disorders, as well as subclinical variants of these conditions (e.g., subsyndromal PTSD, subclinical depression). Similarly, an expert who rules out the presence of exaggeration or symptom exaggeration should be questioned about those objective data supporting this conclusion.

Expert witnesses frequently allude to heuristics they use in arriving at a diagnosis (e.g., rear-end accidents seldom resulting in PTSD, accelerated heart rate during trauma exposure being necessary for the development of PTSD, loss of consciousness during an MVA precludes subsequent PTSD). Legal counsel should identify these heuristics within expert reports and inquire assertively about the scientific references supporting their use.

A very fruitful area of cross-examination presents itself when forensic assessors offer the opinion that the subject condition did not exist prior to the index trauma. Given the difficulties with human's retrospective memory, legal counsel should take care to examine the expert about the evidence supporting opinions about the absence of a preexisting condition(s) to ensure that the expert is not relying on the claimant's retrospective memory alone.

Given the increasing ethnic diversity of our society and the complex relationships between ethnocultural identity and psychological well-being (see chapter 7), expert witnesses should consistently discuss the limitations of their inferences when offering opinions about the mental health of claimants from ethnocultural minorities.

Many forensic assessors may too easily assume the equivalence between psychological distress and functional disability. Cross-examining counsel should recognize that while PTSD and depression are demonstrated risk factors for reduced employment and worse economic outcomes, the existence of such risk factors is not synonymous with functional disability in the individual case and expert witnesses should be made to demonstrate convincingly that specific behavioral deficits of the claimant that result from the PTSD or other mental health condition logically interfere with work attendance or productivity. A potentially fruitful line of cross-examination would be to inquire along the lines of "Doctor, you indicated that Ms. Jones is disabled from her work as an X by her PTSD. Could you tell me what PTSD symptoms or emotional problems led to this disability? Further, can you explain to the court how it is that these symptoms interfere with the plaintiff (a) getting to work regularly, (b) completing work-related tasks, (c) concentrating on work duties, (d) getting along with coworkers or supervisors, (e) remaining in the work setting for a normal work shift?"

It is clear that there are many pitfalls and vulnerabilities in psychological evidence. Even an exceptionally knowledgeable and thorough forensic assessor may fall prey to some of these vulnerabilities. For the benefit of assessors, we offer in table 5.3 a summary of common vulnerabilities and our suggestions for correcting such vulnerabilities.

Future Avenues for Research in Psychological Injury Assessment

Psychological Injury Assessment Practice

With the recent exception of Boccaccini and Brodsky (1999), no one has actually studied just what forensic personal injury assessors actually do in their offices. Outside of knowing that the MMPI-2 is the favorite psychological test of psychologists performing personal injury assessments, we are ignorant about their practices. We are tempted to say from our own professional experience that forensic assessors in this area seldom use structured diagnostic interviews, seldom use psychological tests normed for the task (other than the ubiquitous MMPI-2 and the BDI), seldom qualify their opinions when faced with an ethnic minority

Table 5.3. Vulnerabilities in Evidence and Potential Solutions for Practitioners

VULNERABILITIES	POTENTIAL SOLUTIONS
Excessively High or Low Base Rate Assumptions	1. Awareness of empirical research on base rates of target conditions. 2. Awareness of empirically known course characteristics of condition (e.g., spontaneous remission following trauma exposure, recurrence of episodes). 3. Awareness of own biases that may conflict with empirical evidence. 4. Specify in writing one's base rate assumptions.
Illusory Correlations	1. Awareness of own practice-based assumptions. 2. Check practice-based assumptions against research literature. 3. Specify in writing which conclusions are based on practice-based assumptions and which on either empirical research or validated methods.
Information-Seeking Biases	1. Use structured assessment methods when available.
Ethnic Biases	1. Awareness of personal ethnic biases. 2. When possible, check research literature for empirical differences in mental health between different ethnic/cultural groups. 3. Formally assess acculturation of ethnic minorities/immigrants. 4. Specify in writing potential limitations of conclusions given ethnic/cultural background of the plaintiff.
Gender Bias	1. Awareness of any personal gender-based biases. 2. Use of valid assessment tools whenever considering diagnoses or problem formulations that are potentially sex-linked (e.g., borderline personality disorder).
Impressionistic Assessments	1. Use structured diagnostic interviews whenever possible and relevant. 2. Supplement interviews with reliable, valid, and relevant tests.
Insufficient Breadth of Problem Coverage	1. Awareness of breadth of diagnoses, problems associated with a given trauma or disability claim based on epidemiological literature. 2. Use of reliable, valid, and relevant assessment tools for all relevant problems. 3. Allocate sufficient time for such a broad assessment.
Inadequate Assessment of Injury Severity	1. Use assessment tools that have a range of severity/frequency options rather than mere symptom checklists. 2. Compare plaintiff data to empirically established norms. 3. Review functioning across life domains (work, home, social life) and investigate impact of symptoms on functioning in each of those domains.

VULNERABILITIES	POTENTIAL SOLUTIONS
Taking Plaintiff's Retrospective Memories at Face Value	1. Review medical, accident, employment, and school records whenever possible. 2. Obtain collateral information from family members or other potential third-party observers.
Overlooking Alternative Contributions to Injury	1. When possible, use validated checklists or other tools to assess the plaintiff's exposure to both traumatic and nontraumatic stressors. 2. Review other stressors or adverse life events with plaintiff and collateral observers.
Presumption of Disability Associated with Distress	1. Awareness of empirical literature on economic correlates of mental health problems. 2. Critically examine ways in which symptoms/problems may result in reduced functioning.
Misuse of Tests	1. Awareness of test norms. 2. Use appropriate norms if available for individual case. 3. Specify in writing limitations of particular tests for individual plaintiffs because of ethnic, cultural, or other reasons.

patient for whom appropriate test norms do not exist, and seldom cite recent research when making their conclusions. However, these are only our impressions; we recommend the following topics of timely research questions to fill at least some of the gaps in our knowledge.

How many psychologists and psychiatrists who assess psychological injuries use structured diagnostic interviews to arrive at diagnoses? Our bias that assessments using such interviews are superior may be transparent to the reader. A determination of how frequently such diagnostic tools are used will become a baseline assessment of the quality of such assessments.

How adequately do psychologists and psychiatrists warn their personal injury claimants about confidentiality limitations, goals of the forensic assessment, and the adversarial nature of such assessments? Remember Melton et al.'s (1997) comments on the distinguishing characteristics of clinical and forensic assessments. The presence of such warnings may have significant impact on the claimant's responses during assessment. While this relates to the ethics of practice more than to assessment procedures, per se, it is still an important element in determining quality control.

To what extent are tests normed for trauma survivors used in psychological injury assessments? It is one thing to use commercially available tests that have a large and diverse psychometric research history such as the MMPI-2. It is a step beyond to use tools that reliably answer questions directly relevant to the legal questions about the existence and prognosis of a psychological injury. It is notable that many of the measures we reviewed in chapter 4 were not used by Boccaccini and Brodsky's (1999) subjects. For example, the CAPS and PCL are perhaps the best validated interview and self-report measures of PTSD status. Given that forensic assessors must frequently make judgments about the presence/absence of PTSD, it is worthwhile knowing how many forensic assessors use these "best practice" tools. On a related theme, anger is a psychological state that is apparently common in PTSD sufferers and appears to be a negative prognostic sign. It is interesting how many forensic assessors use some validated measure of trait, or state anger or even assess anger in an unstructured manner during PTSD evaluations.

How do psychologists and psychiatrists accommodate their assessments to the cultural and ethnic characteristics of claimants that may influence the validity of their forensic opinions? Specific research questions in this area include: (1) how many forensic assessors qualify their interpretation of psychological test data by referencing known limitations in the normative data or studies that suggest caution in interpretation of such test data with particular ethnic minorities, (2) do forensic assessors regularly address the claimant's ethnic/immigration status and acculturation in their reports, and (3) how many forensic assessors qualify their opinions about psychological injury with a discussion of cultural limitations on the expression of emotional distress?

Common Heuristics/Biases

The field desperately needs to know how some of the common clinical biases and heuristics operate among experienced forensic assessors involved in psychological injury evaluations. For example, are there professional (e.g., psychiatry vs. psychology) or other contextual (defense vs. plaintiff-hired), or gender biases that inflate or suppress the diagnosis of psychological injuries? Answering this question takes us a step further toward understanding the influence of assessor characteristics on diagnoses given to claimants.

It would also be enlightening to know if there are heuristics concerning the diagnosis of psychological injuries that are commonly used by forensic assessors and to what degree these heuristics are supported by current research literature. Related to this question is the influence of experience (in terms of years of practice or number of forensic assessments) on the use of such heuristics. Forensic experts may be prone to a number of types of "drift" as they gain more experience. For example, they may increasingly depend on idiosyncratic diagnostic heuristics rather than empirically supported practice. On the other hand, "true" experts may become increasingly sophisticated in their use of state-of-the-art assessment tools, knowledge, and diagnostic heuristics.

The inverse of "drift" is calcification, that is, relying on a personal knowledge base that is increasingly obsolete given burgeoning research within the field and limited continuing education by the practitioner. Given the possibility that calcification of knowledge is a problem within forensic practitioners, it is worthwhile knowing the state of knowledge about recent relevant research findings within the forensic assessment community.

Consumer Satisfaction

There are several different consumers of forensic assessments for psychological injuries, personal injury lawyers, insurance adjusters (e.g., automobile and disability insurers, workers' compensation programs), judges, and juries. Because the vast majority of personal injury cases settle prior to court, the prime consumer groups for psychological injury assessments are legal counsel and insurance adjusters. Therefore, it seems important that psychological science address the extent to which these consumers understand the content of such assessments, value them, and perceive them as (a) improving their own knowledge of the claimant and (b) helping to resolve claims. It also would be worthwhile to know the extent to which these consumers discriminate between the credentials, assessment content, or assessment quality of different forensic assessors. Finally, it would be illuminating to determine the extent to which lawyers and insurance adjusters express their own biases and heuristics concerning psychological injuries that may color their interpretation of forensic assessments.

With respect to juries and judges, it would be of some interest to know the extent to which professional credentials (e.g., psychiatrists vs. psychologists), professional experience, and professional roles (independent consultant vs. treating professional) influence judges' and jury members' receptivity to expert evidence with respect to psychological injuries. It would also be useful to know what mode of communicating evidence is most understandable to judges and juries, and leads to the highest comprehension. Because juries are chosen from the general public, the biases and beliefs of the general public about the veracity and associated disability of psychological injuries are also interesting topics for future research.

6

Gender, Trauma, and Distress

> There is perhaps no variable that is easier to measure than biological sex and more difficult to know what its values—male or female—mean . . . sex, the biological factor becomes utterly confounded with gender, a sociocultural construction.
>
> —Norris, Perilla, Ibañez, and Murphy (2001a)

Gender has a complex relationship with trauma, posttraumatic stress disorder (PTSD), and more generally with psychological distress. Conclusions regarding the implications of gender for differences in the prevalence and intensity of post-traumatic responses have variously been described as "consistent" (Gavranidou & Rosner, 2003, p. 131) and "limited and confusing" (Freedman et al., 2002, p. 407; also see Pimlott-Kubiak & Cortina, 2003). In our view, relative consensus exists on several chief points, but considerable debate with regard to other issues concerning women's experiences of psychological stressors continues.

Although the prevalence of PTSD in women is consistently about double what it is in men—causing some writers to conclude that female gender is a vulnerability factor for PTSD (Gavranidou & Rosner, 2003)—we believe that there is still insufficient evidence to draw concrete conclusions about the relationship of gender to posttraumatic adjustment (also see Cloitre, Koenen, Gratz, & Jakupcak, 2002; Saxe & Wolfe, 1999) or to describe female gender as a "risk factor" for PTSD (also see Cusack, Falsetti, & de Arellano, 2002, p. 172).

As our opening quote by Norris et al. (2001a) alluded, most current knowledge addresses *biological sex* differences in the *prevalence* of PTSD, without adequately accounting for *gender* differences (e.g., social influences) that potentially underlie variations in posttraumatic coping. "To date, no empirical study of PTSD has measured the construct of gender and associated correlates. . . . One can thus only indirectly surmise the effect of gender on PTSD from their results" (Saxe & Wolfe, 1999, p. 164). The field awaits an increased understanding of the toxicity of the stressor (e.g., subjective level of fear or risk of serious harm or death in males and females exposed to the same trauma category) and the event characteristics (see Cloitre, Koenen, Gratz, & Jakupcak, 2002, p. 121), as well as the social, cultural, and economic factors influencing trauma exposure and posttrauma adjustment (Kimerling, Ouimette, & Wolfe, 2002). In addition, research to date has not sufficiently controlled for age at exposure, the impact of chronic traumas (e.g., child abuse, partner abuse), attachment, and/or traumas involving betrayals of trust (e.g., child sexual abuse, abuse by intimate partners, sexual harassment, and stalking, which affect women disproportionately). Similarly, postexposure variables (e.g., availability of social support, impact of daily hassles, socioeconomic status) and cognitions (e.g., self blame, belief in a just world) must be measured to allow researchers to conclude with any confidence that women are uniquely vulnerable to posttraumatic maladjustment when such other variables are accounted for.

Exposure to Potentially Traumatic Events and the Risk of PTSD

Gender Differences in the Frequency of Traumatic Stressors

By definition, PTSD, acute stress disorder (ASD) (American Psychiatric Association, 2000), and adjustment disorders are mental illnesses that can be explicitly associated with a precipitating incident. Thus, a logical starting point for considering the influence of gender on psychological injuries is a possible difference in the rate of exposure to potentially traumatic events (PTE) among men versus women. Recent theoretical reviews consistently conclude that women are less likely than men to be exposed to PTE (Criterion A1, DSM-IV-TR, American Psychiatric Association, 2000) (e.g., Ballenger et al., 2000; Gavranidou & Rosner, 2003; Norris, Foster, & Weisshaar, 2002).

Several epidemiological studies of trauma exposure and PTSD that compare male and female respondents have been conducted, primarily in the United States (for reviews, see Breslau, 2002b; Norris et al., 2002). The most commonly used diagnostic tools for assessing PTSD in such studies are the National Institute of Mental Health-Diagnostic Interview Schedule (NIMH-DIS) and the World Health Organization-Composite International Diagnostic Interview (WHO-CIDI), based on the Diagnostic Interview Schedule (DIS) (Breslau, 2002b). In these interviews, respondents are asked to nominate the worst event they have ever experienced, or a randomly selected stressor is chosen from the respondent's list of reported PTE and PTSD symptoms associated with the selected event. The lifetime prevalence of exposure and conditional risk for PTSD determined across epidemiologic studies reflects discrete and combined effects of differences in stressor definitions and diagnostic criteria (see Breslau, 2002b; Kessler, Sonnega, Bromet, Hughes, & Nelson, 1995). Perhaps the most commonly reported factor believed to contribute to between-study prevalence differences has been the modifications to the DSM-IV/DSM-IV-TR stressor criteria, which broadened considerably the types of stressors that qualified for a *Diagnostic and Statistical Manual of Mental Disorders* (DSM) diagnosis of PTSD. For instance, sudden unexpected death of a loved one accounts for nearly one-third of PTSD cases (Breslau, Kessler, & Chilcoat, 1998). This change has been associated with a substantial increase (e.g., 68.1% to 89.6%) in the lifetime rate of exposure to PTE in the general population (see Breslau & Kessler, 2001); readers should be mindful of these differences when comparing studies described below.

The Epidemiologic Catchment Area (ECA) Study (Helzer, Robins, & McEvoy, 1987; Robins & Regier, 1991) was the first to use the original DIS (Robins, Helzer, Croughan, & Ratcliff, 1981), a highly structured interview based on DSM-III criteria (American Psychiatric Association, 1980). The DIS was the first measure developed to provide reliable psychiatric diagnoses in samples drawn from the general population. This groundbreaking study included interviews with more than 20,000 community participants over a series of five community survey sites. Respondents were asked if they had experienced an event that frightened them so much that they had one or more of the PTSD symptoms. Events considered to fit the criteria ("a psychologically traumatic event that is generally outside the range of usual human experience," American Psychiatric Association, 1980) were grouped into seven categories: combat, serious accident, physical attack, seeing someone hurt or die, threat or close call, natural disaster, other. Results suggested that PTSD was relatively uncommon in the general population with 5 men and 13 women per 1,000 meeting diagnostic criteria (Helzer et al., 1987). Subsequent critiques of the DIS resulted in its revision and initiated a generation of research demonstrating substantially higher rates of PTSD in community samples; however, gender differences persisted.

The Health and Adjustment in Young Adults study (HAYA) (Breslau, Davis, Andreski, & Peterson, 1991) demonstrated the ubiquity of traumatic events, and the extent of the burden of PTSD in the general population. In that sample of 1,007 young (ages 21–30) male and female health maintenance organization (HMO) members in the United States, 39.1% of respondents ($n = 394$) reported experiencing a PTE, defined according to the DSM-III-R (American Psychiatric Association, 1987). Using the PTSD section of the NIMH-DIS (version III, revised) (Robins, Helzer, Cottler, & Golding, 1989), men (43.0%) were more likely than women (36.7%) to report exposure to a traumatic stressor. These results were further substantiated in the findings of the National Comorbidity Survey (NCS) of trauma (Kessler et al., 1994). The NCS was the first to administer a structured psychiatric interview to a representative national sample in the United States. Using the modified version 1.0 of the CIDI (World Health Organization [WHO], 1990) for the DSM-III-R, the NCS asked Whites, Blacks, and Hispanics, 15–54 years old, from 48 states about 12 trauma categories. Consistent with the earlier studies, men (60.7%) reported a significantly higher rate of exposure to traumatic events than women (51.2%).

According to the Detroit Area Survey (DAS) of Trauma ($N = 2,181$, age range = 18–45 years; Breslau et al., 1998), few people in the United States have *never* encountered a PTE. Telephone interviews in the DAS began by using a list of 19 types of PTE according to DSM-IV criteria to determine the lifetime prevalence of specific traumatic events. The four categories included assaultive violence (e.g., combat, rape), other injury or shocking experience (e.g., motor vehicle accident, diagnosed with life threatening illness), learning about traumas to others (e.g., friend/relative physically attacked), and the sudden unexpected death of a close friend or relative. According to DSM-IV, PTSD was assessed using the DIS (version IV) and the WHO CIDI, with respect to a randomly selected event from the list of reported PTE; lifetime exposure for any trauma was 92.2% for men and 87.1% for women (Breslau et al., 1998). On average, men ($n = 5.3$) also reported significantly more distinct events than women ($n = 4.3$). The dramatically high rates, in contrast to earlier studies, are attributed primarily to the changes in the DSM-IV. Other research (see chapter 3) suggests that the lifetime prevalence for PTE exposure hovers above 60%. Kessler (2000) recently commented it is not entirely clear how the results of these American studies generalize to other developed countries given that the United States has substantially higher rates of violent crimes.

A brief review of research in other developed nations also suggests a high prevalence of PTE, with slightly higher rates in men than in women. In a sample of 1,002 Canadian adults (> 18 years), Stein, Walker, and Forde (2000) reported that men (82%) evidenced a greater rate of lifetime exposure to at least one traumatic event than women (74%). Men (55%) also were more likely to report multiple events than women (46%). Using the CIDI and DSM-IV criteria, Perkonigg, Kessler, Storz, and Wittchen (2000; also see Perkonigg & Wittchen, 1999) found the lifetime prevalence of traumatic events in a prospective survey of a large ($N = 3021$), representative, young (14–24 years) community sample from metropolitan Munich, Germany, was much lower than in prior U.S. studies. With regard to gender differences, however, the results were relatively consistent with North American research. Male subjects were more likely than female subjects to report lifetime exposure to at least one traumatic event (25.2% vs. 17.7%, respectively). The Australian National Survey of Mental Health and Well-Being ($N = 10,641$) similarly demonstrated that substantially more men (64.6%) than women (49.5%) experienced trauma over their lifetime (Creamer, Burgess, & McFarlane, 2001).

While the perceptive reader may believe that these high prevalence estimates reflect an overestimation of disorders (e.g., due to nonclinicians administering the diagnostic interviews in large studies), this does not seem to be the case (Kessler et al., 1997). Validation studies from the DIS (e.g., Wittchen, Kessler, Zhao, & Abelson, 1995) and the CIDI (WHO, 1990) demonstrate that blind clinical interviewers are in agreement with the vast majority of diagnoses (Kessler et al., 1997). In fact, the more common concern may be underreporting (Wittchen, Uestuen, & Kessler, 1999). Alternatively, the critical reader might query whether apparent gender differences reflect underreporting bias in males and/or overreporting bias in females. In an effort to combat underreporting in general, researchers use memory enhancement and motivational procedures to reduce underreporting; evidence suggests these approaches are successful (e.g., see Kessler et al., 1997); however, extensive research demonstrates that men and women tend to have different reporting styles. Saxe and Wolfe (1999) asserted women might be more willing to disclose PTE, and research confirms that women tend to report more symptoms of physical and emotional distress than men. Gender differences in reporting styles have not been adequately addressed in the PTSD literature and such biases might affect prevalence rates (Saxe & Wolfe, 1999).

A review of the literature suggests that men have a higher (Breslau et al., 1991, 1998; Kessler et al., 1995; Stein et al., 2000) or fairly equivalent (Breslau, Davis, Andreski, Peterson, & Schultz, 1997a) risk of exposure to traumatic stressors when compared to women. While women are less likely than men to experience PTE across many developed countries, there are significant cross-cultural differences with respect to PTE prevalence. For example, women in the United States are at higher risk of exposure to trauma than men in Germany. The risk of lifetime exposure to PTE does not appear to explain the unique burden of PTSD for women.

Gender Differences in the Prevalence of PTSD in the General Population

Generally, women are reported to have approximately twice the risk of developing PTSD compared to men (Davidson et al., 1991; for reviews, see Brewin, Amdrews, & Valentine, 2000; Foa & Street, 2001; Gavranidou & Rosner, 2003; Norris et al., 2002; Seedat & Stein, 2000; Wolfe & Kimerling, 1997). For highly noxious events (e.g., rape), gender differences appear to be ameliorated (Gavranidou & Rosner, 2003; Kessler et al., 1995: Perkonigg & Wittchen, 1999) and the probability of PTSD is high for both sexes. A large body of data converges to support this conclusion.

To study the frequency and impact of different types of PTE on a variety of demographic groups, Norris (1992) used a sampling procedure that assured approximately equal numbers of Blacks and Whites, men and women, and younger (18–39), middle-aged (40–59), and older (60+) participants. The sample was drawn from 12 neighborhoods across four mid-sized southeastern U.S. cities. Because the sample was not drawn randomly, it cannot be described as necessarily representative of the general population, but likely much more so than many PTSD studies that often draw on samples of convenience. Consistent with previous research, men (73.6%) were more likely than women (64.8%) to experience most categories of trauma (with the exception of sexual assault). *Current* PTSD was higher, though not significantly, among women (8.5%) than among men (6.1%); lifetime frequency of PTSD was not reported.

In the HAYA study (Breslau et al., 1991), the cumulative incidence of PTSD (DSM-III-R, American Psychiatric Association, 1987) was significantly higher in women (30.2%) than in men (13%) (also see Breslau & Davis, 1992; Breslau, Davis, Andreski, Peterson, & Schultz, 1997a). Lifetime prevalence rates were 11.3% in women, 6% in men (Breslau et al., 1991). Perhaps the best estimate of the prevalence of PTSD in the U.S. general population is the NCS (Kessler et al., 1995), a nationwide study that yielded a lifetime prevalence rate of 7.8% (applying DSM-III criteria). The NCS demonstrated that men (60.7%) were more likely to be exposed to trauma than women (51.2%), but women (10.4%) were more likely than men (5.0%) to experience clinically significant symptoms (Kessler et al., 1995; also see Purves & Erwin, 2002).

To truly appreciate the burden of PTSD, Kessler (2000) recommends reporting the point prevalence estimate (i.e., how many people in the population have PTSD at one point in time). Though we see considerable value in reporting point prevalence estimates, we direct the reader to Phelan and Link (1999) for a discussion of the potential limitations of this approach. Specific to the current topic, it is to be expected that the conditional risk is higher among women given that women experience more chronic courses of PTSD (Norris et al., 2002). The DAS (Breslau et al., 1998) is one of the only studies to use the necessary methodology to capture this information (Kessler, 2000). The results of the DAS suggested the lifetime prevalence and mean number of traumas are both lower in women than in men (Breslau, Chilcoat, Kessler, & Davis, 1999a; Breslau, Chilcoat, Kessler, Peterson, & Lucia, 1999b). Despite less exposure to PTE, the overall conditional risk of PTSD among women was double that for men. Consistent with prior studies, Breslau et al. (1998) reported that women were nearly twice as likely as men to develop PTSD after exposure to a PTE. The conditional risk of PTSD was 13.0% in women and 6.2% in men, when estimated based on a randomly selected trauma. PTSD resulting from the respondent's nominated worst events was 17.7% in women and 9.5% in men. Breslau (2001) contends that PTSD is not a rare disorder and estimates that PTSD affects as many as 1 in 12 adults over the course of their lifetime.

As previously noted, the bulk of this research has been conducted in the United States and the prevalence of PTSD in general populations in other countries has not been studied widely (Kessler, 2000; Norris et al., 2002). For the most part, research that has been conducted in other nations is consistent with the U.S. data, indicating that females are significantly more likely to develop PTSD. According to the Modified PTSD Symptoms Scale, Stein, Walker, Hazen, & Forde (1997) found that 5% of Canadian women compared to 1.7% of Canadian men met symptom criteria. In subsequent analyses of the same data, Stein et al. (2000) reported that Canadian women were more vulnerable to PTSD following nonsexual assault but not in response to nonassaultive traumas. Lifetime exposure (to at least one trauma) resulted in full or partial *current* PTSD in 8.2% of women and 1.8% of men (Stein et al., 2000).

Research outside of North America yields relatively consistent findings with regard to gender differences, but much lower base rates of PTSD in the community, consistent with the evidence reviewed above demonstrating lower rates of exposure to PTE. In a German study of 3,021 adolescents and adults (Perkonigg & Wittchen, 1999) the lifetime prevalence of PTSD was 1.3%. Consistent with data from the United States, the lifetime risk for PTSD after trauma was substantially higher for women (2.2%) than for men (0.4%). Epidemiological research in Australia similarly reveals a much lower prevalence of PTSD (12-month prevalence of PTSD at 1.3%) in the general population (Creamer, Burgess, & McFarlane, 2001) than generally is reported in North American research (e.g., 12-month prevalence of 3.9%, Kessler, Mickelson, & Williams, 1999). Australian women (1.4%) were somewhat more likely than their male counterparts (1.2%) to have PTSD in the past 12 months. When examining a specific trauma, women (2.9%) were significantly more likely than men (1.9%) to be diagnosed with PTSD in the prior 12 months.

Recent empirical (e.g., Brewin, Andrews, & Valentine, 2000b) and theoretical (Ballenger et al., 2000; Breslau et al., 1999b; Gavranidou & Rosner, 2003; Yehuda, 2002) reviews confirm that women have about a twofold greater lifetime risk of PTSD than do men (for a thorough review, see Kimerling, Ouimette, & Wolfe, 2002); the same also has been found with panic disorder and generalized anxiety disorder (Kessler et al., 1994). For present purposes, it is most essential to consider that despite differences in methodology, culture, the prevalence of exposure to traumatic events across studies, and so on, the lifetime prevalence of PTSD varies within a narrow range and is consistently found to be more common among women (also see Breslau, 2002a).

Gender Differences in the Risk of Exposure to Multiple Traumas

Epidemiological surveys indicate that the unique risk for PTSD among women is not because they are more likely than men to have a history of multiple trauma exposures (Freedman et al., 2002; Pimlott-Kubiak & Cortina, 2003). To the contrary, men often are found to have a greater mean number of prior traumas. In the DAS, the mean number of distinct events was 5.3 for men and 4.3 for women

(Breslau et al., 1998). In the NCS (Kessler et al., 1995) considerably more men (34%) than women (25%) reported multiple traumas. Similarly, Creamer et al. (2001) found that a significantly greater proportion of Australian men than women reported two (18.3% vs. 11.8%), three (10.2% vs. 6.2%), four (6.5% vs. 2.9%) and more than four (4.7% vs. 2.4%) traumas, respectively. A related area of study is the impact of chronic or serial traumas (e.g., childhood abuse, abuse in intimate relationships, combat) (see Kaysen, Resick, & Wise, 2003).

Gender Differences in PTE and the Conditional Risk of PTSD

As discussed elsewhere in this book, knowledge of the prevalence of PTSD within the general population is of less utility for the practitioner than knowledge of the *conditional prevalence* of PTSD. While women's exposure to trauma (lifetime or mean number of events) is less than that for men, these findings do not necessarily indicate that female gender, *per se*, is a risk factor for PTSD. Simple examination of PTE exposure rate may mask important differences in the nature of traumas experienced by women versus men. The fundamental issue is whether women are more likely than men to encounter the *kinds* of aversive events that trigger traumatic responses (Kessler et al., 1995) or whether women's experiences of the "same" event differ in some manner from men's experiences (Yehuda, 2002).

Research confirms that men and women are prone to exposure to distinctive types of PTE. Stein et al. (2000) excluded respondents with a history of sexual abuse, controlled for number of lifetime exposures and trauma types (i.e., sexual traumatization, nonsexual assaultive violence, nonassaultive trauma), and examined features associated with the trauma (e.g., physical injury, fear of death). Controlling for trauma-related variables in this manner led these authors to conclude that men and women are exposed to unique stressors.

In their review of gender differences in PTSD, Gavranidou and Rosner (2003) asserted that women more often experience sexual abuse and rape, men more frequently experience physical attacks and serious accidents, and there are no apparent gender differences in the prevalence of traumas like natural disaster or sudden death of close family members. We would add that the most common cause of PTSD among men reported in the literature is exposure to combat (see Breslau et al., 1999a; Seedat & Stein, 2000). Provided below is a brief review of gender differences in the conditional risk of PTSD associated with various forms of PTE within categories of trauma likely to give rise to forensic assessments with women.

Nonsexual Interpersonal Violence

Interpersonal violence is more likely to result in posttraumatic maladjustment than other types of events (e.g., natural disasters, motor vehicle accidents) (e.g., Ballenger et al., 2000; Breslau et al., 1998; Kessler et al., 1995; Shercliffe, 2001).

Given that women are twice as likely as men to suffer from PTSD over their lifetime, some have speculated that this might simply reflect the fact that women are at greater risk of being assaulted. On the contrary, crime records, national victimization surveys (e.g., Tjaden & Thoennes, 2000), and epidemiological studies of trauma (e.g., Breslau et al., 1998, 1999b; Norris, 1992; Kessler et al., 1995) indicate that women are actually less likely than men to be the victims of *non-sexual* interpersonal violence. Further, although men are the predominant victims of nonsexual physical assaults, several studies suggest that women are substantially more likely to develop PTSD secondary to a physical attack (e.g., Breslau et al., 1998; Kessler et al., 1995; Perkonigg et al., 2000).

In their reanalysis of data from the National Violence Against Women survey, Pimlott-Kubiak and Cortina (2003) found that men reported more childhood physical abuse (54% vs. 40%) and adult physical assaults (45% vs. 31%) than women (also see Freedman et al., 2002). Males are also substantially more exposed to combat violence (Breslau et al., 1998, 1999a; Creamer et al., 2001; Freedman et al., 2002).

Norris (1992) reported the conditional risk of PTSD to be similar for men and women, with the exception of criminal violence. Similarly, the results of the NCS (Kessler et al., 1995) suggested that differences in the response to traumatic interpersonal events might account for gender differences in the clinical outcome. Women (6.8%) sampled in the NCS (Kessler et al., 1995) were significantly less likely than men (19.0%) to report having been threatened with a weapon over their lifetime, or to be the victim of a physical attack (women = 6.9%, men = 11.1%). However, women who did report these experiences had significantly higher rates of PTSD than men (weapon = 32.6% vs. 1.9%; attack = 21.3% vs. 1.8%, respectively). A relatively unique sample of trauma survivors from the general population further bolsters this interpretation of the data. North, Smith, and Spitznagel (1994) reported that women (36%) were significantly more likely than men (20%) to suffer from PTSD after surviving a mass murderer's attack.

Recent qualitative (e.g., Norris et al., 2002) and quantitative reviews (Tolin & Foa, 2002) provide further evidence that "even within trauma types, females still appear to be at somewhat greater risk for PTSD" (p. 90). While these findings are generally consistent across studies, the extant literature is not particularly compelling. Research examining gender differences in the nature of PTE really is in its infancy—studying broad categories of trauma types is just a preliminary step in the right direction. Cusack et al. (2002) recommend an assessment of the relationship with the perpetrator, the victim's perception of potential serious harm or death, the chronicity of the trauma, and the extent of injury. To date, the trauma literature has not sufficiently examined Criterion A2 to determine the role of subjective distress. Recent reviews suggest that the subjective risk perceived by a woman versus a man in response to an otherwise identical stressor might account for gender differences (e.g., Pigott, 2003). Breslau (2002a) and Yehuda (2002) both hypothesized that a woman's fear of injury or death may exceed that of a man's, providing the two targets were facing an identical attacker. Women do, in fact, face a substantially greater threat of injury than men during physical attacks, suggesting that women's disproportionate fear is based on an accurate evaluation of their differential risk of harm compared to men facing the same threat. In the Violence Against Women survey (VAWS), 39.0% of female physical assault victims compared to 24.8% of male physical assault victims reported being injured during their most recent assault (Tjaden & Thoennes, 2000).

There are at least two forms of nonsexual interpersonal violence that present a relatively unique risk of trauma to women in terms of the rate of exposure and the associated risk of harm: abuse in intimate relationships and stalking/criminal harassment. Although these PTE are included here under "nonsexual" interpersonal violence, it is important to note that physically abusive relationships and stalking often include some element of sexual violence.

Abusive Intimate Relationships
Approximately 25–30% of North American women report experiencing physical abuse by an intimate partner (e.g., in dating, common law, or marital relationships) over their lifetime (Canadian Violence Against Women Survey, Johnson, 1998; U.S. National Violence Against Women survey, Tjaden & Thoennes, 2000). While the *rate* of abuse experienced in romantic relationships is comparable for men and women, there is less consensus regarding men's and women's experiences of domestic violence and the resulting physical, psychological, and economic damages experienced by male and female victims. (e.g., Nicholls & Dutton, 2001; Straus, 1999). It is not surprising that female victims of intimate partner abuse have exceptionally high rates of PTSD (31%–60%, Cascardi, O'Leary, Lawrence, & Schlee, 1995; 33%–84%, Golding, 1999) and other trauma related symptoms (e.g., depression, suicide) compared to women in the general population (for a review, see Rhodes & McKenzie, 1998). Highlighted are several important issues for cross-examination in court and in the assessment and treatment of women with abusive partners.

First, psychopathology among abused women is consistently found to postdate the abuse (i.e., it is considered a consequence of the abuse) (Cascardi et al., 1995; Gondolf, 1998). Using data from the NCS, Kessler, Molnar, Feurer, and Appelbaum (2001) found no evidence of elevated rates of premarital mental disorders among women in abusive relationships. Attempts to identify a typology of battered women have been unsuccessful, meaning that there is no "typical" battered woman, and pathology models are poor predictors of who will enter into or remain in abusive relationships (Campbell, Miller, Cardwell, & Belknap, 1994).

Second, because stress symptoms during and immediately following a PTE can be considered a normal response (Simon, 1996), applying the diagnosis of depression or PTSD to a woman in an ongoing violent situation "lacks common sense" (Koss, Bailey, Yuan, Herrara, & Lichter, 2003, p. 135). Similar to using bereavement as a factor to rule out applying the diagnosis of depression during the normal grieving period, women's reactions to the *ongoing* threat of danger in abusive intimate relationships might preclude a mental disorder diagnosis (Koss et al., 2003). Mental health problems among women currently experiencing abuse should be considered relevant to the extent that they place a woman at risk for ongoing abuse by interfering with her ability to engage in safety planning and help seeking.

Third, concepts such as learned helplessness and posttraumatic stress disorder (Koss et al., 2003; Mechanic, Kaysen, & Resick, 2002) might be of limited utility when dealing with women *currently* in abusive relationships and women whose ex-partners continue to abuse, stalk, or harass them following dissolution of the relationship. A diagnosis of PTSD implies that the threat of abuse has been alleviated and the woman is now in a safe interpersonal situation. In fact, women often are at increased risk of abuse and severe violence when attempting to seek help or to leave an abuser, and over the period of time shortly after a separation (e.g., Coleman, 1997). Hyperarousal might be an adaptive response to a chronic abusive relationship (Mechanic et al., 2002). Decreasing a battered woman's arousal level might reduce her awareness of her partner's level of risk, inadvertently increasing her level of danger.

Fourth, many women "choose" to remain in an abusive relationship for fear of escalating abuse, because the abuser has made specific threats to harm her or others if she attempts to leave, or because she believes authorities and/or family cannot protect her. Considerable research demonstrates that these fears are justified, and leaving an abuser does not necessarily end the violence (e.g., Coleman, 1997; LaViolette & Barnett, 2000). As many as one in three women with former abusive partners experience a physical assault after separation (Fleury, Sullivan, & Bybee, 2000), some women experience abuse for the first time following a separation (Kurcz, 1996) and the risk of murder and attempted murder is highest during this time (Campbell, 1992; Coleman, 1997; McFarlane et al., 1999; Meloy, 1998).

Finally, professionals carry the substantial burden of ensuring that they do not inadvertently undermine a woman's credibility in criminal and civil proceedings (e.g., reducing the woman's chances of obtaining custody of her children; Gondolf, 1998). Advocates need to be aware of the limits of confidentiality and share that information and the associated risks with their clients (see Carlson & Dutton, 2003).

Stalking

According to Tjaden & Thoennes (2000, p. 5), stalking or criminal harassment involves, "a course of conduct directed at a specific person that involves repeated visual or physical proximity; nonconsensual communication; verbal, written, or implied threats; or a combination thereof that would cause fear in a reasonable person (with *repeated* meaning on two or more occasions)." It is little wonder, therefore, that one of the major associated mental health problems is PTSD. Stalking can result in chronic stress due to repeated trauma, a loss of control, mistrust, and/or fear (Pathé & Mullen, 1997).

Douglas and Dutton (2001) estimated that as many as 1 in 20 people in the general population will be stalked in the course of their lifetime. Official criminal records and self-report victim surveys suggest that women are the predominant victims of this form of interpersonal aggression. Gill and Brockman (1996) examined 601 stalking cases spanning a 3-year period (1993–1996) in Vancouver, Edmonton, Winnipeg, Montreal, and Halifax, Canada. Their data revealed that 88% of the victims were women. More recent data released by Statistics Canada (Johnson & Au Coin, 2003) indicated that rates of criminal harassment have increased (up 53% between 1995 and 2001; Schell, 2003), with women still accounting for the vast majority of victims (male victims increased 8% to 12%). Findings from the National Violence Against Women Survey (NVAWS) in the United States indicated that 1% of all adult women are stalked each year and that 8% (1 in 12) of all women have been stalked at least once in their lifetime, compared with 1 in 45 men.

The most common victim of stalking is an ex-intimate partner (Douglas & Dutton, 2001; Meloy, 1998). In their sample of 144 battered women, Mechanic, Weaver, and Resick (2000) found 13% to 29% reported being stalked in the 6 months immediately following separation from the abuser. According to the NVAWS, slightly more than half (54%) of all stalking is done by current or former partners. The prevalence of prior intimate partner stalking is particularly troubling because ex-intimate stalkers engage in more dangerous behavior than nonintimate relationship stalkers (Palarea, Zona, Lane, & Langhinrichsen-Rohling, 1999). Of note, male victims (32%) are about half as likely as female victims (59%) to have had a prior intimate relationship with the stalker (Tjaden & Thoennes, 2000), suggesting that females are not only more likely to be harassed, but also are more likely than their male counterparts to experience violence by the stalker.

Research in Australia (Pathé & Mullen, 1997), the United States (Tjaden & Thoennes, 2000), Canada (Abrams & Robinson, 1998), and the Netherlands (Blaauw, Winkel, Arensman, Sheridan, & Freeve 2002), for example, demonstrates that stalking is a significant risk factor for posttraumatic reactions even a year or more after such activity has ceased (Blaauw et al., 2002; Draucker, 1999). As many as one-third of stalking victims experience PTSD. Pathé and Mullen (1997) reported that 83% of stalking targets responding to an interview questionnaire had increased anxiety, 37% had PTSD, and 18% had subsyndromal PTSD. According to Kamphius and Emmelkamp (2001), in a community-based study of Dutch female help-seeking stalking victims, more than half the women had clinically significant distress, as measured by the General Health Questionnaire. The authors concluded that stalking was associated with psychological morbidity in 59% of the women, including PTSD. In one of the few studies to examine both male and female victims of stalking, Davis, Coker, and Sanderson (2002) reported that the physical and mental health repercussions of stalking were not differentiated by gender. That said, it must be recalled that women are more likely to experience stalking by an ex-partner and to be the targets of serious threats and/or violence.

In summary, women are disproportionately exposed to stalking, as well as to stalking in a manner (when the offenders are ex-intimate partners) in which they are objectively at risk of serious physical harm. Stalking appears to have significant negative emotional consequences for the victim. Further research is required to elucidate the psychological impact of stalking, and to further explore gender differences and similarities.

Sexual Violence

In the United States, the NVAW survey concluded that females comprised more than 90% of the victims of childhood and adult sexual violence (Tjaden & Thoennes, 2000; also see Pimlott-Kubiak & Cortina, 2003). Tjaden and Thoennes (2000) estimated that 14.8% of women and 2.1% of men in the United States had experienced a completed rape and another 2.8% of women and 0.9% of men suffered an attempted rape over their lifetime. The disparity in the rate of sexual violence experienced by women versus men raises the issue of whether sexual violence might account for the association between gender and PTSD.

Adult Sexual Assault and Rape

Most authors distinguish between sexual assaults (i.e., any unwanted sexual acts) and rape (i.e., forced vaginal, oral, or anal penetration). The majority of epidemiological and national studies have examined rape (see Breslau et al., 1998; Koss et al., 2003; Tjaden & Thoennes, 2000). The NVAWS showed that 0.3% of women and 0.1% of men had been raped in the 12 months prior to the survey. The incidence of rape (i.e., the number of separate victimizations) exceeded its prevalence (i.e., the number of victims reporting rape; $n = 734$ women, 62 men) because some respondents reported multiple rapes. In the previous 12 months, women reported an average of 2.9 rapes and men reported an average of 1.2 rapes (Tjaden & Thoennes, 2000), although these data must be viewed with caution given the small sample sizes. In the NVAWS, 31.5% of female rape victims compared to 16.1% of male victims reported being injured during their most recent assault (Tjaden & Thoennes, 2000).

Posttraumatic stress disorder is a common consequence of sexual assault; in fact, sexual assaults are more closely associated with the onset of PTSD than other forms of trauma (Breslau et al., 1998, 1999a; Kessler et al., 1995; Norris, 1992; Norris et al., 2002). Estimates of the conditional risk of PTSD following rape range from one-third (Resnick, Kilpatrick, Dansky, Saunders, Best, 1993) to 94% (Rothbaum, Foa, Murdock et al., 1993). In a retrospective national probability sample of women in the United States (National Women's Study), Resnick et al. (1993) found that rates of PTSD were highest among women whose traumas included rape or assault. One in 3 rape survivors (31%) developed PTSD over their lifetime, a rate 6.2 times higher than women who had never been crime victims (current PTSD = 11% vs. 2%, respectively). Prospective studies indicate that as many as 94% of female rape victims meet criteria at two weeks (dropping to 47% at 3 months) (e.g., Rothbaum, Foa, Riggs, Murdock, & Walsh, 1992; Riggs, Rothbaum, & Foa, 1995). Foa (1997) concluded that rape is uniquely traumatic, resulting in PTSD in 48% versus 25% of nonsexual crime victims three months after the trauma. Of note, the conditional prevalence of PTSD in the NCS (Kessler et al., 1995) did not differ between men and women exposed to a sexual assault. Of the women sampled, 9.2% reported a rape, nearly half (49.5%) of whom developed PTSD (Kessler et al., 1995). In contrast, of the 0.7% of men reporting a rape over their lifetime, 65.0% developed PTSD (also see Creamer et al., 2001; Freedman et al., 2002). Rape in marital or cohabiting relationships is estimated at 10–14% of the general population of women, and about 50% of women who are physically abused by a male partner also report sexual assaults (Koss et al., 2003; Smith, Thornton, DeVellis, Earp, & Coker, 2002). Importantly, rapes committed in the context of intimate relationships are associated with mental health effects as deleterious as the psychological impact of being raped by a stranger (Campbell et al., 1999) and a *greater* likelihood of injury than rapes committed by nonintimates (Tjaden & Thoennes, 2000).

In summary, adult sexual assault is disproportionately suffered by women, female victims are more likely to suffer multiple sexual assaults than are men, and sexual assaults within cohabiting or married relationships are more likely to be associated with other forms of abuse and with physical injury. All of the above suggests that sexual assault poses a more toxic influence on women's mental health than it does for men.

Childhood Sexual Abuse
Girls and women are at substantially greater risk of sexual assault throughout their lifetime than their male counterparts, beginning in childhood. Large national surveys in the United States indicate that as many as 1 in 3 women (27%), compared to 1 in 10 men (8–16%), experienced at least one incident of childhood sexual abuse (CSA) (Breslau et al., 1997a; Finkelhor, 1994; Finkelhor, Hotaling, Lewis, & Smith, 1990). The NVAWS (Tjaden & Thoennes, 2000) similarly demonstrated that 9% of women and 1.9% of men were raped before the age of 18. Female respondents (13.5%) to the NCS (Molnar, Buku, & Kessler, 2001) also were much more likely than male respondents (2.5%) to report CSA.

Epidemiological studies and large national surveys in other developed nations similarly indicate that the prevalence and incidence of CSA is no less alarming in other countries (e.g., Fergusson, Swain-Campbell, & Horwood, 2002; Finkelhor, 1994). The World Health Organization (WHO) recently carried out a review of prevalence estimates of CSA from 39 countries. "After controlling for differences between studies, the prevalence of non-contact, contact and intercourse types of CSA in females was about 6%, 11% and 4%, respectively. In males it was about 2% for all categories. Thus, over 800 million people worldwide may have experienced CSA, with over 500 million having experienced contact or intercourse types of abuse" (WHO, 2002, p. 10).

Professionals should be aware that it is still being debated in the literature whether or not *all* instances of CSA satisfy DSM-IV criteria for PTSD. Although sexual contact between adults and children is morally repugnant, research suggests that every such instance might not be "traumatic" as such, particularly when the abuse does not involve physical force (e.g., Rind, Tromovitch, & Bauserman, 1998; cf., Dallam, Gleaves, & Cepeda-Benito, 2001). Moreover, it is difficult to disentangle long-term effects specific to CSA from the larger body of childhood adversities often facing sexual abuse targets (e.g., mother's psychopathology, poverty, parental substance abuse, interparental violence) (e.g., Browne & Finkelhor, 1986; Molnar et al., 2001). This methodological issue is particularly challenging when the perpetrator is a previously trusted family member. Finkelhor (1979) suggested that the matter should be framed in terms of the ethical and legal issues. He asserted that asymmetrical power makes informed consent by a child impossible; and, therefore, inherently wrong. Although many CSA survivors go on to be well adjusted, a large body of literature demonstrates a link between CSA and immediate and long-term negative outcomes, including PTSD (see Breslau, Peterson, Kessler, & Schulz, 1999c; Fergusson et al., 2002; Molnar et al., 2001).

Community samples (e.g., Saunders, Villeponteaux, Lipovsky, Kilpatrick, & Veronen, 1992) suggest that the psychological sequelae of CSA often involve PTSD and appear to differ as a function of the aspects of the experience. Saunders et al. (1992) reported 33.3% of survivors of CSA that involved physical contact without penetration versus 64.1% of those who experienced penetration developed PTSD. The duration of CSA, use of physical force or threats, and fear of injury or death have been found to differentiate the risk of PTSD and/or the severity of symptoms (e.g., Rowan, Foy, Rodriguez, & Ryan, 1994; Wolfe, Schnurr, Brown, & Furey, 1994).

Most epidemiological studies to date have not evaluated the conditional risk of PTSD following CSA. Creamer et al.'s study (2001) indicated that while females (10.2%) were significantly more likely than males (3.5%) to report CSA, male victims were significantly more likely to suffer from PTSD (11.8% vs. 5.5%). In sum, exposure to adult or childhood sexual victimization almost certainly accounts for some, but not all, of the variance we witness in the prevalence of posttrauma maladjustment among men and women (see Stein et al., 1997, 2000).

Sexual Harassment

Sexual harassment is a pervasive problem. McKinney (1990) estimated that 20–75% of female college students are the targets of harassing behaviors of a sexual nature. Ilies, Hauserman, Schwochau, and Stibal (2003) found that 58% of women reported having experienced potentially harassing behaviors at work in the United States. Sexual harassment appears to be no less prevalent in Canadian industry; in a cross-section of 46 Canadian companies responding to a questionnaire (Schell, 2003), 43.5% indicated that a reported incident (i.e., the target made an official complaint) of sexual harassment occurred from January 1995 through January 2000. The vast majority of these reported incidents (including 53 cases in 20 companies) involved male perpetrators and female targets (91.7%). Given that this study examined cases reported to the companies' human resources departments, it likely underestimated the prevalence of sexual harassment. As discussed, men tend to experience potentially sexually harassing behaviors very differently from women; as such, the study likely overestimated the proportion of cases involving female targets. Simon (1996) estimated that complaints by men account for about one-tenth the number of complaints by women.

Although power and hierarchical status are considered important antecedents to sexual harassment, there also is considerable research documenting "contrapower" sexual harassment (i.e., harassment by objectively less powerful persons against more powerful persons) (McKinney, 1992). DeSouza and Fansler (2003) found that almost one-third of university students ($N = 158$) admitted to having sexually harassed a professor and more than half of the 209 professors surveyed reported having been sexually harassed by students. Male and female professors experienced similar rates of harassment, though the psychological impact was greater for women (DeSouza & Fansler, 2003).

Some authors assert that Criterion A1, as defined in the DSM-IV, does not necessarily require a life-threatening event, and many victims of sexual harassment show a pattern of PTSD-like symptoms (for a review, see Avina & O'Donohue, 2002). Theorists further assert that sexual harassment has a trauma-like impact and exists on the same continuum as sexual assault (e.g., Koss, 1990). Empirical support for the traumatic impact of sexual harassment has been obtained in workplace (e.g., Dansky & Kilpatrick, 1997) and university contexts (McDermut, Haaga, & Kirk, 2000). Controlling for prior traumas, lifetime PTSD (measured with the Structured Clinical Interview for DSM-IV [SCID]) is associated with sexual harassment, and the severity of harassment is positively correlated with current PTSD symptoms (McDermut et al., 2000). As would be expected, PTSD symptom scores on average are lower than among samples of rape victims, and the research indicates that sexual harassment likely falls on the low severity end of the sexual trauma continuum (McDermut et al., 2000).

It is important to consider that the operational definitions of sexual harassment used in research and psychology do not always translate well to legal definitions. These differences are particularly compelling if one considers, for instance, gender differences in response to potentially harassing behaviors (e.g., Berdahl, Magley, & Waldo, 1996; Koedam, 2000; Waldo, Berdahl, & Fitzgerald, 1998). It might well be the case that a female target found a sexually harassing experience to be emotionally taxing, though the experience might not satisfy legal definitions. In contrast, a male target might experience more severe harassing behavior, which satisfied legal criteria, but was not distressing to him (Waldo et al., 1998). Professionals should be conversant in relevant legal standards in their jurisdictions.

Nonassaultive Traumas

Motor Vehicle Accidents

Data from large-scale epidemiological studies that have examined PTSD following motor vehicle accidents (MVAs) and other serious accidents (e.g., Breslau, 2002b; Creamer et al., 2001; Kessler, 1995; Norris, 1992) offer little evidence that gender plays an important role in psychological recovery following accidents. In contrast, several convenience and clinical samples have yielded more mixed results.

Freedman et al. (2002) examined gender differences in response to MVAs in 275 emergency room patients ($N = 93$ men and 104 women). Lifetime exposure to 24 potentially traumatic events was examined using the Trauma History Questionnaire. This prospective study indicated that subsequent to MVAs, there was no gender difference in the incidence of PTSD. Using regression analyses, the authors reported that gender did not add significantly to the prediction of PTSD above trauma severity and previous trauma exposure. The authors also found no statistically significant difference in the occurrence of major depressive disorder or dysthymia, though women were significantly more likely to have postaccident generalized anxiety disorder (GAD), as well as a lifetime history of GAD. The authors concluded that gender differences in response to PTE reflect "gender-specific attributes" of the events. Their results are somewhat unique from other convenience samples, suggesting that women demonstrate poorer recovery than males following MVAs (e.g., Ehlers, Mayou, & Bryant, 1998; Fullerton et al., 2001).

In a recent review of the predictors of PTSD in MVA survivors, Douglas and Koch (submitted) concluded that there is consistent evidence for the relationship between female gender and MVA-PTSD, although they postulate that other factors identified in the literature might account for the apparent relationships. For instance, Almeida, Wethington, and Kessler (2002) and Almeida and Kessler (1998) have found that gender differences in daily levels of psychological distress might be explained by different frequencies of daily nontraumatic stressors. Douglas and Koch further postulated that peritraumatic dissociation (see Fullerton et al., 2001) and the generally higher rate of psychological distress among women (e.g., Kessler, McGonagle, Swartz, Blazer, & Nelson, 1993) might account for different rates of PTSD (also see Cusack et al., 2002).

Natural Disasters

Biological sex also has not emerged as an important predictor of recovery following natural disasters. Though epidemiological data suggest that women typically fare somewhat more poorly than men, these differences tend not to be statistically significant (e.g., Kessler, 1995; Norris, 1992; for a review, see Yehuda, 2002). Similar to the epidemiological literature, research with disaster victims generally points to small, nonsignificant gender main effects (e.g., Benight, Swift, Sanger, Smith, & Zeppelin, 1999; Norris et al., 2001a; Thorunn & Ask, 2002).

Summary of the Conditional Risk of PTSD: Are Women Uniquely Vulnerable?

When it comes to trauma, are women the "weaker" sex (Gavranidou & Rosner, 2003)? We opened the chapter by alluding to the relative lack of agreement in the literature regarding women's vulnerability to PTSD. While this debate still rages in the literature (e.g., Bresleau, 2002a; Kimerling et al., 2002; Yehuda, 2002), substantial progress has been made in the field, and speculations regarding sex differences in posttraumatic responses have begun to converge, demonstrating several consistent findings:

1. Women are about twice as likely as men to develop PTSD over their lifetime.
2. Gender differences in the prevalence of PTSD cannot be accounted for by sex differences in the prevalence or incidence of trauma exposures or in exposure to multiple traumas.
3. An examination of diverse forms of trauma reveals that the conditional risk of PTSD in women appears to be relatively similar to men, with a trend for higher rates among women than men exposed to the same PTE.
4. Interpersonal violence appears to have a unique impact on posttraumatic recovery, generally, but presents a greater threat of PTSD to women than to men.
5. Sexual traumas, in particular, contribute disproportionately to the development of posttrauma symptoms in men and women; women are at substantially greater risk of exposure to this form of interpersonal violence.
6. Sex differences in the threat associated with interpersonal violence (i.e.,

risk of injury) likely account for some of the variance in the prevalence of PTSD among men and women.

Several researchers contend that women are more prone than men, irrespective of the nature of the trauma, to develop PTSD and other posttraumatic disorders (e.g., Breslau, 2002a; Kessler et al., 1995; Stein et al., 2000). Gavranidou and Rosner (2003) concluded, "Even when the conditional probabilities for amount and type of traumatic events (toxicity) are considered, the relative risk for women of developing PTSD is elevated" (p. 135). They suggest that women display a higher risk of developing PTSD across categories of trauma, with the exception of highly toxic events such as rape and childhood neglect. Others contend it is possible that the quality of the traumatic events experienced by women and the subjective interpretation of those experiences is what makes women more likely than men to experience subsequent psychopathology (e.g., Cusack et al., 2002; Freedman et al., 2002; Pimlott-Kubiak & Cortina, 2003; Tolin & Foa, 2002; Wolfe & Kimerling, 1997). Yehuda (2002) asserted, "Although women have a higher prevalence of PTSD, it is not clear whether this finding reflects an increased vulnerability to the disorder or the fact that seemingly similar events are experienced differently by men and women" (p. 109). Results of a recent meta-analysis (Tolin & Foa, 2002) demonstrated several significant differences in the conditional risk of PTSD for men and women by trauma category; however, with the exception of sexual assault, CSA, and combat, all of the effect sizes were small. These authors concluded that a general trend toward greater PTSD among females appeared to exist, but that more research was needed to link specific aspects of the traumatic experience with the onset of PTSD.

In sum, we contend that the research does not support the "feminine vulnerability" to PTSD hypothesis (Pimlott-Kubiak & Cortina, 2003, p. 528; Yehuda, 2002); or, perhaps more accurately, the methodology of existing studies is not yet sophisticated enough to conclude that the conditional risk of PTSD is higher among women, without other alternative hypotheses (e.g., greater toxic exposure to a categorically similar trauma) (also see Saxe & Wolfe, 1999). The following discussion should provide some clarity regarding methodological and clinical issues that might account for discrepant findings in the literature, as well as offer some recommendations for future research.

Limitations of Current Knowledge and Future Research Directions

General Methodological Issues

The conventional approach in assessing PTSD prevalence is to specify symptoms in the past month as *current* and those that occurred prior as during the subject's *lifetime* (Litz, Miller, Ruef, & McTeague 2002). To the extent that researchers examine *current* as opposed to *lifetime* prevalence of PTSD in men and women, apparent gender differences in prevalence rates could reflect an artifact of the differential course of PTSD across the sexes as opposed to a true susceptibility in women (Stein et al., 2000). In a similar vein, some research has examined PTSD from the perspective of the victim's *most* distressing event (Stein et al., 2000). As discussed above, women are the predominant victims of sexual violence, which appears to be uniquely predictive of PTSD. Results from studies inquiring about the respondent's most distressing event may provide biased comparisons of PTSD prevalence between men and women. That being said, even within broad trauma categories, there is some evidence of significant gender differences in the conditional risk of PTSD (Tolin & Foa, 2002). How might such gender-related differences be accounted for? Saxe and Wolfe (1999) hypothesized that diagnostic biases (i.e., research demonstrates that health-care practitioners are more likely to diagnose women with some mental illnesses) and reporting styles (i.e., research confirms that women are more likely to disclose PTE and tend to report more severe symptoms) might be to blame. Below we offer some further possible explanations.

The Nature of the Trauma

Criteria A1 and A2

With regard to assessment and diagnostic criteria, the DSM-IV is still relatively vague. As Litz et al. (2002) noted, "threat to physical integrity of self or others" (American Psychiatric Association, 1994, pp. 427–428) is "particularly ambiguous and subject to interpretation" (p. 220). Furthermore, Vogel and Marshall (2001) emphasized that distinguishing different types of traumas is an important goal given that multiple stressors, trauma severity, and revictimization all have been demonstrated to predict PTSD symptoms. While some authors assert that gender differences in the risk of PTSD exist even after controlling for trauma types, (i.e., typically defined broadly as combat, MVA, rape), there is a great deal of variability within classes of traumatic experiences (e.g., Cusack et al., 2002; Foa & Tolin, 2002; Norris et al., 2002; Stein et al., 2000). Norris (1992) similarly noted that one assault is not necessarily like another assault and, therefore, victims may have qualitatively different experiences.

Our review of sex differences in sexual harassment, stalking, and abuse in intimate relationships indicates that a more detailed analysis of PTE features might advance our understanding of women's vulnerability to PTSD. Other authors have similarly recommended such a finer-grained analysis of PTE. Yehuda (2002) concluded that the most salient characteristics of PTE for the development of PTSD are the severity, predictability, duration, and type of trauma.

The necessity of furthering PTSD assessment approaches to more accurately reflect the perspective of the victim is evident in the DSM-IV-TR diagnostic criteria. Criterion A2 requires that "The person's response to the event must involve intense fear, helplessness or horror" (American Psychiatric Association, 2000, p. 463). The few studies that have begun to examine Criterion A2 support our assertion that this will be an important area of study to clarify gender differences. To demonstrate, Perkonigg and Wittchen (1999) reported that rates of exposure to PTE were significantly higher for men (25%) than women (18%); however, once Criterion A2 was accounted for, gender differences were substantially reduced (men = 19%; women = 15%). Norris et al. (2002) reported that an examination of Criteria A1 and A2 in a Mexican sample (N = 1,289, two-thirds female) assessed using the CIDI version 2.1 for DSM-IV resulted in very similar findings. An assessment of A1 yielded 83% of men and 74% of women experiencing at least one lifetime PTE; however, nearly identical percentages of men (60%) and women (61%) met Criterion A2. King, King, Gudanowski, and Vreven (1995) also found that perceived threat was a better predictor of PTSD in men and women than other traditional means of assessing combat exposure.

The differential meaning of interpersonal violence, such as spouse abuse or sexual harassment, for men versus women has received considerable attention in the literature for those fields, yet these issues have yet to be adequately addressed in the trauma/PTSD literature. For instance, speaking to sexual harassment, Waldo et al. (1998) wrote, "similar behavioral experiences are likely to have different meanings for men and women, given gender differences in socialization and in social, organizational, and physical power" (p. 60). In fact, some research demonstrates that men often describe potentially sexually harassing experiences as benign or even welcome, and are significantly less likely than women to find such experiences distressing (e.g., Cochran, Frazier, & Olson, 1997; DeSouza & Fansler, 2003; Waldo et al., 1998).

Threat to physical safety and cognitive perceptions (e.g., the perceived likelihood of being injured or killed; see Blanchard et al., 1995; Shalev, Peri, Canetti, & Schreiber, 1996) have been demonstrated to increase risk for PTSD. Moreover, factors that contribute are evaluated based on the victim's feelings of control over the circumstances, predictability, and the extent of the perceived risk. Further examination of Criterion A–related factors—such as perceived risk, feelings of control versus helplessness, and predictability—might explain, in part, why women are at greater risk than men of developing PTSD following nonsexual assaultive violence (e.g., mugging, robbery, domestic violence), but not following nonassaultive violence (e.g., MVA, fire) (see Stein et al., 2000). Litz et al. (2002) critiqued the DSM-IV for its categorical approach and failure to assess dimensional features of PTE and the person's response. They recommended that clinicians provide clients the opportunity to evaluate the event subjectively; appropriate measures for this type of evaluation are available (e.g., the Severity of Violence against Women Scales; Marshall, 1992), though to our knowledge have not been utilized for this purpose.

Cumulative and Chronic Traumas—Considering Dose Response

Intuitively, the extent or length of exposure to a PTE should predict mental health problems. Evidence of a dose-response relationship and PTSD has been demonstrated in several studies of partner abuse (e.g., Astin, Lawrence, & Foy, 1993; Cascardi & O'Leary, 1992; Cascardi, O'Leary, & Schlee, 1999), and also has been found in studies of the impact of CSA on psychological functioning (e.g., Rowan et al., 1994; Saunders et al., 1992; Wolfe et al., 1994; for a model see Briere, 1992), for instance. Future research should serve to quantify the chronicity of traumatic events when attempting to make gender comparisons (e.g., see Herman, 1992; Kaysen et al., 2003; also see Litz et al., 2002). Most experts agree (e.g., Breslau, 2002a; Yehuda, 2002) that contrasting the experience of a man who is repeatedly involved in physical fights with other men against a woman's experience of being battered repeatedly by a male partner is inappropriate. Metaphorically, it is like contrasting the likelihood of injury to a heavyweight boxer fighting other heavyweights to a lightweight boxing above his weight in the heavyweight class. One would logically expect more frequent and severe injuries to the lightweight. Yet, these essential distinctions are not made in the bulk of the literature—typically, a female abuse victim and a man in a barroom brawl would both be categorized as having experienced a physical assault. Litz et al. (2002) recommended asking clients to describe the timing of the stressor, to determine if it was (a) serial or chronic in nature, or (b) if the individual experienced repeated similar events over their lifetime. Within forensic assessments, it is particularly important to detect multiple PTE and their temporal relationship to psychological distress.

Traumatic Betrayals—Relationship to Perpetrators of Violence

The relationship of the victim to the perpetrator of interpersonal violence also has received relatively little research attention in the PTSD literature. Some research suggests that CSA has worse outcomes if the perpetrator is a father figure versus a trusted adult outside the immediate family or a stranger (e.g., Friedrich, Urquiza, & Beilke, 1986). On a related matter, the relationship between the child and the perpetrator has been found to affect mothers' reactions to disclosures of CSA, subsequent family discord, and family composition. According to the CSA (Friedrich et al., 1986; Quas, Goodman, & Jones, 2003; cf., Lucenko, Gold, & Cott, 2000), domestic violence (Tjaden & Thoennes, 2000), and stalking (e.g., Palarea et al., 1999) literatures, closer affiliation to the perpetrator generally increases the target's risk of chronic abuse, severe abuse, and physical injury. It is as yet unclear whether it is the victim's relationship to the perpetrator or associated risks (e.g., age, duration of abuse, or penetration) that increase the risk for psychopathology in CSA survivors (Lucenko et al., 2000). Similarly, much of the extant epidemiological literature assesses physical assault experiences without considering that many of the incidents reported reflect familial abuse, which likely carries substantially different meanings (e.g., trustworthiness of close family members, shame, implications of reporting the abuse) for the victims.

Gender differences in PTSD might reflect women's greater risk of PTE that involve a betrayal of trust (also see DePrince & Freyd, 2002), reporting (i.e., disclosure), and cognitive differences associated with family abuse and sexual violence (e.g., self-blame or victim blaming; see Quas et al., 2003), or the importance of relationships to women's construct of self (Saxe & Wolfe, 1999). To clarify the role of betrayal, DePrince and Freyd (2002) called for further research to elucidate the influence of gender role socialization, the experience of unique PTE across the genders, or some combination of these factors (also see Cusack et al., 2002).

The Context in Which Trauma and Recovery Occurs

As noted in chapter 3, trauma recovery occurs in the context of the individual's everyday life. Measuring the social (e.g., social support, economic resources) and cultural (e.g., attitudes around gender roles, sexual assault) context in which PTE and recovery occur is likely to provide further clarity regarding the true influence of gender (e.g., see Norris et al., 2001a). Almeida and Kessler (1998) asserted that it is necessary to obtain both richer descriptions of external triggers, as well as internal appraisals of traumatic events to better understand the relationship between gender and well-being. Litz et al., (2002) similarly advised clinicians that the current nosological systems (i.e., DSM-IV-TR, American Psychiatric Association, 2000) and existing assessment tools for rendering a decision about the client's exposure and extent of trauma are insufficient in their coverage of the victim's social context. They recommend that clinicians should ask, at a minimum, "What was going on in your life at the time that this event occurred?" and "What were the responses of those around you?" (pp. 220–221).

Social Support

The reactions of significant others to trauma survivors appear to predict shifts from normal responses to chronic posttraumatic reactions. Social-psychological theories suggest that social support tends to buffer people who experience PTE (for a review, see Turner, 1999). On the other hand, research examining negative social support also points to the deleterious impact of some social relationships (e.g., see Turner, 1994).

Survivors of interpersonal violence are more likely than survivors of other types of PTE (e.g., MVAs or nonsexual assaults) to encounter negative reactions from others, including accusations that the incident(s) did not occur (e.g., in the case of incest) and victim blaming (e.g., following sexual assault, domestic violence) (Janoff-Bulman, 1992). Research from the general social support literature indicates that women tend to report greater perceived support and derive greater benefits from that support than men, but that women also are more likely than men to experience negative social support (Turner, 1994). In the trauma literature, PTSD symptoms are more strongly associated with negative or harsh reactions from significant others (e.g., rejection, denial) than with positive reactions from the social environment (e.g., Ullman & Filipas, 2001; Zoellner et al., 1999b). Societal responses to victims of sexual PTE in contrast to other types of trauma survivors are more likely to be unsupportive or even hostile (Campbell, Ahrens, Sefl, Wasco, & Barnes, 2001; Zoellner et al., 1999b). Such negative social support may be particularly relevant to minority women whose cultures place great value on chastity (Ullman & Filipas, 2001).

In a recent meta-analysis of risk factors for PTSD, of the 14 risk factors examined, social support was found to have the largest weighted average effect size (Brewin, Andrews, & Valentine, 2000). The first known study to compare gender differences in levels and benefits of social support among trauma victims (Andrews, Brewin, & Rose, 2003) found that negative social support mediated the relationship between distress and gender (i.e., women might be more likely to experience negative support). Alternatively, the authors postulated that support might moderate the relationship between distress and gender (i.e., women might be more vulnerable to negative support and/or derive more benefit from positive support). Presumably, as Andrews et al. (2003) asserted, the impact of negative perceptions will be more evident in the longitudinal course of posttraumatic reactions than in the immediate response to trauma. Negative responses from others can serve to exacerbate avoidance behaviors and reinforce maladaptive attitudes (e.g., shame, self-blame) (e.g., see Janoff-Bulman, 1989; Quas et al., 2003). Further appreciation of the differential impact of social support might broaden our understanding of women's consistently higher rates of PTSD.

Daily Hassles and Nontraumatic Stressors
Gender role theoretical perspectives posit that women are more likely than men to experience distress due to their role in providing nurturing and empathy to a broad range of people and unique role-related stressors (e.g., Gove & Tudor, 1973). For most individuals, even a short period of adjustment and recovery can compound the impact of a PTE (e.g., an increased workload due to time off). Research suggests that the burden for women recovering from mental health problems may be even greater than for men (Allen & Webster, 2001). Almeida and Kessler (1998) used daily diary methods to demonstrate that women are more likely than men to report any distress on a given day and to have a greater prevalence of high-distress days. Longitudinal research has found that assaulted women subsequently face higher rates of poverty, divorce, and unemployment

than do male assault victims (e.g., Byrne, Resnick, Kilpatrick, Best, & Saunders, 1999). Almeida and Kessler (1998) concluded that future research should use more sophisticated assessments of daily stressors (e.g., frequency, style, and outcome of marital disagreements), a measure of respondents' appraisals of daily events, daily responding to assure actual daily reporting of events (e.g., e-mail responses), and combined gender role and cognitive behavioral approaches (also see Almeida et al., 2002).

Gender Roles and Socialization

Gender role socialization shapes how we understand our environment and ourselves; as noted above, gender role theories are believed to have considerable applicability to improving our understanding of gender differences in PTSD. Norris et al. (2001a) found nonsignificant gender differences in cultures that value egalitarian roles for women (i.e., women who are expected to be resourceful, contribute to wage earning; e.g., African American women) versus large gender differences in cultures that are more likely to socialize women to be compliant and passive (e.g., Mexican women). This is an area of study that likely has important implications for reporting PTE (DePrince & Freyd, 2002), victim attributions of responsibility, help-seeking, coping strategies (DePrince & Freyd, 2002), micro-explanations of gender differences (e.g., trauma processing, see Almeida & Kessler, 1998; DePrince & Freyd, 2002; Krause, DeRosa, & Roth, 2002) and treatment (e.g., Cason, Grubaugh, & Resick, 2002).

Posttraumatic Reactions, Cognitive Distortions, and Coping

It is normal for individuals exposed to traumatic events to experience a short-lived stress reaction (Litz et al., 2002). The extent to which the individual experiences normal recovery is determined in part by the psychological processes he or she employs following the trauma. Wolfe and Kimerling (1997) proposed that the assessment of trauma in women requires a multidimensional approach, and urged clinicians to consider the impact of schemata and distorted cognitions related to the self and the world on women's posttrauma coping. As reviewed above, examples of victims for whom distorted cognitions might be particularly relevant include domestic violence victims, incest, and other sexual assault survivors (for a cognitive model, see Tolin & Foa, 2002). Empirical evidence of the impact of these types of traumas on women's attributions and cognitions (e.g., self-blame, shame, self-efficacy) indicates that clinicians need to consider posttrauma adjustment beyond the circumscribed DSM-IV criteria including "event type, frequency, overall severity ... individual attributions about stressor causality" (Wolfe & Kimerling, 1997, p. 210). Research further suggests that female gender may account for more cases of PTSD through the pathway of rumination (e.g.,

Ehlers, Mayou, & Bryant, 1998) and peritraumatic dissociation (e.g., Fullerton et al., 2001).

Clinical Presentation and Course of Recovery

As reviewed above, epidemiological studies have yielded higher rates of PTSD in women than in men in the general population; a greater number of comorbid diagnoses and gender differences in clinical presentation after traumatic events also have been reported (Wong & Yehuda, 2002). Some authors contend that women with PTSD have a higher rate of comorbidity (Wong & Yehuda, 2002), express more symptoms (Lavik, Hauff, Skrondal, & Solberg, 1996; North, Smith, & Spitznagel, 1997), have unique symptoms (Norris et al., 2001a), and/or that PTSD persists longer for them than for men (Breslau et al., 1998; McFarlane, 1988; Perkonigg et al., 2000; Saxe & Wolfe, 1999). Wolfe and Kimerling (1997) asserted that women show clinically significant disruption in health status (e.g., sexual dysfunctions, eating disorders, somatization), substantial comorbid substance abuse, as well as depression, and family and social disruption.

Despite the fact that comorbidity with PTSD is the norm (Orsillo, Raja, & Hammond, 2002; see chapter 3), very few studies have examined it in relation to gender differences. Kessler et al. (1995) reported that among individuals with a lifetime history of PTSD, men (88.3%) had a higher likelihood than women (79.0%) of having at least one other disorder. Men (59%) also were more likely than women (44%) to have more than three comorbid disorders. Similarly, Kessler et al. (1995) reported that comorbidity among their NCS sample was not differentiated by gender; for instance, lifetime history of depression (men = 47.9%, women = 48.5%) and dysthymia (men = 21%, women = 23.3%), were nearly identical. Based on their review of the literature, Orsillo et al., (2002) concluded that specific prevalence rates vary widely between studies, but a general pattern suggests that for most disorders, comorbidity does not differ "dramatically" for men and women.

With regard to substance-use disorders (SUD) specifically, Stewart, Ouimette, and Brown (2002) summarized the literature by stating that SUD might be somewhat more likely to appear in women, but that its presence appears to be related to the severity of the trauma. Data on this question are equivocal. There are two means of examining co-occurring disorders—the prevalence of people with PTSD who also have SUD (for instance) or the prevalence of people with SUD who also have PTSD. Data from the NCS (Kessler et al., 1995) indicated that 51.9% of men and 27.9% of women with PTSD had co-occurring alcohol abuse/dependence. Of participants without PTSD, 34.4% of men and 13.5% of women had alcohol abuse/dependence (Kessler et al., 1995). Kessler, Davis, and Kendler (1997) found that among people with lifetime alcohol dependence, women (26.2%) were much more likely than men (10.3%) to have PTSD. Najavits, Weiss,

Shaw, and Muenz (1998) noted that 30% to 59% of women with a current substance-use disorder have PTSD, while women with current PTSD are 1.4 to 5.5 times more likely to have SUD than women without PTSD. Najavits et al. (1998) noted that while these rates are remarkable on their own, they are particularly striking if one considers the prevalence rates are double that found in men.

Stewart et al. (2002) summarized the empirical literature and suggested that women appear to develop SUD subsequent to PTSD, while men appear more likely to develop PTSD subsequent to SUD, possibly reflecting impulsive or risky behaviors increasing their level of risk for exposure to PTE. In general, they suggest that "In mental health treatment settings geared for SUDs or trauma related problems, approximately half of the men and one-third of the women will evidence this dual diagnosis" (p. 235).

Comorbidity research also has examined gender differences in medical or health-related outcomes for PTSD clients. In contrast to the general population, recent reviews indicate that male and female trauma victims show few differences in number or severity of physical symptoms (Brand, 2003; Kimerling, Clum, McQuery, & Schnurr, 2002). It should be noted, however, that much of the comorbidity research does not include control groups, has been conducted on males, and relies on retrospective reports of symptom onset (increasing susceptibility to biased reporting).

While research suggests that there are gender differences in the PTSD symptom constellation, it is not entirely clear yet if women necessarily fare "worse." Davis and Breslau (1998) reported that women experience PTSD symptoms for longer than men. Similarly, the Detroit Area Survey (DAS) (Breslau et al., 1998) concluded that women suffered from PTSD for approximately 4 years compared to men who remitted after about one year. Freedman et al. (2002) also found that 10 of 24 men (42%) and 18 of 29 women (62%) who met PTSD at one month no longer met CAPS PTSD criteria at a 4-month follow-up, indicating a trend for faster recovery among women. Future research with larger samples and longer follow-up periods is called for.

With regard to symptoms/severity of PTSD, Pimlott-Kubiak and Cortina (2003) found that women were not more likely to score higher than men on continuous measures of PTSD. In their sample of MVA survivors, Freedman et al. (2002) reported that male and female victims had similar symptom expression: men's and women's scores on the Clinical Administered PTSD Scale, the Impact of Events Scale, and the Beck Depression Inventory showed that no gender differences remained statistically significant after taking into account multiple comparisons.

Brady and Back (2002) suggested that gender differences might be evident in the PTSD Clusters. For instance, they postulated that men might evidence more Cluster D symptoms (i.e., irritability, angry outbursts) and women might report higher rates of Cluster B (i.e., re-experiencing) or Cluster C (i.e., avoidance/numbing) symptoms (e.g., see Davis & Breslau, 1998). Considerable research confirms that men and women respond differently to trauma exposures, typically described as internalizing (e.g., self-harm, depression) versus externalizing (e.g., anger, antisocial personality disorder) symptoms or disorders. Further research is necessary to examine gender differences in symptom expression and chronicity, both important issues for assessment and treatment.

The Psychometric Assessment of PTSD in Women

As previously discussed, PTSD has a brief history (introduced in DSM-III, American Psychiatric Association, 1980), and the first measure to assess the prevalence in the general population followed shortly thereafter (Diagnostic Interview Schedule, Robins et al., 1981). Litz et al. (2002) commented on the proliferation of PTSD assessment instruments in the 1990s. Limitations of such rapid development of assessment measures have been, as mentioned previously, the inadequate norms for litigating or compensation-seeking samples, and germane to the current discussion, gender-based normative data. Compared to the explosion of prevalence data reviewed in this chapter, there has been relatively less work on the psychometric assessment and diagnosis of PTSD in women (for recent reviews, see Cloitre, Koenen, Gratz, & Jakupcak, 2002; Cusack et al., 2002).

Assessment of PTSD has included measures intended to diagnose PTSD using interview schedules such as the Structured Clinical Interview for DSM (SCID; Spitzer et al., 1989) and the Diagnostic Interview Schedule (DIS; Robins et al., 1981). In addition, several self-report measures to assess PTSD are available, including the Minnesota Multiphasic Personality Inventory (MMPI; Keane, Mallaoy, & Fairbank, 1984). Methods for evaluating the severity of symptoms have emerged, including the Impact of Events Scale (IES; Horowitz, Wilner, & Alvarez, 1979) and measures that quantify symptom severity and allow for diagnosis (e.g., PTSD Symptom Scale-Interview, PSS-I/PSS-SR; Foa, Riggs, Dancu, & Rothbaum, 1993). Often, these tools don't address Criterion A (i.e., exposure to a trauma; e.g., PSS-I/PSS-SR); as such, more recently, tools to screen for traumatic experiences have emerged (Stressful Life Events Questionnaire, SLESQ; Goodman, Corcoran, Turner, Yuan, & Green, 1998).

The Importance of Using Behaviorally Specific Assessment Methods

In a treatment-seeking sample of battered women ($N = 43$), Weaver (1998) compared two methods of screening for physical and sexual assaults. Using the PTSD module from the SCID (Spitzer, Williams, & Gibbon, 1986, cited in Weaver, 1998), respondents were asked "Have you ever had an experience that was really frightening or traumatic, like having your life threatened, seeing someone dead or badly hurt, or having your house burn down?" (Spitzer et al., 1986, p. 20, cited in Weaver, 1998); women were asked to list all of their life experiences they felt met the criteria. A second assessment relied on behaviorally specific questions (e.g., "Has a man or boy ever made you have sex by *using force* or threatening to harm you or someone close to you? Just so there is no mistake, by sex we mean putting a penis in your vagina"). Respondents were invited to describe as many as nine experiences from childhood, six different experiences from their adolescence, and five from their adulthood. In response to the single SCID question, women reported a total of 71 traumas. A comparison of the mean number of CSA, childhood physical abuse, adult rape, and adult physical battery experiences indicated that the behaviorally specific assessment methodology identified significantly more childhood sexual abuse ($n = 23, 53\%$; $n = 3, 7\%$, respectively) and childhood physical abuse ($n = 4, 9\%$; $n = 32, 74\%$) than the SCID. There was also a trend for the SCID to miss adult rape ($t\,(72) = 1.88$, $p = .067$), while there was a nonsignificant difference for adult physical battery ($t\,(83) = 1.48$, $p = .14$). Weaver (1998) concluded the results demonstrated that the context of an assessment might influence the nature of traumas reported and serves as a reminder of the "importance of detailed and separate assessment of traumatic life events in conjunction with assessment of diagnostic symptomatology" (p. 184). The importance of behaviorally specific questions is widely recognized in the child abuse, rape, partner abuse, and trauma literatures (for a discussion of interview construction, see Johnson, 1998).

Assessment of Potentially Traumatic Events—Criterion A

The diagnosis of PTSD requires detailed assessment of a PTE (Criterion A1). The DSM-IV-TR (American Psychiatric Association, 2000), although substantially improved over prior volumes, still is lacking in certain respects (for a review, see Litz et al., 2002). Of particular relevance to assessments with women is the ambiguous definition of a PTE provided in the DSM-IV: "an event that involves actual or threatened death or serious injury, or other threat to one's physical integrity; or witnessing (a similar event)" (American Psychiatric Association, 2000, p. 463). The necessity of actual or threatened physical harm is problematic because some PTE, such as some cases of CSA, might not satisfy these criteria although they might give rise to emotional distress that is symptomatically identical to PTSD.

Given that many of the instruments developed to evaluate exposure to potentially traumatizing events are relatively new, psychometric data is limited, generally (Litz et al., 2002) and for women, specifically (Cusack et al., 2002). Moreover, the strategies to evaluate the validity and reliability of these measures are necessarily unique (see Litz et al., 2002). Based on their review of measures available to assess exposure to PTE, Cusack et al. (2002) recommended that the

Traumatic Assessment for Adults (TAA; Resnick, Best, Kilpatrick, Freedy, & Falsetti, 1993), the Life Stressor Checklist (LSC; Wolfe & Kimerling, 1997), and the Trauma History Questionnaire (THQ; Green, 1996) are preferable for use with women.

Beyond the use of specific psychometric assessment techniques, one must consider the emotional response of the woman exposed to specific traumas and how it might realistically differ because of the social and physical characteristics of female gender. "Threat to physical integrity" is a particularly vague concept. Thus, given women's smaller stature and increased risk of physical injury during assaults, it is worthwhile questioning more closely a female claimant's subjective perception of risk of physical injury, even under circumstances when the resulting physical injury was nonexistent or minor. Given society's long-standing differential attitudes about sexual experiences of men and women (e.g., valuing virginity in women more so than in men, devaluing women who are more sexually experienced), women who have experienced sexual victimization need to be questioned concerning their perception of permanent harm accrued by involuntary sexual experiences. Such perceived harm may be greater in religious or ethnic subcultures that place a special premium on female virginity. Similarly, in most cultures, women are valued at least partially on their physical attractiveness. Thus, disfiguring scars may pose a differential threat to women's physical integrity in comparison to men.

PTSD Assessment Instruments—Interviews

Diagnostic Interview Schedule (DIS)
Designed for use by trained lay interviewers, the original Diagnostic Interview Schedule (DIS; Robins et al., 1981) assessed just two categories of PTE—lifetime military service and physical assault within the six months preceding the interview. Some of these weaknesses were addressed in the revised DIS-R (Robins, Helzer, Cottler, & Golding, 1989); however, the PTE still evaluates exposure using broad questions (e.g., "A few people have terrible experiences that most people never go through—things like being attacked, being in a fire or flood or bad traffic accident") rather than using behavioral anchors, which, as discussed above, are essential to obtaining an accurate appraisal of exposure to PTE. Authorities caution that the instrument still has some important limitations, some of which have particular relevance to assessments with women.

Resnick, Falsetti, Kilpatrick, and Freedy (1996) identified the following problems with the DIS: (1) the preface suggests that PTE are rare, which is problematic given the statement's factual inaccuracy and also because it might reduce reporting; and (2) the measure fails to use behaviorally specific questions to assess sexual assaults, which likely results in large underestimates of the prevalence of such experiences. The DIS might have utility for confirming a diagnosis of PTSD, but its utility as a screening interview is limited (Litz et al., 2002) and it is not a particularly sensitive measure for use with women (Cusack et al., 2002).

Structured Clinical Interview for DSM-IV (SCID-PTSD Module)

An advantage of the Structured Clinical Interview for DSM-IV (SCID-IV, SCID-IV/P—First, Spitzer, Gibbon, & Williams, 1995, 1996) is that it is particularly useful for evaluating comorbidity because the module comprises one component of the SCID, which was designed to assess most mental disorders. Symptom evaluation is based on the "worst" event, which might inadvertently contribute to apparent gender differences in prevalence rates (e.g., due to the high prevalence of sexual assaults among females, a longer course of PTSD in some women). Resnick et al. (1996) further proposed that reference to the worst PTE might limit the assessor's ability to develop an appreciation of how multiple traumas are reflected in the development and course of PTSD. Further, as with the DIS-R, a failure to normalize exposure to PTE (i.e., preface the assessment with a comment about the ubiquity of trauma) and to use behaviorally specific questions to assess trauma exposure are important limitations. Cusack et al. (2002) recommended that the SCID should be used in conjunction with a Criterion A measure. In addition, the utility of the SCID is somewhat limited in that a trained clinician must administer it.

Clinician Administered PTSD Scale (CAPS)

The CAPS (Blake et al., 1990, 1995) is a structured interview that assesses the 17 DSM-IV symptoms and severity. As indicated by the title, it was intended for use by mental health professionals, but there is some evidence that it may be used by other trained interviewers (Blake et al., 1995). The CAPS has several compelling strengths and is considered a useful measure for assessing women (Cusack et al., 2002). It assesses multiple events, uses behavioral anchors, and has excellent validity and reliability in diverse samples of men and women (e.g., schizophrenic women, Gearon, Bellack, & Tenhula, 2004; female victims of civilian traumas, MVA survivors, Weathers, Keane, & Davidson, 2001 (Keane et al., 1995). This measure's excellent psychometric properties have been demonstrated in sophisticated studies (e.g., Weathers, et al., 2001) and recently were documented in an extensive review of a decade of research and more than 200 studies (e.g., Weathers et al., 2001). Perhaps one of this measure's few limitations is that it is sometimes considered lengthy and cumbersome (see Foa & Tolin, 2000; Weathers et al., 2001 for a discussion), though it is "often referred to as the 'gold standard' measure for PTSD" (Foa & Tolin, 2000, p. 182).

Composite International Diagnostic Interview (CIDI)
The CIDI (WHO, 1993) contains a PTSD module similar to the DIS; as such, many of the limitations of the DIS apply to the CIDI, as well. In their extensive review of psychometric assessment of PTSD in women, Cusack et al. (2002) concluded that the CIDI should not be used to screen for PTSD in women and would be appropriate only if used in conjunction with other measures, given the high rate of false negatives. They recommended further validation research because of the instrument's promise resulting from its development and validation with multicultural samples.

PTSD Symptom Scale (PSS-I/PSS-SR)
The PTSD Symptom Scale is available as a semistructured interview (PSS-I; Foa, Riggs, Dancu, & Rothbaum, 1993) and a self-report version (PSS-SR; Foa et al., 1993) to assess frequency and severity of PTSD symptoms over the two weeks prior to the assessment. Both contain 17 items that correspond to the 17 DSM-III-R diagnostic criteria and the scoring is identical on the self-report and interview. Trained lay assessors administer the semistructured interview version. The authors assert that advantages of the PSS include the fact that in contrast to measures such as the SCID or CAPS, it is brief to administer (20–30 minutes) and interviewers can be trained to use the PSS-I in 2 to 3 hours (e.g., see Foa & Tolin, 2000). Foa and Tolin (2000) recommended the PSS-I as a suitable alternative to the CAPS. Cusack et al. (2002) noted that despite the instrument's many strengths (e.g., psychometric properties, provides dichotomous and continuous scores, validated with rape victims and general clinical samples of women) it assesses symptoms over the prior 2 weeks, contrary to PTSD criteria (at least one month), and it also does not allow for lifetime diagnoses and limits the assessment to one index trauma.

The PSS has been validated with victims of rape and nonsexual assault (e.g., Foa, Riggs, Dancu, & Rothbaum, 1993; Saunders, Arata, & Kilpatrick, 1990). In a sample of primarily African American (70.7%) women who had been assaulted within 2 weeks of the initial assessment (46 rape victims and 72 nonsexual assault victims—excluding women assaulted by family members or partners) Foa et al. (1993) studied the internal consistency, test-retest reliability, inter-rater reliability, and concurrent and convergent validity of the PSS-I and PSS-SR, and reported adequate to good results on each domain. Convergent validity of both the PSS-I and PSS-SR was tested by comparing diagnostic agreement with the SCID in 64 women. According to the SCID, 16 of the 64 women had a diagnosis of PTSD, and 14 of those women also were diagnosed with PTSD by the PSS-I (sensitivity = 88%, specificity = 96%, positive predictive power = 88%, negative predictive power = 96%). The PSS-SR also demonstrated good convergent validity, though as the authors acknowledged, it is a more conservative measure with a fairly high false negative rate (38%). When a brief interview is needed or if the assessor is interested in one event, Cusack et al. (2002) recommend the PSS-I for use with women.

Self Report Measures—Not Corresponding to DSM Criteria

Impact of Events Scale (IES)

The IES (Horowitz et al., 1979) is a 15-item self-report measure intended to assess posttraumatic *symptoms* of intrusion and avoidance (i.e., not PTSD diagnosis). The revised version (IES-R; Weiss & Marmar, 1997) added 7 items to evaluate hyperarousal; however, it still assesses just 14 of the 17 PTSD symptoms. Neither version is suitable for diagnosing PTSD; the IES is useful as a screen or to monitor treatment progress. The scale has been validated with diverse samples including male and female assault victims, combat survivors, female sexual assault survivors, and women at risk for breast cancer. Both versions of the scale have adequate psychometric properties (see Cusack et al., 2002; Joseph, 2000). Although some studies have reported that women receive significantly higher scores than men (particularly on the IES intrusion scale), a recent meta-analysis of 66 studies indicated that gender, age, and culture did not contribute significantly to regression models (Sundin & Horowitz, 2003). In contrast, results indicated that type of event and time elapsed since the event accounted for a substantial proportion of the variance in IES intrusion (total $R^2 = .29$) and IES avoidance (total $R^2 = .22$) (Sundin & Horowitz, 2003). As Sundin and Horowitz acknowledged, however, there is still a substantial proportion of variance unaccounted for by the variables considered in the study.

The IES has the advantage of measuring the client's *subjective* psychological distress associated with the PTE. We see this as particularly important for assessments with female clients, and an important avenue of future research to clarify gender differences (also see Resick, 1993). However, the IES has been criticized for potentially measuring the memorability of an event or the cognitive accessibility of the "stressor" rather than psychopathology (e.g., Lees-Haley, Price, & Williams, 2001) and because it contains just one item to assess numbing (Foa, Cashman, Jaycox, & Perry, 1997).

Self Report Measures—Corresponding to DSM Criteria

The Posttraumatic Stress Diagnostic Scale (PDS)

The PDS (Foa et al., 1997) is a self-report measure of PTSD (DSM-IV); it also assesses Criterion A. None of the previously examined self-report measures correspond to DSM criteria and on their own cannot be used as diagnostic instruments; the PDS was developed to rectify this gap in the assessment literature (Foa et al., 1997). The PDS was validated in a community sample of primarily Caucasian (65%) or African American (31%) men (55%) and women (45%) who had diverse trauma histories (Foa et al., 1997). Using the SCID-PTSD module (Spitzer et al., 1990) as the criterion against which the PDS was evaluated, convergent validity was satisfactory (kappa = .65; sensitivity = .89, specificity = .75). Test-retest reliability was measured over 2- to 3-week retest intervals, with satisfactory results on all four scales (α = .83 for total symptom severity).

PTSD Checklist (PCL-C)

The PTSD Checklist-Civilian Version (PCL-C; Weathers, Litz, Herman, Huska, & Keane, 1991; Weathers & Ford, 1996) is a 17-item measure of PTSD originally based on DSM-III-R and revised to correspond to the three DSM-IV symptom clusters (Criteria B, C, and D). The PCL has been used with breast cancer survivors, MVA survivors, parents of pediatric cancer patients, cancer patients, and veterans, and has been found to have excellent reliability and validity with men and women (e.g., Cusack et al., 2002; Dobie, Kivlahan, & Maynard, 2002). The PCL-M is the military version and also has been found to be useful with women. Dobie et al. (2002) reported that the PCL performed well as a screening measure for PTSD in a sample (n = 282) of female Veterans Affairs patients. Using the CAPS as the gold standard for comparisons, the area under the Receiver Operating Curve (ROC) was 0.86 (sensitivity = .79, specificity = .79), demonstrating very good agreement between the two measures.

Minnesota Multiphasic Personality Inventory-2 (MMPI-2)

The Keane MMPI-PTSD Scale (PK) has 49 items and was developed to assess PTSD in combat veterans (Keane, Malloy, & Fairbank, 1984). Perrin, Van Hasselt, Basilio, and Hersen (1996) studied the validity of the Keane scale in a sample of 66 primarily Caucasian (73%) battered women referred to an outpatient Interpersonal Violence Program in Florida. Consistent with their hypothesis, battered women diagnosed with PTSD (n = 48) on the MMPI scale had significantly higher scores on the three primary measures of PTSD: the IES intrusion (t (60) = 5.1, p = .0001) and avoidance subscales (t (59) = 5.2, p = .0001) and the SCL-90-R CR PTSD subscale (t (60) = 5.1, p = .0001), suggesting that the MMPI-PTSD scale has utility as a screening measure with abused women.

The MMPI scales for diagnosing acute and chronic PTSD in civilians do not appear to be influenced by gender (Gaston, Brunet, Koszycki, & Bradwejn, 1996), but assessors should consider that mental health professionals and forensic assessors have been cautioned that the PK scale has an unsatisfactory hit rate based on existing validation data (e.g., Gaston et al., 1996).

Caveat

It is important to recognize that a diagnosis of PTSD might be less critical than the degree of impairment experienced by the individual. The International Consensus Group on PTSD (Ballenger et al., 2000) recommended that clinicians consider partial PTSD (e.g., the individual fails to meet one criterion, most often avoidance), which can be associated with substantial impairment. The past decades have resulted in profound advancements in the assessment of PTSD; in particular, many measures have been developed. The challenge now is to validate these existing measures rather than developing more instruments (also see Cusack et al., 2002).

Summary and Closing Comments

The literature examining gender differences in the risk of PTSD is at a crossroads. To date, researchers have used gender as a crude sorting variable, but emerging research concerning biological and cognitive moderator variables are likely to increase our understanding of how individual differences influence posttraumatic distress. Our current rudimentary knowledge suggests several conclusions. Women face twice the risk of developing PTSD over their lifetime. However, simple prevalence rates should not be misinterpreted as confirmation that female gender is a risk factor or vulnerability for PTSD. The DSM-IV resulted in substantial changes to the assessment of PTSD, some of which (addition of Criterion A2) were meant to account for differences in the individual response to trauma exposure. However, to date there is no "gold standard" means for evaluating Criterion A1 (i.e., exposure to a PTE), and the ambiguity of Criterion A2 is problematic. More specific to gender issues, little attention has been given to the significance of Criterion A2 (i.e., the subjective experience of the victim), in particular how characteristics of female gender (greater risk for physical injury from assault, women's socially based different appraisals of the consequences of involuntary sexual experience) might affect posttraumatic emotional distress. A rapidly maturing empirical literature directed by firmly established theories likely will provide greater understanding of gender differences in PTSD.

Given the relative youth of this field, practitioners have a duty to ensure that they consider our limited empirical knowledge and the limits of available methodology, thus not rushing to judgment in any individual case. While on the surface it might seem a relatively minor issue to conclude that women (or minorities— see chapter 8) are more susceptible to PTSD or other posttraumatic emotional distress, such an assumption could have important and far-reaching implications both for the individual claimant and for these specific populations. Much as it would be inaccurate and reprehensible to conclude that educational achievement or criminal offending simply reflect group ethnic differences rather than social inequalities (e.g., poverty, child abuse), it is essential in the area of trauma to discover the unique factors about women or women's experiences that place them at greater risk for posttraumatic distress (also see Cusack et al., 2002, pp. 172–173).

To assert that gender differences in the likelihood of adaptive versus maladaptive responses to stress are due to an inherent vulnerability is to suggest that the "cause" of the susceptibility lies within the individual, potentially contributing to biased conclusions. In large part, that perspective relinquishes society from having to intervene responsibly to relieve social inequalities that might actually be contributing to apparent gender differences. It might also adversely impact the response of mental health professionals to female claimants or patients. As such, we recommend further consideration of methodological issues that currently limit our understanding of the meaning of gender for adaptation to PTE, and consideration of social status differences (e.g., daily hassles) and dynamic risk factors (i.e., that are changeable, amenable to intervention) that the extant literature suggests might account for gender differences in posttraumatic response. A better understanding of the factors that masquerade as gender differences may shed light on the etiology of PTSD (also see Seedat & Stein, 2000), the nature and course of the disorder (Cloitre, Koenen, Gratz, & Jakupcak, 2002) and useful treatment approaches.

7

Ethnocultural Minorities

> Life's pain and tragedy is not evenly, randomly, or fairly distributed over the population but falls disproportionately on a concentrated segment which is beset by increased risk of all forms of ill fortune and personal agony, both of which are compounded by stigma.
>
> —Rosenheck (2002)

Trauma can affect individuals' psychological well-being, independent of ethnicity, race, or cultural affiliation. Marsella, Friedman, Gerrity, and Scurfield (1996; also see Norris, Murphy, Baker, & Perilla, 2003) concluded that PTSD occurs in a considerable range of non-Western cultures. PTSD appears to be a valid mental health condition even in nonindustrialized, hunter-gatherer cultures that are isolated from Western media influences (e.g., Kalahari Bushmen; McCall & Resick, 2003). That said, ethnocultural differences abound with respect to the nature of traumatic stressors encountered and in clinical presentation, coping strategies, and barriers to the receipt of treatment. Rosenheck's (2002) observation above should remind us to routinely consider the unique impact of trauma on the lives of minority group members, who frequently lack social influence, economic power, and often confront stereotypes and discrimination. While exposure to potentially traumatic events (PTE) is common in our society, only a minority of people exposed to such events develop PTSD or related emotional disorders (see chapters 3 and 5). Foa and Street (2001) summarized the state of the literature nicely: "Individuals differ in their ability to recover from a traumatic experience, and traumas differ in their likelihood to produce PTSD" (p. 29). This chapter considers how ethnicity, culture, or race (referred to as ethnocultural status or affiliation) impacts uniquely on the risk of PTSD.

The chapter begins with a brief discussion of the necessity of considering ethnocultural status in mental health assessments and the limitations of our current knowledge. We then review the impact of ethnocultural affiliation on the risk of exposure to PTE and the lifetime prevalence and conditional risk of PTSD in non-White, non Euro-American groups. This is followed by a discussion of how ethnocultural status is reflected in the expression of psychological injuries or symptoms and subsequent coping and help-seeking responses. We also provide a brief examination of cross-cultural assessment issues and ethics. The chapter closes with a discussion of current controversies and recommendations regarding future directions in the field.

Importance of Considering Ethnocultural Identity

How many "Cablinasians" do you know? Tiger Woods coined the term after he won the Masters Golf Tournament in 1997. It was "Tigerspeak" for Caucasian-Black-Indian-Asian; Woods explained that his father is half Black, one-quarter American Indian, and one-quarter White, and his mother is half Thai, half Chinese (Castro, 2003). The 2000 Census in the United States was the first to allow people like Tiger to select multiple races, and results show that he is one of many Americans embracing their diverse heritage (Population Reference Bureau, 2001). In contemporary society, diversity may be more the rule than the exception. It is anticipated that over the next 25 years, 40% of adults and 48% of children in the United States will be from ethnic "minority" groups (U.S. Census Bureau, 2001).

Many other nations also are experiencing similarly dramatic transformations in the cultural compositions of their populations. Immigration accounts for more than 50% of Canada's population growth. Visible minorities currently comprise 10% of Canada's population, and it is predicted that by 2016, one in five Canadians will be a visible minority (Statistics Canada Census, 2001a). Australia's multicultural society also is increasing at an accelerating pace. In 1947, virtually the entire population of Australia (98%) had been born in Australia or another English-speaking nation. This had declined to 86% by 1996, and diversity is expected to continue to flourish as a result of recent major immigration policy changes (Hugo, 2003). The Statistical Office of the European Communities (Eurostat, 2003) reported that in 2002, more than three-quarters of the population increase in the European Union (including Belgium, Germany, Greece, Spain, France, Ireland, Italy, Luxembourg, the Netherlands, Austria, Portugal, and Finland) came from cross-border migration.

Given the pluralistic nature of many countries' populations, it behooves mental health professionals to be aware of, and sensitive to, cultural mores and differences relevant to their clients (Sue, Bingham, Porche-Burke, & Vasquez, 1999). While recognizing the influence of cultural affiliation on mental health, the U.S. surgeon general's report on mental health (U.S. Department of Health and Human

Services, 2001) cautioned that sweeping statements about cultural characteristics might invite stereotyping of individuals based on physical appearance or reported cultural affiliation. There is usually more diversity within ethnocultural groups than there is between groups, for example, in terms of education, income, attitudes, and beliefs (see Marsella et al., 1996). Ethnocultural affiliations should *not* be treated as a stereotype applied broadly to individual members of a group (Draguns & Takana-Matsumi, 2003). While the focus of this chapter is on non-White and non–Anglo-American individuals, we encourage mental health professionals to give adequate consideration to religious beliefs, ethnicity/race, and cultural heritage in all assessments. Service providers should assess, in collaboration with the client, the relevance of cultural status/affiliation for the individual and the extent of acculturation to the predominant culture (Manson, 1996; Weaver, 1998; for models of culturally competent psychotherapy, see Kirmayer, Groleau, Guzder, Blake, & Jarvis, 2003; Lo & Fung, 2003). An appreciation of the claimant's subjective experience of trauma doubtless will reflect these experiences, traditions, and beliefs.

Limitations of Knowledge about PTSD and Minority Groups

A number of methodological hurdles complicate the study of cross-cultural issues in trauma victims (Sattler et al., 2002). First, there is a lack of large, rigorous epidemiological (Norris et al., 2003; Sue, 2002) and longitudinal studies with minority groups (Lee, Lei, & Sue, 2001). As Lee et al. (2001) noted, longitudinal and cross-sectional studies are important for revealing intergenerational effects of trauma exposure and to explore developmental issues. Second, although minority groups are growing in many industrialized nations, individual minority groups still often represent a small proportion of the population. Because it is often difficult to obtain sufficient and representative samples, many studies rely on convenience samples (e.g., ethnic organizations, snowball sampling); in particular, we have little research examining subgroups of ethnic minorities (Lee et al., 2001). Third, as discussed below in greater detail, ethnocultural groups are extremely heterogeneous (Sue, 2002) and they are constantly evolving (Lee et al., 2001), for instance, due to changes in immigration and group acculturation; study samples rarely reflect this diversity. Fourth, it is not yet entirely clear how well many existing assessment instruments translate for cross-cultural use (e.g., Lee et al., 2001; Manson, 1996). Fifth, cross-cultural differences in response styles, values, and self-disclosure (Lee et al., 2001), as well as "cognitive processes, social structure and person-environment" (Manson, 1996, pp. 239–240) have not been adequately addressed in the literature.

At the most basic level, there is a lack of research examining anything but the most rudimentary descriptive indices of ethnicity or culture, making any conclusions about the relationship of ethnicity to PTSD tentative, at best. To clarify, there is increasing recognition of the limitations of large descriptive categories such as "Asian" or "Hispanic" for classifying cultural affiliation (e.g., Marsella et al., 1996; Weaver, 1998). As illustrated by Tiger Woods's comment above, many individuals identify with multiple ethnocultural groups, which tend not to be reported or considered when designating group status in trauma-related research. Broad cultural categories likely exaggerate similarities and overlook variabilities within groups. For instance, the label "African American" might be applied to Haitian, Black Cuban, Jamaican, or Ethiopian subjects, not to mention Black Americans whose families have lived in the United States for many generations. The category "Asian/Pacific Islander" would treat as culturally identical a Punjabi Sikh immigrant farmworker, a Chinese immigrant entrepreneur from Hong Kong, and a fifth-generation Chinese university student. Categorizing individuals by place of birth or broad racial characteristics also seriously restricts the validity of the conclusions we can draw from the research (Marsella et al., 1996).

Studying the impact of culture on mental health requires careful *a priori* definitions of the boundaries of each ethnocultural group, as well as the measurement of defining group characteristics (e.g., with a questionnaire assessing beliefs, attitudes, identity, traditions, etc.). In their review of ethnocultural aspects of PTSD, Marsella et al. (1996) asserted that much of the extant literature had actually failed to truly control for ethnocultural factors.

Culture as defined by Marsella (1998) refers to "shared learned behavior which is transmitted from one generation to another to promote individual and group adjustment and adaptation. Culture is represented externally as artifacts, roles, and institutions, and is represented internally as values, beliefs, attitudes, cognitive styles, epistemologies, and consciousness patterns" (p. 10). As the term suggests, cultural affiliation refers to a shared set of norms and traditions; it is reflected in our cultural identity, and our use of an identified group to whom we look for standards of behavior (Cooper & Denner, 1998).

A competent assessment with a person who is an immigrant or an individual from a minority group should also consider the extent to which the claimant has been acculturated. The term "acculturation" originated in anthropology and refers to changes in cultural patterns associated with contact between members of different cultural groups (Salant & Lauderdale, 2003). To determine accurately an individual's cultural affiliation requires an assessment of these multiple, overlapping, and complex constructs. To our knowledge, few studies of trauma exposure and PTSD to date have assessed respondents' degree of acculturation, despite the existence of several such measures (see Marsella, 1998; Salant & Lauderdale, 2003).

Cross-cultural studies in trauma also have failed to control for other potential sources of variance. Marsella et al. (1996) critiqued the extant literature for inattention to variations in trauma exposure, education, social class, residence, and income; factors that are likely to vary as greatly within cultural groups as they do between them. Despite these serious limitations, the literature examining trauma exposure and PTSD in minority populations has expanded rapidly in recent years (e.g., Marsella et al., 1996).

Trauma Exposure among Minorities

Minorities Are More Likely to Be At Risk Due to Marginalization

Of all the mental disorders in the DSM-IV-TR (American Psychiatric Association, 2000), PTSD probably is most influenced by cultural and social influences. Social dominance theory asserts that racism, classism, and patriarchy reflect a common social hierarchy that is found in many cultures (Sidanius & Pratto, 1999). According to this conceptualization, groups without access to prestige and valued resources are more likely to be oppressed and exposed to victimization (e.g., women, Aboriginals, African Americans, immigrants, refugees, the homeless). People who belong to minority groups are at increased risk for trauma exposure due to lower social status and economic vulnerability (e.g., Shupe, Cortina, Ramos, Fitzgerald, & Salisbury, 2002). Worldwide, people of certain groups are disproportionately represented among refugees, concentration camp survivors, the homeless, incarcerated, and impoverished—people who are or have been at heightened risk of experiencing trauma.

People of color comprise the vast majority of refugees and report high rates of exposure to preimmigration trauma such as torture and forced relocation (e.g., Porter & Haslam, 2001). The proportion of refugees subjected to torture is estimated to be between 5% and 30% (Burnett & Peel, 2001). Although many refugees adapt well, preimmigration stressors often are exacerbated by relocation stressors (e.g., loss of educational credentials), separation from social supports, the conditions inherent in refugee camps (e.g., overcrowding), and the socioeconomic and acculturative stressors encountered upon resettling in a new country (e.g., racism, separation from loved ones) (Porter & Haslam, 2001).

Theories of marginalization and social dominance also find support in analytic investigations of poverty, homelessness, and reported rates of incarceration, which demonstrate that those conditions affect minorities to a disproportionate extent in comparison to people of Anglo-American heritage. Phelan and Link's (1999) review of homelessness based on three large American surveys and a review of 18 other published studies conducted in the United States indicated that 50–66% of currently homeless individuals were minorities and 20% of previously homeless individuals were racial/ethnic minorities. The U.S. surgeon general (U.S. Department of Health and Human Services, 2001) reported that African Americans comprise 40% of the homeless, despite being only 12% of the U.S. population. Rosenheck (2002) asserted, "It is not news that homelessness affects minorities, especially African Americans, more than Whites, any more than it is news that African Americans are so much more likely than Whites to be in prison (7% of Black males vs. 1% of White males), or to live in poverty (over 20% of Blacks and less than 10% of Whites)" (p. 1005). In the United States, Latino men are nearly four times more likely than White men to be imprisoned at some point during their lifetimes (U.S. Department of Health and Human Services, 2001). The surgeon general further noted that poverty rates are 14% for Cuban Americans, 31% for Puerto Ricans, and 27% for Mexican Americans, compared to 13.5% of all Americans.

Although minorities are overrepresented in disenfranchised groups, whether they experience a disproportionate number of PTE is still an empirical question. Doubtless, experiences such as homelessness, poverty (e.g., living in low-income neighborhoods), and incarceration are associated with high rates of traumatic experiences (e.g., Wenzel, Leake, & Gelberg, 2001). However, drawing conclusions about minority groups fails to take into account substantial within-group heterogeneity. Moreover, these issues do not impact all ethnic minority groups equally, making it difficult to draw conclusions about the significance of "minority" status or being "non-White" as a risk factor for trauma exposure (see Shupe et al., 2002). Data from the U.S. surgeon general (U.S. Department of Health and Human Services, 2001) clarifies our point: African Americans were noted to be at significantly greater risk of being homeless than non-Hispanic Whites. In comparison, Asian American/Pacific Islanders (AA/PI) and Hispanics were not disproportionately represented among the homeless, but they comprised a large proportion of refugees. In comparison, Hispanics reportedly have high rates of poverty, but AA/PI do not (U.S. Department of Health and Human Services, 2001; also see Tjaden & Thoennes, 2000).

Risk of Trauma Exposure Among Minorities

A small number of studies have examined the differential risk of trauma exposure among diverse ethnic groups using large, representative samples of the general population. Among 1,000 adults in four southern U.S. metropolitan cities damaged by Hurricane Hugo, Norris (1992) found that African American respondents (60.2%) were less likely to report a lifetime history of exposure to PTE than Caucasian respondents (67.6%). Significantly more White than Black respondents reported prior physical assaults (18.4% vs. 11.6%), exposure to disasters (21.8% vs. 4.6%), hazards (23.6% vs. 6.8%), and tragic deaths (36.3% vs. 24.1%). Rates were not significantly different between Whites and Blacks for exposure to combat, robberies, and motor vehicle accidents (MVAs). Notably, with the exception of African Americans reporting a higher rate of MVAs than Whites in the prior 12 months, no significant ethnic differences were reported for past-year traumas. It should be recalled that Norris's sample was not random; however, she noted that it was quite heterogeneous and approximated the cultural, gender, and age composition of the southeastern United States.

In a random sample of young adults (21–30 years of age) from southeast Michigan, Breslau, Davis, Andreski, and Peterson (1991) reported no ethnic differences at baseline, but found that African Americans had a higher rate of PTE at the three-year follow-up. In the 1996 Detroit Area Survey (DAS, Breslau, Kessler, & Chilcoat, 1998) non-Whites had double the risk of PTE that Whites had over their lifetime. In that community survey, non-Whites were not only at greater risk of being victims of physical violence, but also were more likely to report knowing someone who had suffered violence; controlling for socioeconomic differences or location of residence did not eliminate ethnic differences (Breslau et al., 1998).

National victimization surveys also can provide substantial insight into this issue. The National Violence Against Women Survey in the United States (NVAWS, Tjaden & Thoennes, 2000) found that ethnic minority men and women were no more likely than White men and women to be the victims of rape, physical assault, or stalking. However, disaggregating the five ethnic minority groups resulted in an interesting pattern of ethnocultural differences. African American women were no more likely to report violent victimization histories than White women. In stark contrast, the rate of rape among American Indian/Alaska Native women (34.1%) was nearly double that reported by White (17.7%) or African American women (18.8%) (mixed race = 24.4%; Asian/Pacific Islander = 6.8%). The proportion of American Indian/Alaska Native women reporting physical assault (61.4%) and stalking (17.0%) also was strikingly higher than that reported by women of the other ethnic groups. These data suggest that various minorities might be at differential risk for specific forms of PTE. This study did not take into account neighborhood or socioeconomic status differences.

Some authors have hypothesized that specific ethnocultural groups might face a greater risk of some forms of trauma. For example, Black American males 18–24 years of age have a homicide risk nearly 17 times their representation in the general population (Pallone & Hennessy, 2000). Considerable evidence suggests that minorities also are at unique risk of violence as a result of race-hate crimes in many countries (e.g., Clancy, Hough, Aust, & Kershaw, 2001; Federal Bureau of Investigation, 2002; Roberts, 1995). It also has been hypothesized that women of color might face a "double jeopardy" for sexual harassment; however, this has received minimal support in the literature (Cortina, Swan, Fitzgerald, & Waldo, 1998). Large surveys (e.g., U.S. Meritor System's Protection Board, 1988) have failed to demonstrate that non-White women were any more likely than White women to be sexually harassed. Shupe et al. (2002) found that Hispanic women reported less sexual harassment than non-Hispanic White women and that their risk of harassment *increased* as the minority women became more incorporated into the dominant culture. Cortina et al. (1998) asserted that no firm conclusions could be drawn about the interaction between ethnicity, gender, and harassment in academia and the workplace, and further proposed that the same limitations exist with regard to the sexual assault literature. Women of ethnic minorities might be at unique risk for contrapower harassment (i.e., Whites with less organizational power harassing minorities with more power).

Koss, Gidycz, and Wisniewski (1987) reported that while Native American women had greater exposure to sexual assault than White women, African American, Hispanic, and Asian women reported fewer sexual assaults than White women; their findings are consistent with the NVAW reviewed above (Tjaden & Thoennes, 2000). Also, there is little conclusive evidence that minorities are at unique risk of exposure to child abuse (e.g., Fluke, Yuan, Hedderson, & Curtis, 2003), intimate partner violence (e.g., Vogel & Marshall, 2001) or MVAs (e.g., Norris, 1992) once confounding psychosocial indicators are considered (e.g., socioeconomic status, neighborhood, substance abuse).

Research examining exposure to combat (Norris, 1992) and natural disasters (Webster, McDonald, Lewin, & Carr, 1995) suggests that ethnicity might be associated with the severity of PTE (e.g., dose) rather than the rate (i.e., prevalence or incidence) of exposure. For example, the National Vietnam Veterans Readjustment Study (NVVRS; Kulka et al., 1990) found that apparent cross-cultural differences in PTSD disappeared or were substantially reduced once differential war-zone exposure was controlled.

Summary—Is Ethnocultural Minority Status a Risk Factor for PTE?

As our opening quote reminds us, ethnicity is tightly and complexly interwoven with hardship and stigma. We leave the reader with a few essential points: (1) Ethnic minority status per se does not place individuals at greater risk for exposure to PTE (with the exception of specific forms of trauma such as race-hate crimes), but rather points to the influence of related risk factors and socioeconomic predictors of exposure such as immigrant or refugee status, neighborhood, substance abuse, poverty, and education—risks that impact differentially upon ethnic minorities who are dramatically overrepresented among marginalized individuals. In short, ethnicity is a risk marker, not a causal risk factor for exposure to PTE. (2) Exposure to specific traumas is not evenly distributed between ethnocultural groups. (3) Conflicting research findings with regard to the risk of exposure to discrete forms of trauma (e.g., sexual harassment) suggest that minority group affiliation might even serve a protective function in some cases. As Manson (1996) noted, "None of this argues against the importance of ethnicity and culture in regard to risk of PTSD. The field just has not thought critically about the matter or struggled much beyond a static conceptualization of either as independent variables to be accounted for in epidemiological and clinical study designs" (p. 241).

It is unlikely that minority status, or a relatively hollow term such as "non-White," will ever provide much insight into this issue. Future research with respect to PTE exposure should examine narrowly defined ethnocultural subgroups, as well as study the predictive utility of those demographic characteristics (e.g., socioeconomic status) typically confounded with ethnicity. Even then, the heterogeneity within groups is likely to make this a challenging research enterprise (see Sue, 2002).

Ethnoculural Identity and the Conditional Risk of PTSD

Some of the earliest examinations of ethnocultural differences in trauma recovery came from studies of Vietnam veterans. The NVVRS (Kulka et al., 1990; for a critique, see Ruef, Litz, & Schlenger, 2000) entailed a survey of 3,016 non–treatment-seeking Vietnam veterans (including 1,200 male veterans exposed to the war zone) and civilians. In order to ensure adequate statistical power to detect cultural differences, the authors oversampled ethnic minorities; marked ethnic differences in the prevalence of PTSD were reported. Among those who served in Vietnam, 20.6% of Black veterans and 27.9% of Hispanic veterans compared to 13.7% of White/other veterans were diagnosed with PTSD (all statistically significant differences). After adjusting for predisposing factors (e.g., economic disadvantage in family of origin, childhood behavior problems, drug abuse or dependence, and affective disorder), the differences between Black and Hispanic veterans disappeared, but individuals from the minority groups still were significantly more likely to be diagnosed with PTSD than White/other veterans (Kulka et al., 1990, 1991). Black and Hispanic veterans were more likely than White/other veterans to report having experienced high combat stress exposure (e.g., combat, abusive violence, and related conflicts, deprivation, loss of meaning and control, and prisoner of war status). After controlling for combat stress exposure, ethnic group differences disappeared or were substantially reduced; Hispanic veterans still had a higher rate of PTSD than both White/other and Black veterans. To summarize, controlling for confounding early life experience and combat exposure variables greatly reduced, but did not entirely extinguish, cultural differences in the NVVRS (Kulka et al., 1990).

The American Indian Vietnam Veterans Project (AIVVP, Beals et al., 2002) supplemented the NVVRS (Kulka et al., 1990), which had not been able to include a sufficient number of other ethnic minorities to provide enough power for certain statistical comparisons. In a sample of 487 Vietnam veterans assessed with the Structured Clinical Interview for DSM-IV (SCID), the prevalence of one-month and lifetime PTSD was higher among American Indian veterans than among White veterans. Regression analyses indicated that ethnicity was no longer a substantial risk factor once the authors accounted for war-zone stressors. These studies both demonstrate that the greater risk of PTSD in minority veterans was primarily a function of their greater exposure to trauma and point to the importance of a more detailed examination of trauma exposure.

As discussed previously, in some studies, affiliation with a traditional minority culture has actually been found to moderate the incidence of sexual harassment and to have no significant interaction with psychological distress. A random sample of 207 non-Hispanic White women and 124 Hispanic women employed in a northwestern U.S. organization were administered the Sexual Experiences Questionnaire (SEQ) as part of a sexual harassment education initiative (Shupe et al., 2002). To examine incidence rates, Shupe et al. (2002) compared respondents who had experienced at least one harassing behavior: 23% of Hispanic women with low affiliation to the dominant culture, compared to 61% of Hispanic women with high affiliation and 77% of non-Hispanic White women reported experiencing harassment during the previous 2 years. As sexual harassment experiences increased, women of all cultural affiliations reported worse psychological outcomes. The authors hypothesized that the collectivist Hispanic culture may involve coworkers watching out for one another or that Hispanic women were perceived as having little organizational power and, therefore, experienced less harassment. Alternatively, it may be that Hispanic women with low affiliation were less likely to report harassing experiences.

In a comprehensive review of predictors of PTSD following vehicular accidents, Douglas and Koch (2000) found little evidence that ethnic status was a substantial predictor of PTSD for MVA victims. However, they concluded there is some evidence to suggest that minority status among MVA victims might predict a higher level of PTSD symptoms (e.g., Norris, 1992).

The Epidemiologic Catchment Area (ECA) survey examined the prevalence of PTSD in five urban centers in the United States. Helzer, Robins, and McEvoy (1987) reported that ethnic minorities were not overrepresented among people satisfying PTSD criteria on the Diagnostic Interview Schedule. Using data from North Carolina residents in the ECA ($N = 2,985$, ages 18–95), Davidson, Hughes, Blazer, and George (1991) found that fewer White residents met diagnostic criteria for lifetime PTSD (1.02%) than non-White residents (1.69%), though the difference did not reach statistical significance. Norris (1992) similarly reported that according to her Traumatic Stress Schedule (Norris, 1990), African American (7.6%) and Caucasian (7.2%) respondents evidenced comparable rates of current PTSD. The proportion of respondents meeting current PTSD criteria who reported a lifetime history of exposure to potentially traumatic crimes (7.2%, 10.4%), hazards (5.1%, 6.9%), or accidents (8.2%, 9.2%) did not differ significantly between the groups (Norris, 1992).

The National Comorbidity Survey (NCS, $N = 5,877$; Kessler et al., 1994) examined trauma exposure among White, Black, and Hispanic Americans. Similar to Norris's (1992) findings and the ECA (Horwath, Johnson, & Hornig, 1993), there was no evidence of Black-White or Hispanic-White differences in anxiety disorders. Controlling for income and education did not alter the results. Kessler, Sonnega, Bromet, Hughes, and Nelson, (1995) reported that lifetime prevalence rates for PTSD (7.8%) did not differ by ethnicity once sociodemographic correlates of PTSD (sex, age, marital status) were controlled.

In the 1996 DAS (Breslau et al., 1998), Black subjects (14%) were reported to be twice as likely as White subjects to meet diagnostic criteria for PTSD; however, the statistical significance of the difference in the DAS was negated when the person's place of residence was controlled. People of different cultural affiliations who resided in the same neighborhoods exhibited similar rates of PTSD. Other studies similarly indicate that once exposure is controlled for, the rate of current and lifetime PTSD is relatively equivalent across different ethnocultural groups (e.g., Beals et al., 2002).

One of the few studies to look at the combined effect of culture and gender, Norris, Perilla, Ibanez, and Murphy (2001a) found both a sex main effect and a sex-by-cultural-group interaction (White, Black, and Mexican). Using data six months after Hurricanes Paulina ($N = 200$) and Andrew ($N = 270$), Norris et al. (2001a) assessed respondents with the Revised Civilian Mississippi Scale (RCMS). There was no statistical difference in the likelihood that a Black woman (23.2%) and a Black man (19.7%) would meet all criteria for PTSD. In comparison, White women (19.4%) and Mexican women (43.8%) were significantly more likely than their male counterparts (5.9% and 14.4%, respectively) to be diagnosed with PTSD. The authors concluded that the study provided strong evidence for their hypothesis that the traditional culture of Mexico would amplify sex differences. The study also provided tentative evidence that sex differences are attenuated among Blacks, who, the authors asserted, socialize females to be strong and resourceful.

Our review converges with other recent scholarly reviews to suggest that ethnic status has not been demonstrated to be a significant risk factor for PTSD (e.g., Ballenger et al., 2000; Brewin, Andrews, & Valentine, 2000; Douglas & Koch, 2000; Perilla, Norris, & Lavizzo, 2002). Following their meta-analysis of PTSD in trauma-exposed adults, Brewin et al. (2000) concluded, "Race (minority status) was one of the few demographic variables to be a weak predictor across all of the studies" (p. 754). Although the authors cautioned against drawing strong conclusions due to serious limitations in the study (e.g., minority status was coded dichotomously as White majority vs. non-White minority groups), they noted that several other studies have similarly failed to uncover evidence that minority status is a risk factor for PTSD once confounds (e.g., exposure, neighborhoods) were controlled.

To date, research indicates, "ethnic differences may interact with (Norris, 1992) or be attributable to (Breslau et al., 1991) other factors" (Halligan & Yehuda, 2000, p. 1). Disparities in the nature of the trauma exposure (e.g., extent of war combat or the level of risk associated with combat assignments; Beals et al., 2002), related socioeconomic characteristics (e.g., neighborhoods characterized by crime), and the influence of culture (e.g., collectivism vs. individualism, sex role socialization) have not been sufficiently studied to allow us to draw anything more than tentative conclusions about the conditional risk of PTSD among specific groups of non-White, non–Anglo-Americans. Sweeping statements about the differential risk of PTSD among "minorities" have been demonstrated to provide little useful information if one considers the unique findings that emerge when data are disaggregated.

Despite the relative lack of evidence to suggest that ethnocultural status influences trauma exposure and subsequent risk of PTSD, experts agree it is important for practicing clinicians and forensic assessors to consider the client's ethnocultural identity (Carlson & Dutton, 2003; Sue et al., 1999). Regardless of whether there are large demonstrable cross-cultural *group* variations, the clinician must consider the impact of race, ethnicity, and culture for the *individual* client (see DSM-IV, American Psychiatric Association, 2000). Cultural identity might have significance for the individual's history of prior traumas, reporting style, coping styles, help-seeking behavior, family and community resources, symptom expression, and clinicians' responses to the individual.

Assessment of Ethnocultural Minority Individuals

Professional Cross-Cultural Assessment Policies and Ethics

Evaluating individuals from non-White, non–Anglo-American backgrounds is likely to become the norm rather than the exception in North America and elsewhere, in the very near future. A select review of the ethical and professional standards guiding psychologists might be of particular interest to lawyers faced with the task of cross-examining expert witnesses in cases involving ethnoculturally diverse claimants.

The Canadian Code of Ethics for Psychologists (Canadian Psychological Association, 2000), the Ethical Principles of Psychologists and Code of Conduct of the American Psychological Association (American Psychological Association, 2002c), and the Australian Psychological Society Ethical Guidelines (Australian Psychological Society, 2003), for instance, articulate the ethical principles guiding both clinical practice and scientific research by psychologists. These guidelines speak directly to the conduct of cross-cultural assessments. For instance, Ethical Standard 9.02(b) of the American Psychological Association's Ethics Code requires psychologists to consider available evidence when choosing, administering, and evaluating test results in specific populations (e.g., gender, age, race, ethnicity, national origin, religion, language, and socioeconomic status). Mental health professionals conducting forensic assessments also should be familiar with the Specialty Guidelines for Forensic Psychologists (Committee on Ethical Guidelines for Forensic Psychologists, 1991).

In response to evidence of the import of culture for clinical assessment, the American Psychological Association's Board of Ethnic Minority Affairs (BEMA) established a Task Force on the Delivery of Services to Ethnic Minority Populations in 1988. The task force developed "Guidelines for Providers of Psychological Services to Ethnic, Linguistic, and Culturally Diverse Populations" (American Psychological Association, 1993). These guidelines were intended to address issues that might arise when working with American Indians/Alaska Natives, Asian Americans/Pacific Islanders, Blacks/African Americans, and Hispanics/Latino Americans. Relevant populations also included refugee and immigrant groups and established subcultures such as Amish, Hasidic Jewish, and rural Appalachian people (American Psychological Association, 1993). The guidelines reflect general principles and were intended to be aspirational in nature. For example, it should be clear that the assessor considered language fluency (written and oral) in choosing and administering assessment instruments, in conducting interviews, and in drawing conclusions from psychometric tests, which may have limited validation data for the claimant's ethnocultural group. Similarly, the individual's sociopolitical history and prior trauma experiences must be considered in the overall clinical picture. For instance, a tendency to be suspicious or hypervigilant that might reflect a response style that has been developed in reaction to prior negative experiences with persons in a position of authority (e.g., torture by criminal justice authorities) should be clearly indicated in the ensuing report.

At about the same time the American Psychological Association guidelines emerged, the fourth edition of the *Diagnostic and Statistical Manual of Mental Disorders* (DSM-IV, American Psychiatric Association, 1994) was published. This was the first edition of the DSM to give careful consideration to cross-cultural and multiethnic assessment. The DSM-IV-TR (American Psychiatric Association, 2000) presents four types of information pertaining to cross-cultural assessments: (1) a systematic overview of cultural variations in the clinical presentation of many disorders; (2) a glossary of idioms of distress or "culture-bound syndromes"; (3) an appendix, which provides an outline for cultural formulation; and (4) expanded definitions of psychosocial and environmental factors in Axis IV to include acculturation and discrimination. The outline is intended to assist clinicians in identifying the cultural issues relevant to an individual case (for a discussion of DSM-IV and culture, see Lopez-Ibor, 2003). More recently, the American Psychological Association published its *Guidelines on Multicultural Education, Training, Research, Practice and Organizational Change for Psychologists* (2002b). Similar advances are occurring in Canada (e.g., development of the Cultural Consultation Service, see Kirmayer, Groleau, Guzder, Blake, & Jarvis, 2003) and the United Kingdom (Nippoda, 2003).

A few principles that apply in any forensic assessment (generally, see Heilbrun, 2001) or any psychological assessment, for that matter, seemingly have particular importance to conducting ethnoculturally sensitive assessments. First, the American Psychological Association's Ethical Principles (2002c) require that psychologists accept referrals only within their area of expertise (e.g., education, training, experience). Divorced from guidelines and professional requirements, this issue is particularly salient in forensic assessments, given that the courts will apply legal criteria to determine whether or not a clinician can testify as an expert witness (Heilbrun, 2001). Thus, it should be clear that the mental health professional has expertise in the relevant legal issues (e.g., sexual assault, partner abuse, workplace discrimination) and in conducting evaluations with the relevant ethnocultural group. Second, it is a general tenet in forensic psychology that the strengths and limitations of the report should be discussed in such a way "so that they need change little under cross-examination" (Heilbrun, 2001, p. 226). In addition to evaluating and reporting general limitations in the assessment, the unique impact of the client's ethnocultural status should be afforded special attention (e.g., conducting interviews with an interpreter).

Considerations for Culturally Competent Assessments

Plaintiffs and their lawyers tend to prefer that a single causative factor (i.e., the index PTE) is reported to have led to the diagnosed psychological difficulties and functional impairments. In conducting an unbiased and competent assessment, however, the mental health expert must evaluate and compare the client's pre-PTE and post-PTE mental health status and functioning. Below, we provide several examples of issues that might differentially impact ethnically diverse clients over White, Euro-American claimants. The mental health professional should consider the claimant's unique life history and how ethnocultural identity is or is not relevant to postexposure adjustment.

Immigration and Acculturation

Although immigration can be stressful, research results do not suggest that immigration, in the absence of PTE, results in higher rates of mental disorders (for a discussion, see U.S. Department of Health and Human Services, 2001); the fact that a client is an immigrant does not necessarily imply that the experience was traumatic. In contrast, trauma among adults and children from war-torn countries before and after immigrating is associated with disproportionately high rates of PTSD (Eisenman, Gelberg, Honghu, & Shapiro, 2003; U.S. Department of Health and Human Services, 2001). In particular, refugees who had little control over their decision to immigrate and the circumstances surrounding their departure, and those who experienced political violence are at risk for psychological distress (Eisenman et al., 2003; U.S. Department of Health and Human Services, 2001). Emerging research suggests that the process of adapting to a new culture might also result in acculturative stress (for a review, see Rudmin, 2003). For instance, Nippoda's (2001) questionnaire research with a random sample of Japanese people living in the United Kingdom indicated high rates of disillusionment (36%); stress from interacting with non-Japanese people (30%); worries about loved ones in Japan (29%); feelings of frustration or inferiority due to the language barrier (59%); and isolation, loneliness, or social withdrawal (28%). Simon (1996) cautioned that while base rates such as those above can be informative, it should not be presumed that an experience was necessarily distressing for the individual.

Racism and Discrimination

Despite evidence of improvements in cross-cultural relations, racism is ubiquitous, and available evidence suggests that, both intergroup (e.g., White Canadians discriminating against Black or Chinese Canadians) and intragoup (e.g., African Americans discriminating on the basis of skin tone) (e.g., Clark, Anderson, Clark, & Williams, 1999) racism persists. Racism and discrimination can be traumatic in their own right (e.g., physical assaults, workplace discrimination) or can add to the stress experienced in relation to other PTE (Clark et al., 1999; Marsella et al., 1996; Penk & Allen, 1991). Experiences linked to racial/ethnic discrimination are hypothesized to contribute to the likelihood that ethnic minority individuals will develop posttraumatic symptoms (Butts, 2002); there is some research to support this position (e.g., Norris, 1992; Penk & Allen, 1991). In a nationally representative telephone survey, Kessler et al. (1999) found that "major discrimination" (e.g., being hassled by police, fired from a job) was significantly higher (50%) among African Americans, in contrast to White Americans (31%). "Day-to-day perceived discrimination" was experienced "often" among African Americans (almost 25%) and rarely among Whites (3%). Day-to-day discrimination was related to the development of distress and related diagnoses of generalized anxiety and depression in both Black and White Americans. The magnitude of the association between these two forms of discrimination and diminished mental health was similar to other commonly studied stressful life events, such as death of a loved one, divorce, or job loss.

Racism and discrimination also have been demonstrated to impact the extent or nature of a trauma. For instance, several authors have discussed at length how combat experiences during the Vietnam War were uniquely distressing for minority veterans (e.g., Lee et al., 2001; Manson, 1996; Penk & Allen, 1991). These challenges included racial stigmatization by fellow comrades, "bicultural conflict" (e.g., referring to Asians as "gooks"), cognitive dissonance as a result of identifying with the Vietnamese culture, and being mistaken for the enemy (e.g., Manson, 1996; Penk & Allen, 1991).

Dose Response

Minority groups may be at greater risk than nonminority groups to experience a unique dose (e.g., length of time, proximity) of what otherwise appear to be similar stressors (e.g., a hurricane or store robbery). As discussed above, evidence of trauma exposure and dose differences have been noted among individuals exposed to combat. Research with veterans demonstrates several potential confounds including differential exposure to war zone and the level of danger involved in assignments, as well as the greater potential for individuals of ethnic minority status to identify with the enemy due to their physical appearance, which may account for a large proportion of the variance in posttraumatic adjustment (e.g., Penk & Allen, 1991).

Family Collectivism and Social Support

The focus on the individual within Western cultures is in dramatic contrast with the collectivism evident in many other cultures. Greek, Latino, African American, Asian, and Aboriginal cultures, for instance, often are described as sharing collectivism and family solidarity as common characteristics (e.g., Chatzifotiou & Dobash, 2001; Nippoda, 2003; Perilla, et al., 2002; Sue, 2002). Collectivism emphasizes familial ties and responsibilities and reflects a shared feeling of belonging or oneness with other people. In collectivist cultures, the self is primarily defined as part of the group; the role of extended family, religious traditions, and interdependence are central in many communities (e.g., Sue, 2002).

While family cohesiveness can represent a significant source of support when an individual encounters stress, it also has been found to be associated with poor recovery in certain circumstances. For example, familial support may be depleted when natural disasters occur (see Perilla et al., 2002). Furthermore, when the source of trauma is in the family (e.g., elder, wife, or child abuse) this interconnectedness and a reluctance to seek sources of support outside the family can have serious implications for the individual's risk of further trauma exposures, the likelihood of disclosure, help seeking, and recovery. Behaviors by members of the social network, such as ostracizing or victim blaming, can influence the individual's distress (Simon, 1996). For example, many women with abusive partners report that help seeking from friends and family often is useless (e.g., women are told that it is their responsibility to keep the family together). Women from cultures with strong patriarchal beliefs are more likely to encounter such responses and to be less likely to engage in active coping strategies such as formal help seeking than women from less patriarchal societies (e.g., Chatzifotiou & Dobash, 2001). The shame associated with divorce in some cultures may interfere with women's attempts to escape from abusive relationships (Roysircar-Sodowsky & Kuo, 2001). Similarly, minority survivors of childhood sexual abuse often experience social, familial, and cultural pressures (e.g., the importance attached to female virginity) that make disclosure exceptionally difficult.

Symptom Expression

Psychiatric symptoms can be linked to collective attitudes, which sometimes vary between cultures (Draguns & Tanaka-Matsumi, 2003). Unique or characteristic modes of expressing psychological discomfort are termed culture-bound syndromes or "idioms of distress" (American Psychiatric Association, 2000, p. 897). Somatization, for example, is widely regarded as a common means of expressing psychological discomfort and is particularly apparent among ethnic minorities. Keane, Kaloupek, and Weathers (1996) similarly recommend that professionals consider that trauma symptoms may be expressed differently. For instance, they note that it might be difficult to develop one instrument that could measure rape across different cultures because the effects of rape might reflect diverse mores and religious and cultural beliefs.

In their recent review of three decades of literature on psychopathology across and within cultures, Draguns and Tanaka-Matsumi (2003) concluded that somatization and guilt were prominent examples of cross-cultural variation in expressed well-being and psychopathology. Somatic dysfunction, general malaise, pain, and discomfort appear to function as important avenues of communicating mental experience for individuals from non-Caucasian states (e.g., Japan, India, Latin America, and Africa). Marsella (1988) hypothesized that with increasingly severe psychological disturbance, cross-cultural variability in symptoms is likely to decrease. Differential symptom profiles might decrease cross-cultural validity in qualitative assessments (e.g., semistructured clinical interviews) and also in quantitative assessments (e.g., structured assessment instruments). For example, the client's behavior might not fit the mental health professional's culturally biased stereotype of a typical domestic violence victim. Similarly, the client's symptoms might not cluster as expected on psychological tests developed with Euro-Americans.

Response Styles

Between-group differences in values and beliefs about mental health (e.g., stigma and shame, fear of losing face) might affect self-disclosure of both PTE and symptoms of psychological distress. Lee et al. (2001; also see Roysircar-Sodowsky & Kuo, 2001) described seven response styles relevant to cross-cultural assessments: (1) acquiescence—a tendency to agree, (2) social desirability—a tendency to respond in normative or socially favorable ways, (3) oppositional—a tendency to endorse neutral responses or to respond aggressively (e.g., answering "no" to all questions), (4) evasiveness—unwillingness to commit to a response, (5) carelessness—a tendency to respond inconsistently, (6) impression management—or other deception, and (7) self-deception—denying to the self the relevance of items, significance of symptoms. Lee et al. (2001) caution that response styles might differ between ethnocultural groups, between acculturated and unacculturated individuals, and so on, which can invalidate test results and between study comparisons. For example, efforts on the part of the client to avoid reexperiencing the event or to save face might lead to underreporting of symptoms and increase the risk of a false negative diagnosis when conducting a PTSD evaluation, though these behaviours are not unique to minority individuals.

Socioeconomic Status

Poverty is a risk factor for poor mental health in relation to both the risk of PTE and the "dose" of PTE experienced (e.g., resources to escape when a natural disaster occurs, insurance). Socioeconomic status can moderate the impact of potentially stressful events or, conversely, trauma can result in "resource spirals" (Sattler et al., 2002). Hobfoll (1989) coined the term "loss spirals" to describe secondary stressors or additional strains and hassles that develop in the wake of a disaster; the term similarly can be applied to other trauma exposures. People of low socioeconomic status are more likely to be exposed to stressful social environments (e.g., crime, overcrowding) and to be cushioned less by social or material resources (e.g., medical insurance, respite child care) to prevent these cycles (McLeod & Kessler, 1990).

Following Hurricane George, Sattler et al. (2002) reported that resource loss accounted for a significant portion of acute stress disorder variation in all locations studied: the U.S. Virgin Islands, Puerto Rico, Dominican Republic, and the United States. Large interethnic differences in the adequacy of insurance were reported. Similarly, in their random sample of non-Hispanic White and Hispanic women discussed previously, Shupe et al. (2002) found that Hispanic women who were least acculturated were the least likely to consider quitting their jobs in response to sexual harassment. The authors hypothesized that high rates of unemployment among Hispanic women might influence work-related outcomes among harassment victims.

A further element of distress associated with financial resources is the strain and expense of the litigation process and the cost of treatment. Herman (2003) speculated, "Indeed, if one set out intentionally to design a system for provoking symptoms of posttraumatic stress disorder, it might look very much like a court of law" (p. 159). She further commented that the adversarial system is stressful for the most robust individual, but is likely exceptionally troubling for crime victims. We would further speculate that the distress and expense associated with obtaining legal representation, and attending serial interviews and assessments is likely particularly arduous for many individuals of minority ethnocultural affiliation. In particular, immigrants who might be unfamiliar with the civil and criminal justice systems, for whom English is not their native language, or who justifiably distrust government authority (e.g., refugees) may find navigating the courts overwhelming. Similarly, claimants of restricted financial resources might find it difficult to obtain adequate legal representation, obtain timely and effective mental health resources, and otherwise utilize available resources.

Low socioeconomic status (SES) might also explain cultural differences in health or health care utilization. Most experts agree that poverty and SES do play a strong role in disparities in the use of mental health services (e.g., Chow, Jaffee, & Snowden, 2003), but evidence contradicts the notion that lower SES alone explains ethnic and racial disparities in treatment seeking (see U.S. Department of Health and Human Services, 2001). We turn now to an examination of these issues.

Barriers to Help Seeking among Minority Groups

Attitudes, Beliefs, and Stigma

Cultures vary with respect to the meaning they impart to illness, and their subjective understanding of distress (Kleinman, 1988a; Sue, 2002). Mental health problems in China, for example, traditionally were not considered indicative of a need to seek professional intervention (Sue, 2002; Sussman, Robins, & Earls, 1987; Zhang, Snowden, & Sue, 1998). Within Japanese communities, mental health problems are seen as a weakness (Nippoda, 2003) and among Chinese people, like many groups, mental illness can result in a significant loss of face (Sue, 2002). Koenen, Goodwin, Struening, Hellman, and Guardino (2003) examined barriers and predictors of treatment seeking among community participants who met DSM-IV (American Psychiatric Association, 1994) criteria for PTSD ($N = 2, 713$) identified through the National Anxiety Disorders Screening Day (NADSD) survey in 50 states across the United States. Individuals who had ever ($n = 2,045$) versus never ($n = 668$) received treatment were compared on *enabling* (e.g., employment, residence), *need* (interference with daily life measured in response to "How much of the time does your anxiety interfere with your daily life" using a six-point Likert scale), and *predisposing* factors (e.g., age, gender, race—White vs. minority), as well as *barriers* to treatment seeking (e.g., "afraid of what others might think," "not sure where to get help"). Minority race was associated with a decreased likelihood of having been in treatment, even after taking into account need factors and enabling factors.

Stigma surrounding mental health problems is pervasive and can have dramatic effects on coping strategies, social support, and treatment seeking; this appears to be somewhat more pronounced among some ethnic minorities than it is among Whites. In a sample of Asian Americans, Zhang et al. (1998) found that just 12% of Asians, in contrast to 25% of Caucasians, reported they would mention their mental health problems to a friend or relative. Even fewer Asians (4%) stated they would seek help from a psychiatrist or specialist, or physician (3%) (versus 26% and 13% of Caucasians, respectively) (also see Chow et al., 2003; Sue, 2002). Conversely, studies with African Americans have found that they did not differ from Caucasians in the amount of embarrassment associated with seeking treatment for mental illness (e.g., Sussman et al., 1987). Taken together, these results suggest that minorities hold similar, and in some cases stronger, stigmatizing attitudes toward mental illness than do Caucasians, but that the term "minority" is too broad to yield much clarity as there is great diversity within and between ethnocultural groups.

One issue that has been neglected in the research literature is the extent to which members of ethnocultural minorities utilize different health providers (e.g., more culturally connected but perhaps less professionally recognized counselors) than do members of the Caucasian majority. For example, reserve-dwelling Aboriginals in Canada are more likely to seek and receive mental health care via lay counselors within Aboriginal healing centers than they are to seek and receive care from licensed psychiatrists or psychologists (Brasfield, 2004).

Family Factors and Collectivism

As we noted above, some minority individuals/groups might be more likely to seek out culturally specific treatment providers than Whites; they also may be more likely to rely on friends and family. Koenen et al. (2003) called for further inquiry into whether minorities are truly underserved or whether they simply make use of other resources such as clergy, friends, or family. We would add that assessors should carefully evaluate the utility of these kinds of alternative sources of support, considering for instance the nature of the PTE and the client's relationship to the perpetrator (if relevant) and how the beliefs and attitudes of the individuals involved might impact the client (Chatzifotiou & Dobash, 2001). As noted previously, the interconnectedness of ethnocultural personal networks can make help seeking within the family/social network of some ethnic minority groups difficult because of the extensive sharing of personal information and the expectation that family members be productive in order to support family members either in the host country or in the country of origin (Sue, 2002). Sue (2002) noted that having a mental health problem that might reduce productivity would result in a significant loss of face, exacerbating the person's shame. In addition to sharing the same struggles as White victims, some people from non–Euro-American backgrounds also describe unique pressures (e.g., the value of a girl's virginity) and how social, family and cultural experiences impact on their coping and help-seeking decisions (Lee & Law, 2001).

Mistrust

In comparison to the White majority, ethnic minorities are more likely to report a reluctance to seek treatment due to prior negative experiences with health-care professionals, mistrust of government authorities, or fear of deportation due to lack of documentation (e.g., Sussman et al., 1987; U.S. Department of Health and Human Services, 2001). Sue, Nakamura, Chung, & Yee-Hradbury (1994) concluded that underutilization of mental health services among minorities reflects limited English proficiency, stigma (i.e., embarrassment/losing face), lack of access to culturally competent services, and mistrust. Research with African Americans and North American Aboriginals, for instance, suggests that their histories of discrimination by the majority Euro-American population has had long-lasting detrimental effects on the trust required to seek assistance from primarily White service providers and to develop rapport in therapy (e.g., Fenster & Fenster, 1998).

Expertise in Cross-Cultural Services and Clinician Bias

Koenen et al. (2003) hypothesized that a minority group member's reluctance to seek treatment may reflect a lack of cross-cultural expertise among mental health professionals. Related to this issue, the surgeon general (U.S. Department of Health and Human Services, 2001) estimated that just 2% of psychiatrists, 2% of psychologists, and 4% of social workers in the United States are African American. Minority groups report a reluctance to seek treatment due to a lack of clinicians familiar with either the client's culture or language (see Nippoda, 2003; Sue et al., 1994; Sue, 2002). Some research suggests that dropping out of treatment is more common if therapists and clients are of different ethnicities (Rosenheck, Fontana, & Cottrol, 1995).

A lack of faith in clinicians' skills with non-White patients might be at least partially justified: Ethnicity-related bias has been found to result in overdiagnosis, underdiagnosis, or misdiagnosis of mental disorders among African Americans (e.g., Garretson, 1993) and underdiagnosis among Asian Americans (e.g., Takeuchi & Uehara, 1996; also see Sue, 2002) (generally, see Kirmayer et al., 2003; Lin & Lin, 2002). These errors likely reflect Euro-American biases inherent in the psychiatric and psychological professions (e.g., the notion that Asians are better adjusted than other ethnocultural groups) and the failure of mental health professionals and educators to evolve with the rapidly diversifying population in developed nations (Lin & Lin, 2002; Sue et al., 1999; Sue, 2002). The need to train culturally competent practitioners and address the influence of culture on current nosological systems has been widely recognized, but developments have been slow (e.g., Kirmayer et al., 2003; Lin & Lin, 2002; Lo & Fung, 2003; Sue, Bingham, Porché-Burke, & Vasquez, 1999; U.S. Department of Health and Human Services, 2001).

Evaluating Measures for Use in
Cross-Cultural Assessments

Given the overabundance of diverse cultures and ethnicities both within nations and cross-nationally, it is impossible for clinicians to have instruments that have been validated for every ethnicity or culture (Ritsher, Struening, Hellman, & Guardino, 2002). A variety of methods are available for developing measures suitable to evaluate mental health in minority populations. Researchers/clinicians have developed new measures for the express purpose of evaluating a specific ethnocultural group (emic or culture-specific measures); alternatively, existing measures are translated and modified as necessary to capture the same construct (in this case, PTSD) in the population of interest (etic or universal measures). Suggestions are provided below for determining whether a measure might be appropriate for use with a particular client. This information should be of value to legal counsel as well as forensic assessors, clinicians, and researchers who intend to develop, validate, or use PTSD assessment instruments in their work.

There are several psychometric issues to be considered if existing tools are to be used cross-culturally. Measurement equivalence refers to several interrelated issues (Marsella & Kameoka, 1989): (a) content equivalence, (b) linguistic and semantic equivalence, (c) conceptual equivalence, (d) scale and technical equivalence, and (e) normative equivalence (also see Keane, Kaloupek, & Weathers, 1996). Other issues include: score interpretation, the use of nonrepresentative samples, and the selection criteria used to establish separate norms and response sets (see Roysircar-Sodowsky & Kuo, 2001).

Content equivalence refers to the extent to which two ethnocultural groups respond to the same trauma in the same way, expressing the same signs and symptoms (Keane et al., 1996); or, put another way, whether the content of the questionnaire or interview taps the same construct when used with different ethnocultural groups (Lee et al., 2001). Moreover, some constructs might not exist in some cultures. To the extent that there is equivalence, one measure might be suitable; if the two groups respond differently, there may be a need to develop a completely different measure to accomplish the same goal (Keane et al., 1996).

To ensure linguistic and semantic equivalence, it is preferable for measures to be translated and back-translated by individuals who are fluent in both languages, as well as knowledgeable about the relevant culture and mental health issues (Keane et al., 1996). Cultural and mental health experts should then review the translated version to evaluate the extent to which the measure accurately represents the mental health construct in the intended cultural group. There may be no dictionary equivalent in some languages for certain mental health descriptors including, for example, "depression" (Draguns & Tanaka-Matsumi, 2003, p. 761). Moreover, when such words exist, their connotations may be inconsistent across ethnocultural groups. The issue of cultural appropriateness deserves consideration when using DSM disorder criteria and in the selection and use of scales and interviews (i.e., given that most were designed using middle- to upper-class White Americans). To demonstrate, if a client does not satisfy all criteria for PTSD, it might be useful to probe to determine if symptoms are being expressed in a culturally unique manner; for example, by asking: "is there any other way that the crime event comes back to you?" (Carlson & Dutton, 2003, p. 140).

Conceptual equivalence is central to measure equivalence but difficult to attain (Keane et al., 1996). For instance, concepts such as numbing, depression, or rape might have very different meanings across cultures. Similarly, it is essential that the measurement methods for specific constructs are evaluated for cross-cultural equivalence. Scales such as Likert scales or true/false questions are commonplace in Western nations; however, they might have different interpretations in other cultures (Keane et al., 1996; Roysircar-Sodowsky & Kuo, 2001).

The final essential aspects of cross-cultural validation are to use indigenous people in validation studies and to develop norms that are relevant for the population of interest. Most psychological measures are developed, validated, and normed with White, middle-class individuals (Roysircar-Sodowsky & Kuo, 2001). According to Keane et al. (1996, p. 189): "Norms are often the bases for determining abnormality and normality . . . making comparisons between non-Western individuals' performance(s) on tests or instruments developed with Western norms risks two major problems. First, it gives precedence to the Western way of experiencing life. Second, it does not inform the investigator of the relative status of individuals compared to their ethnic or cultural peers." Apparent mean differences between the ethnoculturally different client and the established norms on such a measure might provide little valid information. Roysircar-Sodowsky and Kuo (2001) suggest that two interpretations might be considered: (1) the ethnoculturally unique group might be experiencing greater psychopathology, or (2) psychometric nonequivalence is being reflected in apparent group differences. The interpretation of test results derived from research on one cultural group should not be applied to a different cultural group; this is particularly relevant when cutoffs are used (i.e., when scores above or below a certain value are used to identify pathology).

Even when there are norms available for a specific minority group, there is reason to be skeptical. As discussed previously, it is difficult to obtain sample sizes large enough in some cases to ensure they are representative. Furthermore, the extent to which the norms derived from a validation study are relevant to a particular claimant must be carefully considered. Often, selection criteria or methods used for identifying the ethnocultural group are questionable. Roysircar-Sodowsky and Kuo (2001) delineated several examples of problematic selection criteria. Self-selected, referred individuals, or snowball sampling (e.g., referrals by friends or family who participated in the study) within minority group research may result in nonrepresentative samples because of cultural variations in help seeking or accessibility to researchers. Categorizations of samples based on family names will miss important within-group differences such as acculturation and SES. Norming samples are sometimes recruited from relatively unique settings that actually do not reflect the education, occupation, SES, language proficiency, values, and beliefs of the more general group. In some cases, the classification of groups is nothing short of arbitrary, reflecting little if any information about ethnocultural affiliation. For instance, the restandardization of the Minnesota Multiphasic Personality Inventory-2 (MMPI-2) included only African Americans from military bases and the "Hispanic" individuals were arbitrarily classified as "White" or "other" (Roysircar-Sodowsky & Kuo, 2001). Minorities are overrepresented among people residing in households without telephones, the home-less, and incarcerated—groups who fail to get measured in the vast majority of epidemiological and national surveys.

If the forensic assessor/clinician is compelled to use assessment instruments that have not been validated with the client's ethnocultural group, he/she should: (a) interpret the results cautiously, (b) use multiple measures of the relevant con-struct to ensure theoretically adequate coverage, and/or (c) use the results of such measures primarily as a way to generate hypotheses about the claimant that can be confirmed by collateral information (also see Roysircar-Sodowsky & Kuo, 2001). In particular, conclusions should reflect information drawn from the recent empirical literature (e.g., ethnocultural differences in response to the relevant PTE).

A Checklist for Evaluating Ethnocultural Sensitivity in Minority Assessment

Provided below is a select list of recommendations for increasing ethnocultural sensitivity in forensic assessments of PTSD. Readers are cautioned, however, that no instrument, checklist, or other tool is sufficient to replace professional judg-ment, and no measure or guideline is culture free.

1. Evaluate your own competence to work with the client. This includes at least two essential considerations. First, an *awareness of one's own eth-nocultural identity*, values, and biases, and an honest examination of how that might detract from an effective, ethical, objective, and competent as-sessment.
2. An evaluation of your *expertise in the relevant legal and clinical issues*. Professional and ethical guidelines require that psychologists accept refer-rals only when they have the *necessary expertise*. The Association of Mul-ticultural Counseling and Development has developed guidelines for eval-uating awareness, knowledge, and skills necessary to provide services to culturally and racially diverse clients (Lo & Fung, 2003). When appropriate, seek out supervision or consider making referrals. The PTSD and ethno-cultural literatures are expanding exponentially, making continuing educa-tion essential.
3. *Evaluate the claimant's cultural identity* (e.g., the Cultural Identity Check-list, Ibrahim, 1993, cited in Ibrahim & Ohnishi, 2001) to determine the client's affiliation with the culture of origin and the extent of acculturation (see, Marsella, 1998; Salant & Lauderdale, 2003). If relevant, it might be useful to consider how long the client has been in the country.
4. Consideration in interviews and regarding the choice, use, and evaluation of results from assessment instruments should be given to *reading fluency, and comprehension* for ethnocultural minority claimants. Assessors should

not mistake verbal fluency for reading level. Clients might be reluctant to admit such a perceived deficiency.

5. Use *professional interpreters* when necessary. Choosing an interpreter requires identification of the correct subcultural language group and, in some cases, an interpreter whose gender and ethnocultural status will make the claimant feel most comfortable. It is preferable to use one interpreter for all interviews. The assessor should be sure to stipulate in his/her written conclusions and testimony: (a) when testing and interviews were conducted in a language other than that in which the client was reared, and/or (b) if an interpreter was used during the assessment.

6. In any PTSD assessment, a *multidimensional approach* is preferable. A multicultural assessment will require a flexible integrative approach wherein the qualitative data available from interviews is reconciled with the quantitative data available from psychometric assessment tools.

7. A *multimethod approach* (e.g., paper and pencil self-reports, structured interviews) will help in (a) reducing potential bias (see chapter 4) that may arise from less structured assessment methods, (b) ensure a broader range of coverage of potential psychological injuries, and (c) increase the accuracy of conclusions (Keane, Buckley, & Miller, 2003); this is particularly relevant to assessments involving ethnoculturally different individuals. When assessing minority individuals, it is likely best to use multiple measures to ensure that the relevant constructs are adequately assessed.

8. As with any forensic assessment, it is essential that the assessor *obtain data from multiple sources* including, for example: the client (it is recommended that the assessor conduct multiple interviews); collaterals (e.g., friends, family, coworkers, employer); and medical, employment, and academic records (see Heilbrun, 2001; Simon, 2003). Use of multiple external sources might help to corroborate the claims of the client, but discrepant findings will need to be integrated into the final clinical picture; the importance of external sources cannot be exaggerated in forensic assessments (see chapters 4 and 5; Heilbrun, 2001; Simon, 2003).

9. In conducting cross-cultural assessments, in particular, *knowledge of the current qualitative and quantitative literature* should be used to guide the assessment and temper the conclusions. For instance, although large-sample studies might not be available from the client's ethnocultural group, research involving case studies or focus groups can be useful for understanding the client's response to the PTE, their response styles in an interview, and so on.

10. The assessment should be guided by *multiple hypothesis testing*, which should generally conform to the criteria for PTSD in the DSM-IV-TR and should also be guided by the professional and research literatures. It is essential to *consider other diagnoses* (e.g., depression, other anxiety dis-

orders, and malingering); while forensic clinicians have a duty to remain vigilant to the *possibility of exaggeration and malingering*, it is also important to consider that apparent exaggeration might reflect cultural differences in symptom expression, or cultural problems with respect to the testing procedures. Consider *culture-bound syndromes*. For instance, dissociative phenomena, a central component of PTSD assessment and diagnosis (Simon, 2003), are not considered pathological in all cultures (DSM-IV-TR, American Psychiatric Association, 2000).

11. Consider the possible contribution of *multiple stressors*. Seemingly low-magnitude stressors that result in considerable functional impairment should be scrupulously investigated (Simon, 2003), but in a multicultural context, consideration also should be given to the *unique cognitive perspective of the claimant*. What appears to be a minor assault might result in extreme fear in an African American male who has heard about acquaintances being severely injured or killed as a result of interpersonal violence; thus, he anticipates a significant threat of harm or death associated with even seemingly low-level physical aggression. That is, the vicarious experience of severe or deadly violence may place the individual at risk of a greater sense of personal threat and greater likelihood of developing PTSD or other psychological injuries from a less-severe victimization experience.

12. Assessor characteristics, environment, and the like can serve to enhance or weaken *rapport*. Conduct the assessment at a location that will enhance the comfort of the claimant. Consideration should be given to *cultural elements in the patient-clinician relationship* reflecting differences in gender, culture, and social status, for instance, and how such cultural factors may affect the clinical encounter. Monitor the client's behavior during interviews and testing to *ensure comfort and understanding*. Apparent discomfort might signify problems in either communication or rapport.

13. Thoroughly *investigate seemingly subthreshold PTSD or nonprototypical variants*. The assessor should consider the phasic nature of the disorder (Simon, 2003) and structure the assessment to detect disabling subthreshold cases of PTSD as well as other, perhaps culturally related, consequences of the trauma. This will surely involve the assessor allowing the claimant to describe in his/her own words how the trauma has affected his/her well-being and functioning.

14. *Evaluate the trauma exposure in a culturally sensitive manner*. For instance, the threatening nature of an MVA or disaster might be significant for a client without insurance or social support, and the perceived threat posed by objectively minor assaults might be greater for recent immigrants from countries with notable human rights violations.

15. *Consider cultural factors that might impact symptoms*. While recognizing that PTSD is a universal response to human suffering, it is important to

remain vigilant about recognizing *diversity in individual responses*. Simon (2003) reported that some attorneys view the DSM-IV as the black letter definitive authority, but reminds the reader that diagnostic criteria reflect knowledge available at the time of publication and that specific diagnostic criteria are guidelines requiring clinical expertise in assessment and diagnostic formulation. Assessors should consider culturally specific expressions such as somatization.

16. Consider *cultural influences on coping, help seeking, and reporting* with respect to victimization experiences. Frequently, expert witnesses are asked to elaborate on the nature of the trauma (e.g., what is wife abuse, sexual harassment?) and how a "typical" victim might respond (e.g., the likelihood of reporting the experience to authorities). A history of discriminatory, institutional, and social barriers to equitable treatment, as well as prejudice and discrimination might be useful for explaining delays in reporting victimization.

17. There is no maximum quota on the traumas or other stressors to which we may be exposed. Claimants may experience *ongoing, concurrent, or overlapping PTE* resulting from traumatic stressors such as conflict in the country of origin or fear for missing or separated family members, as well as from psychosocial stressors such as racism/discrimination and socioeconomic disadvantage.

18. *Consult with colleagues* who have expertise in cross-cultural assessments—in the ethnocultural group of interest and in the index PTE.

19. The term *eggshell plaintiff* refers to the litigant's preexisting degree of vulnerability (see chapter 2). The eggshell plaintiff is a person who is extremely vulnerable to even a minor trauma, but has remained asymptomatic prior to the injury. This issue might be of considerable importance for minority individuals wherein an assessor will have to tease apart and educate the trier of fact about the distinction between preexisting psychiatric histories, multiple traumas, and the litigant's pretrauma vulnerability.

20. No assessment measure or assessor is culture free. Forensic assessors have a responsibility to *communicate culturally related limitations of their assessments and opinions* so as to not misinform consumers (e.g., lawyers, judges, juries).

Future Directions in Research and Practice

Past research intended to elucidate the influence of ethnocultural affiliation upon posttraumatic adjustment has been methodologically inadequate. There are relatively few prospective studies of PTSD (Brewin, Andrews, & Valentine, 2000; for exceptions, see Macklin et al., 1998; Freedman et al., 2002), epidemiological

research with people from minority groups lags significantly behind that of research with Caucasians (Norris et al., 2003; Sue, 2002), and there is little evidence
that existing measures have cross-cultural validity (Norris et al., 2003). Further,
researchers have relied upon broad categories of "ethnicity" that tend not to reflect
shared culture and fail to consider other multiple confounding factors (Marsella
et al., 1996).

It makes no sense that ethnic minority status per se would be associated with
increased exposure to PTE. However, these relationships appear to exist and need
to be recognized; in particular, we need to understand what variables are confounded with ethnic minority status and how those confounded variables affect
trauma exposure or PTSD. Identified below are several categories of research that
might provide some clarity as to why ethnicity might be an important risk marker
for PTSD and why some studies reveal few if any differences in rates of PTSD
while others suggest important differences.

Measuring Ethnocultural Identity and Acculturation

While many researchers measure and control for SES, most do not carefully define
and measure aspects of ethnicity or cultural affiliation. Studies often report the
ethnic or racial backgrounds of study participants as shorthand for their culture,
without systematically examining more specific information about their living
circumstances, attitudes, beliefs, and behavior. Furthermore, assimilation to the
dominant culture rarely is considered. The limitations in this realm are so significant that one of the most prolific writers on ethnicity and trauma went so far as
to state that most culture and trauma research has not actually studied "culture"
(Marsella et al., 1996). As we noted previously, many acculturation measures
exist and can be used to address this deficit in the literature (e.g., for reviews see,
Marsella, 1998; Salant & Lauderdale, 2003). Future research with respect to individuals' responses to trauma should use more detailed and valid measures of
culture and acculturation.

The Impact of Racism, Discrimination, and
Multiple Stressors

Future research must attend to the potentially mediating aspects of daily stressors
or other discrimination-related experiences on the expression of psychological
distress, as well as to potential biases in forensic assessment related to claimants'
or assessors' ethnocultural status. Few studies consider the influence of ethnocultural status on PTE exposure (see Ibrahim & Ohnishi, 2001), for example,
events that occur in a racist or discriminatory context, such as workplace harassment or hate crimes and the impact of prior traumas on recovery from PTE. Our
review of the literature suggests that minority groups may be more likely to
experience posttraumatic symptoms due to elevated pretrauma levels of stress
and/or due to the impact of day-to-day stressors. Wyatt (1990) postulated that

assessments of multiple victimization experiences are particularly warranted when studying minority groups. Moreover, ethnic minority status alone may be a stressor in itself (see Comas-Diaz, 1990). Exposure to racism likely has significant implications for susceptibility to posttraumatic maladjustment and help seeking. Minority status and degree of acculturation may not only influence individuals' responses to traumatic stress; they may also influence the judgments of mental health professionals providing forensic assessments (e.g., diagnostic bias).

Defining the Trauma—Accounting for Dose Response or Severity

One of the most promising areas for advancing research in trauma appears to be examination of the characteristics of the stressor (see Litz, Miller, Ruef, & McTeague, 2002, pp. 216–217; Norris et al., 2003; cf., Bowman, 1999). Similar to other populations (e.g., women—see chapter 6), apparent ethnic differences in posttraumatic adjustment might be accounted for by a failure to operationalize adequately the index stressor. Few studies sufficiently assess the severity of the trauma (Stein, Walker, & Forde, 2000), or examine individual differences in the experience of apparently similar traumas. This appears to be a profitable avenue of research for understanding apparent ethnocultural differences (Manson, 1996; Marsella et al., 1996; Penk & Allen, 1991).

Interactions Among Race, Poverty, and Gender

> The symptoms experienced by these groups have been misclassified as anxiety disorders, adjustment disorders, affective disorders, and so on. This has occurred due to the misperception that we have a level playing field
> —Ibrahim and Ohnishi (2001, p. 98)

Socioeconomic status, education, and poverty are widely regarded as important risk factors for PTSD (Breslau et al., 1991; U.S. Department of Health and Human Services, 2001). Wealth, education, and high-status positions are all underrepresented among women and non-White individuals. Minorities tend to be overrepresented among incarcerated, homeless, and economically disadvantaged groups and individuals with alcohol and drug problems; these marginalized groups are at unique risk for trauma exposure. "Any analysis that fails to control for income may present findings that reflect the influence of poverty rather than culture" (Koss, Bailey, Yuan, Herrera, & Lichter, 2003, p. 133). Similarly, race and gender work together to influence trauma exposure. For instance, some commentators assert that the line between gender and racial discrimination and harassment in the workplace often is blurry (e.g., Texeira, 2002).

Bergman and Drasgow (2003) examined a rich data set of more than 20,000 women from the U.S. military using the Sexual Experiences Questionnaire (SEQ) (Gelfand, Fitzgerald & Drasgow, 1995). They found that White women reported the fewest harassment experiences, and noted that, "the experience of race and gender is intertwined, resulting in distinct experiences" (Bergman & Drasgow, 2003, p. 142). Sexual harassment and other forms of workplace discrimination often are rooted in power differences between majority and minority group members. The extent to which cultural affiliation, gender, and poverty interact is an under-researched area that conceivably has important implications for the prevalence of trauma exposure, coping, help seeking, and recovery (e.g., Chow et al., 2003).

Possible Protective Factors

Few studies have considered that minority status might contribute to vulnerability to PTE or subsequent psychological trauma in some cases, but that conversely some ethnocultural affiliations might reduce an individual's risk or exposure to PTE and/or subsequent distress. It might well be that communal living and social embeddedness serve to reduce the risk of exposure to some forms of PTE and/or increase resiliency postexposure in some groups.

The influence of constructs such as hardiness and resilience and investigations of protective factors have not been fully explored with regard to ethnocultural differences following exposure to trauma. For instance, some cultures, such as Mexican Americans, or Asian Americans might "normalize" stress and present as stoic, resigned, or indifferent to suffering, which reduces the extent of stress associated with PTE. To the contrary, in cultures where control is considered important a PTE might be experienced as more extreme (Ibrahim & Ohnishi, 2001) if the individual experienced extreme helplessness, for instance.

In summary, to attribute differences to ethnicity requires measures of ethnocultural identity, acculturation, multiple traumas (e.g., racism, immigration/acultural stress), trauma severity/dose, and a consideration of other confounds (e.g., socioeconomic status, daily stressors, culturally unique resilience factors). These issues have not been thoroughly researched, and may, in part, account for conflicting research results to date.

Assessment Issues and PTSD Diagnostic Criteria

Other research priorities should involve the investigation of equitable provision of services to minorities, such as validating instruments for use across ethnic groups (Ritsher et al., 2002) and treatment outcome studies demonstrating the utility of various approaches to ensure culturally competent services (e.g., Kirmayer et al., 2003; Lo & Fung, 2003). Research priorities to ensure evidence-based practice for minorities must be a priority. The surgeon general's (U.S. Department of Health and Human Services, 2001) report on mental health in the United States demonstrated that empirically supported therapies for minorities have received little research attention. Research consistently indicates that minorities are less likely to receive treatment that adheres to clinical practice guidelines and more likely to suffer uncomfortable side effects from psychotherapeutic medications (Lin & Cheung, 1999; U.S. Department of Health and Human Services, 2001).

As we discussed, cultural affiliation likely influences the manner in which traumas are experienced and the subsequent expression of psychological distress (Perilla et al., 2002, p. 22; Sue, 2002). Kleinman (1988) asserted that clients of varying cultural affiliations likely describe and express their symptoms in unique ways. There are some well-recognized differences in symptom presentation across cultures. Asian patients, for instance, are noted to be more likely to report somatic symptoms (Sue, 2002), while not reporting the emotional symptoms that they do acknowledge having when probed (Lin & Cheung, 1999). As such, cultural differences might have significant import for the manner in which clinicians conduct their assessments and make diagnostic decisions; in particular, several authors cite cultural bias in Criterion C in the DSM-IV (e.g., Marsella et al., 1996; McCall & Resick, 2003; for a review, see Kirmayer et al., 2003).

Some preliminary research on the cultural implications for posttraumatic symptom expression has been conducted (Norris, Perilla, & Murphy, 2001b; Norris et al., 2001c; Norris et al., 2003). Results to date suggest that current PTSD criteria are salient for Mexicans. In a qualitative study of Mexican disaster victims, Norris et al. (2001c) found that unprompted, subjects reported 14 of the 17 criteria for PTSD in the DSM-IV (American Psychiatric Association, 2000); nonetheless, these authors reported some interesting differences from U.S. samples. Controlling for the severity of the trauma, Norris et al. (2001c) reported that the Mexican sample ($N = 200$) had higher intrusion and avoidance scores, in contrast to the U.S. non-Hispanic Whites ($n = 270$), who had higher arousal scores. The authors point out that their results are consistent with Marsella et al.'s (1996) hypothesis that intrusive thoughts might be common across cultures, whereas avoidance/numbing and hyperarousal might be culturally specific expressions. These results are consistent with those of McCall and Resick (2003), who found very low rates of avoidance/numbing symptoms such as psychogenic amnesia, reduced interest, and emotional numbing in Kalahari Bushmen exposed to traumatic assault. As Norris et al. (2001c) asserted, their results demonstrate that important findings can be masked if PTSD is examined as a unidimensional construct.

While changes to the DSM-IV reflect some substantial improvements, there is still considerable room for advancement. In their review of the literature, Roysircar-Sodowsky and Kuo (2001) noted that the DSM-IV glossary of culture-bound syndromes might be of little utility when making diagnoses. Indigenous afflictions might still result in substantial functional distress, and as such, coding these conditions as part of a multiaxial diagnosis similar to that used in DSM-IV Axes IV and V might be useful.

Perhaps the greatest cultural barrier to accurate assessment is the availability of validated measures. A review of the literature seems to indicate uncertainty as to whether the etic (i.e., cross-validated existing measures) or the emic approach is preferable. Of note, Roysircar-Sodowsky and Kuo (2001) pointed out that some third-party payers and mental health settings require the use of "mainstream instruments"; this seems to reflect ethnocentricity on the part of those agencies, but it also raises an important issue for PTSD litigants. We disagree with Roysircar-Sodowsky and Kuo on the issue of needing etic measures in order to provide a common language across cultures. If unique measures are developed to determine PTSD in different groups, it will be essential that statistical procedures (e.g., item-response theory) are able to demonstrate cross-cultural content equivalence (i.e., that the instruments are measuring the same thing). More research is needed in these areas in order to provide further insights into how the expression of post-trauma psychopathology differs between and within cultural groups (see Sue, 2002).

Closing Comments

Meeting the needs of the rapidly evolving client population in developed nations requires that mental health professionals, educators, professional associations, and policy makers are prepared to evolve with the changing landscape of the mental health profession (Sue et al., 1999). Public education, training, and research are needed to ensure the provision of adequate mental health care to non-White, non–Anglo-American cultural groups. Mental health professionals should reflect on their own identities and biases. Respect for cultural diversity is critical for ensuring that minorities will seek services (e.g., marketing, outreach strategies), remain in treatment, and ultimately benefit from interventions (e.g., people must appreciate how the intervention addresses their needs). Culturally sensitive public education is needed to reduce the stigma of mental illness among both Whites and non-Whites (Nippoda, 2003). Increasing the availability of culturally responsive mental health providers should be a priority of educators, professional organizations (e.g., American Psychiatric Association), and policy makers (see Sue et al., 1999).

Minority groups are more likely to fall victim to certain forms of trauma (e.g., torture), but research demonstrates that there are substantial differences between heterogeneous minority groups and within trauma categories (e.g., sexual harassment, MVA). We found virtually no evidence that ethnocultural status is a risk factor for PTSD once risk factors such as extent of exposure and socioeconomic status are controlled. Like gender, ethnocultural minority status is a risk marker, not a causal risk factor, for PTSD. This is an essential distinction that needs to be carefully translated into public policy. Labeling ethnicity as a risk factor for trauma and PTSD suggests that a particular group is uniquely vulnerable to stressful experiences rather than identifying the real underlying risk factors. This seems to be a very seriously misinformed conclusion.

The challenge of advancing multicultural psychology has been taken up with great enthusiasm, as reflected by recent developments in the diversification of organizational, educational, and research agendas (e.g., American Psychological Association, 2002b; Kirmayer et al., 2003; Lo & Fung, 2003; Nippoda, 2001; Sue et al., 1999). We hope these research agendas encourage the reduction of stigmatization and isolation associated with elevated rates of trauma exposure and subsequent psychopathology among disadvantaged groups.

8

Prevention and Rehabilitation of
Psychological Injuries

> We shall have to learn to refrain from doing things merely because we know
> how to do them.
> —Theodore Fox, Speech to Royal College of Physicians (1965)

The perceived need to prevent and rehabilitate psychological injuries has encouraged the development of a variety of psychological and pharmacological
interventions in the last two decades. This chapter provides an overview and
analysis of these interventions.

Prevention of Psychological Injuries

The perceived high prevalence of psychological injury following traumatic events
encouraged the development of early intervention for posttraumatic stress symptoms. Rachman (1980) and others have argued that maladaptive cognitive, affective, and behavioral patterns may be less entrenched immediately following the
experience of trauma and thus more amenable to change. This, and society's
compassion for victims of workplace and disaster-related trauma, has led to the
increased popularity of early intervention and prevention initiatives such as critical incident stress debriefing (CISD) and psychological debriefing (PD). As
shown, such attempts at prevention of PTSD may, in fact, result in unintended
negative outcomes.

Critical Incident Debriefing

CISD was first described by Mitchell (1983) and developed for emergency service workers such as paramedics and firefighters. Debriefing protocols presume that normalizing and ventilation shortly after a traumatic stressor can inhibit subsequent stress responses (Mitchell, 1983). CISD is a structured intervention conducted by trained mental health professionals in either group or individual format. The process typically occurs 2 to 3 days following the traumatic event and can last 3 to 5 hours. Victims are encouraged to recount their thoughts and feelings with the ultimate goal of processing and making sense of the trauma (Mitchell, 1983). These debriefing protocols are now recommended as standards of care for a multitude of national and international government and military organizations (Mitchell & Everly, 1997).

While growing anecdotal support for CISD enhanced its popularity and use, methodologically sound studies testing the effectiveness of CISD lagged behind clinical implementation. Since two randomized controlled trials were published in 1979 (Bordow & Porritt, 1979; Bunn & Clarke, 1979), empirical evaluations of debriefing have resulted in uniformly disappointing results, and several reviewers have commented on such continued failures (e.g., Bisson, 2003; Ehlers & Clark, 2003). We briefly review the empirical studies of PD to illustrate the range of outcomes with trauma victims.

Accident Victims

Bordow and Porritt (1979) allocated 70 males who had been hospitalized subsequent to motor vehicle accident (MVA)-related injuries to either a 3- to 4-month follow-up assessment, immediate short debriefing interview and follow-up assessment, or a social work intervention of 2 to 10 hours. The subjects receiving the social work intervention fared better than the other two groups, while the subjects given the initial debriefing interview fared better at follow-up than the subjects given only follow-up assessment. There were multiple problems with this study, including the absence of baseline measures of psychological distress, and the absence of blind assessment of subjects (the outcome measures were administered by the same people conducting the intervention). Bunn and Clarke (1979) randomly assigned 30 relatives of seriously ill/injured emergency room patients to either a 20-minute counseling session or to no intervention. Five-minute audiotaped verbal samples of pre- and post-intervention discussion were analyzed for features of anxiety. Subjects receiving the 20-minute intervention were said to be less anxious based on these speech samples. These are, to date, the success stories for psychological debriefing.

Hobbs, Mayou, Harrison, and Worlock (1996) randomly assigned 106 MVA survivors to either one hour of debriefing within 2 days of the accident or to no treatment, and assessed them on established measures of psychological distress and PTSD symptoms at baseline, 4 months, and (in a subsequent paper) three years post-MVA (Mayou, Ehlers, & Hobbs, 2000). The debriefed subjects fared marginally *worse* at the 4-month follow-up, and, alarmingly, had *more* self-reported PTSD symptoms three years later. Hobbs and Adshead (1996) reported an unpublished study by Stevens and Adshead in which 63 emergency room patients were allocated to either debriefing or control groups and assessed at one-week, one-month, and three-month follow-up on self-report measures of depression, anxiety, and the Impact of Event Scale (IES). While most patients found the intervention useful, there were no between-group differences on any of the measures of psychological distress or PTSD symptoms. Bisson, Jenkins, Alexander, and Bannister (1997) randomly assigned 130 burn victims to debriefing within three weeks of injury or to a control group. Subjects were assessed prior to debriefing, as well as at 3- and 13-month follow-up. There were no between-group differences in general distress or PTSD symptoms at the 3-month follow-up, but the debriefing group fared *worse* on PTSD symptoms at 13 months. Conlon, Fahy, and Conroy (1999) assigned 40 MVA survivors to either a 30-minute debriefing or no intervention, and assessed subjects at baseline and at 3-month follow-up. The small sample size of this study made it difficult to obtain meaningful results. While four control subjects met criteria for PTSD at follow-up and only two debriefing subjects met such criteria, this was not a statistically significant or clinically meaningful difference.

Other Trauma Victims
Lee, Slade, and Lygo (1996) randomly assigned 40 women who had miscarried to either one hour of debriefing within 2 weeks of miscarriage or no intervention and assessed them at baseline and at 4-month follow-up on self-report measures of psychological distress and PTSD symptoms. While women who received debriefing considered it helpful, there were no differences between groups in PTSD symptoms or psychological distress at the 4-month follow-up. Rose, Brewin, Andrews, and Kirk (1999) randomly assigned 157 crime victims to a control group, to a 30-minute educational session on normal responses to trauma, or to a one-hour debriefing session approximately 3 weeks postassault. Subjects were assessed at baseline, and at 6- and 11-month follow-up. No differences were found between groups on any measures. Deahl et al. (2000) non-randomly allocated British soldiers returning from duty in Bosnia to either two-hour group debriefings or to a control condition, and assessed subjects at baseline, as well as at 3-, 6-, and 12-month follow-up. The debriefed group fared *worse* with respect to reductions in PTSD symptoms. This is a problematic study because of the non-random assignment of subjects to conditions and because the nondebriefed group was significantly more distressed at baseline (therefore making their greater improvement on the IES explainable by regression to the mean).

Given emerging empirical findings of equivocal efficacy and participants' positive opinions of CISD, Raphael, Meldrum, and McFarlane (1995) recommended carefully considering the most cost-effective and helpful intervention options for different groups of people and traumas. Ehlers and Clark (2003) have suggested that debriefing typically occurs too early, that it may reinforce an individual's maladaptive appraisals of his/her intrusive memories (e.g., having this recurrent upsetting memory means I'm losing my mind), and that patients may use the debriefing exposure to memories maladaptively (e.g., as an opportunity to ruminate).

Treating Acute Stress Disorder

Acute stress disorder (ASD, American Psychiatric Association, 2000) was introduced as a diagnostic category into the *Diagnostic and Statistical Manual of Mental Disorders* (DSM-IV) to help identify those at risk of developing PTSD. ASD is defined as a reaction to traumatic stress that occurs up to four weeks after the index trauma. Although ASD focuses more on dissociative symptoms than PTSD, it also includes symptoms of reexperiencing, avoidance, and hyperarousal. Preliminary prospective studies suggest that between 60% and 80% of individuals meeting criteria for ASD following a traumatic event will meet criteria for PTSD up to 2 years later (e.g., Harvey & Bryant, 2000a). The ASD diagnosis has been contentious since its inception. It has been criticized on the grounds of being conceptually and empirically redundant with PTSD, as well as pathologizing common symptoms of psychological distress in the immediate aftermath of trauma.

To date, there have only been a few controlled treatment trials for ASD. Bryant, Harvey, Dang, Sackville, and Basten (1998) randomly assigned 24 participants with ASD following either a motor vehicle or industrial accident to either five sessions of cognitive behavioral therapy (CBT) or supportive counseling (SC) within two weeks of the trauma. Seventeen percent of participants in the CBT group compared with 67% in the SC group met criteria for PTSD at the 6-month follow-up assessment. Similar results with 45 participants were found when Bryant, Sackville, Dang, Moulds, and Guthrie (1999) compared prolonged exposure, exposure with anxiety management, and supportive counseling. Bryant, Moulds, and Nixon (2003) followed 41 participants who had received these two treatments over a four-year period. Eight percent of CBT clients and 25% of SC clients met PTSD criteria at the 4-year follow-up assessment.

Echeburua, de Corral, Sarasua, and Zubizarreta (1996) randomly assigned 20 sexual assault victims with acute PTSD (1 to 3 months posttrauma) to five sessions of either cognitive restructuring and coping skills training or progressive muscle relaxation. Therefore, these patients did not meet the ASD duration criterion, but were sufficiently acute that they could be considered to have received early intervention. There were no differences between groups on any postassessments, except for the cognitive restructuring group having a significantly lower PTSD symptom score at the 12-month follow-up assessment. Foa, Hearst-Ikeda, and

Perry (1995) found that survivors of recent sexual assault who received four sessions of CBT had lower rates of PTSD, and reduced depressive and reexperiencing symptoms than did a matched assessment control group.

More recently, Foa et al. (unpublished data cited in Ehlers & Clark, 2003) found that four 2-hour weekly sessions of CBT beginning an average of 21 days posttrauma did not have superior results to mere repeated assessments of patients. CBT was marginally superior to supportive counseling in this study. The Bryant group's most recent study (Bryant, Moulds, Guthrie, & Nixon, 2005) found that 5 to 6 sessions of CBT as well as a combination of CBT and hypnosis were more effective than supportive counseling.

In short, brief (four to six sessions) CBT provided to trauma survivors meeting diagnostic criteria for either ASD or acute PTSD appears relatively effective in reducing the rate of chronic PTSD. Therefore, ASD and acute PTSD cases may benefit from early intervention, but only if it is of a specific CBT nature. CISD, while receiving positive consumer satisfaction ratings, appears unlikely to have reliable benefits with respect to reduced PTSD symptoms or general psychological distress. At this time, SC has not been demonstrated to have any benefit for symptomatic trauma survivors.

Despite the relative superiority of CBT of 4 to 6 sessions duration to supportive counseling, there are some strikingly unanswered questions about such early intervention. According to Ehlers and Clark (2003), it is still unclear whether CBT beginning within one month of the trauma is superior to simple repeated assessments, which themselves may potentially be an effective treatment. Second, it is still unclear whether supportive counseling administered within the first few weeks posttrauma is worse than no treatment. If this were the case, it would have serious implications for trauma rehabilitation as it is currently practiced.

Pharmacological Prevention of PTSD

There have been only limited research trials evaluating pharmaceutical prevention of PTSD. Pitman et al. (2002) found that 40 mg of propanolol administered 4 times daily for 10 days beginning within 6 hours of accident trauma resulted in decreased heart rate and skin conductance reactivity to mental imagery of the trauma, as compared to a placebo group. There were, however, no differences in PTSD symptoms between the two groups. Saxe et al. (2001) found that amount of morphine administered during initial hospitalization due to burn injury predicted lower PTSD symptoms at 6-month follow-up, despite there being no significant correlation between pain and later PTSD outcome. This is a curious result given the many studies that have shown a potentiating relationship between pain and PTSD. There is some evidence that short-term use of sedative benzodiazepines may be helpful with PTSD cases in their early stages. Mellman, Byers, and Augenstein (1998) found that use of benzodiazepines for sleep disturbance in PTSD patients between 1 and 3 months posttrauma resulted in reduced PTSD symptoms. It is clear that much more research is necessary before pharmaceutical treatments can be confidently prescribed as preventative interventions for trauma victims.

Psychological Treatment of PTSD

The controlled and open trials of treatment for PTSD are reviewed below so that the reader may appreciate the current standards for optimal treatment.

Treatment Efficacy Studies for Chronic PTSD

Cognitive behavioral therapy (CBT) appears to be the main efficacious psychological treatment for chronic PTSD. Four variations of CBT have demonstrated significant efficacy. These include stress inoculation training (SIT, Veronen & Kilpatrick, 1983), prolonged exposure (PE, Foa, Dancu, Hembree, Jaycox, Meadows, & Street, 1999), cognitive processing therapy (CPT, Resick & Schnicke, 1992), and cognitive behavioral therapy based on Ehlers and Clark's (2000) cognitive model of PTSD (e.g., Ehlers et al., 2003). The efficacy of cognitive behavioral interventions for chronic PTSD has been demonstrated in a number of different studies with various different trauma populations. These include sexual assault victims (e.g., Foa et al., 1999; Resick & Schnicke, 1992), adult survivors of childhood abuse (Cloitre, Koenen, Cohen, & Han, 2002), motor vehicle accident survivors (e.g., Blanchard et al., 2003), and veterans (e.g., Frueh, Turner, Beidel, Mirabella, & Jones, 1996).

Limited studies included the following criteria necessary to be defined as a randomized controlled treatment trial: clearly defined target symptoms; random assignment of patients to different treatments or control conditions; reliable and valid measures of symptoms or clinical status; blind evaluators of outcome; assessor training; manualized, replicable, specific treatment programs; unbiased assignment of patients to specific treatments or control conditions; and monitored adherence by therapists to treatment protocols. Such criteria are important because they ensure that any variations in outcome between patients in different treatment or control conditions can be validly attributed to the treatment and not to extraneous variables. The reader will recall the difference between widespread consumer satisfaction with CISD and the equivocal evidence for symptomatic improvement following CISD in randomized trials. Such well-controlled trials are thus critical to our acceptance of the efficacy of any particular treatment.

PE-based interventions have largely been developed by Foa, Rothbaum, and Steketee (1993) and include education about PTSD; breathing retraining; in vivo hierarchy construction and graded repeated exposure (e.g., to different driving situations for MVA-PTSD victims); prolonged imaginal exposure to trauma memories (e.g., to the assault or subject MVA); and imaginal exposure debriefing. Imaginal exposure encourages the client to relive the trauma in imagination, in present tense, for a prolonged period of time (typically 45–60 minutes). Therapists use various techniques to titrate the imaginal recounting for maximal exposure and habituation. Some protocols tape the reliving and encourage clients to listen daily for increased emotional processing.

Stress inoculation training (SIT) interventions focus on skills to cope with trauma-related anxiety and other difficulties. This includes education about PTSD, breathing retraining, applied relaxation, thought stopping, cognitive restructuring, and guided self-dialogue. The behavioral rehearsal techniques include covert modeling, role-play, and exposure, which are designed to decrease the patients' avoidance of trauma-related stimuli (Kilpatrick, Veronen, & Resick, 1982).

Cognitive processing therapy (CPT) interventions focus mainly on cognitive therapy and exposure for victims of sexual assault. Resick and Schnicke (1992) implemented exposure through detailed written accounts of the index trauma that sexual assault survivors read to both themselves and the therapist. Consistent with traditional cognitive therapy, CPT therapists identify distorted beliefs that the individual may have about the assault, him/herself, and other matters (e.g., other people's evaluation of the rape victim); challenge these beliefs; and work to create more balanced, yet realistic beliefs. These authors found that CPT significantly reduced both PTSD and depressive symptoms compared to a wait-list control.

Ehlers et al. (2003) showed that up to 12 weekly sessions of CBT with their particular emphasis on cognitive therapy was superior to one session with a clinician and bibliotherapy, as well as superior to repeated assessments with MVA-PTSD patients recruited approximately three months post-MVA. This particular study is important because it better controlled for repeated assessments, which appears to be a mildly effective procedure in reducing PTSD symptoms (cf., Tarrier, Somerfield, Reynolds, & Pilgrim, 1999).

While SIT appears to be an efficacious treatment, when it is compared to PE, effect sizes measuring PTSD symptoms, depression, and general anxiety are generally lower (see Foa, Dancu, et al., 1999). Recent theoretical and empirical efforts suggest that thought stopping, one of the interventions in the SIT package, may actually be harmful for persons with anxiety problems. Thought stopping is now understood to be a form of thought control or suppression that unexpectedly increases the frequency and intensity of intrusive thoughts (e.g., O'Neill & Whittal, 2002). Thus, the inclusion of thought stopping in these trials may explain the marginally worse outcomes. This also has implications for interventions applied by many general clinicians with trauma victims, given that thought stopping is still widely used.

Nevertheless, because SIT does not incorporate any imaginal exposure to trauma memories, some clients may prefer this form of treatment. It may also prove useful for trauma survivors who tend to dissociate easily or who experience extremely high levels of emotional arousal in response to trauma memories. SIT could provide a helpful set of coping skills in which to train PTSD patients prior to PE treatment. While it is intuitively plausible that such improved stress management skills would enhance patients' responses to PE treatment, this hypothesis has not yet been empirically tested.

Resick, Nishith, Weaver, Astin, and Feuer (2002) compared CPT, PE, and wait-list conditions with female sexual assault victims. Overall, it appears that both treatments were highly efficacious and superior to the wait-list control. The two active treatments were largely equivalent with respect to symptom reduction. Tarrier et al. (1999) compared CPT and PE for a mixed-trauma sample, finding that both treatments were effective, but neither superior to the other.

When Nishith, Resick, and Griffin (2002) examined the pattern of change, they found several interesting results. First, for both the PE and CPT, reexperiencing symptoms were often initially exacerbated before they lessened. Foa, Zoellner, Feeny, Hembree, and Alvarez-Conrad (2002), on the other hand, found only a minority of individuals experiencing symptom exacerbation following imaginal exposure and that such exacerbation was unrelated to the probability of treatment termination or symptomatic change. Therapists should therefore educate their patients about such short-term effects and reassure them that such symptom exacerbations will be temporary. Second, for both treatment conditions, overall symptom levels exhibited a dramatic decrease following the first exposure session. This finding, as Nishith et al. (2002) concluded, leads us to suspect that the exposure element of treatment is the active ingredient in symptomatic improvement.

CBT also appears effective for MVA survivors with PTSD. For example, Blanchard et al. (2003) examined CBT, supportive psychotherapy, and wait-list control in a sample of 78 MVA survivors with chronic PTSD. The CBT treatment contained components of exposure, progressive relaxation, training in coping self-statements, and behavioral activation. CBT significantly reduced PTSD symptoms and diagnosis, as well as reduced comorbid diagnoses of major depression and generalized anxiety disorder in comparison to the other two conditions.

Overall, it appears that the different variants of cognitive behavioral therapy are all efficacious and generally equivalent. The International Consensus Group on Depression and Anxiety along with a group of PTSD experts recommend exposure therapy as the first-line psychological treatment for PTSD with the therapy being continued for six months and follow-up provided on an as-needed basis (Ballenger et al., 2000). This has important implications for therapists involved in PTSD rehabilitation. Treatment that does not include some form of PE, SIT, or CPT may not meet minimum standards and, thus, is a disservice to patients and to third-party insurers.

Open Treatment Trials for Chronic PTSD

There are a number of studies not meeting randomized controlled trial criteria. These are typically referred to as open trials. Najavits, Weiss, Shaw, and Muenz (1998) examined the effectiveness of cognitive behavioral group therapy for women with PTSD and concurrent substance dependence. Compared with pre-treatment, the women showed significant improvements across a wide variety of adjustment measures including PTSD symptoms, depression, substance use, and social and familial adjustment. Frueh et al. (1996) developed trauma management therapy (TMT) for combat veterans with PTSD. TMT uses exposure and social and emotional skills training over 29 sessions. These authors found significant pre- and post-differences across PTSD symptom scores in a sample of 15 veterans.

CBT interventions have also been investigated in women with PTSD related to domestic violence. Kubany, Hill, and Owens (2003) examined the preliminary effectiveness of cognitive trauma therapy (CTT) in 37 women who had left an abusive relationship. CTT focuses on modifying the irrational beliefs and eval-uative language associated with chronic PTSD. Thirty of the 32 women who completed CTT did not meet criteria for PTSD at posttest. Kubany et al. (2004) replicated their first study in a larger sample of 125 battered women. Eighty-six (69%) of these women completed treatment, with 87% of the latter remitting from PTSD status. Gains were maintained at six-month follow-up. Of note, women who failed to complete treatment differed at the beginning of treatment from completers by being younger, less educated, and more depressed. Noncompleters also experienced lower self-esteem and greater guilt and shame.

The largest open trial of CBT for PTSD following MVAs is that of Taylor et al. (2001). These authors completed an uncontrolled study of group CBT for chronic PTSD in 50 MVA survivors, and found significant reductions in PTSD symptomatology with 44% of PTSD patients no longer meeting formal criteria for PTSD at follow-up. This study was significant for two results: (a) the reason-able success rate (44% remission) for group-administered CBT, and (b) the var-iables that were found to predict worse outcome. Taylor et al. (2001) used cluster analysis to group patients into those who made substantial symptomatic improve-ments and those who had less symptomatic improvement. Pain severity, comorbid depression, and anger all predicted worse outcome. Interestingly, presence of litigation or compensation claims did not predict outcome.

Pharmacological Treatment of PTSD

Increasing evidence supports the effectiveness of selective serotonin reuptake in-hibitors (SSRIs) and monoamine oxidase inhibitors (MAOIs) in reducing PTSD symptomatology. Davidson, Rothbaum, van der Kolk, Sikes, and Farfel (2001) compared sertraline and placebo in a double-blind multicenter trial for moderate to severe PTSD. A 60% versus 38% responder rate for sertraline compared with placebo was found for 208 patients over a 12-week period. Davidson, Landerman, Farfel, and Clary (2002) examined the impact of sertraline on the individual symptoms of PTSD using data from two 12-week placebo-controlled trials. Sertraline outperformed placebo on the vast majority of PTSD symptoms, particularly with the numbing and arousal clusters of symptoms.

There are a number of open-trial studies for the treatment of PTSD with various SSRIs. Fluvoxamine has demonstrated some effectiveness for PTSD symptoms, particularly with combat-related trauma (e.g., Escalona, Canive, Calais, & Davidson, 2002). Citalopram has demonstrated symptom reduction in a preliminary study with 14 adults (Seedat et al., 2002). There is also evidence that nefazodone decreases PTSD symptoms in combat veterans (Garfield, Fichtner, Leveroni, & Mahableshwarkar, 2001). However, Lubin, Weizman, Shmushkevitz, and Valevski (2002) completed an open-label preliminary study of naltrexone and found that the side effects did not support the minor clinical improvements found. Overall, it appears that the family of SSRIs demonstrates moderate but clinically significant improvement in PTSD symptomatology and overall functioning across a wide variety of trauma populations. Gaffney (2003) suggests that SSRIs may be more effective with the depressive symptoms that are often associated with PTSD. The International Consensus Group on Depression and Anxiety along with a group of PTSD experts recommend SSRIs as the first-line class of pharmaceutical treatment for PTSD, with such treatment recommended for at least 12 months (Ballenger et al., 2000). To date, within the United States, both paroxetine and sertraline have received the label of having a PTSD-specific indication.

Special Issues in Psychological Treatment of PTSD

Several articles discuss specific techniques for increasing treatment success with cognitive behavioral interventions. Resick and Schnicke (1992) recommend a focus on "stuck points" within trauma narratives as a key element in aiding treatment. Moderate to high levels of emotional engagement throughout the imaginal exposure exercise have also been shown to improve treatment outcomes for PTSD and depression (Jaycox, Foa, & Morral, 1998). For less severe cases of PTSD, Reynolds and Tarrier (1996) found that simple monitoring of symptoms could result in improvement. All of the points above emphasize the importance to successful treatment of imaginal exposure, associated writing assignments, and elicitation of adverse emotional responses contained in the trauma memory.

There is increasing evidence that panic attacks, whether spontaneous or triggered by exposure to reminders of the index trauma, occur frequently in PTSD patients. For example, Falsetti and Resnick (1997) found that 69% of a sample of 62 adults seeking treatment for trauma-related symptoms had experienced at least one panic attack in the two weeks prior to assessment. Bryant and Panasetis (2001) found that more than half of civilian trauma sufferers reported panic attacks during their index trauma, and that those who met criteria for acute stress disorder had more panic symptoms. Such findings led Falsetti, Resnick, Davis, and Gallagher (2001) to develop a specific PTSD treatment protocol (multiple-channel exposure therapy) for comorbid PTSD and panic. This implies that PTSD patients who also suffer significantly from panic attacks may require specific treatment for panic and thus may require more treatment in total.

Specific Trauma Populations

Specific trauma populations such as veterans, victims of sexual assault, childhood abuse, and vehicular or industrial accidents may require variations or additions to the psychological protocols described above in order to maximize functional improvement.

Combat-Related PTSD

Perhaps unique within the general PTSD population, many combat-related PTSD survivors experience feelings of both victimization and perpetration of trauma (Foa & Meadows, 1997). Guilt and shame may be justifiably present around the frequently violent acts that can be carried out while in combat, and standard interventions such as cognitive restructuring should be initiated with caution because of the potential for strengthening maladaptive beliefs about oneself (e.g., guilt over one's actions). Foa and Meadows (1997) suggest using more creative interventions such as exploring different acts in the interests of reparation (e.g., volunteering). Frueh et al. (1996) describe a number of interventions in their trauma management therapy unique to veteran populations.

Childhood Abuse and Sexual Assault

There are a number of issues for victims of childhood abuse and sexual assault. Victims of chronic, long-term childhood abuse may suffer delays or aberrations of emotional and social development (e.g., sexual trust, intimacy) that result in interpersonal skill deficits. Therapists may have to spend 1 or 2 sessions conducting assertiveness skills training. With victims of sexual assault, the uncertainty of possible revictimization, particularly for women living in troubled neighborhoods or relationships, is a reality to be addressed throughout the course of treatment (Foa & Meadows, 1997). Treatment should focus on differentiating safe from unsafe situations, particularly when conducting the in vivo exposure aspect of the therapy (Foa & Meadows, 1997).

PTSD secondary to domestic violence has a number of complications, including many social, economic, and emotional obstacles to leaving the abusive relationship. While in a violent relationship, victims are justified in viewing their situation as dangerous and, thus, most of the elements of PE, intended to give the patient an increased sense of safety, are inappropriate for both ethical and practical reasons. Victims of domestic violence may also be more prone to guilt and shame related to their perceived "choice" of the abusive relationship (Kubany, Hill, & Owens, 2003) and, thus, require cognitive interventions concerning such emotions. Even if a victim of domestic violence has left the abusive relationship, he/she may be stalked by the perpetrator, thus continuing to be in a legitimately dangerous situation. Finally, well-intentioned family members may interfere with domestic violence victims' attempts to leave the relationship, stay away from the perpetrator, or develop appropriate safety measures.

Motor Vehicle Accident Victims
While PTSD sufferers following automobile collisions are as heterogeneous as other PTSD sufferers; there are some more common presentations that are important for treatment and rehabilitation professionals to consider.

First, MVA-PTSD patients will frequently suffer from concurrent pain conditions secondary to orthopedic or soft-tissue injuries. The severity of continuing pain complaints will interfere with CBT for PTSD (e.g., Taylor et al., 2001) and thus CBT of MVA-PTSD should perhaps be coordinated with the patient's pain management program.

Second, approximately 50% of MVA-PTSD patients will have a concurrent major depression. Even those who do not suffer a clinically severe depression may have sufficient depressive symptoms to complicate their recovery. Because depressive affect compromises individuals' tolerance of emotional distress and impairs motivation, many MVA-PTSD patients will require help with their depressive condition. This may be most parsimoniously dealt with through behavioral activation such as pleasant event scheduling (e.g., Blanchard et al., 2003) and exercise or through pharmacological assistance. It appears unwise to ignore depressive affect when treating MVA-PTSD patients.

Mobility restrictions are a striking part of the functional disability of MVA-PTSD patients. As well, there are many MVA survivors who do not meet formal criteria for PTSD, yet suffer disabling phobic avoidance of automobile travel. Ehlers, Hofmann, and Herda (1994) noted three routes of acquisition of driving phobias: (a) fear of auto travel secondary to panic disorder, (b) traumatic onset fear of auto travel secondary to an MVA and a fear of being in yet another MVA, and (c) fear of auto travel secondary to performance anxiety (e.g., low confidence in driving ability, fear that one might become confused/lost). Because these different routes of acquisition are not mutually exclusive, and because of the difficulty in controlling the environment in which driving phobias express themselves, overcoming the phobic avoidance that is common following traumatic MVAs has unique complexities. Ascertaining the core fear(s) for individual patients (e.g., fear of reinjury and worse physical outcomes, lowered confidence in one's driving ability, fear of panic symptoms while driving) is a necessary early step in developing a treatment plan. Ascertaining these core fears and other factors maintaining patients' driving fears requires not only detailed interviewing, but also structured questionnaires (e.g., Posttraumatic Cognitions Inventory, Foa, Ehlers et al., 1999), and behavioral assessments such as observing the patient when he/she is driving or riding as a passenger.

In vivo exposure therapy that involves both therapist- and spouse-accompanied drives is frequently necessary to return MVA-PTSD patients to optimal functioning. Basic principals of in vivo exposure treatment include: (a) remaining in the feared situation until one's fear/anxiety declines in intensity, (b) altering danger and safety appraisals through repeated and prolonged benign exposure to the feared situation, and (c) suppressing maladaptive safety behaviors that increase the patient's sense of safety but become "crutches." Because the auto traffic environment is neither easily controlled nor constant, in vivo exposure treatment requires that the patient repeat his/her exposure to specific situations that elicit fear (e.g., intersections, driving by cars parked on a narrow street, freeway on-ramps), rather than just spending a certain amount of time driving. The therapist must keep in mind that the feared situation is not just being in a car, it is those frequently short-lived traffic situations that elicit rushes of fear in the individual patient.

Accompanying such a patient in a vehicle will allow the therapist to assess the particular situations in which the patient experiences fear, as well as those maladaptive safety behaviors exhibited by individual patients. We have previously used the term "safety compulsions" to describe specific behaviors such as grabbing door handles and bracing oneself against the dashboard. We believe these behaviors in accident phobics serve the same function as compulsions in obsessive-compulsive patients—temporarily increasing the patient's sense of safety, but ultimately maintaining fear and avoidance. As in the treatment of obsessive-compulsive disorder, we believe it is important to block these safety compulsions during in vivo exposure treatment in order to achieve maximal improvement. In vivo exposure to auto traffic may require a graduated approach (e.g., initial repeated short drives in a safe residential neighborhood leading to longer drives in heavier traffic or inclement weather conditions). We recommend a procedure we refer to as "looping exposure," in which patients drive several times through particular locations (e.g., specific intersections) or driving situations (e.g., heavy commercial truck traffic); this maximizes exposure to the situations that elicit fear and allows fear to gradually decline during such repeated within-session exposures.

While the scientific jury is still out on the benefits of specific cognitive therapy procedures for enhancing the effects of exposure therapy for PTSD, we believe there are specific cognitive change exercises therapists should prescribe for their driving phobic patients. Consistent with cognitive behavioral models of PTSD, we believe that accident phobics suffer a change in their perception of the safety of automobile travel and an increased expectancy of collisions. We also believe that they "filter" information while driving in a manner that highlights danger cues (e.g., cars running red lights, illegal lane changes by others), and overlooks safety cues (e.g., cars following a safe distance behind other vehicles, courteous merging behavior). Thus, we frequently ask patients to spend time at a given intersection and to count the number of cars passing through and the number of collisions to get an objective sample of the probability of automobile collisions. Similarly, we frequently ask patients to count the number of "good driving behaviors" or examples of courteous driving in order to shift their attention. Hickling and Blanchard (1996) train their MVA-PTSD patients in coping self-statements such as, "In particular, you need to remind yourself that you are a good driver and a careful and safe driver" (p. 15).

Despite our knowledge of general principles of treating phobias, the therapist must keep in mind that individual differences in coping with fear are very common. One of the authors once simultaneously had two accident phobic patients, one of whom vigilantly scanned oncoming traffic when riding as a passenger so that she could better warn the driver of impending disaster, while the other consistently rode as a passenger with her eyes closed so that she could avoid the sight of oncoming traffic. Treating both of these behaviors as safety compulsions led to prescribing assignments for the vigilant accident phobic to ride with her eyes closed while relaxing, and the "eyes-closed" patient to watch oncoming traffic while practicing relaxation.

Domestic Violence

Because domestic violence (DV) has a high prevalence of PTSD and other emotional distress, it is somewhat surprising that treatments for DV-related PTSD have only very recently been conducted (Kubany, Hill, & Owens, 2003; Kubany et al., 2004). This variant of CBT for PTSD, referred to as cognitive trauma therapy for formerly battered women (CTT-BW), incorporates a unique focus on cognitions (attitudes and beliefs) that revolve around the concepts of guilt and shame. CTT-BW also includes specific treatment modules around assertiveness, managing unwanted contacts with the abuser, and avoidance of future abusive relationships. As well, Kubany and Watson (2002) emphasize the importance of their cognitive therapy intervention for guilt, which targets the following issues thought to plague domestic violence victims: (a) perceived self-responsibility for negative events in the relationship, (b) difficulties justifying self-protective actions, (c) victims' perception that they may be violating other values (e.g. "marriage is supposed to be forever"), and (d) hindsight bias and self-blame (e.g., "I should have been able to predict"). It is important to note here that the two successful trials of treatment to date with domestic violence victims have excluded battered women who were still in the violent relationship (must have been 30 days or more postseparation) or who were considering reconciling. This is important for two reasons. First, treatment of PTSD demands that patients not be in current danger, but women in physically abusive relationships appear to remain at heightened risk of physical harm for some time following the cessation of their violent relationship. Second, it appears (see chapter 6) that women in violent relationships have a significant remission of emotional distress after leaving the violent relationship. Thus, use of CTT-BW would not be recommended for women currently in a violent relationship.

Eye Movement Desensitization and Reprocessing

The efficacy and mechanism of action behind eye movement desensitization and reprocessing (EMDR, Shapiro, 1999) remain highly contentious. EMDR was originally designed for the treatment of PTSD, but has more recently been applied to an increasing variety of disorders and difficulties including phobias, panic disorder, depression, interpersonal conflict, and eating problems.

EMDR has clients engage in lateral eye movements while recalling, in imagination, important portions of a traumatic or disturbing event. As originally described by Shapiro in 1989, the therapist uses lateral movements of their index finger to guide clients in making between 10 and 20 rhythmic eye movements while verbally reporting sensations, cognitions, and emotions. This process is repeated until desensitization occurs. The trauma memory is then paired with a positive cognition until the client reports significant levels of belief in the new thought.

Interestingly, in 1999, Shapiro retracted much of the focus on eye movements as the critical component of the treatment, stating that, "this is incorrect and unfortunate interpretation of the method can be explained by the author's concentration on the concrete actions in which she was engaging during therapy, rather than on the attendant complexity of the methodology actually employed and the underlying processes thought to be engendered by it" (p. 37). Shapiro (1999) indicated that EMDR has been significantly modified over the years through clinical observation to now include 8 phases of treatment that draw from a variety of theoretical and empirical orientations. These include client history and treatment planning, preparation, assessment, desensitization, installation, body scan, closure, and reevaluation.

EMDR's claim of rapid recovery from PTSD, often within one session, sparked significant empirical investigations. Currently, we know EMDR is often associated with treatment gains when compared to no treatment conditions in the treatment of PTSD (e.g., Boudewyns & Hyer, 1996; Carlson, Chemtob, Rusnak, Hedlund, & Muraoka, 1998; Rothbaum, 1997). In contrast, a number of studies have found that EMDR is not superior to supportive counseling (e.g., Devilly, Spence, & Rapee, 1998; Lytle, Hazlett-Stevens, & Borkovec, 2002). Whether EMDR is as effective as already established treatments for PTSD (i.e., PE, SIT, CPT) remains unclear. After a review of the literature, Cahill, Carrigan, and Frueh (1999) concluded that the active ingredient of EMDR is repeated imaginal exposure to the trauma and that EMDR has greater effects on subjective ratings of anxiety made by the patient rather than on established psychometric scales.

A recent meta-analysis of 34 empirical studies of EMDR (Davidson & Parker, 2001) led to several conservative conclusions. First, when EMDR is compared to no treatment, clients appear to be better off with respect to improvement on reliable measures of PTSD symptoms. In addition, EMDR appeared to be reliably superior to nonspecific therapies such as applied relaxation. Third, EMDR was not found to be superior to treatments utilizing different forms of exposure therapy or cognitive behavioral therapy. Fourth, EMDR procedures not utilizing the eye movements that gave the treatment its name are as effective as EMDR with eye movements. Fifth, EMDR proponents have in the past explained away negative findings of trials claiming that the therapists in these negative outcome studies were not appropriately trained in EMDR. The meta-analytic data showed that EMDR results were equivalent independent of whether therapists were trained by the EMDR Institute.

More recently, Taylor et al. (2003) compared EMDR, exposure therapy (a documented treatment of choice for PTSD), and relaxation training with 60 chronic PTSD patients. Therapists were trained via the EMDR Institute. Of the 19 patients assigned to EMDR, 15 completed treatment. Fifteen of 22 patients assigned to exposure therapy completed their treatment and 15 of 19 patients assigned to relaxation training completed treatment. Treatments were structured to involve equivalent amounts of in-session work (eight 90-minute sessions) and equivalent amounts of homework. In brief, PTSD symptoms declined for all treatments, but exposure therapy was superior to EMDR and relaxation in reduction of both reexperiencing symptoms and avoidance behavior, leading to a lower rate of active PTSD cases in the exposure therapy group at follow-up (15%) than for EMDR (35%), or relaxation (55%). Exposure therapy also led to more rapid reduction in avoidance behavior. This particular empirical study adds to the evidence that exposure therapy is beneficial for chronic PTSD cases, and that EMDR has little unique to offer PTSD cases beyond marginal improvement over the effects of nonspecific treatments. EMDR should not be considered a treatment of choice for PTSD sufferers by rehabilitation coordinators and insurers.

The Effects of Litigation on Treatment

Many clinicians decline to treat individuals who have ongoing compensation claims, are on work disability payments, or who are involved in personal injury litigation with respect to their mental health. Specifically, many clinicians believe that litigants or compensation-seeking patients are unlikely to improve clinically and functionally until their litigation resolves or they are awarded compensation. The beginning of this belief is usually attributed to Miller (1961) who, based on a sample of 50 accident victims, concluded that the prospect of compensation was the primary cause of what he called "accident neurosis." Weissman (1990) seconded Miller's positions, stating, "Involvement in litigation renders plaintiffs susceptible to stressors and to influences that may lead to increased impairment, biased reportage, and retarded recovery" (p. 67). There appear to be two hypotheses underlying these writings: (a) that compensation seeking is the primary cause of symptom overendorsement for many if not all claimants (i.e., secondary gain), and (b) that litigation may contribute to plaintiffs' experience of stress, thus contributing directly to their clinical disability.

There is certainly some evidence that personal injury litigation and compensation seeking are associated with elevated reports of emotional distress and disability (e.g., Frueh, Gold, & de Arellano, 1997). However, few methodologically rigorous studies exist that have tested Miller's initial inference that cessation of litigation will result in cessation of symptoms.

One recent study by Blanchard et al. (1996) tested this hypothesis with MVA survivors. These authors followed 132 subjects for 12 months following their initial assessment one to four months after MVA, using the Clinician Administered PTSD Scale (CAPS) interview, self-report measures of distress, and measures of role functioning including employment status. Of these 132 subjects, 18 had their litigation settled during the 12-month follow-up, 49 litigants had not yet settled at 12 months, and 65 had never litigated. Nonlitigants did have significantly lower PTSD symptom scores (from the CAPS) at initial assessment compared to the two litigant groups. This is consistent with Miller's hypothesis, notwithstanding the alternative hypothesis that less-distressed/injured persons will appropriately be less likely to initiate legal claims. However, these interviewer-assessed PTSD symptoms did decrease at the 6- and 12-month assessments for both litigant groups, as well as for the nonlitigant group. While the litigation-pending group had more PTSD symptoms at 12 months than the nonlitigating group, the litigants had clearly improved over the 12 months despite ongoing litigation. Initial differences on the CAPS between litigants and nonlitigants were replicated with self-report measures of subjective distress, role performance, social relationships, and recreational activity. However, in this study, the litigants had also suffered more severe physical injuries as objectively assessed, thus offering some support for the view that severity of injury itself predicts decisions to litigate. At 12-month follow-up, litigants were no worse off with respect to role functioning or to PTSD symptoms as assessed by the CAPS than were nonlitigants, although they were more distressed as measured by self-report tests. In short, Blanchard et al. (1998) provided some limited support for Miller's hypothesis in that MVA survivors with pending litigation reported higher levels of distress on self-report inventories. Contrary to Miller's prediction, however, role functioning and PTSD symptoms assessed via a reliable interview improved despite pending litigation.

Very few trials of psychological treatment have evaluated the effects of litigation or compensation status on treatment success. One such study was that of

Taylor et al. (2001), an open trial of CBT for PTSD following MVAs. Study participants were chronic PTSD sufferers, with almost 90% of subjects involved in litigation. The authors used cluster analysis to identify two clusters of patients: full responders to treatment ($n = 30$) and partial responders ($n = 20$). The authors assessed a broad array of other potential predictor variables for differentiating the two clusters of patients who had differential success in group CBT treatment. Subjects pretreatment global functioning, anger about the MVA, severity of depression, and comorbid major depression, pain severity and pain-related interference, and use of psychotropic medications during CBT all predicted membership in the partial responding cluster. Litigation did not predict cluster membership; in fact, the percentage of patients in litigation was numerically higher in the responders cluster than in the partial responders cluster. However, it should be recognized that this study had a lower rate of full PTSD remission (44%) than the 70% of Blanchard et al. (2003), a study utilizing relatively similar treatment strategies. Other differences between these two studies included group (Taylor et al., 2001) versus individual (Blanchard et al., 2003) administration of treatment, and the handling of motor vehicle claims in the two jurisdictions. The Blanchard et al. study was conducted in New York State, a no-fault jurisdiction, while the Taylor et al. study was conducted in British Columbia, a torts jurisdiction where psychological services are excluded from reimbursement other than through a lawsuit. The differences in outcome could be accounted for by the methodological or legal differences between these two studies, or some other related factor. The extent to which personal injury litigation is stressful has not been studied in detail. One study (Koch, Shercliffe, Fedoroff, Iverson, & Taylor, 1999) collected survey data from both lawyers ($n = 50$) and psychologists ($n = 50$). They found that both lawyers (57%) and psychologists (80%) believed that stress secondary to the litigation process had moderate to major effects on plaintiffs' psychological status. In an attempt to understand whether different aspects of personal injury litigation would predict psychological outcome, these authors correlated pretreatment values of a number of putative litigation stress variables with prepost change on PTSD symptoms following cognitive behavioral therapy. The only items correlating with PTSD symptom change were (a) slowness of physical recovery ($r = -.38$), (b) optimism about recovery ($r = -.39$), number of health-care appointments since the subject MVA ($r = -.39$), and pre-MVA hours worked ($r = -.45$). Thus, those stressors related to litigation that predict PTSD symptom change appear to involve physical recovery and negative changes in how much time the person spent in health-care appointments and at work. Thus, perhaps the most stressful aspect of personal injuries is the change in how the person spends his/her time following injury.

In any event, a number of studies now suggest that litigation leads to over-endorsement of self-reported psychological distress, but there is little convincing support for Miller's (1961) hypothesis that accident neurosis is primarily mediated by the litigation process. It appears that MVA survivors spontaneously remit even when pursuing litigation and make gains in CBT treatment for PTSD despite concurrent involvement in litigation. Therefore, it does not appear wise to withhold effective treatment for PTSD from litigants.

Ethnicity and Treatment Outcome

The role of ethnicity in treatment outcome for sufferers of PTSD is scarce. The literature that does exist focuses, almost exclusively, on the differences between Caucasians and African Americans. Two studies looked at PTSD treatment for veterans. Rosenheck, Fontana, and Cottrol (1995) found that African American veterans participated less in therapy, showed poorer attendance, and had less improvement on outcome measures compared to Caucasian veterans, even after controlling for a number of important variables. However, Rosenheck and Fontana (1996) investigated male veterans again and found no differences between groups in treatment response.

One study examined chronic PTSD treatment in 95 female victims of sexual and nonsexual assault (Zoellner, Feeny, Fitzgibbons, & Foa, 1999). They found no differences between Caucasian and African American women on several measures including pretreatment functioning, dropout rates, and overall treatment efficacy. In short, there is one study indicating that African American combat-related PTSD sufferers may respond less well to treatment, but other studies that show no effects of African American ethnicity on treatment response. Socioeconomic factors may be more important predictors than ethnicity of treatment involvement and success, and all those professionals involved in PTSD rehabilitation should be alert to financial and other resource obstacles to PTSD sufferers entering and successfully completing treatment. Other prominent ethnic minorities (e.g., East Asians, South Asians, Aboriginal peoples) have been neglected in this treatment literature.

Comorbidity and Treatment Outcome

Comorbidity refers to the joint occurrence of two or more health problems simultaneously in the same patient. As discussed in chapter 3, PTSD has a very high rate of comorbidity of both other mental health conditions and of physical health problems. What are the implications of this comorbidity for successful rehabilitation of psychological injury claimants? Three types of studies have addressed the implications of comorbid problems in the treatment outcome of PTSD sufferers. A few treatment outcome studies have used pretreatment characteristics of patients to predict response to therapy (e.g., Taylor et al., 2001). Other studies have evaluated the efficacy of multicomponent treatments that target both PTSD and specific comorbid problems (e.g., Blanchard et al., 2003). Chemtob, Novaco, Hamada, and Gross (1997) have also evaluated the efficacy of anger treatment strategies on anger problems within PTSD samples.

Predictors of Worse PTSD Outcome

Taylor et al. (2001) conducted a large ($n = 50$) open trial of group-administered CBT for PTSD following MVAs. As part of this study, all patients completed an extensive pretreatment assessment battery and a CAPS interview. Following treatment, the authors performed a statistical cluster analysis to separate those patients who showed significant improvement in their PTSD symptoms (termed "responders," $n = 30$) and those patients who showed relatively little improvement ("partial responders," $n = 20$). Partial responders were characterized by more severe numbing symptoms on the pretreatment CAPS, greater depression, more severe pain, and greater trait anger expression. Blanchard et al. (2003) examined predictors of outcome for both their CBT and supportive psychotherapy conditions in a large Randomized Controlled Trial (RCT) for MVA-PTSD. It is of interest that these two different treatments with differential effectiveness had slightly different predictors of outcome. For patients receiving CBT, the pretreatment CAPS score and number of days of work missed following the MVA contributed 43% of the variance in posttreatment CAPS scores. For patients receiving supportive psychotherapy, approximately 70% of the variance in posttreatment CAPS scores was explained by pretreatment CAPS, a diagnosis of major depression at intake, and the patient's subjective fear that they might die in the MVA. Foa, Riggs, Massie, and Yarczower (1995) found that angry female rape victims receiving exposure treatment for their PTSD expressed less fear during such imaginal exposure sessions and benefited less from treatment. Tarrier et al. (2000) found that worse outcome was predicted by higher suicide risk, male gender, living alone, and comorbid generalized anxiety disorder.

On the other hand, van Minnen, Arntz, and Keijsers (2002), using two samples of mixed-trauma PTSD patients (n's $= 59$ and 63), found that no demographic or pretreatment variables predicted outcome. However, benzodiazepine use was related to both poorer outcome and dropout, while alcohol use was related to dropout.

Taken as a whole, there is some evidence that comorbid physical pain, depression, generalized anxiety disorder, high levels of anger, benzodiazepine use, and extent of initial work impairment may all limit the effectiveness of CBT or exposure therapy for PTSD. Because there is good reason to believe that depression, other anxiety disorders, and anger are commonly comorbid conditions in

PTSD patients, good clinical practice will involve screening for, and concurrent treatment of, these comorbid conditions. In addition, those involved in the rehabilitation of trauma survivors should note the potential negative predictive status of initial work impairment and of benzodiazepine use.

Treatment of Anger with PTSD Patients

Chemtob, Novaco, Hamada, and Gross (1997) allocated 28 Vietnam War veterans with PTSD and high levels of anger to either 12-session stress inoculation intervention for anger devised by Novaco (1983) or usual clinical care. Alarmingly, 13 of 28 participants who began treatment subsequently dropped out, leaving 8 in the anger control treatment and 7 in the control condition. The anger treatment consisted of self-monitoring of anger, completing an anger provocation hierarchy (i.e., situations that resulted in different degrees of anger), relaxation training, cognitive restructuring and self-instruction training, role-played assertiveness and communications training, and practicing new coping skills within session in role-played vignettes from their anger hierarchies. Participants completed several measures of anger, anxiety, and depression pre- and posttreatment, as well as at 18-month follow-up. The treated subjects showed greater reduction in anger control, but no other differences on measures of anger disposition, anxiety, or depression. Interpretation of this study is hampered by the high dropout rate (perhaps a natural consequence with this particularly impaired sample) and the resulting small sample size.

Treatment of Substance Abuse with PTSD Patients

Of special interest, recent efforts have been made in evaluating treatments for individuals with comorbid PTSD and substance abuse (e.g., Najavits, Weiss, Shaw, & Muenz, 1998). Najavits et al. (1998), in perhaps the best-described treatment for PTSD and substance abuse, conducted an open trial of a 24-session CBT treatment for these comorbid conditions on 27 women (17 completers, 10 dropouts). Completers improved from pretreatment to three-month posttreatment follow-up on measures of substance use, PTSD symptoms, and somatic complaints. While the dropout rate of 37% was alarming, treatment completers were paradoxically more impaired at pretreatment assessment than dropouts.

In short, while controlled trials of treatment for PTSD and substance abuse are still limited in number, there is growing evidence that psychological treatments can be tailored to include effective interventions for comorbid problems as well as for PTSD.

Future Directions

Despite the progress of the last decade, there are many unanswered questions about the prevention and rehabilitation of psychological injuries. With respect to prevention, four questions need to be addressed. First, given the number of trauma survivors who improve secondary to simple repeated assessments, any proposed preventive interventions must demonstrate that they improve upon such simple repeated assessment.

Second, both single-session psychological debriefing and supportive counseling need more stringent tests in which they are pitted against repeated assessments and CBT. Both supportive counseling and PD, when applied as early interventions, may now be in the position of having to prove they are not harmful. Such evaluations may benefit from being conducted in multisite trials in which the impact of treatment allegiance on treatment outcome can be empirically evaluated. Such studies should also use more diverse outcome evaluations to determine whether their muted or negative effects on symptomatic status are counterbalanced by positive effects on other dimensions. For example, such early interventions, while being neutral with respect to symptom reduction, may lead to better relationships between trauma survivors and employers or insurers because of the recipients' perception of having their psychological concerns heard. The latter phenomenon may have beneficial effects on work attendance and productivity, as well as litigation propensity, all of which may be independent of clinical status. If debriefing and supportive counseling continue to have neutral or negative outcomes, insurers and employers will have to grapple with a substantial policy issue. Is it, in fact, ethical insurance or employment policy to apply such well-intended but perhaps ineffective prevention strategies to unselected trauma survivors?

Third, stringently evaluated pharmacological prevention trials must be conducted and compared with appropriate comparison groups such as repeated assessment and 4- to 6-session CBT. Fourth, even in the presence of apparently positive results from the 4- to 6-session CBT trials, cost-benefit research concerning prevention of psychological distress following trauma is necessary to guide policy. Identifying symptomatic cases shortly following trauma is an expensive and time-consuming business, and many trauma survivors appear reluctant to seek help early. The cost of screening for and then soliciting such early survivors into preventative treatment must be weighed against the benefits associated with later decreased distress and disability. This is particularly the case given (a) the high rate of spontaneous remission during the first year posttrauma and (b) the relative success of different CBT interventions in treating chronic PTSD.

There are also substantial remaining questions with respect to the treatment of more chronic psychological injuries. Treatment trials need more stringent controls including such minimalist treatments as repeated assessments (e.g., Ehlers et al., (2003). In the absence of this type of control group, randomized controlled trials of PTSD treatment may give overly optimistic results. Unlike treatment trials for depression, we have yet to see head-to-head trials of psychological and pharmacological treatments to determine relative efficacy. Such comparative trials will likely emerge within the next few years. Moreover, given the extensive comorbidity of PTSD with depression and particularly with chronic pain in accident survivors, the field needs controlled evaluations of more intensive treatments that combine therapy for PTSD with focused treatments for chronic pain, depression, anger, and/or substance abuse. Some inroads have been made (e.g., including depression treatment components in CBT for PTSD, evaluating anger control treatments with PTSD samples), but much more remains to be done before the results of treatment efficacy studies can be used to guide individual rehabilitation programs for claimants with complex psychological injuries.

An important step in evaluating PTSD treatment may involve examining the impact that treatment choice has on treatment outcome. Clients may have better symptomatic outcomes when allowed to choose their own treatment from an array of evidence-based treatments. Because personal injury claimants have a duty to ameliorate their losses through following appropriate professional advice, it behooves us to understand whether patient treatment preferences predict better outcome. Some individuals will have an adverse response to exposure therapy for PTSD or will reject it out of hand for diverse personal reasons. Rather than apply different treatments to individual claimants on a trial and error basis, it would be helpful to understand better what works for whom. In addition, matching treatment type to patient preference would increase external validity because such matching more closely mimics the usual process of treatment initiation in non–research-based clinics. One way to answer this question would be to utilize a randomized design comparing "choice" to "no choice" treatment types, and the three known effective treatments. Zoellner and colleagues at the University of Washington are beginning to explore this important question.

Rehabilitating psychological injuries is about more than treating symptoms of disorders such as PTSD. The fundamental purpose of rehabilitation is to return claimants to a state of good functioning vocationally and socially, as well as to reduce their general distress. For that reason, future treatment trials will have to more carefully evaluate vocational and social outcomes, as well as more diverse psychological variables (e.g., quality of life, emotional resiliency). Throughout our field, many clinicians assume that remission of a clinical disorder will automatically result in amelioration of the vocational and social deficits seen in psychological injury claimants. While there may be some truth in this assumption, it has yet to be tested directly, and one suspects that many variables other than mere symptomatic status will control claimants' return to optimal functioning.

Finally, it is apparent to us that few clinicians who treat trauma victims use treatments that have been found efficacious in clinical trials. In fact, it is clear that the vast majority of licensed psychologists do not use prolonged imaginal exposure (perhaps the most consistently documented efficacious treatment for PTSD) on any of their PTSD patients. In a survey of 207 licensed psychologists from the northeastern United States and Texas, Becker, Zayfert, and Anderson (2004) found that 83% of their sample never used imaginal exposure therapy with their PTSD patients. As the increasing popularity of EMDR, a marginally effective treatment, shows, practitioners treat many PTSD patients and other personal injury claimants by less-than-ideal methods. Dissemination of better treatments and policy development by insurers and employers to mandate reimbursement of only the more efficacious treatments cannot come too soon for those individuals who suffer with psychological injuries. It is now 40 years since Theodore Fox encouraged physicians to be discriminating in the treatments they provide their patients. In the area of trauma rehabilitation, this advice continues unheeded.

9

Psychological Injury Cases

> When one has finished building one's house, one suddenly realizes that in the process one has learned something that one really needed to know in the worst way—before one began.
>
> —Friedrich Nietzsche

Writing an expert opinion about psychological matters is much like building Nietzsche's house. After their written opinions are in the hands of other professionals, experts often learn something important that they should have known about the plaintiff or the phenomenon under scrutiny. Then, having to own their opinions with possibly negative consequences, experts may face embarrassment in the witness box or ethics complaints. This series of case descriptions is intended to alert forensic assessors to problematic areas of forensic opinion. The following cases all illustrate issues in psychological injury assessment that have been addressed in some form in previous chapters.

Biases and Heuristics

Biases

We start with a case that illustrates the potential for biased assessment decisions, presumably based on an implicit diagnostic heuristic held by the assessor. The reader should remember that a diagnostic heuristic is, in its simplest form, a sorting device that assessors use to shorten the evaluation process. Such sorting devices may be formally agreed upon and part of standard diagnostic rules. Alternatively, such heuristics may be idiosyncratic biases of individual clinicians.

Case 1. A young woman was physically injured in a severe motor vehicle accident (MVA) and was later assessed by Dr. Quick Assessment as having an acquired "driving phobia" caused by the MVA. The plaintiff complained of fear and avoidance of driving on bridges, in highway traffic, and in crowded inner urban traffic. Subsequently, the plaintiff was assessed by Dr. Defense (hired by the auto insurer), who diagnosed a panic disorder with agoraphobia (American Psychiatric Association, 2000), and documented that the plaintiff had been a driver of limited experience and confidence prior to the MVA. In the opinion of Dr. Defense, the plaintiff's fear of driving was not traumatically induced, but rather was a joint product of the plaintiff's preexisting panic disorder (including fear of being away from safe places in the event of biological catastrophe—e.g., heart failure) and low confidence in her driving ability.

As the reader can tell from this example, Dr. QA may have been overly influenced by an illusory correlation (see chapter 5) stemming from his own forensic practice that would read, more or less, as "Most MVA survivors I see have driving phobias, so driving phobias must be uniquely related to MVA trauma." Unfortunately, such is not necessarily the case. Taylor and Deane (2000) compared 140 individuals who had experienced at least one MVA in their lives with 50 individuals who had never had an MVA and found no group difference in fear of driving or interference by such fear. Ehlers, Hofmann, Herda, and Roth (1994) found that self-defined driving phobics varied in the reasons they gave for their fear, with only 15% attributing their fear to an MVA, and 53% attributing it to a fear of panic attacks occurring while driving. It is notable that Taylor, Deane, and Podd (2002) concluded that the association of driving competence/confidence with driving fears has been largely neglected by the research literature, but that low driving confidence may mediate such fear. Some clinicians and forensic assessors may believe that driving phobias occur uniquely in MVA survivors; however, the scientifically sophisticated assessor will understand that it is necessary to investigate other explanations for the plaintiff's driving fears.

The next case further illustrates the causality conundrum.

Case 2. An elementary school teacher was verbally abused and physically intimidated by a parent in the classroom and on the school grounds. The teacher was already aware through her colleagues that this parent was suspected of significant criminal and gang involvement. Subsequent to these incidents at the school, the teacher coincidentally met the parent on public transit where he again threatened her. She subsequently became frightened whenever she saw adult males of the same ethnic minority group in public places. This case is of forensic interest because the teacher claimed PTSD and fear of: (a) work attendance at the school, and (b) traveling on public transit in the nearby community. Thus, she was unable to work at the particular school and initiated a claim with the Workers' Compensation Board.

The forensic question in this case is whether this teacher's fear and other mental health symptoms are part of a PTSD secondary to the parent's threats (which arguably occurred because of her work as a teacher) and thus deserving of intervention by the Workers' Compensation Board or whether it is part of an unrelated fear of crime. Some forensic examiners might normalize this teacher's fear as general apprehension about crime and not consider such avoidance a symptom of PTSD. Such a decision will make a diagnosis of PTSD less likely and would also fail to connect such avoidance to her workplace experiences. Alternatively, an assessor might consider this to be partial evidence for PTSD Criterion B4—"intense psychological distress at exposure to internal or external cues that symbolize or resemble an aspect of the traumatic event" (American Psychiatric Association, 1994, p. 425)—requiring further investigation. Other examiners might consider such a reaction to meet Criterion B4 without any further elaboration. This latter decision ignores the alternative explanation that the teacher may have an unfortunate fear of crime that is causally unrelated to the workplace incidents. Either of the two extremes (normalization or acceptance without elaboration) would show confirmatory bias, and potentially lead to confirmatory information-seeking bias. See chapter 5 for a discussion of these forms of diagnostic bias.

The case below illustrates how gender bias may influence psychological injury assessments.

> *Case 3.* A young woman with severe panic disorder (PD, American Psychiatric Association, 1994) was referred for her first treatment for this condition to Dr. Unique Therapy. Dr. UT and the patient then had a brief sexual relationship, following which the patient's emotional state allegedly deteriorated, she made a suicide gesture, and became more avoidant. The patient launched a personal injury suit to seek compensation for the worsening of her psychological state. As would be expected, there was disagreement both about the degree of the patient's consent to the sexual relationship and the emotional consequences to the patient. The defense expert diagnosed a borderline personality disorder (BPD, American Psychiatric Association, 1994) and PD, and concluded that the alleged worsening of the plaintiff's symptoms were a naturally evolving product of her personality disorder rather than any consequence of Dr. UT's professional misbehavior.

Much has been made of the potential for women with BPD to become involved in untoward sexual interactions and to make sexual harassment complaints (e.g., Feldman-Schorrig, 1994). However, making a diagnosis in a case like this necessitates structured assessments of BPD, PD, and other potential conditions such as PTSD and depression, both historically and with respect to current status. For example, forensic assessors considering personality disorder diagnoses as alternative explanations for claimants' distress should use formal assessment instruments such as structured interviews (e.g., First, Spitzer, Gibbon, & Williams, 1995; Widiger, Mangine, Corbitt, Ellis, & Thomas, 1995). Such structured interviews can be supplemented by multiscale assessment tools relevant to personality assessment (e.g., Personality Assessment Inventory [PAI]—Morey, 1991; Minnesota Multiphasic Personality Inventory-2 [MMPI-2]—Butcher, Dahlstrom,

Graham, Tellegen, & Kaemmer, 1989; Millon Clinical Multiaxial Inventory-III [MCMI-III]—Millon, 1994). All of the latter self-report instruments have some validity in assessing BPD, although the reader should consider the critical study of Rogers, Salekin, and Sewell (1999) that suggests the MCMI is not yet well validated for use in forensic settings. The defense expert in this case would need to carefully examine his/her own potential diagnostic biases given the results of Becker and Lamb (1994). The latter authors found that psychiatrists, psychologists, and social workers, when given vignettes of patients with symptom patterns equally representative of either borderline personality disorder (BPD) or post-traumatic stress disorder (PTSD), more frequently gave BPD diagnoses to female cases than to male cases. That is, female gender itself led to the clinicians preferring the diagnosis of BPD rather than PTSD when symptomatic status was identical.

Forensic assessors must specify prognoses for the plaintiff's injuries. While estimates of prognosis are at best probabilistic, experts should relate their opinions to the scientific literature. Following is an example of what *not* to do:

> *Case 4.* Dr. Pessimist assessed a survivor of a rather gruesome MVA two months following the accident with a comprehensive assessment battery. The claimant met criteria for PTSD, but not major depression, during interview. While having PTSD, he had no residual physical injuries or excessive anger. Dr. P. then opined, "This patient requires extensive therapy and will suffer some permanent disability from his PTSD."

Assessing and communicating prognosis for psychological problems is a three-step process. First, one must understand and communicate the prognoses for similar cases as documented in the psychological, psychiatric, and related research literatures. This allows the assessor to communicate what is known in general about the probability and speed of recovery from specific mental health problems. Second, the assessor must systematically assess factors known to predict the improvement or worsening of such problems, and subsequently describe the claimant's status with respect to such scientifically established predictors. Third, the assessor must communicate a clinical opinion about the individual claimant's prognosis based on the results of steps 1 and 2. To take a simple example, anger about the trauma and general anger-proneness have been shown to predict worse outcome for PTSD sufferers (e.g., Ehlers, Mayou, & Bryant, 1998; Taylor et al., 2001). In our experience, however, very few forensic assessors routinely assess for anger problems in PTSD claimants. In the example above, Dr. P. would have been wise to note the positive prognostic implications of the absence of depressed mood in the claimant, and would also have been well advised to assess for anger problems and the presence of chronic pain, both of which have been shown to predict worse outcome for PTSD (Taylor et al., 2001). Moreover, given that PTSD, particularly that arising from MVAs, has a steep remission curve within the first year (Blanchard, Hickling, Vollmer et al., 1995; Blanchard, Hickling, Forneris et al., 1997; Blanchard, Hickling, Barton et al., 1996; Ursano et al., 1999), Dr. P. should have noted that PTSD sufferers in general have a substantial probability of remitting without treatment during the first several months post-MVA. Also of note in this particular example: PTSD of less than three months in duration does not qualify as chronic in DSM terms (American Psychiatric Association, 1994, 2000). This is not to say that Dr. P. could not justify her negative prognosis, but she would have to speak to known risk factors for such a negative prognosis and the extent to which these risk factors characterized the individual plaintiff. It is important to remember that overly optimistic prognostic opinions also may fail to consider scientific research.

Idiosyncratic Heuristics

All clinicians and forensic assessors likely show some "drift" in their diagnostic methods over time. Part of such drift involves the use of heuristics. Use of idiosyncratic heuristics is to be expected as busy professionals try to achieve their assessment goals within a tight schedule; however, such heuristics can reduce the validity of expert opinions. We give an example of a forensic examiner's context-specific heuristic below.

> *Case 5.* Dr. Rear-End Heuristic sees a patient who suffered a severe whiplash injury following a rear-end collision, and who also reported fear of motor vehicle travel, becoming upset when traveling near the MVA scene, becoming less interested in her social and recreational activities, and being easily startled, among other psychological symptoms. Dr. Heuristic opined, "Individuals who suffer rear-end MVAs seldom develop PTSD because they have no visual image of the car approaching," and subsequently concluded that the plaintiff had no PTSD or driving phobia.

One presumes that this professional uses this heuristic to guide her assessment activities and the interpretation of subsequent assessment data. Such a heuristic would likely work toward lowering the rate of vehicular PTSD she diagnoses because it would automatically rule out some cases as potential PTSD sufferers without the benefit of a diagnostic interview. It is important to compare this particular heuristic to what we know of the predictors of PTSD. In brief, the nature of the subject MVA (amount of property damage to vehicles, nature of vehicular accident) has not been shown to predict subsequent PTSD (see review by Douglas & Koch, 2001). Therefore, use of objective trauma characteristics to exclude further inquiry about PTSD when plaintiffs exhibited subjective severe fear, helplessness, or horror runs against our current scientific understanding of PTSD.

The following illustrates a case involving the designation of a particular MVA-related trauma as a Criterion A stressor. As we discussed in chapter 3, forensic assessors of PTSD claimants must take care with respect to assessing the putative stressful event. According to DSM-IV-TR (American Psychiatric Association, 2000), a person suffering from PTSD must have been exposed to:

An extreme traumatic stressor involving direct personal experience of an event that involves actual or threatened death or serious injury, or other threat to one's physical integrity; or witnessing an event that involves death, injury, or a threat to the physical integrity of another person; or learning about unexpected or violent death, serious harm, or threat of death or injury experienced by a family member or other close associate (Criterion A1). The person's response to the event must involve intense fear, helplessness, or horror (Criterion A2). (American Psychiatric Association, 2000, p. 463)

The reader should examine carefully the logic presented by the forensic assessor involved in the case below.

Case 6. Dr. Pseudoscience assessed an MVA claimant and stated (in part), "PTSD is a syndrome resultant upon an extremely traumatic stressor where actual or threatened death or serious injury to oneself or another may occur. In this respect, once again quoting from the ambulance crew report, there was 'moderate damage' reported. Thereafter there must be a response on the part of the victim, which will involve intense fear, helplessness, or horror . . . although she was shaky and felt sick with a hollow sickness, scared and shocked she was able to grab her son in the backseat and, very importantly, her vital signs in the Emergency Department were all within the norm. Specifically, her blood pressure and respiratory rates were within the norm within half an hour of being seen and in this respect, quoting the literature, following such a traumatic event there is an enormous autonomic discharge occurring in response to fear. This autonomic surge would include a very rapid heartbeat, termed tachycardia, rapid respiration, and increased blood pressure. This autonomic arousal persists for days, weeks, or even months if the stressor is extreme or catastrophic as in PTSD."

The forensic assessor's reference here to autonomic arousal as an important facet of PTSD assessment has some validity. Some studies (reviewed by Yehuda, McFarlane, & Shalev, 1998) have shown that increased heart rate (HR) and lower cortisol levels subsequent to the trauma are associated with PTSD. The predictive utility of posttrauma HR has been investigated in MVA-PTSD by three different labs. In an Israeli sample of 86 patients (34 women, 52 men) attending an Emergency Department following a trauma (83% MVAs), Shalev et al. (1998) obtained HR and blood pressure (BP) measures and Clinician Administered PTSD Scale (CAPS) assessments following the trauma. They reported that HR assessed in the Emergency Department was higher in PTSD patients (average of 95.5 BPM) than non-PTSD patients (83.3 BPM) diagnosed at one month (for HR $\geq$ 85, positive predictive power = 85%, negative predictive power = 79%). The Australian group, Bryant, Harvey, Guthrie, and Moulds (2000), measured HR and BP on the day of discharge for 113 MVA survivors, and found that it was significantly higher for the PTSD group (82.9 BPM) than for non-PTSD subjects (76.3 BPM). Heart rate greater than 90 BPM at hospital discharge was a strong predictor of PTSD at 6 months.

These findings suggest that immediate posttrauma resting HR *may* be a reliable predictor of later PTSD status. Unfortunately, the only study to attempt to replicate these findings using hospital Emergency Department vital signs (Blanchard, Hickling, Galovski, & Veazey, 2002) found negative results. These authors examined the relationship of emergency personnel-obtained vital signs (HR, systolic BP, and diastolic BP) to CAPS and PTSD Checklist (PCL) diagnoses of PTSD an average of 13 months post-MVA in 74 treatment-seeking MVA victims. Contrary to predictions, HR and DBP were negatively related to PTSD diagnosis in this sample.

Bearing in mind the data above, and the strongly held opinion of the expert witness, it is of note that the ambulance crew assessing vital signs for the claimant in Case 6 found her to have a heart rate of 92 beats per minute. According to Yehuda et al. (1998), use of a heart rate of > 85 BPM in diagnosing PTSD led to a positive predictive power of 85%, meaning that 85% of HR-predicted PTSD cases were actual PTSD cases. Thus, if the forensic assessor above were both committed to this model of PTSD and more knowledgeable about this physiological research, he/she would have to say that "Ms. Doe's heart rate response at the time of the accident (92 BPM) was predictive of her later having PTSD." An expert assessor cannot have his/her cake and eat it too. One cannot assert that a claimant did not have sufficient physiological arousal at the time of the MVA to qualify for a PTSD without comparing her heart rate to the research studies concerning this topic. This is a good example of an expert engaged in pseudoscientific posturing.

The reader will be cognizant of our discussion in chapter 1 about the high level of comorbidity of PTSD and traumatic brain injury. We repeat our two conclusions from that review: the presence of traumatic brain injury (TBI) or amnesia for the traumatic event does not render persons immune to PTSD; and the majority of studies show some substantial comorbidity of TBI and PTSD (e.g., 25% to 26%, Bryant & Harvey, 1999; Bryant, Marosszeky, Crooks, & Joseph, 2000). The following case illustrates an adverse consequence of a forensic assessor using the loss of consciousness–PTSD incompatibility heuristic.

Case 7. A middle-aged successful retailer was exiting a shopping mall parking lot after a late lunch with her adult daughter. Another vehicle was turning left into the parking lot when it was struck by an oncoming, third, vehicle and propelled into the eventual claimant's car. Minor damage to the claimant's vehicle ensued, but when she went to help the driver of one vehicle she began to feel faint from seeing blood (the other driver's nose had broken and the claimant had a preexisting blood-injury phobia). After an ambulance arrived, the paramedic observed the claimant appearing faint and asked her to recline in the ambulance while wearing an oxygen mask.

Unfortunately, while doing so, the claimant became nauseous, vomited the contents of her stomach into the mask, and aspirated it. She subsequently stopped breathing and her heart stopped beating for a brief period of time. Luckily, she was discovered in short order and rushed to the hospital where she stayed in a coma for some days prior to awaking. She suffered some cognitive impairment from the anoxia, but more importantly developed a range of anxiety and fear symptoms. Thus, she complained of a significant fear and avoidance of motor vehicle travel, and was bothered by intrusive thoughts and upsetting dreams, not of the MVA (which she did not recall at all), but of her family sitting by her side during the time she was in intensive care during her coma. The latter intrusive memories would appear to qualify as pseudo-memories (Bryant, 1996). The claimant was later seen by a forensic assessor who opined, "She did not suffer a posttraumatic stress disorder, because PTSD and a cerebral concussion are two mutually exclusive disorders."

The reader should note a few important issues with respect to this case. First, this lady did, in fact, experience a life-threatening event (Criterion A1, American Psychiatric Association, 1994, 2000). In fact, she was momentarily dead. Second, she had no recall of either the MVA, some period of time preceding the collision, or of the first several days of her hospitalization. Nonetheless, she later appreciated how close to death she had been, arguably fulfilling Criterion A2, had intrusive reexperiencing symptoms (in particular of pseudomemories of her family grieving at her hospital bed, but also of emotional distress when in a car), and had related phobic fear and avoidance. Third, the forensic assessor's strong statement about the incompatibility of PTSD and cerebral contusion cannot be supported by the research literature (see chapter 1).

Breadth of Assessment

Because of the broad range of emotional problems trauma survivors can develop, competent forensic assessors should not arbitrarily limit the scope of investigation. An example of a common type of narrow assessment follows:

Case 8. Dr. Narrow & Focused, acting as a defense expert, uses the CAPS interview for PTSD as well as an MMPI-2 to assess a woman claiming damages for a sexual assault by a church official. Dr. Narrow used no other structured diagnostic interviews or tests. Scale 2 (depression) of the MMPI-2 was marginally elevated (T = 67), and the CAPS interview resulted in the claimant falling one symptom short on Cluster C (avoidant/numbing symptoms) of a full PTSD diagnosis. This led Dr. Narrow to conclude that the claimant had no PTSD and, consequently, no psychological injury.

A separate forensic assessment of the same claimant included (a) the Anxiety Disorders Interview Schedule, (b) MMPI-2, (c) Posttraumatic Diagnostic Scale (PDS), and (d) collateral interviewing of the woman's husband about her emotional state and her responses to physical intimacy. This assessment replicated the elevated score on MMPI-2 scale 2 and the findings of subsyndromal PTSD. However, this broader assessment found evidence of (a) clinically severe depressive symptoms, (b) clinically elevated scores on the PDS, and (c) collateral evidence from the plaintiff's partner that she was fearful and avoidant of church and other authority figures, as well as avoidant of sexual intimacy.

While we approve of the use of a CAPS interview in such cases because of its superior psychometric qualities for assessing PTSD (see, e.g., Blanchard, Jones-Alexander, Buckley, & Forneris, 1996), limiting a forensic interview to just the CAPS precludes documentation of other mood or anxiety disorders. These two experts varied in their diagnoses, but more importantly they varied in their methods. One can argue that the first expert's assessment was too narrow to find evidence of the full range of the claimant's injuries, which were detected by the second expert's more detailed assessment strategy. Note that some of the losses documented by the second assessor did not necessarily conform to DSM-IV diagnoses. Psychological injuries that are either of subclinical severity or which do not easily conform to psychiatric nosology may cause significant disability and require documentation, even if assessment methods previously proven to be reliable are not always available. Guidelines for psychological assessment favor using the second expert's method because it is consistent with the multitrait, multimethod assessment model that is at the heart of psychological measurement (Campbell & Fiske, 1959; see also Meyer, 2002).

Estimations of Functional Disability

Expert opinions with respect to disability may be more credible and valid for individual cases if the expert can trace individual claimant's symptoms and behaviors to important functional deficits that hinder employment or other duties. Casual observation of many forensic and clinical assessments suggests that this is a relatively neglected area. Remember from our previous discussion that occupational disability may be mediated by a number of psychological characteristics, including impaired social interactions and fear-mediated avoidance behavior. We give some examples below of ways in which different plaintiffs may express their disabilities.

Case 9. A 35-year-old man with PTSD following injuries suffered in an MVA was able to sustain employment as a sales manager in a large retail auto dealer, but was vulnerable to job loss/disability through: (a) fear and avoidance of driving, and (b) extreme irritability and angry verbal outbursts. His employment appeared to be saved by: (a) living within walking distance of the car dealership, (b) being able to avoid test drives with customers given his managerial status, and (c) an understanding employer who accommodated his angry outbursts because of his previous positive work history.

Case 10. Another MVA-PTSD sufferer, a 30-year-old woman with pronounced travel fear and avoidance, was on long-term disability because the large retail chain in which she held a middle management position had no job opportunities within easy pedestrian or mass transit access, and also required her to drive between different stores during the workday. She had a marked avoidance of motor vehicle travel secondary to two separate MVAs, related orthopedic injuries, and a fear of reinjury if she were to be involved in another MVA.

The cases above illustrate not only how different problems within the same diagnosis differentially affect employment functioning, but also how accommodations made by employers for the behavioral deficits of their employees may impact on disability claims. The employment disability associated with PTSD in Case 9 were mitigated by both living close to work and by a sympathetic employer. However, the PTSD illustrated in Case 10 resulted in greater economic damages because of both a longer commuting distance and work demands involving automobile travel. The reader should note that despite having the same mental health diagnosis, these cases had strikingly different employment disability.

The following case illustrates how individuals who suffer criminal assaults may also suffer occupational disability related to their trauma.

Case 11. A 45-year-old Aboriginal man was assessed in the context of litigation concerning his sexual and physical abuse as a child in a residential school. At the time of evaluation, 35 to 40 years postabuse, he still met criteria for subsyndromal PTSD based on CAPS interview. By history, he had met full criteria for PTSD during his adolescence and early adulthood. While he had little residual occupational disability at the time of the evaluation, he described a history of social avoidance of Caucasian males, particularly authority figures. This avoidance behavior was apparently motivated by fear of adverse treatment and by triggering of upsetting memories of his sexual abuse by male caregivers in the residential school. This fear-motivated avoidance figured prominently in his avoidance of postsecondary education and of applying for work outside his Aboriginal reserve. In fact, early in his working life, he took up work that allowed him to not leave the reserve. Such restriction arguably had significant negative effects on his earning capacity.

The reader of forensic assessments about disability must consider such opinions carefully to ensure that a logical pathway has been demonstrated between observed deficits of the claimant and the interaction of such deficits with specific occupational demands. As illustrated in the cases above, fear-related avoidance can impact negatively on employment, as can problematic anger or other interpersonal deficits.

Inadequate Historical Data Collection

The following case illustrates the risks inherent in offering opinions without adequate collateral data about a plaintiff's history. It is well accepted that forensic assessment requires the collection of collateral information to confirm plaintiff self-report and that a review of the plaintiff's past history is especially important (see, e.g., Melton, Petrila, Poythress, & Slobogin, 1997).

> *Case 12.* A plaintiff claimed the onset of his panic disorder to be an MVA that occurred when he was in his mid-thirties. Plaintiff's counsel requested an independent assessment from Psychologist A, who conducted a diagnostic assessment, including measures of response bias (validity scales of MMPI-2). All interview measures (Anxiety Disorders Interview Schedule for DSM-IV [ADIS-IV]) and tests pointed to a severe panic disorder, without evidence of symptom over endorsement. Plaintiff's counsel did not, however, provide complete health records predating the subject's MVA. Psychologist A opined, "Mr. X currently meets criteria for a panic disorder with agoraphobia, which appears to have arisen subsequent to the subject MVA. There is no evidence that he is overendorsing or exaggerating mental health problems, and by his report, these symptoms began following the index MVA." However, defense counsel later obtained both childhood and earlier adult health records that showed a history of childhood sexual abuse, somatic preoccupation, and anxious apprehension predating the subject MVA.

Psychologist A would have been well advised to have qualified his initial forensic opinion given the absence of pre-MVA health records and/or to have delayed writing a final opinion until he obtained such records. However, use of collateral health records also requires that the forensic assessor admit when such records suggest the absence of similar psychological conditions preceding the subject trauma. The case below illustrates the apparent reluctance of a defense expert to admit the absence of evidence for a preexisting condition, and demonstrates the role of individual risk factors in the development of trauma-precipitated psychopathology.

Understanding Preexisting Vulnerabilities

Given that only a minority of individuals exposed to potentially traumatic events (PTE) develop chronic PTSD (see chapter 3), it behooves forensic assessors to appreciate how preexisting vulnerabilities may influence the development of psychological distress following trauma. The reader will also recall the discussion in chapter 2 of eggshell personality. The two cases below illustrate this phenomenon, and the forensic decision making inherent in answering the causality question.

Case 13. Ms. Vulnerability had a pre-MVA history of victimization by sexual assault and intimate partner abuse. She also espoused some thought action fusion beliefs (TAF, Rachman, 1993). TAF beliefs are those in which individuals believe that thoughts may be harmful because of some combination of the moral culpability of certain beliefs or the potential for thoughts to lead to actual events (e.g., having a catastrophic thought or image may make the actual event more likely to occur). Unfortunately, Ms. V.'s TAF beliefs dovetailed with a traumatic MVA in which she accompanied a friend with a newborn child. The friend had expressed worries about untoward accidents or illness harming her baby (e.g., Sudden Infant Death Syndrome). Ms. V. reassured her friend and, in so doing, warned her against thinking such bad thoughts because they might come true. Shortly afterward, the two adults and infant were struck by a motor vehicle in a crosswalk, resulting in life-threatening injuries to the new mother and her infant and less-severe physical injuries to Ms. V. Subsequently, Ms. V. developed: (a) a PTSD which eventually partially remitted; and (b) an obsessive-compulsive disorder (OCD), in which she became fearful of caring for small children (she ran a home-based day care), and of becoming contaminated through others' malevolence or negligence. There was no evidence from pre-MVA health records of any disabling anxiety or affective disorder, although there were very limited family physician references to modest complaints of stress. Historical interview did not lead to the report of any significant anxiety or mood disorders predating the subject MVA, despite the sexual assault and domestic violence history in the distant past.

Plaintiff's expert diagnosed a PTSD and an OCD evidently triggered by the subject MVA, and noted that Ms. V. had some preexisting vulnerability to: (a) PTSD from her previous history of assault, and (b) OCD from her preexisting TAF.

Defense's expert stated (in part), "It is evident from the data that Ms. V. probably did not have any major psychiatric illness prior to the (subject) events." However, the defense expert then stated, "Ms. V. has hyper reactions to stressful events stemming from preexisting difficulties with her thought form" and "Ms. V. is simply biologically predisposed to having marked anxiety responses to events."

This case should be reviewed with three principles in mind. First, it is important that forensic experts clarify whether they believe the plaintiff had a preexisting disorder and subsequently are prepared to defend such a conclusion based on objective data concerning the plaintiff. It is neither logical nor ethical to indicate in the body of one's report that the previous health records suggest the plaintiff had no preexisting mental health diagnoses and then in the same breath opine that he/she had such a disorder pre-MVA because of some unusual presentation or trait that may have predisposed the plaintiff to develop such a disorder. Second, forensic assessors must be able to differentiate between factors that are putative vulnerability or risk factors and the actual characteristics of the health condition (e.g., PTSD, OCD) being litigated. The logical corollary of considering risk factors for OCD such as TAF synonymous with OCD itself is to consider the presence of TAF (without further evidence of OCD) as a mental health condition. Given the ubiquity of risk factors for developing psychological distress, assumption of risk factor–disorder equivalence is a dangerous precedent. Third, forensic assessors owe it to the courts, the legal counsel who retain them, and to the plaintiffs they assess to continually educate themselves about the factors influencing mental health conditions about which they are offering expert opinions.

The case below is less complicated, yet illustrates the differentiation of psychological damages that can and cannot be attributed to a tortuous act.

> *Case 14.* Ms. Cautious was a 30-year-old, well-educated, and employed professional, who suffered some soft-tissue injuries from a head-on MVA in which she was a passenger. She had no preexisting history of mental health treatment or use of psychotherapeutic medications. Shortly after the MVA, and while suffering frequent headaches and upper back pain, she began to show fear and avoidance of passenger travel in a car, with lesser fear of driving (which she insisted on describing as "being cautious" because she did not feel comfortable labeling this as fear). She also began suffering upsetting nightmares involving traumatic death or injury of her or family members (husband, father). Structured interview revealed (a) current subsyndromal PTSD; (b) current subclinical depression; and (c) current severe fear and avoidance of car passenger travel; as well as (d) past and current generalized anxiety disorder (GAD) and (e) past and current severe specific phobias of dogs and cats. The forensic assessor's conclusion was that (a) neither the GAD nor animal phobias were attributable to the MVA; (b) the GAD (characterized by excessive worrying, perfectionism, need for control, and tension) served as a predisposing condition for the development of distress following trauma; and (c) the specific phobias of dogs and cats were evidence for a predisposition toward developing phobic avoidance; but that (d) the subsyndromal PTSD and depression, including the car travel fear and avoidance were causally linked to the traumatic MVA and her resulting physical injuries. That is, the MVA and subsequent physical injuries were the direct precipitants to the latter conditions.

The latter case presents what may be a more prototypical case of psychological injury causality. Take an eggshell personality (e.g., preexisting anxiety disorder, or avoidant coping style), expose the person to a life-threatening trauma, and wait for the potential blossoming of new anxiety or mood disorders when the person's coping resources are exceeded or lead to maladaptive responses to the new challenges. The inference of the forensic assessor in this case rests heavily on the empirical differentiation of the diagnoses of PTSD and depression from GAD.

Understanding Comorbid Conditions

PTSD seldom occurs by itself, and claims for psychological injuries usually involve multiple emotional losses, as well as possibly physical losses (discussed in chapter 3). Therefore, it behooves the forensic assessor to appreciate the scientific research concerning the interrelationships among these problems, as well as the temporal onset of such conditions. The following case illustrates inadequate consideration of the comorbidity of different mental health problems.

> *Case 15.* A defense expert assessed a plaintiff in a legal action emanating from putative sexual assaults in a residential school for Aboriginal children some 30 years previous to the assessment. The defense expert noted the plaintiff's adolescent and young adult history of alcohol abuse, as well as the biological family's history of alcohol abuse, but gave cursory attention to the plaintiff's PTSD symptoms. This expert then asserted that the plaintiff's primary mental health problem was alcohol abuse and that it arose from his Aboriginal background and family history of alcohol abuse rather than from his abuse in the residential school. Plaintiff's expert noted that the temporal onset of the plaintiff's alcohol and substance use followed the beginning of his sexual abuse history by several years, that he had relatively modest exposure to his parent's alcohol problems (given that he was living away from home for most of his childhood), and that his alcohol use reportedly was motivated by a need to sedate himself when emotionally distressed.

Such sexual abuse assessments pose difficulties for forensic assessors because of the vagaries of retrospective memory and the passage of time and life experiences between the alleged trauma and the actual assessment. Putting aside issues related to the accuracy of retrospective memory, this case illustrates some of the interpretive problems forensic assessors may encounter if they do not have an adequate appreciation of the comorbidity of mental health conditions. First, it is important to appreciate that substance abuse is highly comorbid with PTSD (Breslau, Davis, & Schultz. 2003; Kilpatrick et al., 2003; Stewart, 1996). This is a case in which the defense expert appeared to not appreciate recent research concerning the comorbidity of PTSD and substance abuse, in particular, those studies suggesting that in PTSD sufferers, substance use is more often used to cope with negative emotion than for other reasons (e.g., social activities) (Stewart, Conrod, Pihl, & Dongier, 1999; Stewart, Conrod, Samoluk, Pihl, & Dongier, 2000).

Forensic assessors must also consider the temporal onset of comorbid conditions, especially if causality is a relevant legal issue.

> *Case 16.* Subsequent to a vehicular accident in which the plaintiff suffered a fractured leg, she presented as very distressed to three separate forensic assessors. The first assessor opined (on the basis of a neuropsychological test battery, an MMPI-2, and a clinical interview) that the plaintiff had no organic neuropsychological impairment, but likely had a PTSD accounting for both her emotional distress and some impairment of her concentration and short-term memory. The former expert did not comment on the extent of the plaintiff's prescription and nonprescription drug use. The second assessor, on the basis of a clinical interview, noted the plaintiff's extreme distress and a long-term history of daily cannabis use, and concluded that she had suffered a PTSD and a mild traumatic brain injury (TBI). A third expert, using a structured diagnostic interview and different psychological tests, noted that the plaintiff did not meet criteria for PTSD (because of a lack of sufficient emotional distress

at the time of the incident), but was in a severely depressed state. The third expert also noted that the plaintiff had substantial, daily use of both cannabis and Tylenol #3 (containing codeine) both prior to and following the index trauma. He then questioned the causality issue, suggesting that the plaintiff's preexisting cannabis and codeine use might contribute substantially to her depression.

This last case is notable because it brings to the fore the issue of preexisting substance use and its impact on psychological distress. There is evidence in the research literature suggesting that both cannabis use (Troisi, Pasini, Saracco, & Spalletta, 1998; Reilly, Didcott, Swift, & Hall, 1998; Patton et al. 2002; Rey & Tennant, 2002) and codeine use (Sproule, Busto, Somer, Romach, & Sellers, 1999; Bakal, 1997) increase the risk of depressive symptoms. Thus, forensic assessors must not only account for comorbid substance abuse and dependence problems when assessing for other psychological injuries, but they must also use available information to determine the relative dates of onset of substance use and other emotional problems.

Summary

The cases above and related discussion were intended to alert both forensic assessors and consumers of expert opinions to a number of important issues. Idiosyncratic diagnostic heuristics and outright biases (e.g., gender bias, confirmatory bias) constitute serious limitations to the validity of forensic assessments. Assessors should monitor their use of such heuristics and biases, and readers of forensic opinions should be alert to them.

Some assessors may offer opinions on prognosis without careful consideration of the known early course of spontaneous remission for PTSD or of scientifically established predictors of remission. Forensic assessors need to integrate both what is known about the temporal course of specific disorders (e.g., PTSD, depression) from the scientific literature and individual characteristics of the plaintiff that indicate positive or negative prognoses in the individual case.

Forensic assessments need to be of both adequate breadth and historical perspective to describe the plaintiff and changes in him/her before and after the index trauma. Very narrow assessments or those that do not adequately sample historical data or collateral sources of information are a disservice to plaintiffs and their defense, as well as to the courts. Forensic assessors should ensure that their evaluation methods are sufficiently broad and incorporate sufficient historical and collateral data that they can adequately describe the plaintiff's difficulties; and readers must hold experts accountable on these assessment practices.

The pathways from mental health problems to employment disability are multiple. A symptom that interferes with one plaintiff's ability to work may not interfere with another plaintiff's work status. This may be a result of either the demands of the job or accommodations made by the employer. Forensic assessors must attend to the task of relating symptoms or diagnoses to work disability for individual plaintiffs. Readers of such expert opinions must consider them critically to determine if a logical case has been made for claiming work disability associated with a psychological injury.

Cases 13 and 14 illustrate issues in inferring causality. While Case 14 illustrates what might be considered a prototypical case of psychological injury and the contributions of preexisting conditions, many cases are as complicated as that illustrated in Case 13. All of Cases 13 through 16 illustrate the complexity with which psychological injury plaintiffs may present and the need for broad assessment methods, understanding the contributions of preexisting vulnerability factors, the nature of comorbidity among different mental health conditions, and adequate historical assessment. Readers of forensic assessments should critically examine expert opinions in complex cases, and hold experts accountable for understanding the complex relationships among different mental health conditions, as well as for explicating the temporal courses of such conditions with regard to the same plaintiff.

10

Current Status and Future Trends

> If I have seen further, it is by standing on the shoulders of giants.
> —Isaac Newton (1676)

Newton was referring to the fact that knowledge of our world develops incrementally and through the influences of individual scholars and the evolving scientific and social zeitgeist. There are many scholars who have added to our understanding of what we call psychological injuries. Progress in the understanding of this intersection of human misery, science, and law has come in a gradual and often nonsystematic manner, sometimes necessitating the merger of thinking from quite different scholarly traditions (e.g., law, clinical and social psychology, psychiatry). In particular, the "giants" to whom we refer involve the prolific researchers in trauma, PTSD, and other areas of the anxiety and mood disorders (see our references), as well as the remarkable changes in legal precedents arising over the past century. For example, 166 citations for PTSD were found via the American Psychological Association's Psych Info search engine between 1980 and 1984. In contrast, in an identical time period (1995–1999), 3,093 citations for PTSD were found via this same search engine (American Psychological Association, 2004).

Society's interest in psychological injuries such as PTSD, depression, other anxiety disorders and their association with work disability also plays a substantive role in the growth of this area of research, practice, and legal precedent. Numerous professions are beset with stress-related work disability (e.g., nursing, Canadian Institutes of Health Information, 2001), and other professional groups, like lawyers, claim what appear to be high rates of depression (e.g., see Mounteer, 2004). Thus, society's interests in this phenomenon, whether gullible, self-interested, or skeptical (e.g., Lilienfeld, Lynn, & Lohr, 2003) have played a major role in the growth of intellectual and legal interest in psychological injuries.

In this chapter, we will briefly discuss where the field (or rather intersection of several related fields) now stands. Subsequently, we describe what we anticipate to be the future trends and necessary research to move this field forward.

Current Status

Treatment of Psychological Injuries in Law

Not long ago, the law simply did not acknowledge psychological injuries. That is, psychological injuries to persons were considered noncompensable. The law considered such injuries too ephemeral, excessively subject to malingering, and impossible to prove. There was great worry that allowing recovery for psychological injuries would open the metaphorical floodgates and permit litigation premised upon shaky and unverifiable grounds. Terms such as "compensation neurosis" were commonly applied by doubtful critics who thought that untrustworthy plaintiffs would abuse such injuries in an attempt to get something for nothing.

However, the twentieth century—particularly the latter half—witnessed drastic legal changes. In fact, there has been a correlation between the growth of the science and practice surrounding psychological injuries and its acceptance by the law. We hesitate—as one always should in the realm of correlation—to draw firm causal connections between the progress in science and practice concerning psychological injuries and the acceptance by the law. However, it seems likely that there is some meaningful connection between the development of the mental health field and the responsiveness of the legal arena.

Currently, psychological injuries are compensable in many areas of law. The earliest examples were in the area of tort law. Psychological injuries were compensable to the extent that they were parasitic to established, independent torts such as battery. That is, if one suffered battery at the hands of another, one could be compensated for the psychological injuries sustained, as well as for any physical ones. However, in the absence of a traditional, independent tort, psychological injuries had no "standing" under tort law.

This changed with the 1948 supplement of the Restatement (Second) of Torts, which introduced the tort of intentional infliction of emotional distress. This was the first example under tort law in which psychological injuries (or "severe emotional distress") were independently compensable.

The area of negligent tort followed suit shortly thereafter, though typically required that in order to be compensable, the psychological injury had to be caused by physical contact or injury, or had to manifest physical sequelae. In some jurisdictions, these requirements have been loosened. The Hawaii case of *Rodrigues* in 1970 is commented upon by some as the first time a negligent infliction of emotional distress case was not required to have either a physical injury or manifestation. Today, many jurisdictions allow "bystander" negligent infliction of emotional distress cases, which logically precludes the necessity of physical injury as part of the legal calculus. Physical manifestation might still be required in some jurisdictions in bystander cases, and most jurisdictions also narrow the field of compensability as a function of the relationship between the injured and bystander parties, and nearness in space and time with respect to the observation of the injury. Recovery is even allowable in the so-called eggshell personality and crumbling personality contexts, in which some psychological vulnerability or malady might have been present prior to the tortious act.

Psychological injuries are recognized in many other areas of law now as well, many of which have borrowed from (and modified) the more established area of tort law in terms of defining psychological injury. For instance, psychological injuries are recognized in workers' compensation law, particularly when either caused by or leading to a physical injury. Some jurisdictions are less likely to recognize the so-called "mental-mental" case, where a psychological insult is said to cause psychological injury. The primary difference between workers' compensation law and tort law stems from the intent requirement that is absent in workers' compensation law. That is, in tort law, the tortfeasor either must have intended the harm that would ensue from his/her act (in the case of intentional torts), or must have reasonably known what harm could ensue from his/her actions (in the case of negligence). In workers' compensation, harm can be caused by purely accidental means, so long as the injured party can prove a causal connection between the putative injuring agent and the resulting psychological harm.

Psychological injuries also are recognized in sexual harassment, employment discrimination, and housing discrimination contexts. Some commentators have even argued that the harm suffered need not be as serious as in other areas of law, such as tort (Cucuzza, 1999). A movement is evident throughout the last century from a legal position of near-absolute rejection of psychological injuries by the law, to greater and greater acceptance within the law that mental tranquility is a legitimate interest to protect.

Status of Current Assessment Methods

We now understand that exposure to potentially traumatic events (PTE) in modern civilization is relatively common, and that a thorough mental health professional should screen for the occurrence of a wide array of such events in the lives of his/her patients. While the importance of screening for PTE is known to researchers in this field, systematic screening in primary practice or even specialized mental health services appears relatively rare.

Whereas the assessment technology for conditions such as PTSD and depression was once quite unreliable, there is now a wide array of reliable structured interviews and self-report psychological tests available that can help in the diagnosis and description of psychological injuries. We know that use of such instruments provides more reliable, and thus valid, descriptions of people who are being assessed than do mere clinical interviews. Unfortunately, we also know that many tests shown to be reliable and valid in strictly clinical contexts have not yet been validated within litigating or compensation-seeking samples, and often have not been sufficiently validated among ethnic/cultural minority groups, who comprise an increasingly large proportion of Western society. Further, because of the potential of nonclinical influences (e.g., compensation motivation, retrospective memory bias) on the self-report, sophisticated forensic assessors use a multimethod assessment model incorporating collateral information such as medical records and family members' reports, as well as behavioral observation.

Both clinical and forensic practices appear to lag far behind the scientifically supported best practices. Many clinicians and forensic assessors apparently still rely on unstructured interviews and relatively few tests shown to be directly germane to the relative questions. The unstructured nature of many clinical and forensic assessments is made more problematic because of the many potential sources of decision-making bias (e.g., ethnic and gender bias, social distance bias, confirmatory bias) that can unduly influence the conclusions of mental health professionals, especially if they are operating within a vacuum devoid of reliable and valid assessment tools. Despite lagging behind the science of trauma in their utilization of empirically supported assessment methods, many (though not all) practitioners proffer themselves as "experts" about trauma and PTSD to the public, legal counsel, and the courts in a manner that may misinform consumers. The reader will recall from chapter 9 the example of Dr. Pseudoscience who waxed eloquently about the relationship of physiological arousal to the diagnosis of PTSD but did not appear to have up-to-date knowledge about research in this area. One should not presume that self-proclaimed but unjustified expertise is a rarity. For example, if one searches the Canadian Register of Health Service Professionals in Psychology (CRHSP) Web site across major metropolitan areas, fully 54% of CRHSPP registrants designate themselves as having expertise in PTSD (CRHSP, 2004). Given the breadth of psychology and what we know about psychological practice with trauma survivors, one can only presume that some CRHSP listees are setting the threshold for claiming PTSD expertise rather low.

Certain of the types of questions posed to forensic assessors about psychological injuries are likely unanswerable via any straightforward reference to the scientific literature. The inherent biases in humans' retrospective memories and underdocumentation of mental health problems in general health records make forensic opinions about plaintiffs' past mental health guesswork at best. Statements about the prognoses for conditions such as PTSD based on published longitudinal data limit us to actuarial predictions of only a few years in the future. This is obviously inadequate for the purposes of legal counsel and judges, both of whom must take a longer-term view of the plaintiff's prospects for symptom remission and recovery of adequate functioning. Statements about functional disability following psychological injuries at this time must be limited to a review of the correlational data concerning lowered economic functioning for individuals with similar mental health problems. Beyond such general statements, the responsible forensic assessor is once again limited to informed speculation about how an individual plaintiff's particular symptoms may limit his/her ability to attend and function in the workplace.

Women are at disproportionate risk for psychological distress following trauma exposure, and have significantly higher rates of depression. While some may consider female gender, per se, a risk factor for psychological distress, the research literature is throwing more light on the ways in which women inhabit a different social environment than do men. Women's environment is characterized by greater risks for victimization by sexual assault, stalking, harassment, and for physical injury secondary to assault. In addition, the role demands placed on women in industrialized society result in a higher density of daily hassles that may exacerbate the negative influences of traumatic stressors or interfere with the remission of psychological distress.

While there is evidence that PTSD and related psychological injuries exist across diverse cultures, there appear to be some culture-specific differences (e.g., the higher prevalence of PTSD among Mexican than among non-Hispanic Caucasian or Black women). We are only beginning to understand the cultural and gender contributions to the form, frequency, and intensity of psychological injuries following trauma. In particular, the crude sorting categories of race typically used in epidemiological research may do an injustice to our understanding of more subtle cultural/social variables that may be more important in understanding individual differences in psychological distress.

There are significant economic and personal incentives to exaggerate psychological distress. Because the symptoms of conditions like PTSD and depression are known widely in the lay public, many psychological injury claimants are not naïve as to the prototypical characteristics of the conditions for which they are being assessed. Therefore, forensic assessors must be vigilant for symptom exaggeration, overendorsement, or distortion of the chronological history of problems by claimants. Assessors and the consumers of forensic assessments must also understand that symptom exaggeration is not a black and white phenomenon. Claimants may have varying motivations (e.g., seeking treatment resources versus seeking financial compensation), and may exaggerate their symptoms in varying degrees. Claimants may also provide (and even believe) a distorted history of their psychological distress either through compensation motivation, or through a form of retrospective memory bias, as described in chapter 5.

Symptom checklists or other self-report measures of PTSD and depressive symptoms, when used alone, are vulnerable to overdiagnosis of mental health conditions. Superficial reliance on such self-report methods by practitioners who neither collect a wider range of more objective data (e.g., collateral data, past medical records), nor assess the claimant's response set with respect to symptom exaggeration can result in misdiagnosis and inappropriate compensation. Thus, vigilance with respect to potential symptom exaggeration is no more than a specific example of Meyer's (2002) admonition that the accurate description of patients involves the use of "multiple independent methods and multiple independent sources" (p. 97).

At this time, none of our commonly used psychometric measures of symptom exaggeration are sufficiently developed to be used singly to identify individuals who are malingering PTSD or depression. However, research in the malingering of emotional distress is evolving rapidly. Currently, we know that use of some of the MMPI-2 (Butcher, Dahlstrom, Graham, Tellegen, & Kaemmer, 1989) derived measures of symptom overendorsement, in combination with tests of effort, and judicious skepticism in comparing medical records and other collateral sources of information to the claimant's self-report comprise the best current multimethod strategies for ruling out or confirming an exaggerating response set.

Status of Prevention Efforts

A great deal of effort has gone into developing and implementing strategies for preventing psychological disturbance following exposure to traumatic events. The extent to which single session psychological debriefing has become part of the landscape in Western society appears to reflect more the success of marketing than of effective reduction in human suffering. Suffice it to say that single-session debriefing of trauma survivors cannot be scientifically justified at this time. Some relatively brief (4 to 6 hours) cognitive behavioral treatments for PTSD appear to have some benefit when applied to only highly distressed trauma survivors within the first month or so after their respective traumas. This heartening news is muted when one realizes what professional resources must go into identifying such cases, particularly when many trauma survivors (e.g., sexual assault victims) are initially reluctant to seek help.

Status of Treatment Efforts

We now possess some consistently efficacious treatments for PTSD, depression, and some of the other anxiety disorders. Variants of cognitive behavioral therapy, especially those having large doses of exposure therapy for PTSD and other anxiety disorders, consistently have been shown to help sufferers of these mental health conditions. Other treatments such as stress inoculation therapy and cognitive processing therapy for PTSD also appear efficacious. While these treatments have been shown to be effective in the clinical laboratory, they are available to the general public only within the confines of tertiary care clinics, or from some select evidence-based practitioners. Pharmaceutical treatments, particularly those involving the Selective Serotonin Reuptake Inhibitor (SSRI) antidepressants, are showing some promise with PTSD.

Four caveats apply: First, not all patients benefit from even these rather good treatments. For example, it is clear that even when one eliminates known risk factors for poor outcome (e.g., comorbid chronic pain in PTSD sufferers), not all PTSD patients benefit equally from exposure therapy. We need, therefore, to continue to develop additions to these currently efficacious treatments to improve their success rates. Part of this will involve learning what works for whom, and studies that carefully investigate the relationship of pretreatment patient characteristics (including patient treatment preference) to outcome of different therapies.

Second, despite clinical lore, we have not yet conducted appropriate research to determine the impact of litigation, compensation, or receipt of financial compensation on trauma survivors' responses to even the best treatments. Well-designed treatment trials utilizing such compensation-involved patients are required before we can advance in our knowledge of the rehabilitation of psychological injuries.

Third, we have yet empirically to evaluate comprehensive rehabilitation packages that include both treatments described in this text and other interventions for comorbid conditions such as chronic pain. Given that chronic pain is a commonly comorbid condition among MVA-PTSD survivors, such multidimensional rehabilitation programs are necessary to more fully rehabilitate many patients. The evaluation of such comprehensive rehabilitation programs that integrate evidence-based interventions will be a substantial endeavor.

Fourth, practice in this area has lagged far behind the science of treatment development and evaluation. Very few practitioners regularly utilize the most efficacious treatments (e.g., Becker, Zayfert, & Anderson, 2004). Therefore, even if we reliably identify those psychological injury plaintiffs who deserve treatment for their disabling condition, the probability that they will receive an efficacious treatment is, unfortunately, relatively low. Worse, the probability that consumers will receive treatments with either no scientific support (e.g., supportive counseling) or heavily marketed treatments with limited scientific support (e.g., eye movement desensitization processing) is rather high.

Future Trends

Where does the field go from here? It is apparent that over the last quarter century, the courts have become much more welcoming of claims for psychological injuries (see chapters 1 and 2, as well as Shuman, 2003). Parallel to this legal trend has been an explosion of research involving PTSD, depression, and other anxiety disorders. Simultaneously, employment by mental health professionals and legal counsel related to these disorders has also expanded. We believe society's interest in psychological injuries will remain strong, although there is the potential for legal (e.g., tort reform) and professional (improving standards) changes that may rein in the rapid growth of legal claims and professional services for such conditions.

Trends in the Law

Although speculating about trends in the law is almost certain to invite some error, especially because the law sometimes moves more slowly than public opinion or political agendas, we offer some thoughts here on where the law pertaining to psychological injuries might go in the future. First, we think that there will continue to be a correlation between progress in the science and practice surrounding psychological injuries and legal acceptance of them. Legal acceptance of psychological injuries showed a marked increase after PTSD was introduced into the official diagnostic nomenclature. We believe that if further substantial ground is gained in terms of understanding the nature and course of PTSD and other disorders in scientific terms, and if the reliability and validity of concomitant measurement procedures are further enhanced, then the law will maintain or increase its position on the compensability of psychological injuries.

One particular context to watch, we believe, is research on the physical manifestations of PTSD within the brain. Because there is something of a legacy within the law of requiring some physical evidence that the psychological injury is real and not feigned, accurate tests stemming from brain or physiological functioning will likely be welcomed within courtrooms. Pitman, Saunders, and Orr (1994) speculated along these lines approximately a decade ago, and we believe that this remains an area of great legal relevance. Although some jurisdictions have dropped the physical manifestation requirement, we believe that, depending on what science tells us about functional and physiological manifestations of PTSD, more jurisdictions might be willing to accept this as evidence of physical manifestation. More broadly, this might assuage the fears that many legal professionals have about the legitimacy of psychological injuries.

If the previous 100 years are any indication of what is to come, there may be more areas of law that come to recognize psychological injuries. There has been a slow and somewhat meandering momentum accrued by psychological injuries that might find its way more firmly into other areas. For instance, some have argued that psychological damage might play a more prominent role in toxic torts and toxic megatorts than it currently does (Heinzerling, 2001; Tuohey & Gonzalez, 2001). Psychological injuries already are recognized in some breach-of-contract cases, and it is possible that it might play a more prominent role in the future. Similarly, even in ostensibly far-removed areas of law such as bankruptcy, emotional distress is now being recognized, at least under certain circumstances, as a compensable injury (i.e., in the case of a willful violation by a creditor of an automatic stay, McCullough, 2003).

As in any profession, there is an inevitable specialization and splintering of subfields. As this happens in law, we think that psychological injuries will likely keep pace and receive some recognition within the more specialized areas. A good example of this is the recently created tort of stalking in some jurisdictions (i.e., California Civil Code, § 1708.7). Stalking is now recognized as a crime in all jurisdictions; however, a handful of jurisdictions are now giving stalking victims a more direct means by which to be compensated by defining it as a tort as well. Stalking is defined in part by the fear felt by its victims for themselves or family members (as well as whether victims felt "harassed" or "alarmed"), and hence is particularly well suited for psychological evidence pertaining to state of mind and emotional effects of being stalked. Another prime example is tort liability through Internet activities, such as the spreading of hate, which could ostensibly lead to litigation for intentional infliction of emotional distress (Smith, 2002).

Of course, there are wild cards that can affect any forecasts. Part of the future of psychological injuries within the law will depend on the conservatism versus liberalism of future higher courts. More legally conservative judges will tend not to favor expansion of any legal areas, including this one. More "reformist" judges might favor expanding this area of law. This is one factor that also will depend on political agendas, elections, and so forth, and hence is difficult to forecast. There has been another type of legal conservatism playing out as well with respect to proposed revisions to the Restatement of Torts. Some commentators would like to remove liability for emotional distress from the core of tort law, whereas others object to this (see, generally, Chamallas, 2001).

Finally, we may see some limiting of recovery within psychological injury cases in the form of greater expectations put upon plaintiffs to mitigate their damages. It is a general rule within tort law that victims have a duty of their own to minimize—or mitigate—the harm that they have suffered, and tortfeasors can be expected to pay less if mitigation has not taken place. For instance, if a person is seriously injured in a motor vehicle accident and refuses to seek medical treatment, the tortfeasor may only be required to pay the damages that would have occurred *with* medical treatment. Mitigation is not as prominent a feature in psychological injury cases. Some commentators argue that it should be, but recognize that there would be some difficulty in establishing what could be agreed upon as reasonable mitigating efforts (Kontorovich, 2001). For instance, does a person have to seek treatment from a psychologist or psychiatrist in order to have mitigated the psychological effects of a motor vehicle accident or criminal victimization? Would seeking pastoral counseling count? Would just talking to one's spouse suffice? This is relatively uncharted legal water in the psychological injury arena, but water that will someday need navigating.

Advances in Assessment Practice and Important Research Questions

As representatives of the mental health disciplines, we hope that forensic assessment practices will evolve closer to scientifically supported methods. We believe, however, that this will be a slow evolution and will require efforts from several groups. First, a greater emphasis on the training of empirical assessment methods is necessary in clinical, as well as forensic psychology and psychiatry graduate programs. However, given the small number of forensic training programs, improvements in formal training will have only a small impact on the practice of forensic assessment in the field. In the broader training of clinical psychologists and psychiatrists, such improvements will likely be incremental. There is a glimmer of hope for more rapid evolution toward science-based assessment. This hope is provided by the evolution over the past decade of the empirically supported treatments movement (APA Division of Clinical Psychology, 1995). While controversial in some circles, this movement spread within a decade to the accreditation criteria for academic and internship training in psychology (American Psychological Association, 2002a). Practitioner-friendly guidebooks to empirically based assessment tools for anxiety and depression, including PTSD, are becoming more accessible (e.g., Antony, Orsillo, & Roemer, 2001), and hopefully will lead to gradual improvements in the practitioners' utilization of superior assessment measures.

Second, legal counsel and insurance adjusters have important roles to play in a more refined critical appraisal of forensic evidence about psychological injuries. Because they are the consumers of such evidence, they can exert a direct influence on the quality of forensic assessment practice through educated cross-examination and the selection of more empirically oriented assessors. The improvement of professional standards through increasingly specialized credentialing, or through the courts becoming more restrictive on qualifying experts, may eventually enhance the quality of forensic assessment practice. For example, Shuman (2003) has specifically suggested that "Qualification as an expert witness is not generic, but rather issue specific. Licensure as a physician who practices psychiatry, or even board certification in psychiatry should not, without more, result in qualification as an expert on PTSD" (p. 855).

There are also many important questions to answer that will impact on the quality of forensic assessments more generally and allow us a greater understanding of this process. While psychological assessment instruments (e.g., tests, structured interviews) are increasingly sophisticated and psychometrically sound, we still have inadequate normative data for large samples of (a) personal injury claimants, and (b) claimants from ethnic/cultural minority groups. Collection of such normative data is a pressing issue. Comparisons of diagnosis-matched litigating and nonlitigating samples with respect to their responses to empirically validated psychological tests will increase the ecological validity of forensic assessments using such tools.

In addition, we do not yet understand the impact of the different types of bias on expert opinions about psychological injuries. While we understand that clinicians in general may have biases in making mental health diagnoses with respect to certain ethnic minorities and with respect to women, we have no data showing us whether this is a trivial or substantial problem with expert evidence given in psychological injury claims. Early work in this area can be done via clinical vignettes utilizing samples of forensic practitioners and fictional cases. It would also be helpful to know what diagnostic heuristics (e.g., nature/severity of the index trauma, incompatibility of different diagnoses) forensic assessors commonly endorse, and whether such heuristics change with professional experience.

We also need a better database with respect to the prevalence of different psychological injuries within relevant contexts (e.g., conditional prevalence of PTSD following automobile collisions in no-fault vs. torts litigation jurisdictions). These questions can, of course, only be answered in collaboration with the insurers who receive such claims. Related to prevalence of psychological injuries, we need more research on the longitudinal history of such injuries, whether these arise from tortious acts like MVAs or as disability claims among specific occupations. It would also be worthwhile to study the natural course of depression and PTSD-related distress while sufferers are receiving disability compensation. While disability arrangements may superficially appear to assume unchanging levels of distress and functional disability, it seems more likely that both distress and functional disability wax and wane over time and secondary to life events, daily hassles, and other variables. For example, Ronis et al. (1996) studied the records of mental health services to Veterans Administration PTSD patients to track their use of mental health services, and, by implication, their functioning over time. Patients with PTSD were relatively chronic users of mental health services, but did have episodes when they did not use mental health services (average of 2.2 "nonuse intervals" of 100 days or more in duration). The latter suggests that PTSD patients may have episodic bursts of relative well-being. Similar research is needed for a wider range of disabled claimants.

Finally, mental health concepts are admittedly fuzzy, with substantial symptomatic and functional overlap among such putatively separate entities as PTSD, depression, other anxiety disorders, chronic pain, and traumatic brain injury. It is likely that very few psychological injury claims involve just one of the conditions above, and thus the symptomatically complex claimant is more the norm than the exception. Much future work is required on developing assessment tools or packages of tools that enable us to understand this complexity and provide more coherent and helpful descriptions of claimants' psychological problems. Much of this research will be of an experimental nature in which we come to understand, for example, the ways in which two classes of psychological injury like PTSD and pain interact (e.g., Sharp & Harvey, 2001). For example, Rachman (1991) proposed a model for studying the comorbidity of emotional problems, which has implications for the study of the substantial comorbidity between PTSD, depression, other anxiety disorders, pain, and anger.

The Future of Prevention and Rehabilitation

If there are to be advances in the prevention of psychological injuries, we believe they will occur in the following spheres: First, it is our opinion that single-session psychological debriefing as it is currently practiced in many settings will decline in use. It appears to be an intervention that is currently practiced without any empirical support despite multiple attempts to demonstrate its utility with respect to symptom reduction. However, it is possible that better-designed research utilizing a wider array of outcome measures will demonstrate that early debriefing has some benefits (e.g., providing voice to survivors, improving claimant-insurer relations). Second, we believe that 4- to 6-session CBT for selected trauma survivors will continue to be evaluated and will prove to be an efficacious intervention when applied to highly distressed survivors. Third, to make the latter intervention practically useful, much research must be done on cost-effective detection and recruitment of deserving trauma survivors. It does little good to have an efficacious early intervention for a health problem if the cost of early detection is so prohibitive that no one will pay for such screening.

Future research with respect to the rehabilitation of psychological injuries will, we believe, focus much more on the following three topics: First, research attention will focus on what works for whom, and will involve evaluating such innovations as matching patient preference to treatment modality (e.g., psychological vs. pharmaceutical, exposure therapy vs. coping skills training). A second variant of this theme will involve the evaluation of efficacious treatments with high-risk or treatment-resistant patients (e.g., those in litigation, those with high levels of comorbidity).

Second, multicomponent treatment trials that evaluate the effectiveness of treatment across more than one domain of dysfunction (e.g., PTSD symptoms as well as pain complaints) will be published. This will reflect the complexity with which many claimants present and the need for demonstrated effective treatments for the "whole person" as opposed to a set of symptoms reflecting a subset of the claimant's distressing problems.

Third, effectiveness studies will evolve into evaluations of functional rehabilitation, with the critical dependent measures including return to employment and other finer-grained measures of work performance, as well as functioning in important family and social roles.

Summary

In the end, the law is increasingly recognizing the importance and compensability of psychological injuries, albeit this concept is still ill defined. These injuries appear to have a negative economic impact, but the nature and extent of such impact is still inadequately studied. Practice in both forensic assessment and rehabilitative efforts lags behind scientific advances and it behooves the mental health professions, as well as individual practitioners, to improve the quality of such practice. Research over the past few decades has led to a greater understanding of the mental health conditions comprising psychological injuries, to more reliable assessment tools, and to some efficacious interventions. However, both our assessment methods and our treatments lag behind in terms of ecological validity. They have not always been adequately evaluated with the individuals who commonly comprise psychological injury claimants, or in settings that reflect the world in which such claims are typically handled. Moreover, interventions that have only limited scientific support are still popular among practitioners, while empirically supported treatments (e.g., exposure therapy for PTSD) are seldom used. Much work remains to be done, both in the realm of scientific investigation and in the dissemination of scientifically supported assessment and treatment.

References

Abrams, K. M., & Robinson, G. E. (1998). Stalking: Part II: Victims' problems with the legal system and therapeutic considerations. *Canadian Journal of Psychiatry, 43,* 477–481.

Acierno, R., Resnick. S., & Kilpatrick. D. G. (1997). Health impact of interpersonal violence 1: Prevalence rates, case identification, and risk factors for sexual assault, physical assault, and domestic violence in men and women. *Behavior Medicine, 23,* 53–64.

Allen, A. M. (1992). *Effects of race and gender on diagnostic judgments with the DSM-III-R.* Doctoral dissertation, University of South Dakota. *Dissertation Abstracts International, 53/05-A,* 1395.

Allen, S. M., & Webster, P. S. (2001). When wives get sick: Gender role attitudes, marital happiness, and husbands' contribution to household labor. *Gender & Society, 15,* 898–916.

Almeida, D. M., & Kessler, R. C. (1998). Everyday stressors and gender differences in daily distress. *Journal of Personality and Social Psychology, 75,* 670–680.

Almeida, D. M., Wethington, E., & Kessler, R. C. (2002). The daily inventory of stressful events: An interview-based approach for measuring daily stressors. *Assessment, 9,* 41–55.

Amaya-Jackson, L., Davidson, J. R., Hughes, D. C., Swartz, M., Reynolds, V., George, L. K., & Blazer, D. G. (1999). Functional impairment and utilization of services associated with posttraumatic stress in the community. *Journal of Traumatic Stress, 12,* 709–724.

American Educational Research Association, American Psychological Association, and the National Council on Measurement in Education. (1999). *Standards for educational and psychological testing.* Washington, DC: American Educational Research Association.

American Jurisprudence. (1997a). *Fright, shock, and mental disturbance, 38,* ss. 24–36. (Original work published 1968.)

American Psychiatric Association. (1952). *Diagnostic and statistical manual of mental disorders.* Washington, DC: Author.

American Psychiatric Association. (1968). *Diagnostic and statistical manual of mental disorders* (2nd ed.). Washington, DC: Author.

American Psychiatric Association. (1980). *Diagnostic and statistical manual of mental disorders* (3rd ed.). Washington, DC: Author.

American Psychiatric Association. (1987). *Diagnostic and statistical manual of mental disorders* (3rd ed., revised). Washington, DC: Author.

American Psychiatric Association. (1994). *Diagnostic and statistical manual of mental disorders* (4th ed.). Washington, DC: Author.

American Psychiatric Association. (2000). *Diagnostic and statistical manual of mental disorders* (4th ed., text revision). Washington, DC: Author.

American Psychological Association. (1987). General guidelines for providers of psychological services. *American Psychologist, 42,* 1–12.

American Psychological Association. (1990). *Guidelines for providers of psychological services to ethnic, linguistic, and culturally diverse populations.* Washington, DC: Author.

American Psychological Association. (1992). Ethical principles of psychologists and code of conduct. *American Psychologist, 47,* 1597–1611.

American Psychological Association. (1993). Guidelines for providers of psychological services to ethnic, linguistic, and culturally diverse populations. *American Psychologist, 48,* 45–48.

American Psychological Association. (2002a). *Guidelines and principles of accreditation.* Washington, DC: Author.

American Psychological Association. (2002b). *Guidelines on multicultural education, training, research, practice, and organizational change for psychologists.* Retrieved January 12, 2004, from http://www.apa.org/pi/multiculturalguidelines/historical.html.

American Psychological Association. (2002c). Ethical principles of psychologists and code of conduct. *American Psychologist, 57,* 1060–1073.

American Psychological Association (2004). Retrieved July 1, 2004, from PsycInfo. http://www.psycinfo.com/psycinfo/index.

Andreasen, N. C. (1995). Posttraumatic stress disorder: psychology, biology and the manichaean warfare between false dichotomies. *American Journal of Psychiatry, 152,* 963–965.

Andrews, B., Brewin, C. R., & Rose, S. (2003). Gender, social support, and PTSD in victims of violent crime. *Journal of Traumatic Stress, 16,* 421–427.

Andrews, G., & Peters, L. (1998). The psychometric properties of the Composite International Diagnostic Interview. *Social Psychiatry & Psychiatric Epidemiology, 33,* 80–88.

Andrews, G., Peters, L., Guzman, A., & Bird, K. A. (1995). Comparison of two structured diagnostic interviews: CIDI and SCAN. *Australian & New Zealand Journal of Psychiatry, 29,* 124–132.

Annis v. County of Westchester, 136 F.3d 239 (2d Cir. 1998).

Antony, M. M., Bieling, P. J., Cox, B. J., Enns, M. W., & Swinson, R. P. (1998). Psychometric properties of the 42-item and 21-item versions of the Depression Anxiety Stress Scales in clinical groups and a community sample. *Psychological Assessment, 10,* 176–181.

Antony, M. M., Orsillo, S. M., & Roemer, L. (Eds.). (2001). *Practitioner's guide to empirically based measures of anxiety.* New York: Kluwer.

Arbisi, P. A., & Ben-Porath, Y. S. (1995). An MMPI-2 infrequent response scale for use with psychopathological populations: The infrequency-psychopathology scale, F(p). *Psychological Assessment, 7,* 424–431.

Arbisi, P. A., & Ben-Porath, Y. S. (1997). Characteristics of the MMPI-2 F(p) scale as a function of diagnosis in an inpatient sample of veterans. *Psychological Assessment, 9,* 102–105.

Arbisi, P. A., Ben-Porath, Y. S., & McNulty, J. (2002). A comparison of MMPI-2 validity in African American and Caucasian psychiatric inpatients. *Psychological Assessment, 14,* 3–15.

Ashendorf, L., Constantinou, M., & McCaffey, R. J. (2004). The effect of depression and anxiety on the TOMM in community-dwelling older adults. *Archives of Clinical Neuropsychology, 19,* 125–130.

Astin, M. C., Lawence, K. J., & Foy, D. W. (1993). Posttraumatic stress disorder among battered women: Risk and resiliency factors. *Violence & Victims, 8,* 17–28.

Athey v. Leonati, 3 S.C.R. 458 (1996).

Australian Health Ministers. (2003). *National Mental Health Plan 2003–2008.* Canberra, Australia: Australian Government.

Australian Psychological Society. (2003). *Australian Psychological Society ethical guidelines* (3rd revision). Melbourne, Australia: Retrieved January 12, 2004, from http://www.psychology.org.au/members/ethics/aboriginal_ethical_guidelines.pdf.

Averill, P. M., & Beck, J. G. (2000). Posttraumatic stress disorder in older adults: a conceptual review. *Journal of Anxiety Disorders, 14,* 133–156.

Avina, C., & O'Donohue, W. (2002). Sexual harassment and PTSD: Is sexual harassment diagnosable trauma? *Journal of Traumatic Stress, 15,* 69–75.

Bagby, R. M., Buis, T., & Nicholson, R. A. (1995). Relative effectiveness of the standard validity scales in detecting fake-bad and fake-good responding: Replication and extension. *Psychological Assessment, 7,* 84–92.

Bagby, R. M., Nicholson, R. A., Buis, T., & Bacchiochi, J. R. (2000). Can the MMPI-2 validity scales detect depression feigned by experts? *Assessment, 7,* 55–62.

Bagby, R. M., Rogers, R., Buis, T., & Kalemba, V. (1994). Malingered and defensive response styles on the MMPI-2: An examination of validity scales. *Assessment, 1,* 31–38.

Bagby, R. M., Rogers, R., Buis, T., Nicholson, R. A., Cameron, S. L., Rector, N. A., et al. (1997). Detecting feigned depression and schizophrenia on the MMPI-2. *Journal of Personality Assessment, 68,* 650–664.

Bakal, D. A. (1997). Clinical complexities of managing pain, suffering, and analgesic dependence. *Headache Quarterly, 8,* 137–149.

Ballenger, J. C., Davidson, J.R.T., Lecrubier, Y., Nutt, D. J., Foa, E. B., Kessler, R. C., McFarlane, A. C., & Shalev, A. Y. (2000). Consensus statement on posttraumatic stress disorder from the international consensus group on depression and anxiety. *Journal of Clinical Psychiatry, 61,* 60–66.

Bamhill v. Davis, 300 N.W.2d 104 (Iowa 1981).

Barron, F. (1956). An ego strength scale which predicts response to psychotherapy. *Journal of Consulting Psychology, 19,* 239–245.

Bass v. Nooney Co., 646 S.W.2d 765 (Mo. 1983).

Beals, J., Manson, S. M., Shore, J. H., Friedman, M., Ashcraft, M., Fairbank, J. A., & Schlenger, W. E. (2002). The prevalence of posttraumatic stress disorder among American Indian Vietnam veterans: Disparities and context. *Journal of Traumatic Stress, 15*(2), 89–97.

Beck, A. T., & Steer, R. A. (1987). *Beck depression inventory manual.* San Antonio, TX: The Psychological Corporation.

Beck, A. T., Steer, R. A., & Brown, G. K. (1996). *Manual for the BDI-II.* San Antonio TX: The Psychological Corporation.

Becker, C. B., Zayfert, C., & Anderson, E. (2004). A survey of psychologists' attitudes towards and utilization of exposure therapy for PTSD. *Behaviour Research and Therapy 42,* 277–292.

Becker, D., & Lamb, S. (1994). Sex bias in the diagnosis of Borderline Personality Disorder and Posttraumatic Stress Disorder. *Professional Psychology: Research and Practice, 25,* 55–61.

Benedek, E. P. (1985). Children and disaster: Emerging issues. *Psychiatric Annal, 15,* 168–172.

Benight, C. C., Swift, E., Sanger, J., Smith, A., & Zeppelin, D. (1999). Coping self-efficacy as a mediator of distress following a natural disaster. *Journal of Applied Social Psychology, 29,* 2443–2464.

Berdahl, J., Magley, V., & Waldo, C. (1996). The sexual harassment of men? Exploring the concept with theory and data. *The Psychology of Women Quarterly, 20,* 527–547.

Bergman, M. E., & Drasgow, F. (2003). Race as a moderator in a model of sexual harassment: An empirical test. *Journal of Occupational Health Psychology, 8,* 131–45.

Berry, D.T.R., Adams, J. J., Clark, C. D., Thacker, S. R., Burger, T. L., Wetter, M. W., et al. (1996). Detection of a cry for help on the MMPI-2: An analog investigation. *Journal of Personality Assessment, 67,* 26–36.

Berry, D.T.R., Baer, R. A., & Harris, M. J. (1991). Detection of malingering on the MMPI: A meta-analysis. *Clinical Psychology Review, 11,* 585–598.

Bevan v. Fix, 42 P.3d 1013 (Wyo. 2002).

Bisson, J. I. (2003). Single-session early psychological interventions following traumatic events. *Clinical Psychology Review, 23,* 481–499.

Bisson, J. L., Jenkins, P. L., Alexander, J., & Bannister, C. (1997). Randomised controlled trial of psychological debriefing for victims of acute burn trauma. *British Journal of Psychiatry, 171,* 78–81.

Blaauw, E., Winkel, F. W., Arensman, E., Sheridan, L., & Freeve, A. (2002). The toll of stalking: The relationships between features of stalking and psychopathology of victims. *Journal of Interpersonal Violence, 17,* 50–63.

Blake, D. D., Weathers, F., Nagy, L. M., Kaloupek, D. G., Chamey, D. S., & Keane, T. M. (1998). *Clinician-administered PTSD scale for DSM–IV.* Boston: National Center for Posttraumatic Stress Disorder.

Blake, D. D., Weathers, F., Nagy, L. M., Kaloupek, D. G., Gusman, F. D., Chamey, D. S., & Keane, T. M. (1995). Development of a Clinician-administered PTSD scale. *Journal of Traumatic Stress, 8,* 75–90.

Blake, D. D., Weathers, F., Nagy, L. M., Kaloupek, D. G., Klauminzer, G., Chamey, D. S.,

& Keane, T. M. (1990). A clinician ratings scale for assessing clinical and lifetime PTSD: The CAPS-1. *Behavior Therapist, 13,* 187–188.

Blanchard, E. B., Buckley, T. C., Hickling, E. J., & Taylor, A. E. (1998). Posttraumatic stress disorder and comorbid major depression: Is the correlation an illusion? *Journal of Anxiety Disorders, 12,* 21–37.

Blanchard, E. B., Gerardi, R. J., Kolb, L. C., & Barlow, D. H. (1986). The utility of the Anxiety Disorders Interview Schedule (ADIS) in the diagnosis of post-traumatic stress disorder (PTSD) in Vietnam veterans. *Behaviour Research and Therapy, 24,* 577–580.

Blanchard, E. B., & Hickling, E. J. (1997). *After the crash: Assessment and treatment of motor vehicle accident survivors.* Washington, DC: American Psychological Association.

Blanchard, E. B., Hickling, E. J., Barton, K. A., Taylor, A. E., Loos, W. R., & Jones-Alexander, J. (1996). One-year prospective follow-up of motor vehicle accident victims. *Behavior Research and Therapy, 34,* 775–786.

Blanchard, E. B., Hickling, E. J., Devineni, T., Veazey, C., Galovski, T., Mundy, E., Malta, L. S., & Buckley, T. C. (2003). A controlled evaluation of cognitive behavioral therapy for posttraumatic stress in motor vehicle accident survivors. *Behaviour Research and Therapy, 41,* 79–96.

Blanchard, E. B., Hickling, E. J., Fomeris, C. A., Taylor, A. E., Buckley, T. C., Loos, W. R., & Jaccard, J. (1997). Prediction of remission of acute posttraumatic stress disorder in motor vehicle accident victims. *Journal of Traumatic Stress, 10,* 215–234.

Blanchard, E. B., Hickling, E. J., Galovski, T., & Veazey, C. (2002). Emergency room vital signs and PTSD in a treatment-seeking sample of motor vehicle accident survivors. *Journal of Traumatic Stress, 15,* 199–204.

Blanchard, E. B., Hickling, E. J., Malta, L. S., Jaccard, J., Devineni, T., Veazey, C. H., & Gavloski, T. E. (2003). Prediction of response to psychological treatment among motor vehicle accident survivors with PTSD. *Behavior Therapy, 34,* 351–363.

Blanchard, E. B., Hickling, E. J., Mitnick, N., Taylor, A. E., Loos, W. R., & Buckley, T. C. (1995). The impact of severity of physical injury and perception of life threat in the development of post-traumatic stress disorder in motor vehicle accident victims. *Behaviour Research & Therapy, 33,* 529–534.

Blanchard, E. B., Hickling, E. J., Taylor, A. E., Buckley, T. C., Loos, W. R., & Walsh, J. (1998). Effects of litigation settlements on posttraumatic stress symptoms in motor vehicle accident victims. *Journal of Traumatic Stress, 11,* 337–354.

Blanchard, E. B., Hickling, E. J., Taylor, A. E., Fomeris, C. A., Loos, W., & Jaccard, J. (1995). Effects of varying scoring rules of the Clinician Administered PTSD (CAPS) for the diagnosis of posttraumatic stress disorder in motor vehicle accident victims. *Behaviour Research and Therapy, 33,* 471–475.

Blanchard, E. B., Hickling, E. J., Taylor, A. E., & Loos, W. (1995). Psychiatric morbidity associated with motor vehicle accidents. *Journal of Nervous and Mental Disease, 183,* 495–504.

Blanchard, E. B., Hickling, E. J., Vollmer, A. J., Loos, W. R., Buckley, T. C., & Jaccard, J. (1995). Short-term follow-up of post-traumatic stress symptoms in motor vehicle accident victims. *Behavior Research and Therapy, 33,* 369–377.

Blanchard, E. B., Jones-Alexander, J., Buckley, T. C., & Forneris, C. A. (1996). Psychometric properties of the PTSD Checklist (PCL). *Behaviour Research and Therapy, 34,* 669–673.

Boccaccini, M. T., & Brodsky, S. L. (1999). Diagnostic test usage by forensic psychologists in emotional injury cases. *Professional Psychology: Research and Practice, 30,* 253–259.

Bolger, N., DeLongis, A., Kessler, R. C., & Schilling, E. A. (1989). Effects of daily stress on negative mood. *Journal of Personality & Social Psychology, 57,* 808–818.

Bordow, S., & Porritt, D. (1979). An experimental evaluation of crisis intervention. *Social Science and Medicine, 13A*(3), 251–256.

Borough of Media and PMA v. Workmen's Compensation Appeal Bd., 580 A.2d 431 (Pa. 1990).

Boudewyns, P. A., & Hyer, L. (1996). Eye movement and desensitization and reprocessing (EMDR) as treatment for posttraumatic stress disorder (PTSD). *Clinical Psychology and Psychotherapy, 3,* 185–195.

Boudreaux, E., Kilpatrick, D. G., Resnick, H. S., Best, C. L., & Saunders, B. E. (1998). Criminal victimization, posttraumatic stress disorder and comorbid psychopathology among a community sample of women. *Journal of Traumatic Stress, 11,* 665–678.

Bowman, M. L. (1999). Individual differences in posttraumatic distress: Problems with the DSM-IV model. *Canadian Journal of Psychiatry, 44,* 21–33.

Brady, K. T., & Back, S. E. (2002). PTSD and medical comorbidity. In R. Kimerling, P. Ouimette, & J. Wolfe (Eds.), *Gender and PTSD* (pp. 335–348). New York: Guilford.

Brand, B. (2003). Trauma and women. *Psychiatric Clinics of North America, 26,* 759–779.

Brasfield, C. R. (2004, July 24). Personal communication.

Bremner, J. D. (1999). Does stress damage the brain? *Biological Psychiatry, 45,* 797–895.

Breslau, N. (2001). The epidemiology of posttraumatic stress disorder: What is the extent of the problem? *Journal of Clinical Psychiatry, 62* (Suppl. 17), 16–22.

Breslau, N. (2002a). Gender differences in trauma and posttraumatic stress disorder. *Journal of Gender-Specific Medicine, 5,* 34–40.

Breslau, N. (2002b). Epidemiologic studies of trauma, posttraumatic stress disorder, and other psychiatric disorders. *Canadian Journal of Psychiatry, 47,* 923–929.

Breslau, N., Chilcoat, H. D., Kessler, R. C., & Davis, G. (1999a). Previous exposure to trauma and PTSD effects of subsequent trauma: Results from the Detroit area survey. *American Journal of Psychiatry, 156,* 902–907.

Breslau, N., Chilcoat, H. D., Kessler, R. C., Peterson, E. L., & Lucia, V. C. (1999b). Vulnerability to assaultive violence: Further speculation of the sex difference in posttraumatic stress disorder. *Psychological Medicine, 29,* 813–821.

Breslau, N., & Davis, G. (1987). Post-traumatic stress disorder: The stressor criterion. *Journal of Nervous and Mental Disease, 175,* 255–264.

Breslau, N., & Davis, G. (1992). Posttraumatic stress disorder in an urban population of young adults: Risk factors for chronicity. *American Journal of Psychiatry, 149,* 671–675.

Breslau, N., Davis, G. C., Andreski, P., & Peterson, E. L. (1991). Traumatic events and posttraumatic stress disorder in an urban population of young adults. *Archives of General Psychiatry, 48,* 216–222.

Breslau, N., Davis, G. C., Andreski, P., Peterson, E. L., & Schutz, L. R. (1997a). Sex differences in posttraumatic stress disorder. *Archives of General Psychiatry, 54,* 1044–1048.

Breslau, N., Davis, G. C., Peterson, E. L., & Schutz, L. R. (1997b). Psychiatric sequelae of posttraumatic stress disorder in women. *Archives of General Psychiatry, 54*, 81–87.

Breslau, N., Davis, G. C., & Schultz, L. R. (2003). Posttraumatic stress disorder and the incidence of nicotine, alcohol, and other drug disorders in persons who have experienced trauma. *Archives of General Psychiatry, 60*, 289–294.

Breslau, N., & Kessler, R. C. (2001). The stressor criterion in DSM-IV posttraumatic stress disorder: An empirical investigation. *Society of Biological Psychiatry, 50*, 699–704.

Breslau, N., Kessler, R. C., & Chilcoat, H. D. (1998). Trauma and posttraumatic stress disorder in the community: The 1996 Detroit area survey. *Archives of General Psychiatry, 55*, 626–632.

Breslau, N., Peterson, E. L., Kessler, R. C., & Schultz, L. R. (1999c). Short screening scale for DSM-IV posttraumatic stress disorder. *American Journal of Psychiatry, 156*(6), 908–911.

Brewin, C. R., Andrews, B., and Rose, S. (2000). Fear, helplessness, and horror in posttraumatic stress disorder: Investigating DSM-IV criterion A2 in victims of violent crime. *Journal of Traumatic Stress, 13*, 499–509.

Brewin, C. R., Andrews, B., & Valentine, J. D. (2000). Meta-analysis of risk factors for posttraumatic stress disorder in trauma-exposed adults. *Journal of Consulting and Clinical Psychology, 68*, 748–766.

Briere, J. N. (1992). *Child abuse trauma: Theory and treatment of the lasting effects.* Thousand Oaks, CA: Sage.

Briere, J., & Elliott, D. M. (1998). Clinical utility of the Impact of Event Scale: Psychometrics in the general population. *Assessment, 5*, 171–180.

Brown v. Kendall, 60 Mass. 292 (1850).

Brown, J. T. (1996). Avoiding litigation neurosis: A practitioner's guide to defending posttraumatic stress disorder claims. *American Journal of Trial Advocacy, 20*, 29–41.

Brown, T. A., Campbell, L. A., Lehman, C. L., Grisham, J. R., & Mancill, R. B. (2001). Current and lifetime comorbidity of the DSM-IV anxiety and mood disorders in a large clinical sample. *Journal of Abnormal Psychology, 110*, 585–599.

Brown, T. A., Di Nardo, P. A., Lehman, C. L., & Campbell, L. A. (2001). Reliability of DSM-IV anxiety and mood disorders: Implications for the classification of emotional disorders. *Journal of Abnormal Psychology, 110*, 49–58.

Browne, A., & Finkelhor, D. (1986). Impact of child sexual abuse: A review of the research. *Psychological Bulletin, 99*, 66–77.

Bryant, R. A. (1996). Posttraumatic stress disorder, flashbacks and pseudomemories in closed head injury. *Journal of Traumatic Stress, 9*, 621–630.

Bryant, R. A., & Harvey, A. G. (1996). Posttraumatic stress reactions in volunteer firefighters. *Journal of Traumatic Stress, 9*, 51–62.

Bryant, R.A. & Harvey, A.G. (1999a). Postconcussive symptoms and posttraumatic stress disorder after mild traumatic brain injury. *Journal of Nervous and Mental Disease, 187*, 302–305.

Bryant, R. A., & Harvey, A.G. (1999b). The influence of traumatic brain injury on acute stress disorder and post-traumatic stress disorder following motor vehicle accidents. *Brain Injury, 13*, 15–22.

Bryant, R. A., Harvey, A. G., Dang, S. T., Sackville, T., & Basten, C. (1998). Treatment of acute stress disorder: A comparison of cognitive-behavioral therapy and supportive counseling. *Journal of Consulting and Clinical Psychology, 66*, 862–866.

Bryant, R. A., Harvey, A. G., Guthrie, R. M., & Moulds, M. L. (2000). A prospective study of psychophysiological arousal, acute stress disorder, and posttraumatic stress disorder. *Journal of Abnormal Psychology, 109,* 341–344.

Bryant, R. A., Marosszeky, J.E. Crooks, J., & Gurka, J.A. (2000). Posttraumatic stress disorder after severe traumatic brain injury. *American Journal of Psychiatry, 157,* 629–631.

Bryant, R. A., Moulds, M.L., Guthrie, R.M., & Nixon, R.D.V. (2005). The Additive Benefit of Hypnosis and Cognitive-Behavioral Therapy in Treating Acute Stress Disorder. *Journal of Consulting and Clinical Psychology. 7,* 334–340.

Bryant, R. A., Moulds, M. L., & Nixon, R. V. (2003). Cognitive behaviour therapy of Acute Stress Disorder: A four-year follow-up. *Behaviour Research and Therapy, 41,* 489–494.

Bryant, R. A., & Panasetis, P. (2001). Panic symptoms during trauma and acute stress disorder. *Behaviour Research & Therapy, 39,* 961–966.

Bryant, R. A., Sackville, T., Dang, S. T., Moulds, M. L., & Guthrie, R. (1999). Treating acute stress disorder: An evaluation of cognitive behavior therapy and supportive counseling techniques. *American Journal of Psychiatry, 156,* 1780–1786.

Buckley, T. C., Blanchard, E. B., & Hickling, E. J. (1996). A prospective examination of delayed onset PTSD secondary to motor vehicle accidents. *Journal of Abnormal Psychology, 105,* 617–625.

Bunger v. Lawson Co., 741 N.E.2d 121 (Ohio 2001).

Bunn, T. A., & Clarke, A. M. (1979). Crisis intervention: An experimental study of the effects of a brief period of counselling on the anxiety of relatives of seriously injured or ill hospital patients. *British Journal of Medical Psychology, 52*(2), 191–195.

Burges, C., & McMillan, T. M. (2001). The ability of naïve participants to report symptoms of post-traumatic stress disorder. *British Journal of Clinical Psychology, 40,* 209–214.

Burgess, A. W., & Holmstrom, L. L. (1979). Adaptive strategies and recovery from rape. *American Journal of Psychiatry, 146,* 1278–1282.

Burkett, B. G., & Whitley, G. (1998). *Stolen valor: How the Vietnam generation was robbed of its heroes and its history.* Dallas, TX: Verity.

Burnett, A., & Peel, M. (2001). Asylum seekers and refugees in Britain: The health of survivors of torture and organized violence. *British Medical Journal, 322,* 606–609.

Butcher, J. N. (1990). *The MMPI-2 in psychological treatment.* New York: Oxford University Press.

Butcher, J. N. (1998). *Users guide for the Minnesota report: Reports for forensic settings.* Minneapolis, MN: National Computer Systems.

Butcher, J. N., Arbisi, P. A., Atlis, M. M., & McNulty, J. L. (2003). The construct validity of the Lees-Haley Fake Bad Scale: Does this scale measure somatic malingering and feigned emotional distress? *Archives of Clinical Neuropsychology, 18,* 473–485.

Butcher, J. N., Cheung, F. M., & Lim, J. (2003). Use of the MMPI-2 with Asian populations. *Psychological Assessment, 15,* 248–256.

Butcher, J. N., Dahlstrom, W. G., Graham, J. R., Tellegen, A., & Kaemmer, B. (1989). *Minnesota Multiphasic Personality Inventory-2: Manual for administration and scoring.* Minneapolis, MN:University of Minnesota Press.

Butcher, J. N., Graham, J. R., Ben-Porath, Y. S., Tellegen, A., Grant Dahlstrom, W., & Kaemmer, B. (2001). *Minnesota Multiphasic Personality Inventory-2: Manual for administration, scoring, and interpretation* (rev. ed.). Minneapolis, MN: University of Minnesota Press.

Butts, H. F. (2002). The black mask of humanity: Racial/ethnic discrimination and post-traumatic stress disorder. *Journal of the American Academy of Psychiatry & the Law, 30,* 336–339.

Byrne, C. A., Resnick, H. S., Kilpatrick, D. G., Best, C. L., & Saunders, B. E. (1999). The socioeconomic impact of interpersonal violence on women. *Journal of Consulting and Clinical Psychology, 67,* 362–366.

Cahill, S. P., Carrigan, M. H., & Frueh, B. C. (1999). Does EMDR work? And if so, why? A critical review of controlled outcome and dismantling research. *Journal of Anxiety Disorders, 13,* 5–34.

Caldwell, A. B. (1988). *MMPI supplemental scale manual.* Los Angeles: Caldwell Report.

Calhoun, P. S., Earnst, K. S., Tucker, D. D., Kirby, A. C., & Beckham, J. C. (2000). Feigning combat-related posttraumatic stress disorder on the personality assessment inventory. *Journal of Personality Assessment, 75,* 338–350.

California Civil Code § 1714.01; 3333.

California Civil Code § 1708.7.

Campbell, D. T., & Fiske, D. W. (1959). Convergent and discriminant validation by the multitrait-multimethod matrix. *Psychological Bulletin, 56,* 81–105.

Campbell, J., Miller, M. M., Cardwell, M. M., & Belknap, R. A. (1994). Relationship status of battered women over time. *Journal of Family Violence, 9,* 99–111.

Campbell, J. C. (1992). A review of nursing research on battering. In C. M. Sampselle (Ed.), *Violence against women: Nursing research, education, and practice issues* (pp. 69–81). Washington, DC: Hemisphere.

Campbell, R., Ahrens, C. E., Sefl, T., Wasco, S. M., & Bames, H. E. (2001). Social reactions to rape victims. Healing and hurtful effects on psychological and physical health outcomes. *Violence and Victims, 16,* 287–302.

Canadian Human Rights Act. R.S.C. 1985, c. H-6.

Canadian Human Rights Commission. (1987). *Sexual harassment casebook: 1978–1986.* Ottawa, ON: Minister of Supplies and Services.

Canadian Institutes of Health Information. (2001). *New report from CIHI examines current state of Canada's health care providers.* Retrieved May 23, 2004, from http://www.secure.cihi.ca/cihiweb/dispPage.jsp?cw_page=media_26nov2001_e.

Canadian Psychological Association. (1991). *Canadian code of ethics for psychologists.* Ottawa, Canada: Author.

Canadian Psychological Association. (2000). *Canadian code of ethics for psychologists.* Ottawa: Author. Retrieved June 29, 2004, from http://www.cpa.ca/ethics2000.html.

Canadian Register of Health Service Professionals in Psychology. (2004). *Finding a CRHSPP psychologist.* Retrieved March 30, 2004, from http://www.crhspp.ca/findlist.htm.

Carlson, E. B., & Dutton, M. A. (2003). Assessing experiences and response of crime victims. *Journal of Traumatic Stress, 16,* 133–148.

Carlson, J. G., Chemtob, C. M., Rusnak, K., Hedlund, N. L., & Muraoka, M. Y. (1998). Eye movement desensitization and reprocessing (EMDR) treatment for combat related posttraumatic stress disorder. *Journal of Traumatic Stress, 11,* 3–24.

Carrero v. New York City Housing Authority, 890 F.2d 569 (2d Cir. 1989).

Carrion, V. G., Weems, C. F., Ray, R., & Reiss, A. L. (2002). Toward an empirical definition of pediatric PTSD: The phenomenology of PTSD symptoms in youth.

Journal of American Academy of Child and Adolescent Psychiatry, 41, 166–173.

Cascardi, M., & O'Leary, K. D. (1992). Depressive symptomatology, self-esteem, and self-blame in battered women. *Journal of Family Violence, 7,* 249–259.

Cascardi, M., O'Leary, K. D., Lawrence, E. E., & Schlee, K. A. (1995). Characteristics of women physically abused by their spouses and who seek treatment regarding marital conflict. *Journal of Consulting & Clinical Psychology, 63,* 616–623.

Cascardi, M., O'Leary, K. D., & Schlee, K. A. (1999). Co-occurrence and correlates of posttraumatic stress disorder and major depression in physically abused women. *Journal of Family Violence. 14,* 227–249.

Cason, D., Grubaugh, A., & Resick, P. (2002). Gender and PTSD treatment: Efficacy and effectiveness. In R. Kimerling, P. Ouimette, & J. Wolfe (Eds.), *Gender and PTSD* (pp. 305–334). New York: Guilford.

Caspi, A., Bolger, N., & Eckenrode, J. (1987). Linking person and context in the daily stress process. *Journal of Personality and Social Psychology, 52,* 184–195.

Castro, T. (2003, March 5). *I am Tiger Woods: The making of the new America.* Retrieved June 16, 2004, from http://www.beverlyhillsbaseball.com/tonycastro/tiger030503 .html.

Chamallas, M. (2001). Removing emotional harm from the core of tort law. *Vanderbilt Law Review, 54,* 751–765.

Chamberlain Mfg. Corp. v. Workmen's Compensation Appeal Board, 405 A.2d 1375 (Pa. 1979).

Champion v. Gray, 478 So.2d 17 (Fla. 1985).

Chaney v. Smithkline Beckman Corp., 764 F. 2d 527 (8th Cir 1985).

Chapman v. Capoccia, 283 A.D.2d 798 (N.Y. 3rd Dep't. 2001).

Chatzifotiou, S., & Dobash, R. (2001). Seeking informal support: Marital violence against women in Greece. *Violence Against Women, 7,* 1024–1050.

Chemtob, C. M., Novaco, R. W., Hamada, R. S., & Gross, D. M. (1997). Cognitive behavioral treatment for severe anger in posttraumatic stress disorder. *Journal of Consulting and Clinical Psychology, 65,* 184–189.

Chemtob, C. M., Novaco, R. W., Hamada, R. S., Gross, D. M. & Smith, G. (1997). Anger regulation deficits in combat-related posttraumatic stress disorder. *Journal of Traumatic Stress, 10,* 17–35.

Chester, M. (2000). The aftermath of the airplane accident: Recovery of damages for psychological injuries accompanied by physical injuries under the Warsaw Convention. *Marquette Law Review, 84,* 227–249.

Chow, J. C., Jaffee, K., & Snowden, L. (2003). Racial/ethnic disparities in the use of mental health services in poverty areas. *American Journal of Public Health, 93*(5), 792–797.

Civil Rights Act. (1964/1991). Public Law 102–166, U.S. Congress. Washington, DC.

Civil Rights Act of 1968, 42, U.S.C. § 3604–3619 (2003).

Civil Rights Act of 1991, 42, U.S.C. § 1981s (1994).

Clancy, A., Hough, M., Aust, R., & Kershaw, C. (2001). *Crime, policing and justice: The experience of ethnic minorities. Findings from the 2000 British crime survey.* London: Home Office.

Clark, R., Anderson, N. B., Clark, V. R., & Williams, D. R. (1999). Racism as a stressor for African Americans: A biopsychosocial model. *American Psychologist, 54,* 805–816.

Cloitre, M., Koenen, K. C., Cohen, L. R., & Han, H. (2002). Skills training in affective and interpersonal regulation followed by exposure: A phase-based treatment for PTSD related to childhood abuse. *Journal of Consulting and Clinical Psychology, 70,* 1067–1074.

Cloitre, M., Koenen, K. C., Gratz, K. L., & Jakupcak, M. (2002). Differential diagnosis of PTSD in women. In R. Kimerling & P. Ouimette (Eds.), *Gender and PTSD* (pp. 117–149). New York: Guilford Press.

Cochran, C. C., Frazier, P. A., & Olson, A. M. (1997). Predictors of responses to unwanted sexual attention. *Psychology of Women Quarterly, 21,* 207–226.

Coleman, F. L. (1997). Stalking behavior and the cycle of domestic violence. *Journal of Interpersonal Violence, 12,* 420–432.

Comas-Diaz, L. (1990). Hispanic/Latino communities: Psychological implications. *Journal of Training & Practice in Professional Psychology, 4*(1), 14–35.

Committee on Ethical Guidelines for Forensic Psychologists. (1991). Specialty guidelines for forensic psychologists. *Law and Human Behavior, 15,* 655–665.

Conlon, L., Fahy, T. J., & Conroy, R. (1999). PTSD in ambulant RTA victims: A randomized controlled trial of debriefing. *Journal of Psychosomatic Research, 46,* 37–44.

Consolidated Rail Corp. v. Gottshall, 512 U.S. 532 (1994).

Constantinou, M., & McCaffrey, R. J. (2003). Using the TOMM for evaluating children's effort to perform optimally on neuropsychological measures. *Child Neuropsychology, 9,* 81–90.

Convention for the Unification of Certain Rules Relating to International Transportation by Air. Oct. 12, 1929, 49, Stat. 3000, T.S. No. 876 (1934).

Cooper, C. R., & Denner, J. (1998). Theories linking culture and psychology: Universal and community-specific processes. *Annual Review of Psychology, 49,* 559–584.

Cortina, L. M., Swan, S., Fitzgerald, L. F., & Waldo, C. (1998). Sexual harassment and assault: Chilling the climate for women in academia. *Psychology of Women Quarterly, 22,* 419–441.

Cottle v. Superior Court, 5 Cal. Rptr.2d 882 (Cal. Ct. App 1992).

Creamer, M., Burgess, P., & McFarlane, A. C. (2001). Post-traumatic stress disorder: Findings form the Australian National Survey of Mental Health and Well-being. *Psychological Medicine, 31,* 1237–1247.

Cucuzza, M. (1999). Evaluating emotional distress damage awards to promote settlement of employment discrimination claims in the second circuit. *Brooklyn Law Review, 65,* 393–452.

Curtis v. Loether, 415 U.S. 189 (1974).

Cusack, K., Falsetti, S., & de Arellano, M. (2002). Gender considerations in the psychometric assessment of PTSD. In R. Kimerling & P. Ouimette (Eds.), *Gender and PTSD* (pp. 150–176). New York: Guilford Press.

Dallam, S. J., Gleaves, D. H., & Cepeda-Benito, A. (2001). The effects of child sexual abuse: Comment on Rind, Tromovitch, and Bauserman (1998). *Psychological Bulletin, 127,* 715–733.

Daly, R. J. (1983). Samuel Pepys and post traumatic disorder. *British Journal of Psychiatry, 143,* 64–68.

Daniels, N. (1984). Post-traumatic stress disorder and competence to stand trial. *The Journal of Psychiatry & Law,* 5–12.

Dansky, B. S., & Kilpatrick, D. G. (1997). Effects of sexual harassment. In W. O'Donohue (Ed.), *Sexual harassment: Theory, research, and treatment* (pp. 152–174). Boston: Allyn & Bacon.

Daubert v. Merrell Dow Pharmaceuticals, Inc., 113 S.Ct. 2786 (1993).

Davidoff, D.A., Kessler, H.R., Laibstain, D.F., & Mark, V.H. (1988). Neurobehavioral sequelae of minor head injury: A consideration of post-concussive syndrome versus post-traumatic stress disorder. *Cognitive Rehabilitation, 6,* 8–13.

Davidson, J.R.T., & Foa, E. B. (1991). Diagnostic issues in posttraumatic stress disorder: Considerations for the DSM-IV. *Journal of Abnormal Psychology, 100,* 346–355.

Davidson, J. R. T., Hughes, D., Blazer, D. G., & George, L. K. (1991). Post-traumatic stress disorder in the community: An epidemiological study. *Psychological Medicine, 21,* 713–721.

Davidson, J.R.T., Landerman, L. R., Farfel, G. M., & Clary, C. M. (2002). Characterizing the effects of sertraline in posttraumatic stress disorder. *Psychological Medicine, 32,* 661–670.

Davidson, J.R.T., Rothbaum, B. O., van der Kolk, B. A., Sikes, C. R., & Farfel, G. M. (2001). Multicenter, double-blind comparison of sertraline and placebo in the treatment of posttraumatic stress disorder. *Archives of General Psychiatry, 58,* 485–492.

Davidson, P. R. & Parker, K.C.H. (2001). Eye movement desensitization and reprocessing (EMDR): A meta-analysis. *Journal of Consulting and Clinical Psychology, 69,* 305–316.

Davis, G. C., & Breslau, N. (1998). Are women at greater risk for PTSD than men? *Psychiatric Times, XV.* Retrieved April 23, 2005, from http://www.psychiatric times.com/p980765.html

Davis, K. E., Coker. L., & Sanderson, M. (2002). Physical and mental health effects of being stalked for men and women. *Violence and Victims, 17,* 429–43.

Deahl, M. P., Gillham, A. B., Thomas, J., Searle, M. M., & Srinivasan, M. (1994). Psychological sequelae following the Gulf War: Factors associated with subsequent morbidity and the effectiveness of psychological debriefing. *British Journal of Psychiatry, 165,* 60–65.

Deahl, M., Srinivasan, M., Jones, N., Thomas, J., Neblett, C., and Jolly, A. (2000). Preventing psychological trauma in soldiers: The role of operational stress training and psychological debriefing. *British Journal of Medical Psychology, 73*(1), 77–85.

DePrince, A. P., & Freyd, J. J. (2002). The intersection of gender and betrayal in trauma. In R. Kimerling, P. Ouimette, & J. Wolfe (Eds.), *Gender and PTSD* (pp. 98–113). New York: Guilford.

DeSouza, E., & Fansler, A. G. (2003). Contrapower sexual harassment: A survey of students and faculty members. *Sex Roles, 48,* 529–542.

Devilly, G. J., Spence, S. H., & Rapee, R. M. (1998). Statistical and reliable change with eye movement desensitization and reprocessing: Treating trauma within a veteran population. *Behavior Therapy, 29,* 435–455.

Dillman, E. G. (2003). Impairment to earning capacity based on psychological findings. In I. Z. Schultz & D. O. Brady (Eds.), *Psychological injuries at trial* (pp. 342–356). Washington, DC: American Bar Association.

Dillon v. Legg, 68 Cal.2d 728 (1968).

DiNardo, P. A., Brown, T. A., & Barlow, D. H. (1994). *Anxiety disorders interview schedule for DSM-IV: Lifetime version (ADIS-IV-L).* Albany, NY: Graywind Publications.

DiNardo, P. A., O'Brien, G. T., Barlow, D. H., Waddell, M. T., & Blanchard, E. B. (1982). *Anxiety Disorders Interview Schedule (ADIS).* Albany: Center For Stress and Anxiety Disorders, State University of New York at Albany.

Dixon, L., & Gill, B. (2002). Changes in the standards for admitting expert evidence in federal civil cases since the Daubert decision. *Psychology, Public Policy, and Law, 8,* 251–308.

Dobbs, D. B., Keeton, R. E., Owen, D. G., & Keeton, W. P. (1984). *Prosser & Keeton on the law of torts* (5th ed). St. Paul, MN: West Publishing Company.

Dobie, D. J., Kivlahan, D. R., & Maynard, C. (2002). Screening for post-traumatic stress disorder in female Veteran's Affairs patients: Validation of the PTSD Checklist. *General Hospital Psychiatry, 24*(6), 367–374.

Donoghue v. Stevenson, A. C. 562 (HL 1932).

Douglas, K. S., & Dutton, D. G. (2001). Assessing the link between stalking and domestic violence. *Aggression and Violent Behavior, 6,* 519–546.

Douglas, K. S., Huss, M. T., Murdoch, L. L., Washington, D. O., & Koch, W. J. (1999). Posttraumatic stress disorder stemming from motor vehicle accidents: Legal issues in Canada and the United States. In E. J. Hickling & E. B. Blanchard (Eds.), *International handbook of road traffic accidents and psychological trauma: Current understanding, treatment and law* (pp. 271–290). New York: Elsevier Science.

Douglas, K. S., & Koch, W. J. (June, 2000). *Posttraumatic Stress Disorder arising from motor vehicle accidents: A critical review of predictive factors.* Working Paper for the Insurance Corporation of British Columbia.

Douglas, K. S., & Koch, W. J. (2001). Psychological injuries and tort litigation: Sexual victimization and motor vehicle accidents. In R. Schuller and J.R.P. Ogloff (Eds.), *Introduction to psychology and law: Canadian perspectives.* Toronto: University of Toronto Press.

Dozois, D.J.A., Dobson, K. S., & Ahnberg, J. L. (1998). A psychometric evaluation of the Beck Depression Inventory-II. *Psychological Assessment, 10,* 83–89.

Draguns, J. G., & Tanaka-Matsumi, J. (2003). Assessment of psychopathology across and within cultures: Issues and findings. *Behaviour Research and Therapy, 41,* 755–776.

Draucker, C. B. (1999). "Living in hell": The experience of being stalked. *Issues in Mental Health Nursing, 20,* 473–484.

Dutton, D. G., & Nicholls, T. L. (in press). A critical review of the gender paradigm in domestic violence research and theory: Part I—Theory and data. *Aggression and Violent Behavior.*

Eastern Airlines, Inc., v. Floyd, 499 U.S. 530 (1991).

Echeburua, E., de Corral, P., Sarasua, B., & Zubizarreta, I. (1996). Treatment of acute posttraumatic stress disorder in rape victims: An experimental study. *Journal of Anxiety Disorders, 10,* 185–199.

Eden, S. M. (2001). I am having a flashback . . . all the way to the bank: The application of the 'thin skull' rule to mental injuries—*Poole v. Copland, Inc. North Carolina Central Law Journal, 24,* 180–189.

Edens, J. F., Otto, R. K., & Dwyer, T. (1999). Utility of the Structured Inventory of Malingered Symptomatology in identifying persons motivated to malinger psychopathology. *Journal of the American Academy of Psychiatry & the Law, 27,* 387–396.

Ehlers, A., & Clark, D. M. (2000). A cognitive model of posttraumatic stress disorder. *Behaviour Research and Therapy, 38,* 319–345.

Ehlers, A., & Clark, D. M. (2003). Early psychological interventions for adult survivors of trauma: A review. *Biological Psychiatry, 53,* 817–826.

Ehlers, A., Clark, D. M., Dunmore, E., Jaycox, L., Meadows, E., & Foa, E. B. (1998).

Predicting response to exposure treatment in PTSD: The role of mental defeat and alienation. *Journal of Traumatic Stress, 11,* 457–470.

Ehlers, A., Clark, D. M., Hackmann, A., McManus, F., Fennell, M., Herbert, C., & Mayou, R. A. (2003). A randomized controlled trial of cognitive therapy, self-help, and repeated assessment as early interventions for PTSD. *Archives of General Psychiatry, 60,* 1024–1032.

Ehlers, A., Hofmann, S. G., & Herda, C. A. (1994). Clinical characteristics of driving phobia. *Journal of Anxiety Disorders, 8,* 323–339.

Ehlers, A., Mayou, R. A., & Bryant, B. (1998). Psychological predictors of chronic posttraumatic stress disorder after motor vehicle accidents. *Journal of Abnormal Psychology, 107,* 508–519.

Ehrlich v. American Airlines, Inc., 2004 WL 419438 (2nd Cir. N.Y. 2004).

Eisenman, D. P., Gelberg, L., Honghu, L., & Shapiro, M. F. (2003). Mental health and health-related quality of life among adult Latino primary care patients living in the United States with previous exposure to political violence. *JAMA: Journal of the American Medical Association, 290*(5), 627–634.

Elden v. Sheldon, 758 P.2d 582 (Cal. 1988).

Elhai, J. D., Gold, P. B., Frueh, B. C., & Gold, S. N. (2000). Cross-validation of the MMPI-2 in detecting malingered posttraumatic stress disorder. *Journal of Personality Assessment, 75,* 449–463.

Elhai, J. D., Gold, S. N., Sellers, A. H., & Dorfman, W. I. (2001). The detection of malingered posttraumatic stress disorder with MMPI-2 fake bad indices. *Assessment, 8,* 221–236.

Elhai, J. D., Ruggiero, K. J., Frueh, B. C., Beckham, J. C., Gold, P. B., & Feldman, M. E. (2002). The Infrequency-Posttraumatic Stress Disorder scale (Fptsd) for the MMPI-2: Development and initial validation with veterans presenting with combat-related PTSD. *Journal of Personality Assessment, 79,* 531–549.

Elliott, D. M. (1997). Traumatic events: Prevalence and delayed recall in the general population. *Journal of Consulting and Clinical Psychology, 65,* 811–820.

Epstein, R. A. (1995). *Cases and material on torts.* New York: Little, Brown.

Equal Employment Opportunity Commission. (1980). *The federal guideline on sexual harassment* (title VII, section 703). Washington, DC: Author.

Equal Employment Opportunity Commission. (1981 & 1994). Guidelines on sexual harassment. *Code of federal regulations* (S. 1604.11). Vol. 29, chap. XIV (7-1-94 ed.), pp. 196–197.

Equal Employment Opportunities Commission. (2003). Guidelines on discrimination because of sex, 29CFR1604.11(a).

Equal Employment Opportunities Commission. (1980). *Federal Register, 45,* 25025.

Erdman, H. P., Klein, M. H., Greist, J. H., & Bass, S. M. (1987). A comparison of the Diagnostic Interview Schedule and clinical diagnosis. *American Journal of Psychiatry, 144,* 1477–1480.

Escalona, R., Canive, J., Calais, L. A., & Davidson, J. T. (2002). Fluvoxamine treatment in veterans with combat-related post-traumatic stress disorder. *Depression and Anxiety, 15,* 29–33.

Eurostat. (2003). *First results of the demographic data collection for 2002 in Europe.* European Communities. Retrieved January 12, 2004, from http://www.europa .eu.int/comm/eurostat/Public/datashop/print-product/EN?catalogue=Eurostat& product=KS-NK-03-020-_-N-EN&mode=download.

Everingim v. Good Samaritan Center of New Underwood, 552 N.W.2d 837 (SD 1996).

Fairbank, J. A., Ebert, L., & Zarkin, G. A. (1999). Socioeconomic consequences of traumatic stress. In P. A. Saigh & J. D. Bremner (Eds.), *Posttraumatic stress disorder: A comprehensive text* (pp. 180–198). Needham Heights, MA: Allyn & Bacon.

Fairbank, J. A., McCaffrey, R. J., & Keane, T. M. (1985). Psychometric detection of fabricated symptoms of posttraumatic stress disorder. *American Journal of Psychiatry, 142,* 501–503.

Falsetti, S. A., & Resnick, H. S. (1997). Frequency and severity of panic attack symptoms in a treatment seeking sample of trauma victims. *Journal of Traumatic Stress, 10,* 683–689.

Falsetti, S. A., Resnick, H. S., Davis, J., & Gallagher, N. G. (2001). Treatment of posttraumatic stress disorder with comorbid panic attacks: Combining cognitive processing therapy with panic control treatment techniques. *Group Dynamics, 5,* 252–260.

Federal Bureau of Investigation. (2002). Uniform crime reports: Hate crime statistics. Author. Retrieved December 8, 2003, from http://www.fbi.gov/ucr/hatecrime 2002.pdf.

Feeny, N. C., O'Neill, M. L., & Foa, E. B. (under review). PTSD and comorbid Axis I and II disorders.

Feeny, N. C., Zoellner, L. A., & Foa, E. B. (2000). Anger, dissociation, and posttraumatic stress disorder among female assault victims. *Journal of Traumatic Stress, 13,* 89–100.

Feldman-Schorrig, S. P. (1994). Special issues in sexual harassment cases. In J. J. McDonald & F. B. Kulick (Eds.), *Mental and emotional injuries in employment litigation* (pp. 332–390). Washington, DC: The Bureau of National Affairs.

Fenster, A., & Fenster, J. (1998). Diagnosing deficits in "basic trust" in multiracial and multicultural groups: Individual or social psychopathology? *Group, 22,* 81–93.

Fergusson, D. M., Swain-Campbell, N. R., & Horwood, L. J. (2002). Does sexual violence contribute to elevated rates of anxiety and depression in females? *Psychological Medicine, 32,* 991–996.

Finkelhor, D. (1979). What's wrong with sex between adults and children? *American Journal of Orthopsychiatry, 49,* 692–697.

———. (1994). The international epidemiologie of child sexual abuse. *Child Abuse and Neglect, 19,* 409–417.

Finkelhor, D., Hotaling, G., Lewis, I. A., & Smith, C. (1990). Sexual abuse in a national survey of adult men and women: Prevalence, characteristics, and risk factors. *Child Abuse & Neglect, 14,* 19–28.

Finn, S. E., & Kamphuis, J. H. (1995). What a clinician needs to know about base rates. In J. N. Butcher (Ed.), *Clinical personality assessment: Practical approaches.* New York: Oxford University Press.

First, M. B., & Pincus, H. A. (1999). Classification in psychiatry: ICD-10 v. DSM-IV: A response. *British Journal of Psychiatry, 175*(9), 205–209.

First, M. B., Spitzer, R. L., Gibbon, M., & Williams, J.B.W. (1995). The Structured Clinical Interview for DSM-III-R personality disorders (SCID–II): I. Description. *Journal of Personality Disorders, 9,* 83–91.

First, M., Spitzer, R., Williams, J, & Gibbon, M. (2000). Structured Clinical Interview for DSM-IV Axis I Disorders (SCID-I). In American Psychiatric Association, *Handbook of psychiatric measures.* Washington, DC: American Psychiatric Association, (pp. 49–53).

Fleury, R. E., Sullivan, C. M., & Bybee, D. I. (2000). When ending the relationship does not end the violence: Women's experiences of violence by former partners. *Violence Against Women, 6,* 1363–1383.

Fluke, J. D., Yuan, Y. T., Hedderson, J., & Curits, P. A. (2003). Disproportionate representation of race and ethnicity in child maltreatment: Investigation and victimization. *Children & Youth Services Review, 25, Special Issue: The overrepresentation of children of color in the child welfare system,* 359–373.

Foa, E. B. (1997). Trauma and women: Course, predictors, and treatment. *Journal of Clinical Psychiatry, 58,* 25–33.

Foa, E. B., Cashman, L., Jaycox, L., & Perry, K. (1997). The validation of a self-report measure of posttraumatic stress disorder: The Posttraumatic Diagnostic Scale. *Psychological Assessment, 9,* 445–451.

Foa, E. B., Dancu, C. V., Hembree, E. A., Jaycox, L. H., Meadows, E. A., & Street, G. P. (1999). A comparison of exposure therapy, stress inoculation training, and their combination for reducing posttraumatic stress disorder in female assault victims. *Journal of Consulting and Clinical Psychology, 67,* 194–200.

Foa, E. B., Ehlers, A., Clark, D. M., Tolin, D. F., & Orsillo, S. M. (1999). The posttraumatic cognitions inventory (PTCI): Development and validation. *Psychological Assessment, 11,* 303–314.

Foa, E. B., Hearst–Ikeda, D., & Perry, K. J. (1995). Evaluation of a brief cognitive-behavioral program for the prevention of chronic PTSD in recent assault victims. *Journal of Consulting and Clinical Psychology, 63,* 948–955.

Foa, E. B., & Meadows, E. A. (1997). Psychosocial treatments for posttraumatic stress disorder: A critical review. *Annual Review of Psychology, 48,* 449–480.

Foa, E. B., Riggs, D. S., Dancu, C. V., & Rothbaum, B. O. (1993). Reliability and validity of a brief instrument for assessing post-traumatic stress disorder. *Journal of Traumatic Stress, 6,* 459–473.

Foa, E. B., Riggs, D. S., & Gershuny, B. S. (1995). Arousal, numbing, and intrusion: Symptom structure of PTSD following assault. *American Journal of Psychiatry, 152,* 116–120.

Foa, E. B., Riggs, D. S., Massie, E. D., Yarczower, M. (1995). The impact of fear activation and anger on the efficacy of exposure treatment for posttraumatic stress disorder. *Behavior Therapy, 26,* 487–499.

Foa, E. B., Rothbaum, B. O., & Steketee, G. S. (1993). Treatment of rape victims. *Journal of Interpersonal Violence, 8,* 256–276.

Foa, E. B., & Street, G. P. (2001). Women and traumatic events. *Journal of Clinical Psychiatry, 62,* 29–34.

Foa, E. B., Zoellner, L. A., Feeny, N. C., Hembree, E. A., & Alvarez-Conrad, J. (2002). Does imaginal exposure exacerbate PTSD symptoms? *Journal of Consulting and Clinical Psychology, 70,* 1022–1028.

Fox, D., Gerson, A., & Lees-Haley, P. (1995). Interrelationship of MMPI-2 validity scales in personal injury claims. *Journal of Clinical Psychology, 51,* 42–47.

Fox, D. M., Lees-Haley, P. R., Earnest, K., & Dolezal-Wood, S. (1995). Base rates of postconcussive symptoms in health maintenance organization patients and controls. *Neuropsychology, 9,* 606–611.

Fox, N. K. (2003). Through the eyes and ears of children: A significant advance for third parties exposed to domestic violence. *Bevan v. Fix,* 42, P.3d 1013 (Wyo. 2002). *Wyoming Law Review, 3,* 735–768.

Frances, A., First, M. B., & Pincus, H. A. (1995). *DSM-IV guidebook.* Washington, DC: American Psychiatric Press.

Franklin, C. L., Repasky, S. A., Thompson, K. E., Shelton, S. A., & Uddo, M. (2002). Differentiating overreporting and extreme distress: MMPI-2 use with compensation-seeking veterans with PTSD. *Journal of Personality Assessment, 79,* 274–285.

Freedman, S. A., Gluck, N., Tuval-Mashiach, R., Brandes, D., Peri, T., & Shalev, A. Y. (2002). Gender differences in response to traumatic events: A prospective study. *Journal of Traumatic Stress, 5,* 407–413.

Friedland, J.F. & Dawson, D.R. (2001). Function after motor vehicle accidents: A prospective study of mild head injury and posttraumatic stress. *Journal of Nervous and Mental Disease, 189,* 426–434.

Friedrich, W. N., Urquiza, A. J., & Beilke, R. L. (1986). Behavior problems in sexually abused young children. *Journal of Pediatric Psychology, 11,* 47–57.

Frueh, B. C., Gold, P. B., & de Arellano, M. A. (1997). Symptom overreporting in combat veterans evaluated for PTSD: Differentiation on the basis of compensation seeking status. *Journal of Personality Assessment, 68,* 369–384.

Frueh, B. C., Hamner, M. B., Cahill, S. P., Gold, P. B., & Hamlin, K. L. (2000). Apparent symptom overreporting in combat veterans evaluated for PTSD. *Clinical Psychology Review, 20,* 853–885.

Frueh, B. C., Turner, S. M., Beidel, D. C., Mirabella, R. F., & Jones, W. J. (1996). Trauma management therapy: A preliminary evaluation of a multicomponent behavioral treatment for chronic combat-related PTSD. *Behaviour Research & Therapy, 34,* 533–543.

Frye v. United States, 293 F. Supp. 1013 (D.C. Cir. 1923).

Frye v. United States, 54 APP. D.C. 46, 47, 293 F.1013-14 (D.C. Cric. 1923).

Fullerton, C. S., Ursano, R. J., Epstein, R. S., Crowley, B., Vance, K., Kao, T. C., Dougall, A., & Baum, A. D. (2001). Gender differences in Posttraumatic Stress Disorder after motor vehicle accidents. *American Journal of Psychiatry, 158,* 1486–1491.

Gaffney, M. (2003). Factor analysis of treatment response in posttraumatic stress disorder. *Journal of Traumatic Stress, 16,* 77–80.

Garb, H. N. (1998). *Studying the clinician: Judgment research and psychological assessment.* Washington, DC: American Psychological Association.

Garb, H. N., & Boyle, P. A. (2003). Understanding why some clinicians use pseudoscientific methods: Findings from research on clinical judgement. In S. O. Lilienfeld, S. J. Lynn, & J. M. Lohr (Eds.), *Science and Pseudoscience in Clinical Psychology.* New York: Guildford Press.

Garcia-Rill, E., & Beecher-Monas, E. (2001). Gatekeeping stress: The science and admissibility of post-traumatic stress disorder. *University of Arkansas at Little Rock Law Review, 24,* 9–40.

Garfield, D.A.S., Fichtner, C. G., Leveroni, C., & Mahableshwarkar, A. (2001). Open trial of nefazodone for combat veterans with posttraumatic stress disorder. *Journal of Traumatic Stress, 13,* 453–460.

Garretson, D. J. (1993). Psychological misdiagnosis of African Americans. *Journal of Multicultural Counseling & Development, 21*(2), 119–126.

Gaston, L., Brunet, A., Koszycki, D., & Bradwejn, J. (1996). MMPI profiles of acute and chronic PTSD in a civilian sample. *Journal of Traumatic Stress, 9,* 817–832.

Gavranidou, M., & Rosner, R. (2003). The weaker sex? Gender and post-traumatic stress disorder. *Depression and Anxiety, 17,* 130–139.

Gearon, J. S., Bellack, A. S., & Tenhula, W. N. (2004). Preliminary reliability and validity of the clinician-administered PTSD scale for schizophrenia. *Journal of Consulting and Clinical Psychology, 72,* 121–125.

Gelfand, M. J., Fitzgerald, L. F., & Drasgow, F. (1995). The structure of sexual harassment: A confirmatory analysis across cultures and settings. *Journal of Vocational Behavior, 47*(2), 164–177.

Gervais, R. O., Rohling, M. L., Green, P., & Ford, W. (in press). A comparison of WMT, CARB, and TOMM failure rates in non-head injury disability claimants. *Archives of Clinical Neuropsychology.*

Getsinger vs. Owens Corning Fiberglass Corp., 515 S.E.2d 104 (SC 1999).

Gilchrist v. Trail King Industries, 612 N.W.2d 1 (SD 2000).

Gill, R., & Brockman, J. (1996). *A review of section 264 (criminal harassment) of the criminal code of Canada.* Working document. Retrieved May 25, 2004, from http://www.canada.justice.gc.ca/en/ps/rs/rep/wd96-7a-e.html.

Golding, J. M. (1994). Sexual assault history and physical health in randomly selected Los Angeles women. *Health Psychology, 13,* 130–138.

Golding, J. M. (1999). Intimate partner violence as a risk factor for mental disorders: A meta-analysis. *Journal of Family Violence, 14,* 99–132.

Gondolf, E. W. (1998). *Assessing woman battering in mental health services.* Thousand Oaks, CA: Sage Publications.

Goode, V. M., & Johnson, C. A. (2003). Emotional harm in housing discrimination cases: A new look at a lingering problem. *Fordham Urban Law Journal, 30,* 1143–1213.

Goodman, L. A., Corcoran, C., Turner, K., Yuan, N., & Green, B. L. (1998). Assessing traumatic event exposure: General issues and preliminary findings for the Stressful Life Events Screening Questionnaire. *Journal of Traumatic Stress, 11,* 521–542.

Goodman-Delahunty, J. (1997). Forensic psychological expertise in the wake of Daubert. *Law and Human Behavior, 21,* 121–140.

Gough, H. G. (1947). Simulated patterns on the MMPI. *Journal of Abnormal and Social Psychology, 42,* 215–225.

———. (1950). The F minus K dissimulation index for the MMPI. *Journal of Consulting Psychology, 14,* 408–413.

———. (1954). Some common misconceptions about neuroticism. *Journal of Consulting Psychology, 18,* 287–292.

———. (1957). *California psychological inventory manual.* Palo Alto, CA: Consulting Psychologists Press.

Gove, W. R., & Tudor, J. F. (1973). Adult sex roles and mental illness. *American Journal of Sociology, 98,* 812–835.

Graham, J. R. (1993). *MMPI-2 assessing personality and psychopathology* (2d ed.). New York: Oxford University Press.

Graham, J. R., Watts, D., & Timbrook, R. E. (1991). Detecting fake-good and fake-bad MMPI-2 profiles. *Journal of Personality Assessment, 57,* 264–277.

Granowitz v. Vanvickle, 264 N.J.Super. 440, 624 A.2d 1047 (1993).

Green, B. L., (1996). Trauma History Questionnaire. In B.H. Stamm (Eds.), *Measurement of Stress, Trauma and Adaptation* (pp. 366–369). Lutherville, MD: Sidran Press.

Greenberg, P. E., Stiglin, L. E., Finkelstein, S. N., & Berndt, E. R. (1993). The economic burden of depression in 1990. *Journal of Clinical Psychiatry, 54*(11), 405–418.

Greene, R. (1991). *The MMPI-2/MMPI: An interpretive manual.* New York: Grune & Stratton.

———. (1997). Assessment of malingering and defensiveness by multiscale personality inventories. In R. Rogers (Ed.), *Clinical assessment of malingering and deception* (2d ed., pp. 169–188). New York: Guilford Press.

———. (2000). *The MMPI-2: An interpretive manual* (2d ed.). Boston: Allyn and Bacon.

Greene, R. L., Brown, R. C., & Kovan, R. E. (1998). *MMPI-2 adult interpretive system professional manual.* Odessa, FL: Psychological Assessment Resources.

Greiffenstein, M. F., Baker, W. J., Axelrod, B., Peck, E. A., & Gervais, R. (2004). The Fake Bad Scale and MMPI-2 F-Family in detection of implausible psychological trauma claims. *The Clinical Neuropsychologist, 18 (4), 573–590.*

Greiffenstein, M. F., Baker, W. J., Gola, T., Donders, J., & Miller, L. (2002). The fake bad scale in atypical and severe closed head injury litigants. *Journal of Clinical Psychology, 58,* 1591–1600.

Greve, K. W., & Bianchini, K. J. (2004). Response to Butcher et al., The construct validity of the Lees-Haley Fake-Bad Scale. *Archives of Clinical Neuropsychology, 19,* 337–339.

Grieger, T. A., Fullerton, C. S., & Ursano, R. J. (2003). Posttraumatic stress disorder, alcohol use, and perceived safety after the terrorist attack on the Pentagon. *Psychiatric Services, 54,* 1380–1382.

Grinker, R. R., & Spiegel, J. P. (1945). *Men under stress.* Philadelphia, PA: Blakiston.

Grove, W. M., Zald, D. H., Lebow, B. S., Snitz, B. E., & Nelson, C. (2000). Clinical versus mechanical prediction: A meta-analysis. *Psychological Assessment, 12,* 19–30.

Guriel, J., & Fremouw, W. (2003). Assessing malingered posttraumatic stress disorder: A critical review. *Clinical Psychology Review, 23,* 881–904.

Hagood, L. R. (1999). Claims of mental and emotional damages in employment discrimination cases. *University of Memphis Law Review, 29,* 577–600.

Hale, B. (1999). Discrimination in housing: The effects of emotional distress and its remedies. *Law and Psychology Review, 23,* 167–177.

Halligan, S. L., & Yehuda. R. (2000). Risk factors for PTSD. *PTSD Research Quarterly,11*(3), 1–3.

Harrington, R. (1996). The "railway spine" diagnosis and Victorian responses to PTSD. *Journal of Psychosomatic Research, 40,* 11–14.

Harris v. Forklift Systems, Inc., 510 U.S. 17 (1993).

Harvey, A. G., Brewin, C. R., Jones, C., & Kopelman, M. D. (2003). Coexistence of posttraumatic stress disorder and traumatic brain injury: Towards a resolution of the paradox. *Journal of the International Neuropsychological Society, 9,* 663–676.

Harvey, A. G., & Bryant, R. A. (2000a). A two-year prospective evaluation of the relationship between acute stress disorder and posttraumatic stress disorder following mild traumatic brain injury. *American Journal of Psychiatry, 157,* 626–628.

———. (2000b). Memory for acute stress disorder symptoms: A two-year prospective study. *Journal of Nervous and Mental Disease, 1888,* 602–607.

Hayes, J. S., Hilsabeck, R. C., & Gouvier, W. D. (1999). Malingering traumatic brain injury: Current issues and caveats in assessment and classification. In N. R. Vamey & R. J. Roberts (Eds.), *The evaluation and treatment of mild traumatic brain injury* (pp. 249–290). Mahwah, NJ: Erlbaum.

Hedlund, J. L., & Won Cho, D. (1979). [MMPI data research tape for Missouri Department of Mental Health patients.] Unpublished raw data. Cited in Greene, R. (1991). *The MMPI-2/MMPI: An interpretive manual.* New York: Grune & Stratton.

Heilbrun, K. (1992). The role of psychological testing in forensic assessment. *Law and Human Behavior, 16,* 257–272.

————. (2001). *Principles of forensic mental health assessment.* New York: Kluwer Academic/Plenum Publishers.

Heinzerling, L. (2001). Tortious toxics. *William and Mary Environmental Law and Policy Review, 26,* 67–92.

Helzer, J., Robins, L., McEvoy, L. (1987). Post-traumatic stress disorder in the general population: Findings of the epidemiologic catchment area survey. *New England Journal of Medicine, 317,* 1630–1634.

Herman, J. L. (1992). Complex PTSD: A syndrome in survivors of prolonged and repeated trauma. *Journal of Traumatic Stress, 5,* 377–391.

————. (2003). The mental health of crime victims: Impact of legal intervention. *Journal of Traumatic Stress, 16,* 159–166.

Hickling, E. J., & Blanchard, E. B. (1996). *Motor vehicle accident treatment manual: Intensive treatment regimen for MVA-PTSD.* Unpublished manuscript. State University of New York at Albany.

Hickling, E. J., Gillen, R., Blanchard, E. B., Buckley, T., & Taylor, A. (1997). Traumatic brain injury and posttraumatic stress disorder: A preliminary investigation of neuropsychological test results in PTSD secondary to motor vehicle accidents, *Brain Injury, 12,* 265–274.

Higgins, S. A. (1991). Post-traumatic stress disorder and its role in the defense of Vietnam Veterans. *Law & Psychology Review, 15,* 259–276.

Hobbs, M., & Adshead, G. (1996). Preventive psychological intervention for road crash survivors. In M. Mitchell (Ed.), *The aftermath of road accidents: Psychological, social, and legal perspectives* (pp. 159–171). London: Routledge.

Hobbs, M., Mayou R., Harrison, B., & Worlock, P. (1996). A randomised controlled trial of psychological debriefing for victims of road traffic accidents. *British Medical Journal, 313,* 1438–1439.

Hobfoll, S. E. (1989). Conservation of resources: A new attempt at conceptualizing stress. *American Psychologist, 44,* 513–524.

Holeva, V., & Tarrier, N. (2001). Personality and peritraumatic dissociation in the prediction of PTSD in victims of road traffic accidents. *Journal of Psychosomatic Research, 51,* 687–692.

Horowitz, M. J., Wilner, N., & Alvarez, W. (1979). Impact of Event Scale: A measure of subjective stress. *Psychosomatic Medicine, 41,* 209–218.

Horwath, E., Johnson, J., Hornig, C. D., (1993). Epidemiology of panic disorder in African-Americans. *American Journal of Psychiatry, 150,* 465–469.

Huffaker, M. L. (2001). Recover for infliction of emotional distress: A comment on the mental anguish accompanying such a claim in Alabama. *Alabama Law Review, 52,* 1003–1027.

Hugo, G. (2003, June). International migration transforms Australia. *Population Reference Bureau.* Retrieved January 25, 2004, from http://www.prb.org.

Human Rights and Equal Opportunity Commission Australia. (1991). *Racist violence: Report of the national inquiry into racist violence in Australia.* Canberra: Australian Government Publishing Service.

Huxley, T. H. (1877). On elementary instruction in physiology. In Ratcliffe, S. (Ed.) *The little oxford dictionary of quotations.* New York: Oxford University Press.

Ibrahim, F. A., & Ohnishi, H. (2001). Posttraumatic stress disorder and the minority experience. In D. B. Pope-Davis & H.L.K. Coleman (Eds.), *The intersection of race, class, and gender in multicultural counseling* (pp. 89–126). Thousand Oaks, CA: Sage.

Ilies, R., Hauserman, N., Schwochau, S., & Stibal, J. (2003). Reported incidence rates of work-related sexual harassment in the United States: Using meta-analysis to explain reported rate disparities. *Personnel Psychology, 56,* 607–631.

Inkelas, M., Loux, L. A., Bourque, L. B., Widawski, M., & Nguyen, L. H. (2000). Dimensionality and reliability of the Civilian Mississippi Scale for PTSD in a post-earthquake community. *Journal of Traumatic Stress, 13,* 149–167.

Iverson, G. L. (2003). Detecting malingering in civil forensic evaluations. In A. M. Horton & L. Hartlage (Eds.), *Handbook of forensic neuropsychology* (pp. 137–177). New York: Springer.

Iverson, G. L., & Binder, L. M. (2000). Detecting exaggeration and malingering in neuropsychological assessment. *Journal of Head Trauma Rehabilitation, 15,* 829–858.

Iverson, G. L., Franzen, M. F., & Hammond, J. A. (1995). Examination of inmates' ability to malinger on the MMPI-2. *Psychological Assessment, 7,* 118–121.

Iverson, G. L., Henrichs, T. F., Barton, E. A., & Allen, S. (2002). Specificity of the MMPI-2 Fake Bad Scale as a marker for personal injury malingering. *Psychological Reports, 90,* 131–136.

James v. Lieb, 375 N.W.2d 109 (Neb. S.Ct. 1985).

Janiak v. Ippolito, 1 S.C.R. 146 (1985).

Janoff-Bulman, R. (1989). Assumptive worlds and the stress of traumatic events: Applications of the schema construct. *Social Cognition, 7,* 113–136.

———. (1992). *Shattered assumptions: Towards a new psychology of trauma.* New York: Free Press.

Janzen and Governeau v. Platy Enterprises Ltd., 1 S.C.R. 1252 (1989).

Jaycox, L. H., Foa, E. B., & Morral, A. R. (1998). Influence of emotional engagement and habituation on exposure therapy for PTSD. *Journal of Consulting and Clinical Psychology, 66,* 185–192.

Johnson v. May, 585 N.E.2d 224 (Ill. App. Ct. 1992).

Johnson v. Supersave Mkts., Inc., 686 P.2d 209 (Mont. 1984).

Johnson, H. (1998). Rethinking survey research on violence against women. In R. E. Dobash & R. P. Dobash (Eds.), *Rethinking violence against women* (pp. 23–50). Thousand Oaks, CA: Sage.

Johnson, H., & Au Coin, K. (2003, June). *Family violence in Canada: A statistical profile 2003.* Retrieved May 22, 2004, from http://www.hc-sc.gc.ca/hppb/family violence/pdfs/2003famvioprofil_e.pdf.

Jordan, D. G. (2000). Expanding the potential for recovery of mental anguish damages in the employment setting: A case note on *GTE Southwest, Inc. v. Bruce. Baylor Law Review, 52,* 461–485.

Joseph v. Jefferson Parish Fire Department, 761 So.2d 801 (La. 2000).

Joseph, S. (2000). Psychometric evaluation of Horowitz's Impact of Event Scale: A review. *Journal of Traumatic Stress, 13,* 101–113.

Kamphuis, J. H., & Emmelkamp, P.M.G. (2001). Traumatic distress among support-seeking female victims of stalking. *American Journal of Psychiatry, 158,* 795–798.

Kardiner, A. (1947). *War, stress, and neurotic illness.* New York: Paul B. Hoeber.

Kaysen, D., Resick, P., & Wise, D. (2003). Living in danger: The impact of chronic traumatization and the traumatic context on posttraumatic stress disorder. *Trauma Violence & Abuse, 4,* 247–264.

Keane, T. M., Buckley, T. C., & Miller, M. W. (2003). Forensic psychological assessment in PTSD. In R. I. Simon (Ed.), *Posttraumatic stress disorder in litigation: Guide-*

lines for forensic assessment (2d ed., pp. 119–140). Washington, DC: American Psychiatric Publishing.

Keane, T. M., Kaloupek, D. G., & Weathers, F. W. (1996). Ethnocultural considerations in the assessment of PTSD. In A. J. Marsella & M. J. Friedman (Eds.), *Ethnocultural aspects of posttraumatic stress disorder: Issues, research, and clinical applications* (pp. 183–205). Washington, DC: American Psychological Association.

Keane, T. M., Malloy, P. P., & Fairbank, J. A. (1984). Empirical development of an MMPI subscale for the assessment of combat-related posttraumatic stress disorder. *Journal of Consulting & Clinical Psychology, 52,* 888–891.

Keane, T. M., Weathers, F. W., & Foa, E. B. (2000). Diagnosis and assessment. In E. B. Foa, & T. M. Keane (Eds.), *Effective treatments for PTSD: Practical guidelines from the International Society for Traumatic Stress Studies* (pp. 18–36). New York: Guilford Press.

Kessler, R. C. (2000). Posttraumatic stress disorder: The burden to the individual and to society. *Journal of Clinical Psychiatry, 51,* 4–12.

Kessler, R. C., Anthony, J. C., Blazer, D. G., Bromet, E., Eaton, W. W., Kendler, K., Swartz, M., Wittchen, H.-U., & Zhao, S. (1997). The U.S. National Comorbidity Survey: Overview and future directions. Editorial. *Epidemiologia e Psichiatria Sociale, 6,* 4–16.

Kessler, R. C., Davis, C. G., & Kendler, K. S. (1997). Childhood adversity and adult psychiatric disorder in the U.S. National Comorbidity Survey. *Psychological Medicine, 27,* 1101–1119.

Kessler, R. C., McGonagle, K. A., Swartz, M., Blazer, D. G., & Nelson, C. B. (1993). Sex and depression in the National Comorbidity Survey: I. Lifetime prevalence, chronicity and recurrence. *Journal of Affective Disorders, 29,* 85–96.

Kessler, R. C., McGonagle, K. A., Zhao, S., Nelson, C. B., Hughes, M., Eshleman, S., Wittchen, H.-U., & Kendler, K. S. (1994). Lifetime and 12-month prevalence of DSM-III-R psychiatric disorders in the United States, results from the National Comorbidity Survey. *Archives of General Psychiatry, 51,* 8–19.

Kessler, R. C., Mickelson, K. D., & Williams, D. R. (1999). The prevalence, distribution, and mental health correlates of perceived discrimination in the United States. *Journal of Health and Social Behavior, 40,* 208–30.

Kessler, R. C., Molnar, B. E., Feurer, I. D., & Appelbaum, M. (2001). Patterns and mental health predictors of domestic violence in the United States: Results from the National Comorbidity Survey. *International Journal of Law and Psychiatry, 24,* 487–508.

Kessler, R. C., Sonnega, A., Bromet, E., Hughes, M., & Nelson, C. B. (1995). Posttraumatic stress disorder in the National Comorbidity Survey. *Archives of General Psychiatry, 52,* 1048–1060.

Kilpatrick, D. G. & Resnick, H. S. (1993). PTSD associated with exposure to criminal victimization in clinical and community populations. In J. R. Davidson & E. B. Foa (Eds.) *Post-traumatic stress disorder in review: Recent research and future directions* (pp. 113–143). Washington, DC: American Psychiatric Press.

Kilpatrick, D. G., Resnick, H. S., Freedy, J. R., Pelcovitz, D., Resick, P. A., & Roth, S. (1998). The posttraumatic stress disorder field trial: Evaluation of the PTSD Construct—Criteria A through E. In T. Widiger, A. Frances, H. Pincus, R. Ross, M. First, W. Davis, & M. Kline (Eds.), *DSM-IV Sourcebook* (Vol. 4, pp. 803–844). Washington, DC: American Psychiatric Association.

Kilpatrick, D. G., Ruggiero, K. J., Acierno, R., Saunders, B. E., Resnick, H. S., & Best, C. L. (2003). Violence and risk of PTSD, major depression, substance abuse/dependence, and comorbidity: Results from the National Survey of Adolescents. *Journal of Consulting and Clinical Psychology, 71,* 692–700.

Kilpatrick, D. G., Veronen, L. J., & Resick, P. A. (1982). Psychological sequelae to rape: Assessment and treatment strategies. In D. M. Doleys, R. L. Meredith, & A. R. Ciminero (Eds.), *Behavioral medicine: Assessment and treatment strategies* (pp. 473–497). New York: Plenum.

Kimerling, R., Ouimette, P., & Wolfe, J. (Eds.). (2002). *Gender and PTSD.* New York: Guilford.

Kimerling, R. E., & Calhoun, K. S. (1994). Somatic symptoms, social support, and treatment seeking among sexual assault victims. *Journal of Consulting and Clinical Psychology, 62,* 33–340.

Kimerling, R., Clum, G., McQuery, J. & Schnurr, P. P. (2002). PTSD and medical comorbidity. In R. Kimerling, P. Ouimette, & J. Wolfe (Eds.), *Gender and PTSD* (pp. 271–302). New York: Guilford.

King, N. S. (1997). Post-traumatic stress disorder and head injury as a dual diagnosis: "Islands" of memory as a mechanism. *Journal of Neurology, Neurosurgery, and Psychiatry, 62,* 82–84.

King, D. W., King, L. A., Gudanowski, D. M., & Vreven, D. L. (1995). Alternative representations of war zone stressors: Relationships to posttraumatic stress disorder in male and female Vietnam veterans. *Journal of Abnormal Psychology, 104,* 184–196.

Kirmayer, L. J., Groleau, D., Guzder, J., Blake, C., & Jarvis, E. (2003). Culture consultation: A model of mental health service for multicultural societies. *Canadian Journal of Psychiatry, 48,* 145–153.

Klar, L. N. (1996). *Tort law* (2d ed.). Scarborough, Ont.: Carswell.

Kleinman, A. (1988a). *Rethinking psychiatry: From cultural category to personal experience.* New York: Free Press.

———. (1988b). A window on mental health in China. *American Scientist, 76,* 22–27.

Koch, W. J., Shercliffe, R., Fedoroff, I., Iverson, G. L., & Taylor, S. (1999). Malingering and litigation stress in motor vehicle accident victims. In E. J. Hickling & E. B. Blanchard (Eds.), *International handbook of road traffic accidents & psychological trauma: Current understanding, treatment, and law.* New York: Pergamon Press.

Koedam, W. S. (2000). Sexual harassment and stalking. In F. Kaslow (Ed.), *Handbook of couple and family forensics: A sourcebook for mental health and legal professionals* (pp. 120–141). New York: Wiley.

Koenen, K. C., Goodwin, R., Struening, E., Hellman, F., & Guardino, M. (2003). Posttraumatic stress disorder and treatment seeking in a national screening sample. *Journal of Traumatic Stress, 16,* 5–16.

Kontorovich, E. (2001). The mitigation of emotional distress damages. *University of Chicago Law Review, 68,* 491–520.

Koopman, B. J. (2003). A rule of which Procrustes would be proud: An analysis of the physical injury requirement in negligent infliction of emotional distress claims under Iowa law. *Drake Law Review, 51,* 361–384.

Koss, M. P. (1990). Changed lives: The psychological impact of sexual harassment. In M. A Paludi (Ed.), *Ivory power: Sexual harassment on campus* (pp. 73–92). Albany, NY: State University of New York Press.

Koss, M. P., Bailey, J. A., Yuan, N. P., Herrera, V. M., & Lichter, E. L. (2003). Depression and PTSD in survivors of male violence: Research and training initiatives to facilitate recovery. *Psychology of Women Quarterly, 27,* 130–142.

Koss, M. P., Gidycz, C. A., & Wisniewski, N. (1987). The scope of rape: Incidence and prevalence of sexual aggression and victimization in a national sample of higher education students. *Journal of Consulting & Clinical Psychology, 55,* 162–170.

Koury v. Lanier Express, Inc., 528 So.2d 734 (La. App. 3rd Cir. 1988).

Krafka, C., Dunn, M. A., Johnson, M. T., Cecil, J. S., & Miletich, D. (2002). Judge and attorney experiences, practices, and concerns regarding expert testimony in federal civil trials. *Psychology, Public Policy, and Law, 8,* 309–332.

Krause, E. D., DeRosa, R. R., & Roth, S. (2002). Gender, trauma themes, and PTSD: Narratives of male and female survivors. In R. Kimerling, P. Ouimette, & J. Wolfe (Eds.), *Gender and PTSD* (pp. 349–381). New York: Guilford.

Kubany, E. S., Hill, E. E., & Owens, J. A. (2003). Cognitive trauma therapy for battered women with PTSD: Preliminary findings. *Journal of Traumatic Stress, 16,* 81–91.

Kubany, E. S., Hill, E. E., Owens, J. A., Iannce-Spencer, C., McCaig, M. A., & Tremayne, K. J. (2004). Cognitive trauma therapy for battered women with PTSD (CTT-BW). *Journal of Consulting and Clinical Psychology, 72,* 3–18.

Kubany, E. S., & Watson, S. B. (2002). Cognitive trauma therapy for formerly battered women with PTSD: Conceptual bases and treatment outlines. *Cognitive and Behavioral Practice, 9,* 111–127.

Kuch, K., Cox, B. J., & Direnfeld, D. M. (1995). A brief self-rating scale for PTSD after road vehicle accident. *Journal of Anxiety Disorders, 9,* 503–514.

Kulka, R. A., Schlenger, W. E., Fairbank, J. A., Hough, R. L., Jordan, B. K., Marmar, C. R., & Weiss, D. S. (1990). *Trauma and the Vietnam War generation: Report of the findings from the National Vietnam Veterans Readjustment Study.* New York: Brunner/Mazel.

———. (1991). Assessment of posttraumatic disorder in the community prospects and pitfalls from recent studies of Vietnam veterans. *Psychological Assessment: A Journal of Consulting and Clinical Psychology, 3,* 547–560.

Kumho Tire Co., Ltd. v. Carmichael, 526 U.S. 137 (1999).

Kurcz, D. (1996). Separation, divorce, and woman abuse. *Violence Against Women, 2,* 63–81.

Kush v. Lloyd, 616 So.2d 415 (Fla. 1992).

Larrabee, G. J. (1997). Neuropsychological outcome, post concussion symptoms, and forensic considerations in mild closed head trauma. *Seminars in Clinical Neuropsychiatry, 2,* 196–206.

———. (1998). Somatic malingering on the MMPI and MMPI-2 in litigating subjects. *The Clinical Neuropsychologist, 72,* 179–188.

———. (2003a). Exaggerated MMPI-2 symptom report in personal injury litigants with malingered neurocognitive deficit. *Archives of Clinical Neuropsychology, 18,* 673–686.

———. (2003b). Detection of malingering using atypical performance patterns on standard neuropsychological tests. *The Clinical Neuropsychologist, 17,* 410–425.

———. (2003c). Detection of symptom exaggeration with the MMPI-2 in litigants with malingered neurocognitive dysfunction. *The Clinical Neuropsychologist, 17,* 54–68.

Larsen, A. (1993). *Workers' compensation law.* New York: Matthew Bender.

Lavik, N. J., Hauff, E., Skrondal, A., & Solberg, O. (1996). Mental disorder among refugees and the impact of persecution and exile: Some findings from an out-patient population. *British Journal of Psychiatry, 169,* 726–732.

LaViolette, A. D., & Barnett, O. W. (2000). *It could happen to anyone: Why battered women stay* (2d ed.). Thousand Oaks, CA: Sage.

Layton, B. S., & Wardi-Zonna, K. (1995). Posttraumatic stress disorder with neurogenic amnesia for the traumatic event. *Clinical Neuropsychologist, 9,* 2–10.

Leark, R. A., Charlton, D., Allen, M., & Gruber, C. (2000). Efficacy of the Malingering Probability Scale to detect malingering in college aged students. *Archives of Clinical Neuropsychology, 15,* 673.

Lee, C., Slade, P., & Lygo, V. (1996). The influence of psychological debriefing on emotional adaptation in women following early miscarriage: A preliminary study. *British Journal of Medical Psychology, 69,* 47–58.

Lee, D., & Young, K. (2001). Post-traumatic stress disorder: Diagnostic issues and epidemiology in adult survivors of traumatic events. *International Review of Psychiatry, 13,* 150–158.

Lee, J., Lei, A., & Sue, S. (2001). The current state of mental health research on Asian Americans. *Psychosocial Aspects of the Asian-American Experience, 3*(3–4), 159–178.

Lee, M. Y., & Law, P.F.M. (2001). Perception of sexual violence against women in Asian American communities. *Journal of Ethnic & Cultural Diversity in Social Work, 10,* 1–25.

Lees-Haley, P. R. (1992). Efficacy of MMPI-2 validity scales and MCMI-II modifier scales for detecting spurious PTSD claims: F, F-K, Fake Bad Scale, ego strength, subtle-obvious subscales, DIS, and DEB. *Journal of Clinical Psychology, 48,* 681–689.

———. (1997). MMPI-2 base rates for 492 personal injury plaintiffs: Implications and challenges for forensic assessment. *Journal of Clinical Psychology, 53,* 745–755.

Lees-Haley, P. R., & Dunn, J. T. (1994). The ability of naive subjects to report symptoms of mild brain injury, post-traumatic stress disorder, major depression, and generalized anxiety disorder. *Journal of Clinical Psychology, 50,* 252–256.

Lees-Haley P. R., English L. T., & Glenn W. J. (1991). A Fake Bad Scale on the MMPI-2 for personal injury claimants. *Psychological Reports, 68,* 203–210.

Lees-Haley, P. R., & Fox, D. D. (1990). MMPI Subtle-Obvious scales and malingering: Clinical versus simulated scores. *Psychological Reports, 66,* 907–911.

———. (2004). Commentary on Butcher, Arbisi, Atlis, and McNulty (2003) on the Fake Bad Scale. *Archives of Clinical Neuropsychology, 19,* 333–336.

Lees-Haley, P. R., Iverson, G. L., Lange, R. T., Fox, D. D., & Allen, L. M. (2002). Malingering in forensic neuropsychology: Daubert and the MMPI-2. *Journal of Forensic Neuropsychology, 3,* 167–203.

Lees-Haley, P. R., Price, J. R., & Williams, C. W. (2001). Use of the Impact of Events Scale in the assessment of emotional distress and PTSD may produce misleading results. *Journal of Forensic Neuropsychology, 2*(2), 45–52.

Leibovitz v. New York City Transit Auth., 4 F.Supp.2d 144 (E.D.N.Y. 1998).

Leo v. Workmen's Compensation Appeal Bd., 537 A.2d 399 (Pa. 1998).

LePage, J., Iverson, G. L., Koehler, B. E., Shojania, K., & Badii, M. (2004, February). An analog study of exaggerated pain and disability in fibromyalgia. Presented at the Canadian Rheumatology Association: Winter Workshop & Annual Meeting, Lake Louise, Alberta.

Levi, R. B., Drotar, D., Yeates, K. W., & Taylor, H. G. (1999). Posttraumatic stress symptoms in children following orthopedic or traumatic brain injury. *Journal of Clinical Child Psychology, 28,* 232–243.

Levit, N. (1992). Ethereal torts. *George Washington Law Review, 61,* 136–175

Levy, A. (1992). Compensation neurosis rides again. *Brain Injury, 6,* 401–410.

Lewis, J. L., Simcox, A. M., & Berry, D.T.R. (2002). Screening for feigned psychiatric symptoms in a forensic sample by using the MMPI-2 and the Structured Inventory of Malingered Symptomatology. *Psychological Assessment, 14,* 170–176.

Lilienfeld, S. O., Lynn, S. J., & Lohr, J. M. (2003). *Science and pseudoscience in clinical psychology.* New York: Guilford Press.

Liljequist, L., Kinder, B. N., & Schinka, J. A. (1998). An investigation of malingering posttraumatic stress disorder on the Personality Assessment Inventory. *Journal of Personality Assessment, 71,* 322–336.

Lilley v. Bd. Of Supervisors of La. State Univ., 735 So.2d 696 (La. Ct. App., 1999).

Lin, K., & Cheung, F. (1999). Mental health issues for Asian Americans. *Psychiatric Services, 50*(6), 774–780.

Lin, K., & Lin, M. (2002). Challenging the myth of a culture free nosological system. In K. S. Kurasaki & S. Okazaki (Eds.), *Asian American mental health: Assessment theories and methods* (pp. 67–73). New York: Kluwer Academic/Plenum Publishers.

Linden, A. M. (1997). *Canadian tort law* (6th ed.). Vancouver, Canada: Butterworths.

Litz, B. T., Miller, M. W., Ruef, A. M., & McTeague, L. M. (2002). Exposure to trauma in adults. In M. M. Antony & D. H. Barlow (Eds.), *Handbook of assessment and treatment planning for psychological disorders* (pp. 215–258). New York: Guilford.

Lo, H., & Fung, K. P. (2003). Culturally competent psychotherapy (special issue). *Canadian Journal of Psychiatry, 48,* 161–170.

Lopez-Ibor, J. J., Jr. (2003). Cultural adaptations of current psychiatric classifications: Are they the solution? *Psychopathology, 36,* 114–119.

Loring, M., & Powell, B. (1988). Gender, race and DSM-III: A study of the objectivity of psychiatric diagnostic behavior. *Journal of Health and Social Behavior, 29,* 1–22.

Louisiana Personal Injury Awards. (2002). Louisiana personal injury awards. *Loyola Law Review, 48,* 819–892.

Lovibond, S. H., & Lovibond, P. F. (1995). *Manual for the depression anxiety stress scales.* Sydney: The Psychology Foundation of Australia.

Lubin, G., Weizman, A., Shmushkevitz, M., & Valevski, A. (2002). Short-term treatment of post-traumatic stress disorder with naltrexone: An open-label preliminary study. *Human Psychopharmacology, 17,* 181–185.

Lucenko, B. A., Gold, S. N., & Cott, M. A. (2000). Relationship to perpetrator and post-traumatic symptomatology among sexual abuse survivors. *Journal of Family Violence, 15,* 169–179.

Lynch v. Knight, 11 Eng. Rep. 854 (1861).

Lynn, E. J., & Belza, M. (1984). Factitious posttraumatic stress disorder: The veteran who never got to Vietnam. *Hospital and Community Psychiatry, 35,* 697–701.

Lytle, R. A., Hazlett-Stevens, H., & Borkovec, T. D. (2002). Efficacy of eye movement desensitization in the treatment of cognitive intrusions related to a past stressful event. *Journal of Anxiety Disorders, 16,* 273–288.

Macklin, M. L., Metzger, L. J., Litz, B. T., McNally, R. J., Lasko, N. B., Orr, S. P., & Pitman, R. K. (1998). Lower precombat intelligence is a risk factor for posttraumatic stress disorder. *Journal of Consulting & Clinical Psychology, 66,* 323–326.

Maes, M., Delmeire, L., Schotte, C., Janca, A., Creten, T., Mylle, J., Struyf, A., Pison, G., & Rousseeuw, P. J. (1998). Epidemiologic and phenomenological aspects of post-traumatic stress disorder: DSM-III-R diagnosis and diagnostic criteria not validated. *Psychiatry Research, 81,* 179–193.

Malmquist, C. P. (1996). The use and misuse of psychiatry in sexual harassment cases. *Psychiatric Annals, 26,* 146–156.

Manitoba Human Rights Act. S. M. 1974, c. 65.

Manson, S. M. (1996). Cross-cultural and multi-ethnic assessment of trauma. In J. P. Wilson & T. M. Keane (Eds.), *Assessing psychological trauma and PTSD: A handbook for practitioners* (pp. 239–266). New York: Guilford Press.

Marrs, S. D. (1992). Mind over body: Trends regarding the physical injury requirement in negligent infliction of emotional distress and "fear of disease" cases. *Tort and Insurance Law Journal, 28,* 1–39.

Marsella, A. J. (1988). Cross-cultural research on severe mental disorders: Issues and findings (Supp.). *Acta Psychiatrica Scandinavica, 78*(344), 7–22.

Marsella, A. J. (1998). Toward a "global-community psychology": Meeting the needs of a changing world. *American Psychologist, 53*(12), 1282–1291.

Marsella, A. J., Friedman, M. J., Gerrity, E. T., & Scurfield, R. M., (1996). *Ethnocultural aspects of posttraumatic stress disorder: Issues, research, and clinical applications.* Washington, DC: American Psychological Association.

Marsella, A. J., & Kameoka, V. A. (1989). Ethnocultural issues in the assessment of psychopathology. In S. Wetzler (Ed.), *Measuring mental illness: Psychometric assessment for clinicians* (pp. 231–256). Washington, DC: American Psychiatric Association.

Marshall, L. L. (1992). Development of the severity of violence against women scales. *Journal of Family Violence, 7,* 103–121.

Marshall, R. D., Spitzer, R., & Liebowitz, M. (1999). Review and critique of the new DSM-IV diagnosis of acute stress disorder. *American Journal of Psychiatry, 156,* 1677–1685.

Max, J. E., Castillo, C. S., Robin, D. A., Lindgren, S. D., Smith, W .L., Sato, Y., & Arndt, S. (1998). Posttraumatic stress symptomatology after childhood traumatic brain injury. *Journal of Nervous and Mental Disease, 186,* 589–596.

Mayou, R. A., Ehlers, A., & Bryant, B. (2002). Posttraumatic stress disorder after motor vehicle accidents: Three-year follow-up of a prospective longitudinal study. *Behaviour Research and Therapy, 40,* 853–865.

Mayou, R. A., Ehlers, A., & Hobbs, M. (2000). Psychological debriefing for road traffic accident victims. *British Journal of Psychiatry, 176,* 589–593.

McCall, G. J., & Resick, P. A. (2003). A pilot study of PTSD symptoms among Kalahari Bushmen. *Journal of Traumatic Stress, 16,* 445–450.

McCullough, R. C. (2003). Emotional distress damages: Should they be permitted under the bankruptcy code for a wilful violation of the stay? *DePaul Business and Commercial Law Journal, 1,* 339–360.

McCusker, P. J., Moran, M. J., Serfass, L., & Peterson, K. H. (2003). Comparability of the MMPI-2 F(p) and F scales and the SIRS in clinical use with suspected malingerers. *International Journal of Offender Therapy and Comparative Criminology, 47,* 585–596.

McDermut, J. F., Haaga, D.A.F., & Kirk, L. (2000). An evaluation of stress symptoms associated with academic sexual harassment. *Journal of Traumatic Stress, 13,* 397–411.

McDonough v. Workmen's Compensation Appeal Bd., 470 A.2d 1099 (Pa. 1984).

McFarland, C., Ross, M., & DeCourville, N. (1989). Women's theories of menstruation and biases in recall of menstrual symptoms. *Journal of Personality and Social Psychology, 57,* 522–531.

McFarlane, A. C. (1988). The phenomenology of posttraumatic stress disorders following a natural disaster. *Journal of Nervous & Mental Disease, 176,* 22–29.

McFarlane, J. M., Campbell, J. C., Wilt, S., Sachs, C. J., Ulrich, Y., & Xu, X. (1999). Stalking and intimate partner femicide. *Homicide Studies: An Interdisciplincary & International Journal, 3,* 300–316.

McKinney, K. (1990). Sexual harassment of university faculty by colleagues and students. *Sex Roles, 23,* 421–438.

———. (1992). Contrapower sexual harassment: The effects of student sex and type of behavior on faculty perception. *Sex Roles, 27,* 1–17.

McLeod, J. D., & Kessler, R. C. (1990). Socioeconomic status differences in vulnerability to undesirable life events. *Journal of Health & Social Behavior, 31,* 162–172.

Mechanic, M. B., Kaysen, D. L., & Resick, P. A. (2002, March). *Stalking, perceptions of lethality, and post-traumatic responding among recently battered women.* Paper presented at the annual meeting of the American Psychology-Law Society, Austin, TX.

Mechanic, M. B., Weaver, T. L., & Resick, P. A. (2000). Intimate partner violence and stalking behavior: Exploration of patterns and correlates in a sample of acutely battered women, *Violence and Victims, 15,* 55–72.

Mellman, T. A., Byers, P. M., & Augenstein J. S. (1998). Pilot evaluation of hypnotic medication during acute traumatic stress response. *Journal of Traumatic Stress, 11,* 563–569.

Mellman, T. A., David, D., Bustamante, V., Fins, A. I., & Esposito, K. (2001). Predictors of post-traumatic stress disorder following severe injury. *Depression and Anxiety, 14,* 226–231.

Meloy, J. R. (1998). *The psychology of stalking: Clinical and forensic perspectives.* San Diego, CA: Academic Press.

Melton, G. B., Petrila, J., Poythress, N. G., & Slobogin, C. (1997). *Psychological evaluations for the courts: A handbook for mental health professionals and lawyers* (2d ed.). New York: Guilford Press.

Merckelbach, H., & Smith, G. P. (2003). Diagnostic accuracy of the Structured Inventory of Malingered Symptomatology (SIMS) in detecting instructed malingering. *Archives of Clinical Neuropsychology, 18,* 145–152.

Meritor Savings Bank v. Vinson, 106 S. Ct. 2399 (1986).

Metro-North Commuter R. R. Co. v. Buckey, 521 U.S. 424 (1997).

Meyer, G. J. (2002). Implications of information-gathering methods for a refined taxonomy of psychopathology. In L. E. Beutler & M. L. Malik (Eds.), *Rethinking the DSM: A psychological perspective.* Washington, DC: American Psychological Association.

Meyers, J. E., Millis, S. R., & Volkert, K. (2002). A validity index for the MMPI-2. *Archives of Clinical Neuropsychology, 17,* 157–169.

Mezy, G., & Robbins, I. (2001). Usefulness and validity of post-traumatic stress disorder as a psychiatric category. *British Medical Journal, 323,* 561–563.

Miller, H. (1961). Accident neurosis. *British Medical Journal, 1,* 919–925, 992–998.

Millon, T. (1994). *The Millon Clinical Multiaxial Inventory-III manual.* Minneapolis, MN: National Computer Systems.

Miramon v. Bradley, 701 So.2d 475 (La. App. 1st Cir. 1997).

Mitchell, J. T. (1983, January). When disaster strikes . . . The critical incident stress debriefing process. *Journal of the American Medical Society, 336–339.*

Mitchell, J. T. & Everly, G. S. (1997). *The scientific evidence for critical incident stress management. Journal of Emergency Medical Services, 22,* 86–93.

Molien v. Kaiser Found. Hosps., 27 Cal. 3d 916 (1980).

Molnar, B. E., Buku, S. L., & Kessler, R. C. (2001). Child sexual abuse and subsequent psychopathology: Results from the National Comorbidity Survey. *American Journal of Public Health, 91,* 753–760.

Morey, L. C. (1991). *Personality Assessment Inventory: Professional manual.* Odessa, FL: Psychological Assessment Resources.

———. (1996). *An interpretive guide to the Personality Assessment Inventory (PAI).* Odessa, FL: Psychological Assessment Resources.

Mott, F. W. (1919). *War neurosis and shell shock.* London, England: Oxford University Press.

Mounteer, J.E. (2004). Depression among lawyers. *The Colorado Lawyer, 33,* 35.

Najavits, L. M., Weiss, R. D., Shaw, S. R., & Muenz, L. R. (1998). "Seeking safety": Outcome of a new cognitive-behavioral psychotherapy for women with posttraumatic stress disorder and substance dependence. *Journal of Traumatic Stress, 11,* 437–456.

Nemiah, J. C. (1995). A few intrusive thoughts on posttraumatic stress disorder. *The American Journal of Psychiatry, 752*(4), 501–503.

Newman, R. L., & Yehuda, R. (1997). PTSD in civil litigation: Recent scientific and legal developments. *Jurimetrics, 37,* 257–267.

Nezu, A. M., Ronan, G. F., Meadows, E. A., & McClure, K. S. (Eds.). (2000). *Practitioner's guide to empirically based measures of depression.* New York: Kluwer Academic.

Nicholls, T. L., & Dutton, D. G. (2001). Abuse committed by women against male intimates. *Journal of Couples Therapy, 10,* 41–57.

Nippoda, Y. (2001). On working with Japanese clients living in the United Kingdom. *Cross-Cultural Psychology Bulletin, 35*(1), 4–13.

———. (2003). Establishing mental health services for the Japanese community in the United Kingdom. *International Journal for the Advancement of Counselling, 25,* 169–180.

Nishith, P., Resick, P. A., & Griffin, M. G. (2002). Pattern of change in prolonged exposure and cognitive-processing therapy for female rape victims with posttraumatic stress disorder. *Journal of Consulting and Clinical Psychology, 70,* 880–886.

Nixon, R. D., & Bryant, R. A. (2003). Peritraumatic and persistent panic attacks in acute stress disorder. *Behaviour Research and Therapy, 41,* 1237–1242.

Norris, F. H. (1990). Screening for traumatic stress: A scale for use in the general population. *Journal of Applied Social Psychology, Special Issue: Traumatic Stress: New perspectives in theory, measurement, and research, 20*(20, Pt. 2), 1704–1718.

———. (1992). Epidemiology of trauma: Frequency and impact of different potentially traumatic events on different demographic groups. *Journal of Consulting and Clinical Psychology, 60,* 409–418.

Norris, F. H., Foster, J., & Weisshaar, D. (2002). The epidemiology of sex differences in PTSD across developmental, societal, and research contexts. In R. Kimerling, P. Ouimette, & J. Wolfe (Eds.), *Gender and PTSD* (pp. 3–42). New York: Guilford.

Norris, F. H., Murphy, A. D., Baker, C. K., & Perilla, J. L. (2003). Severity, timing, and duration of reactions to trauma in the population: An example from Mexico. *Biological Psychiatry, 53,* 767–778.

Norris, F. H., Perilla, J. L., Ibañez, G. E., & Murphy, A. (2001a). Sex differences in symptoms of posttraumatic stress: Does culture play a role? *Journal of Traumatic Stress, 14,* 7–28.

Norris, F. H., Perilla, J. L., & Murphy, A. D. (2001b). Postdisaster stress in the United States and Mexico: A cross-cultural test of the multicriterion conceptual model of Posttraumatic Stress Disorder. *Journal of Abnormal Psychology, 110,* 553–563.

Norris, F. H., Weisshaar, D. L., Conrad, M. L., Diaz, E. M., Murphy, A. D., & Ibañez, G. E. (2001c). A qualitative analysis of posttraumatic stress among Mexican victims of disaster. *Journal of Trauma Stress, 14,* 741–756.

North, C. S. (2001). The course of post-traumatic stress disorder after the Oklahoma City bombing. *Military Medicine, 166,* 51–52.

North, C. S., Nixon, S. J., Shariat, S., Mallonee, S., McMillen, J. C., Spitznagel, E. L., & Smith, E. M. (1999). Psychiatric disorders among survivors of the Oklahoma City bombing. *Journal of the American Medical Association, 25,* 755–62.

North, C. S., Smith, E. M., & Spitznagel, E. L. (1994). Posttraumatic stress disorder in survivors of a mass shooting. *American Journal of Psychiatry, 151,* 82–88.

———. (1997). One year follow-up of survivors of a mass shooting. *American Journal of Psychiatry, 154,* 1696–1702.

Novaco, R. W. (1983). *Stress inoculation therapy for anger control: A manual for therapists.* Unpublished manuscript, University of California, Irvine.

Novaco, R. W., & Chemtob, C. M. (2002). Anger and combat-related posttraumatic stress disorder. *Journal of Traumatic Stress, 14,* 123–132.

O'Brien, S. (2003). Diagnosis and assessment. In I. Z. Schultz & D. O. Brady (Eds.), *Psychological injuries at trial* (pp. 756–792). Washington, DC: American Bar Association.

O'Donnell, M. L., Creamer, M., Bryant, R. A., Schnyder, U., Shalev, A. (2003). Posttraumatic disorders following injury: An empirical and methodological review. *Clinical Psychology Review, 23,* 587–603.

Ogloff, J.R.P., & Douglas, K. S. (2003). Psychological assessment in forensic settings. In J. R. Graham, J. A. Naglieri, & I. B. Weiner (Eds.), *Handbook of psychology, volume 10: Assessment psychology* (pp. 345–363). New York: Wiley.

O'Neill, M. L., & Whittal, M. L. (2002). Thought stopping. In M. Hersen & W. Sledge (Eds.), *Encyclopedia of psychotherapy.* San Diego, CA: Academic Press.

Orsillo, S. M., Raja, S., & Hammond, C. (2002). Gender issues in PTSD with comorbid mental health disorders. In R. Kimerling, P. Ouimette, & J. Wolfe (Eds.), *Gender and PTSD* (pp. 207–231). New York: Guilford.

Ohry, A., Rattok, J., & Solomon, Z. (1996). Post-traumatic stress disorder in brain injury patients. *Brain Injury, 10,* 687–695.

Padget v. Gray, 727 S.W.2d 706 (Tex. Ct. App. 1987).

Page, H. (1885). *Injuries of the spine and spinal cord without apparent mechanical lesion.* London, England: Churchill.

Palarea, R. E., Zona, M. A., Lane, J. C., & Langhinrichsen-Rohling, J. (1999). The dangerous nature of intimate relationship stalking: Threats, violence, and associated risk factors. *Behavioral Sciences & the Law, 17,* 269–283.

Pallone, N. J., & Hennessy, J. J. (2000). Blacks and Whites as victims and offenders in aggressive crime in the U.S.: Myths and realities. In N. J. Pallone (Ed.), *Race, ethnicity, sexual orientation, violent crime: The realities and the myths* (pp. 1–33). Binghamton, NY: The Haworth Press, Inc.

Parker, R. S. (1996). The spectrum of emotional distress and personality changes after minor head injury incurred in a motor vehicle accident. *Brain Injury, 10,* 287–302.

Parker, R. S. (2002). Recommendations for the revision of DSM-IV diagnostic categories for co-morbid posttraumatic stress disorder and traumatic brain injury. *Neuro-Rehabilitation, 17,* 131–143.

Pathé, M., & Mullen, P. (1997). The impact of stalkers on their victims. *British Journal of Psychiatry, 170,* 12–17.

Patton, G. C., Coffey, C., Carlin, J. B., Degenhardt, L., Lynskey, M., & Hall, W. (2002). Cannabis use and mental health in younger people: Cohort study. *British Medical Journal. 325,* 1195–1198.

Penk, W. E., & Allen, I. M. (1991). Clinical assessment of post-traumatic stress disorder (PTSD) among American minorities who served in Vietnam. *Journal of Traumatic Stress, 4,* 41–66.

Perilla, J. L., Norris, F. H., & Lavizzo, E. A. (2002). Ethnicity, culture, and disaster response: Identifying and explaining ethnic differences in PTSD six months after Hurricane Andrew. *Journal of Social & Clinical Psychology, 21,* 20–45.

Perkonigg, A., Kessler, R. C., Storz, S., & Wittchen, H.-U. (2000). Traumatic events and posttraumatic stress disorder in the community: Prevalence, risk factors and comorbidity. *Acta Psychiatrica Scandinavica, 101,* 46–59.

Perkonigg, A., & Wittchen, H.-U. (1999). Prevalence and comorbidity of traumatic events and posttraumatic stress disorder in adolescents and young adults. In A. Maercker, M. Schutzwohl, & Z. Solomon, *Post-Traumatic Stress Disorder: A lifespan developmental perspective* (pp. 113–133). Seattle, WA: Hogrefe & Huber.

Perrin, S., Van Hasselt, V. B., Basilio, I., & Hersen, M. (1996). Assessing the effects of violence on women in battering relationships with the Keane MMPI-PTSD scale. *Journal of Traumatic Stress, 9,* 805–816.

Peters, L., Slade, T., & Andrews, G. (1999). A comparison of ICD10 and DSM-IV criteria for posttraumatic stress disorder. *Journal of Traumatic Stress, 12,* 335–343.

Phelan, J. C., & Link, B. G. (1999). Who are "the homeless"? Reconsidering the stability and composition of the homeless population. *American Journal of Public Health, 89,* 1334–1338.

Pigott, T. A. (2003). Anxiety disorders in women. *Psychiatric Clinics of North America, 26,* 621–672.

Pimlott-Kubiak, S., & Cortina, L. M. (2003). Gender, victimization, and outcomes: Reconceptualizing risk. *Journal of Consulting and Clinical Psychology, 71,* 528–539.

Pitman, R. K., Sanders, K. M., Zusman, R. M., Healy, A. R., Cheema, F., Lasko, N. B., Cahill, L., & Orr, S. P. (2002). Pilot study of secondary prevention of posttraumatic stress disorder with propranolol. *Biological Psychiatry, 51,* 189–192.

Pitman, R. K., Saunders, L. S., & Orr, S. P. (1994). Psychophysiologic testing for post-traumatic stress disorder. *Trial, 30,* 22–26.

Pokrifchak v. Weinstein, 1998 W. L. 303732 (Wash. App. Div. 3 1998).

Poole v. Copland, Inc., 498 S.E.2d 602 (1998).

Population Reference Bureau. (2001, March). Retrieved October, 31, 2003, from http://www.prb.org/template.cfm?Section=QuickFacts#race.

Porter, M., & Haslam, N. (2001). Forced displacement in Yugoslavia: A meta-analysis of psychological consequences and their moderators. *Journal of Traumatic Stress, 14,* 817–834.

Posthuma, A. B., & Harper, J. F. (1998). Comparison of MMPI-2 responses of child custody and personal injury litigants. *Professional Psychology: Research and Practice, 29,* 437–443.

Potter v. Firestone Tire & Rubber Co., 6 Cal.4th 965 (1993).

Powell, T. J., Collin, C., & Sutton, K. (1996). A follow-up study of patients hospitalized after minor head injury. *Disability & Rehabilitation: An International Multidisciplinary Journal, 18,* 231–237.

Poythress, N. G., Edens, J. F., & Watkins, M. M. (2001). The relationship between psychopathic personality features and malingering symptoms of major mental illness. *Law and Human Behavior, 25,* 567–582.

Price, K. P. (1994). Posttraumatic stress disorder and concussion: Are they incompatible? *Defense Law Journal, 43,* 113–120.

Priebe, S., & Bauer, M. (1995). Inclusion of psychological torture in PTSD Criterion A. *American Journal of Psychiatry, 152*(11), 1691–1692.

Purves, D. G., & Erwin, P. G. (2002). A study of posttraumatic stress in a student population. *Journal of Genetic Psychology, 163,* 89–96.

Quaglio v. Tomaselli, 99 A.D.2d 487, 470 N.Y.S.2d 427 (1984).

Quas, J. A., Goodman, G. S., & Jones, D.P.H. (2003). Predictors of attributions of self-blame and internalizing behavior problems in sexually abused children. *Journal of Child Psychology & Psychiatry & Allied Disciplines, 44,* 723–736.

R. v. Mohan, 114 D.L.R. 4th 419 (S.C.C. 1994).

Rachman, S. (1980). Emotional processing. *Behaviour Research and Therapy, 18,* 51–59.

———. (1991). A psychological approach to the study of comorbidity. *Clinical Psychology Review, 11,* 461–464.

———. (1993). Obsessions, responsibility and guilt. *Behaviour Research & Therapy, 31,* 149–154.

Raphael, B., Meldrm, L., & McFarlane, A. C. (1995). Does debriefing after psychological trauma work? Time for randomised controlled trials. *British Medical Journal, 310,* 1479–1480.

Rees, L. M., Tombaugh, T. N., & Boulay, L. (2001). Depression and the Test of Memory Malingering. *Archives of Clinical Neuropsychology, 16,* 501–506.

Rees, L. M., Tombaugh, T. N., Gansler, D. A., & Moczynski, N. P. (1998). Five validation experiments of the Test of Memory Malingering (TOMM). *Psychological Assessment, 10,* 10–20.

Reilly, D., Didcott, P., Swift, W., & Hall, W. (1998). Long-term cannabis use: Characteristics of users in an Australian rural area. *Addiction, 93,* 837–846.

Resick, P. A. (1993). The psychological impact of rape: Special section: Rape. *Journal of Interpersonal Violence, 8,* 223–255.

Resnick, H. S., Best, C. L., Kilpatrick, D. G., Freedy, J. R., & Falsetti, S. A. (1993). *Trauma assessment for adults—Self report version.* Unpublished scale.

Resick, P. A., Nishith, P., Weaver, T. L., Astin, M. C., & Feuer, C. A. (2002). A comparison of cognitive-processing therapy with prolonged exposure and a waiting condition for the treatment of chronic posttraumatic stress disorder in female rape victims. *Journal of Consulting and Clinical Psychology, 70,* 867–879.

Resick, P. A., & Schnicke, M. K. (1992). Cognitive processing therapy for sexual assault victims. *Journal of Consulting and Clinical Psychology, 60,* 748–756.

Resnick, H. R., Falsetti, S. A., Kilpatrick, D. G. & Freedy, J. R. (1996). Assessment of rape and other civilian trauma-related posttraumatic stress disorder: Emphasis on assessment of potentially traumatic events. In T. W. Miller (Ed.), *Theory and assessment of stressful life events* (pp. 235–271). Madison, CT: International Universities Press.

Resnick, H. S., Kilpatrick, D. G., Dansky, B. S., Saunders, B. E., & Best, C. L. (1993). Prevalence of civilian trauma and posttraumatic stress disorder in a representative national sample of women. *Journal of Consulting and Clinical Psychology, 61,* 984–991.

Resnick, P. J. (1997a). Malingering of posttraumatic disorders. In R. Rogers (Ed.), *Clinical assessment of malingering and deception* (2d ed., pp. 130–152). New York: Guilford.

———. (1997b). Malingered psychosis. In R. Rogers (Ed.), *Clinical assessment of malingering and deception* (2d ed., pp. 47–67). New York: Guilford.

Restatement (Second) of Torts. (1979). New York: The American Law Institute.

Rey, J. M., & Tennant, C. C. (2002). Cannabis and mental health. *British Medical Journal, 325,* 1183–1184.

Reynolds, C. R. (Ed.). (1998). *Detection of malingering during head injury litigation.* New York: Plenum Press.

Reynolds, M., & Tarrier, N. (1996). Monitoring of intrusions in post-traumatic stress disorder: A report of single case studies. *British Journal of Medical Psychology, 69,* 371–379.

Rhodes, N. R., & McKenzie, E. B. (1998). Why do battered women stay? Three decades of research. *Aggression & Violent Behavior, 3,* 391–406.

Rice, D. P., & Miller, L. S. (1998). Health economics and cost implications of anxiety and other mental disorders in the United States. *British Journal of Psychiatry, 173*(suppl. 34), 4–9.

Riggs, D. S., Dancu, C. V., Gershuny, B. S., Greenberg, D., & Foa, E. B. (1992). Anger and post-traumatic stress disorder in female crime victims. *Journal of Traumatic Stress, 5,* 613–625.

Riggs, D. S., Rothbaum, B. O., & Foa, E. B. (1995). A prospective examination of symptoms of posttraumatic stress disorder in victims of nonsexual assault. *Journal of Interpersonal Violence, 10,* 201–214.

Rind, B., Tromovitch, P., & Bauserman, R. (1998). Meta-analytic examination of assumed properties of child sexual abuse using college samples. *Psychological Bulletin, 124,* 22–53.

Ritsher, J. B., Struening, E. L., Hellman, F., & Guardino, M. (2002). Internal validity of an anxiety disorder screening instrument across five ethnic groups. *Psychiatry Research, 111*(2–3), 199–213.

Roberts, J. V. (1995). *Disproportionate harm: Hate crime in Canada.* Canada: Department of Justice. Retrieved January 3, 2005, from http://canada.justice.gc.ca/en/ps/rs/rep/wd95-11a-e.pdf.

Robichaud v. Canada (Treasury Board), 2 S.C.R. 84 (1987).

Robins, L. N., Helzer, J. E., Cottler, L., & Golding, E. (1989). *Diagnostic Interview Schedule, Version III Revised.* St. Louis, MO: Washington University.

Robins, L. N., Helzer, J. E., Croughan, J. L., & Ratcliff, K. S. (1981). National Institute of Mental Health diagnostic interview schedule: Its history, characteristics, and validity. *Archives of General Psychiatry, 38,* 381–389.

Robins, L. N., & Regier, D. A. (1991). *Psychiatric disorders in America: The Epidemiologic Catchment Area study.* New York: Free Press.

Rodrigues v. State, 472 P.2d 509 (Hawaii 1970).

Rogers R. (1997). *Clinical assessment of malingering and deception* (2d ed.). New York: Guilford.

———. (2001). *Handbook of diagnostic and structured interviewing.* New York: Guilford Press.

Rogers, R., Hinds, J. D., & Sewell, K. W. (1996). Feigning psychopathology among adolescent offenders: Validation of the SIRS, MMPI-A, and SIMS. *Journal of Personality Assessment, 67,* 244–257.

Rogers, R., Kropp, P. R., Bagby, M. R., & Dickins, S. E. (1992). Faking specific disorders: A study of the Structured Interview of Reported Symptoms (SIRS). *Journal of Clinical Psychology, 48,* 643–648.

Rogers, R., Ornduff, S. R., & Sewell, K. W. (1993). Feigning specific disorders: A study of the Personality Assessment Inventory (PAI). *Journal of Personality Assessment, 60,* 554–560.

Rogers, R., Salekin, R. T., & Sewell, K. W. (1999). Validation of the Millon Clinical Multiaxial Inventory for Axis II disorders: Does it meet the *Daubert* Standard? *Law and Human Behavior, 23,* 425–443.

Rogers, R., Sewell, K. W., Martin, M. A., & Vitacco, M. J. (2003). Detection of feigned mental disorders: a meta-analysis of the MMPI-2 and malingering. *Assessment, 10,* 160–177.

Rogers, R., Sewell, K. W., Morey, L. C., & Ustad, K. L. (1996). Detection of feigned mental disorders on the Personality Assessment Inventory: A discriminant analysis. *Journal of Personality Assessment, 67,* 629–640.

Rogers, R., Sewell, K. W., & Salekin, R. T. (1994). A meta-analysis of malingering on the MMPI-2. *Assessment, 1,* 227–237.

Rogers, R., Sewell, K. W., & Ustad, K. L. (1995). Feigning among chronic outpatients on the MMPI-2: A systematic examination of fake-bad indicators. *Assessment, 2,* 81–89.

Rogers, S., Silver, S. M., Goss, J., Obenchain, J., Willis, A., & Whitney, R. L. (1999). A single session, group study of exposure and Eye Movement Desensitization and Reprocessing in treating Posttraumatic Stress Disorder among Vietnam war veterans: Preliminary data. *Journal of Anxiety Disorders, 13,* 119–130.

Romeo, L. M. (1997). A case-by-case analysis: Connecticut adopts the foreseeability test for bystander emotional distress in *Clohessy v. Bachelor. Connecticut Law Review, 30,* 325–341.

Ronis, D. L., Bates, E. W., Garfein, A. J., Buit, B. K., Falcon, S. P., & Liberzon, I. (1996). Longitudinal patterns of care for patients with posttraumatic stress disorder. *Journal of Traumatic Stress, 9,* 763–781.

Rose, S., Brewin, C. R., Andrews, B., & Kirk, M. (1999). A randomized controlled trial of individual psychological debriefing for victims of violent crime. *Psychological Medicine, 29,* 793–799.

Rosenheck, R. (2002). Accepting the unacceptable. *Child Abuse and Neglect, 26,* 1005–1006.

Rosenheck, R., & Fontana, A. (1996). Race and outcome of treatment for veterans suffering from PTSD. *Journal of Traumatic Stress, 9,* 343–351.

Rosenheck, R., Fontana, A., & Cottrol, C. (1995). Effects of clinician-veteran racial pairing in the treatment of posttraumatic stress disorder. *American Journal of Psychiatry, 152,* 555–563.

Ross, H. E., Swinson, R., Larkin, E. J., & Doumani, S. (1994). Diagnosing comorbidity in substance abusers. *Journal of Nervous and Mental Disease, 182,* 556–563.

Ross, M. (1989). The relation of implicit theories to the construction of personal histories. *Psychological Review, 96,* 341–357.

Ross, S. R., Millis, S. R., Krukowski, R. A., Putnam, S. H., & Adams, K. M. (2004). Detecting incomplete effort on the MMPI-2: An examination of the Fake-Bad Scale in mild head injury. *Journal of Clinical and Experimental Neuropsychology, 26,* 115–124.

Rothbaum, B. O. (1997). A controlled study of eye movement desensitization and reprocessing for posttraumatic stress disordered sexual assault victims. *Bulletin of the Menninger Clinic, 61,* 317–334.

Rothbaum, B. O., Foa, E. B., Riggs, D. S., Murdock, T., & Walsh, W. (1992). A prospective examination of Post-traumatic Stress Disorder in rape victims. *Journal of Traumatic Stress, 5,* 455–475.

Rothke, S. E., Friedman, A., Dahlstrom, W., Greene, R., Arredondo, R., & Mann, A. (1994). MMPI-2 normative data for the F-K Index: Implications for clinical, neuropsychological, and forensic practice. *Assessment, 1,* 1–15.

Rothke, S. E., Friedman, A. F., Jaffe, A. M., Greene, R. L., Wetter, M. W., & Cole, P., et al. (2000). Normative data for the F(p) scale of the MMPI-2: Implications for clinical and forensic assessment of malingering. *Psychological Assessment, 12,* 335–340.

Rowan, A. B., Foy, D. W., Rodriguez, N., & Ryan, S. (1994). Posttraumatic stress disorder in a clinical sample of adults sexually abused as children. *Child Abuse and Neglect, 18,* 51–61.

Roysircar-Sodowsky, F., & Kuo, P. Y. (2001). Determining cultural validity of personality assessment: Some guidelines. In D. B. Pope-Davis & H.L.K. Coleman (Eds.), *The intersection of race, class, and gender in multicultural counseling* (pp. 213–239). Thousand Oaks, CA: Sage.

Rudmin, F. (2003). Acculturation: Advances in theory, measurement, and applied research. *Journal of Cross-Cultural Psychology, 34,* 751–753.

Ruef, A. M., Litz, B. T., & Schlenger, W. E. (2000). Hispanic ethnicity and risk for combat-related posttraumatic stress disorder. *Cultural Diversity & Ethnic Minority Psychology, 6,* 235–251.

Ruggiero, K. J., Del Ben, K., Scotti, J. R., & Rabalais, A. E. (2003). Psychometric properties of the PTSD Checklist—Civilian Version. *Journal of Traumatic Stress, 16,* 495–502.

Ryan v. Workmen's Compensation Appeal Bd., 707 A.2d 1130 (Pa. 1998).

Saigh, P. A., & Bremner, J. D. (1999). The history of posttraumatic stress disorder. In P. A. Saigh & J. D. Bremner (Eds.), *Posttraumatic stress disorder: A comprehensive text* (pp. 1–17). Needham Heights, MA: Allyn & Bacon.

Salant, T., & Lauderdale, D. S. (2003). Measuring culture: A critical review of acculturation and health in Asian immigrant populations. *Social Science & Medicine, 57,* 71–90.

Samra, J., & Koch, W. J. (2002). The monetary worth of psychological injury: What are litigants suing for? In J.R.P. Ogloff (Ed.), *Taking psychology and law into the twenty-first century.* New York: Kluwer Academic.

Sattler, D. N., Preston, A. J., Kaiser, C. F., Olivera, V. E., Valdez, J., & Schlueter, S. (2002). Hurricane Georges: A cross-national study examining preparedness, resources loss, and psychological distress in the U.S. Virgin Islands, Puerto Rico, Dominican Republic, and the United States. *Journal of Traumatic Stress, 15*(5), 339–350.

Saunders, B. E., Arata, C. M., & Kilpatrick, D. G. (1990). Development of a crime-related post-traumatic stress disorder scale for women within the Symptom Checklist-90—revised. *Journal of Traumatic Stress, 3*(3), 439–448.

Saunders, B. E., Villeponteaux, L. A., Lipovsky, J. A., Kilpatrick, D. G., & Veronen, L. J. (1992). Child sexual assault as a risk factor for mental disorders among women. *Journal of Interpersonal Violence, 7,* 189–204.

Saxe, G., Stoddar, F., Courtney, D., Cunningham, K., Chawla, N., Sheridan, R., King, D., & King, L. (2001). Relationship between acute morphine and the course of PTSD in children with burns. *Journal of the American Academy of Child and Adolescent Psychiatry, 40,* 915–921.

Saxe, G., & Wolfe, J. (1999). Gender and posttraumatic stress disorder. In P. Saigh & J. D. Bremner (Eds.), *Posttraumatic Stress Disorder: A comprehensive text* (pp. 160–179). Boston: Allyn & Bacon.

Sbordone, R. J., & Liter, J. C. (1995). Mild traumatic brain injury does not produce post-traumatic stress disorder. *Brain Injury, 9,* 405–412.

Scheeringa, M. S., Zeanah, C. H., Drell, M. J., & Larrieu, J. A. (1995). Two approaches to the diagnosis of posttraumatic stress disorder in infancy and early childhood. *Journal of American Academy of Child and Adolescent Psychiatry, 34*(2), 191–200.

Scheibe, S., Bagby, R. M., Miller, L. S., & Dorian, B. J. (2001). Assessing posttraumatic stress disorder with the MMPI-2 in a sample of workplace accident victims. *Psychological Assessment, 13,* 369–374.

Schell, B. H. (2003). The prevalence of sexual harassment, stalking, and false victimization syndrome (FVS) cases and related human resource management policies in a cross-section of Canadian companies from January 1995 through January 2000. *Journal of Family Violence, 18,* 251–360.

Schnapper, E. (1999). Some of them still don't get it: Hostile work environment litigation in the lower courts. *University of Chicago Legal Forum, 277–345.*

Schnurr, P. P., & Green, B. L. (2004). *Trauma and health: Physical health consequences of exposure to extreme stress.* Washington, DC: American Psychological Association.

Schültzwohl, M., & Maercker, A. (1999). Effects of varying diagnostic criteria for post-traumatic stress disorder are endorsing the concept of partial PTSD. *Journal of Traumatic Stress, 12,* 155–165.

Scott, W. J. (1990). PTSD in DSM-III: A case in the politics of diagnosis and disease. *Social Problems, 37,* 294–310.

Seedat, S., & Stein, D. J. (2000). Trauma and post-traumatic stress disorder in women: A review. *International Clinical Psychopharmacology, 15,* S25–S33.

Seedat, S., Stein, D. J., Ziervogel, C., Middleton, T., Kaminer, D., Emsley, R. A., & Rossouw, W. (2002). Comparison of response to a selective serotonin reuptake inhibitor in children, adolescents, and adults with posttraumatic stress disorder. *Journal of Child and Adolescent Psychopharmacology, 12,* 37–46.

Seedat, S., Stein, M. B., Oosthuizen, P. P., Emsley, R. A., & Stein, D. J. (2003). Linking posttraumatic stress disorder and psychosis: A look at epidemiology, phenomenology, and treatment. *Journal of Nervous and Mental Disease, 191,* 675–681.

Senior, G., Lange, R., & Douglas, L. (2003). Detecting psychosocial exaggeration: Base rates of the MMPI-2 validity index in community controls and personal injury claimants. *Archives of Clinical Neuropsychology, 18,* 787.

Shalev, A. Y. (2001). What is posttraumatic stress disorder? *Journal of Clinical Psychiatry, 62*(suppl. 17), 4–10.

Shalev, A. Y., Freedman, S., Peri, T., Brandes, D., & Sahar, T. (1997). Predicting PTSD in trauma survivors: Prospective evaluation of self-report and clinician-administered instruments. *British Journal of Psychiatry, 170,* 558–564.

Shalev, A. Y., Peri, T., Canetti, L., & Schreiber, S. (1996). Predictors of PTSD in injured trauma survivors: A prospective study. *American Journal of Psychiatry, 153,* 219–225.

Shalev, A.Y., Sahar, T., Freedman, S., Peri, T., Glick, N., Brandes, D., Orr, S. P., & Pitman, R. K. (1998). A prospective study of heart rate response following trauma and the subsequent development of posttraumatic stress disorder. *Archives of General Psychiatry, 55,* 553–559.

Shapiro, F. (1999). Eye Movement Desensitization and Reprocessing (EMDR) and the anxiety disorders: Clinical and research implications of an integrated psychotherapy treatment. *Journal of Anxiety Disorders, 13,* 35–68.

Sharp, T. J., & Harvey, A. G. (2001). Chronic pain and posttraumatic stress disorder: Mutual maintenance? *Clinical Psychology Review, 21,* 857–877.

Shay, J. (1991). Learning about combat stress from Homer's *Illiad. Journal of Traumatic Stress, 4,* 561–579.

Shercliffe, R. (2001). *Post-traumatic stress disorder in a civilian context: A quantitative review.* Unpublished doctoral dissertation, Simon Fraser University.

Shultz v. Barberton Glass Co., 447 N.E.2d 109 (Ohio 1983).

Shuman, D. W. (2003). Persistent reexperiences in psychiatry and law: Current and future trends in post-traumatic stress disorder litigation. In I. Z. Schultz & D. O. Brady (Eds.), *Psychological injuries at trial* (pp. 756–792). Washington, DC: American Bar Association.

Shuman, D. W., & Daley, C. E. (1996). Compensation for mental and emotional distress. In B. D. Sales & D. W. Shuman (Eds.), *Law, mental health, and mental disorder* (pp. 294–308). Belmont, CA: Brooks/Cole.

Shupe, E. I., Corina, L. M., Ramos, A., Fitzgerald, L. F., & Salisbury, J. (2002). The incidence and outcomes of sexual harassment among Hispanic and non-Hispanic White women: A Comparison across levels of cultural affiliation. *Psychology of Women Quarterly, 26,* 298–308.

Sidanius, J., & Pratto, F. (1999). *An intergroup theory of social hierarchy and oppression.* New York: Cambridge University.

Silverton, L., & Gruber, C. (1998). *Malingering Probability Scale (MPS).* Los Angeles, CA: Western Psychological Services.

Simon, G., Ormel, J., VonKorff, M., & Barlow, W. (1995). Health care costs associated with depressive and anxiety disorders in primary care. *American Journal of Psychiatry, 152,* 352–357.

Simon, R. I. (1996). The credible forensic psychiatric evaluation in sexual harassment litigation. *Psychiatric Annals, 26,* 139–148.

———. (2003). Forensic psychiatric assessment of PTSD claimants. In R. I. Simon (Ed.), *Posttraumatic stress disorder in litigation: Guidelines for forensic assessment* (2d ed., pp. 41–90). Washington, DC: American Psychiatric Publishing.

Sivec, H. J., Lynn, S., & Garske, J. P. (1994). The effect of somatoform disorder and paranoid psychotic role-related dissimulations as a response set on the MMPI-2. *Assessment, 1,* 69–81.

Slick, D. J., Sherman, E.M.S., & Iverson, G. L. (1999). Diagnostic criteria for malingered neurocognitive dysfunction: Proposed standards for clinical practice and research. *The Clinical Neuropsychologist, 13,* 545–561.

Smith, C. E. (2002). Intentional infliction of emotional distress: An old arrow targets the new head of the hate hydra. *Denver University Law Review, 80,* 1–61.

Smith, D. W., & Frueh, B. C. (1996). Compensation seeking, comorbidity, and apparent exaggeration of PTSD symptoms among Vietnam combat veterans. *Psychological Assessment, 8,* 3–6.

Smith, G. P., & Burger, G. K. (1997). Detection of malingering: Validation of the Structured Inventory of Malingered Symptomatology (SIMS). *Journal of the American Academy of Psychiatry & the Law, 25,* 183–189.

Smith, P. H., Thornton, G. E., DeVellis, R., Earp, J., & Coker, A. L. (2002). A population-based study of the prevalence and distinctiveness of battering, physical assault, and sexual assault in intimate relationships. *Violence Against Women, 8,* 1208–1232.

Southwick, S. M., Morgan, C. A., Nicolaou, A. L., & Charney, D. S. (1997). Consistency of memory for combat-related traumatic events in veterans of Operation Desert Storm. *American Journal of Psychiatry, 154,* 173–177.

Sparr, L., & Pankratz, L. D. (1983). Factitious posttraumatic stress disorder. *American Journal of Psychiatry, 140,* 1016–1019.

Spitzer, R. L., Williams, J.B.W., Gibbon, M., & First, M. B. (1990). *Structured Clinical Interview for DSM-III-R.* Washington, DC: American Psychiatric Press.

Sproule, B. A., Busto, U. E., Somer, G., Romach, M. K., & Sellers, E. M. (1999). Characteristics of dependent and nondependent regular users of codeine. *Journal of Clinical Psychopharmacology, 19,* 367–372.

Statistics Canada. (2000). *Family violence in Canada: A statistical profile 2000.* Ottawa: Canadian Centre for Justice Statistics.

Statistics Canada. (2001). *Canadian crime statistics 2000* (cat. 85–205). Ottawa: Canadian Centre for Justice Statistics.

Statistics Canada (not published). *2000 Revised Uniform Crime Reporting (UCR2) survey.* Ottawa: Canadian Centre for Justice Statistics.

Statistics Canada Census. (2001a). *Canada's ethnocultural portrait: The changing mosaic.* Retrieved January 9, 2004, from http://www.12.statcan.ca/english/census01/products/analytic/companion/etoimm/canada.cfm.

Statistics Canada Census (2001b). *Population statistics for greater Vancouver regional district (census division) British Columbia.* Retrieved March 24, 2004, from http://www.12.statcan.ca/english/profil01/detailslpop2.cfm.

Steele v. Title Realty Co., 478 F.2d 380 (10th Cir. 1973).

Stein, M. B., Jang, K. L., Taylor, S., Vernon, P. A., & Livesley, W. J. (2002). Genetic and environmental influences on trauma exposure and posttraumatic stress disorder symptoms: A twin study. *American Journal of Psychiatry, 159,* 1675–1681.

Stein, M. B., Walker, J. R., & Forde, D. R. (2000). Gender differences in susceptibility to posttraumatic stress disorder. *Behaviour Research and Therapy, 38,* 619–628.

Stein, M. B., Walker, J. R., Hazen, A. L., & Forde, D. R. (1997). Full and partial posttraumatic stress disorder: Findings from a community survey. *American Journal of Psychiatry, 154,* 1114–1119.

Steiner, J. L., Tebes, J. K., Sledge, W. H., & Walker, M. L. (1995). A comparison of the

Structured Clinical Interview for DSM-III-R and clinical diagnoses. *Journal of Nervous and Mental Disease, 183,* 365–369.

Sterling v. Velsicol, 855 F.2d 1188 (6th Cir., 1987).

Stewart, S. H. (1996). Alcohol abuse in individuals exposed to trauma: A critical review. *Psychological Bulletin, 120,* 83–112.

Stewart, S. H., Conrod, P. J., Pihl, R. O., & Dongier, M. (1999). Relations between post-traumatic stress symptom dimensions and substance dependence in a community-recruited sample of substance-abusing women. *Psychology of Addictive Behaviors, 13,* 78–88.

Stewart, S. H., Conrod, P. J., Samoluk, S. B., Pihl, R. O., & Dongier, M. (2000). Posttraumatic stress disorder symptoms and situation-specific drinking in women substance abusers. *Alcoholism Treatment Quarterly, 18,* 31–47.

Stewart, S. H., Ouimette, P., & Brown, P. J. (2002). Gender and the comorbidity of PTSD with substance use disorders. In R. Kimerling, P. Ouimette, & J. Wolfe (Eds.), *Gender and PTSD* (pp. 232–270). New York: Guilford.

Stone, A. (1993). Post-traumatic stress disorder and the law: Critical review of the new frontier. *Bull Am Acad Psychiatry Law, 21*(1), 23–36.

Storm, J., & Graham, J. R. (2000). Detection of coached general malingering on the MMPI-2. *Psychological Assessment, 12,* 158–165.

Strain v. Donesky (unreported), B.C.J. 350, New Westminster Registry C871072 (B.C.S.C. February 15, 1991).

Straus, M. A. (1999). The controversy over domestic violence by women: A methodological, theoretical, and sociology of science analysis. In X. B. Arriaga & S. Oskamp (Eds.), *Violence in intimate relationships* (pp. 17–44). Thousand Oaks, CA: Sage Publications, Inc.

Strong, D. R., Greene, R. L., & Schinka, J. A. (2000). A taxometric analysis of MMPI-2 infrequency scales [F and F(p)] in clinical settings. *Psychological Assessment, 12,* 166–173.

Sue, D. W., Bingham, R. P., Porché-Burke, L., & Vasquez, M. (1999). The diversification of psychology: A multicultural revolution. *American Psychologist, 54,* 1061–1069.

Sue, S. (2002). Asian American mental health: What we know and what we don't know. In W. J. Lonner, D. L. Dinnel, S. A. Hayes, & D. N. Sattler (Eds.), *Online readings in psychology and culture* (unit 3, chapter 4). Bellingham, WA: Centre for Cross-Cultural Research, Western Washington University. Retrieved January 12, 2004, from http://www.wwu.edu/culture/SueS.htm.

Sue, S., Nakamura, C. Y., Chung, R. C., & Yee-Hradbury, C. (1994). Mental health research on Asian Americans (special issue). *Journal of Community Psychology, 22*(2), 61–67.

Summerfield, D. (2001). The invention of post-traumatic stress disorder and the social usefulness of a psychiatric category. *British Medical Journal, 322,* 95–98.

Summerfield, D. (2002). ICD and DSM are contemporary cultural documents. *British Medical Journal, 324,* 914.

Sundin, E. C., & Horowitz, M. J. (2002). Impact of Event Scale: Psychometric properties. *British Journal of Psychiatry, 180,* 205–209.

Sussman, L. K., Robins, L. N., & Earls, F. (1987). Treatment-seeking for depression by Black and White Americans. *Social Science & Medicine, 24*(3), 187–196.

Sweet, J. J. (1999). Malingering: Differential diagnosis. In J. J. Sweet (Ed.), *Forensic neuropsychology: Fundamentals and practice.* Lisse, Holland: Swets & Zeitlinger Publishers.

Takeuchi, D. T., & Uehara, E. S. (1996). Ethnic minority mental health services: Current research and future conceptual directions. In B. L. Levin & J. Petrila (Eds.), *Mental health services: A public health perspective* (pp. 63–80). New York: Oxford University Press.

Tan, J. E., Slick, D. J., Strauss, E., & Hultsch, D. F. (2002). How'd they do it? Malingering strategies on symptom validity tests. *The Clinical Neuropsychologist, 16,* 495–505.

Tarrier, N., Pilgrim, H., Sommerfield, C., Faragher, B., Reynolds, M., Graham, E., & Barrowclough, C. (1999). A randomized trial of cognitive therapy and imaginal exposure in the treatment of chronic posttraumatic stress disorder. *Journal of Consulting and Clinical Psychology, 67,* 13–18.

Tarrier, N., Sommerfield, C., & Pilgrim, H. (1999). Relatives' expressed emotion (EE) and PTSD treatment outcome. *Psychological Medicine, 29,* 808–811.

Tarrier, N., Sommerfield, C., Pilgrim, H., & Faragher, B. (2000). Factors associated with outcome of cognitive-behavioural treatment of chronic post-traumatic stress disorder. *Behaviour Research & Therapy, 38,* 191–202.

Tarrier, N., Sommerfield, C., Reynolds, M., & Pilgrim, H. (1999). Symptom self-monitoring in the treatment of posttraumatic stress disorder. *Behavior Therapy, 30,* 597–605.

Task Force on Promotion and Dissemination of Psychological Procedures (1995). Training in and dissemination of empirically-validated psychological treatments: Report and recommendations. *The Clinical Psychologist, 48,* 3–23.

Taylor, J. E., & Deane, F. P. (2000). Comparison and characteristics of motor vehicle accident (MVA) and non-MVA driving fears. *Journal of Anxiety Disorders, 14,* 281–298.

Taylor, J., Deane, F., & Podd, J. (2002). Driving-related fear: A review. *Clinical Psychology Review, 22,* 631–645.

Taylor, S., Fedoroff, I. C., Koch, W. J., Thordarson, D. S., Fecteau, G., & Nicki, R. M. (2001). Posttraumatic stress disorder arising after road traffic collisions: Patterns of response to cognitive-behavior therapy. *Journal of Consulting and Clinical Psychology, 69,* 541–551.

Taylor, S., Kuch, K., Koch, W., Crockett, D. J., & Passey, G. (1998). The structure of posttraumatic stress symptoms. *Journal of Abnormal Psychology, 107,* 154–160.

Taylor, S., Thordarson, D. S., Maxfield, L., Fedoroff, I. C., Lovell, K., & Ogrodniczuk, J. (2003). Comparative efficacy, speed, and adverse effects of three PTSD treatments: Exposure therapy, EMDR, and relaxation. *Journal of Consulting and Clinical Psychology, 71,* 330–338.

Teichner, G., & Wagner, M. T. (2004). The Test of Memory Malingering (TOMM): normative data from cognitively intact, cognitively impaired, and elderly patients with dementia. *Archives of Clinical Neuropsychology, 19,* 455–464.

Terr, L. C. (1985). Children traumatized in small groups. In S. Eth, & R. S. Pynoos (Eds.), *Post-traumatic stress disorder in children* (pp. 45–70). Washington, DC: American Psychiatric Press.

Texeira, M. T. (2002). "Who protects and serves me?" A case study of sexual harassment of African American women in one U.S. law enforcement agency (special issue). *Gender & Society, 16,* 524–545.

Theriault v. Swan, 558 A.2d 369 (Me. 1989).

Thing v. La Chusa, 771 P.2d 814 (Cal. 1989).

Thorunn, F., & Ask, E. (2002). Posttraumatic sequelae in a community hit by an avalanche. *Journal of Traumatic Stress, 15,* 479–485.

Tjaden, P., & Thoennes, N. (2000). *Full report of the prevalence, incidence, and consequences of violence against women: Findings from the Violence Against Women Survey*. Washington, DC: U.S. Department of Justice. Retrieved January 3, 2005, from http://www.ncjrs.org/pdffiles1s/nij/183781.pdf.

Tolin, D. F., & Foa, E. B. (2002). Gender and PTSD: A cognitive model. In R. Kimerling & P. Ouimette (Eds.), *Gender and PTSD* (pp. 76–97). New York: Guilford Press.

Tollefson, G. D., Souetre, E., Thomander, L., & Potvin, J. H. (1993). Comorbid anxious signs and symptoms in major depression: Impact on functional work capacity and comparative treatment outcome. *International Clinical Psychopharmacology, 8*, 281–293.

Tomb, D. A. (1994). The phenomenology of post-traumatic stress disorder. *Psychiatric Clinics of North America, 17*, 237–250.

Tombaugh, T. N. (1997). The Test of Memory Malingering (TOMM): Normative data from cognitively intact and cognitively impaired individuals. *Psychological Assessment, 9*, 260–268.

Trevino v. Southwestern Bell Tel. Co., 582 S.W.2d 582 (Tex. Civ. App.-Corpus Christi 1979).

Troisi, A., Pasini, A., Saracco, M., & Spalletta, G. (1998). Psychiatric symptoms in male cannabis users not using other illicit drugs. *Addiction, 93*, 487–492.

Tsushima, W. T., & Tsushima, V. G. (2001). Comparison of the Fake Bad Scale and other MMPI-2 validity scales with personal injury litigants. *Assessment, 8*, 205–212.

Tuohey, C. G., & Gonzalez, F. V. (2001). Emotional distress issues raised by the release of toxic and other hazardous materials. *Santa Clara Law Review, 41*, 661–775.

Turner, H. (1994). Gender and social support: Taking the bad with the good. *Sex Roles, 30*, 521–541.

Turner, R. J. (1999). Social support and coping. In A. V. Horwitz & T. L. Scheid (Eds.), *A handbook for the study of mental health: Social contexts, theories, and systems* (pp. 198–210). New York: Cambridge University Press.

UK Department of Health. (2003). *Minority Ethnic Communities and Health Publications*. Retrieved January 12, 2004, from http://www.doh.gov.uk/minorityhealth/publications.htm.

Ullman, S. E., & Filipas, H. H. (2001). Predictors of PTSD symptom severity and social reactions in sexual assault victims. *Journal of Traumatic Stress, 14*, 369–389.

The uniqueness of the DSM definition of post-traumatic stress disorder: Implications for research. (2002). *Psychological Medicine, 32*, 573–576.

United States Meritor System's Protection Board. (1988). *Sexual harassment in the federal government: An update*. Washington, DC: Government Printing Office. Retrieved January 3, 2005, from http://www.mith2.umd.edu/WomensStudies/GenderIssues/SexualHarassment/MSPBReport/.

Ursano, R. J., Fullerton, C. S., Epstein, R. S, Crowley, B., Kao, T., Vance, K., Craig, K. J., Dougall, A. L., & Baum, A. (1999). Acute and chronic posttraumatic stress disorder in motor vehicle accident victims. *American Journal of Psychiatry, 156*, 589–595.

U.S. Census Bureau. (2001). *U.S. Census 2000, Summary Files 1 and 2*. Retrieved on January 25, 2004, from http://www.census.gov/main/www/cen2000.html.

U.S. Department of Health and Human Services. (2001). *Mental health: Culture, race and ethnicity—A supplement to mental health: A report of the surgeon general*. Rockville, MD: Office of the Surgeon General. Retrieved January 3, 2005, from http://media.shs.net/ken/pdf/SMA-01-3613/sma-01-3613A.pdf.

Vaidya, N. A., & Garfield, D. A. (2003). A comparison of personality characteristics of patients with posttraumatic stress disorders and substance dependence: Preliminary findings. *Journal of Nervous & Mental Disease, 191,* 616–618.

Vandiver, T., & Sher, K. J. (1991). Temporal stability of the Diagnostic Interview Schedule. *Psychological Assessment, 3,* 277–281.

van Minnen, A., Arntz, A., & Keijsers, G.P.J. (2002). Prolonged exposure in patients with chronic PTSD: Predictors of treatment outcome and dropout. *Behaviour Research & Therapy, 40,* 439–457.

Veronen, L. J., & Kilpatrick, D. G. (1983). Stress management for rape victims. In D. Meichenbaum & M. E. Jaremko (Eds.), *Stress reduction and prevention* (pp. 341–374). New York: Plenum.

Vickery, C. D., Berry, D.T.R., Inman, T. H., Harris, M. J., & Orey, S. A. (2001). Detection of inadequate effort on neuropsychological testing: A meta-analytic review of selected procedures. *Archives of Clinical Neuropsychology, 16,* 45–73.

Vincent, C., Chamberlain, K., & Long, N. (1994). Relation of military service variables to posttraumatic stress disorder in New Zealand Vietnam War veterans. *Military Medicine, 159,* 322–326.

Vogel, L.C.M., & Marshall, L. L. (2001). PTSD symptoms and partner abuse: Low income women at risk. *Journal of Traumatic Stress, 14,* 569–584.

Vreven, D. L., Gudanowski, D. M., King, L. A., & King, D. W. (1995). The civilian version of the Mississippi PTSD Scale: A psychometric evaluation. *Journal of Traumatic Stress, 8,* 91–109.

Waddams, S. M. (1997). *The law of damages* (3d ed.). Toronto, ON: Canada Law Book.

Waldo, C. R., Berdahl, J. L., & Fitzgerald, L. F. (1998). Are men sexually harassed? If so, by whom? *Law & Human Behavior, 22,* 59–79.

Walters, G. L., & Clopton, J. R. (2000). Effect of symptom information and validity scale information on the malingering of depression on the MMPI-2. *Journal of Personality Assessment, 75,* 183–199.

Ward, C. H., Beck, A. T., Mendelson, M., Mock, J. E., & Erbaugh, J. K. (1962). The psychiatric nomenclature. *Archives of General Psychiatry, 7,* 198–205.

Warden, D. L., Labbate, L. A., Salazar, A. M., & Nelson, R. (1997). Posttraumatic stress disorder in patients with traumatic brain injury and amnesia for the event. *Journal of Neuropsychiatry and Clinical Neurosciences, 9,* 18–22.

Watson, D. (1999). Dimensions underlying the anxiety disorders: A hierarchical perspective. *Current Opinion in Psychiatry, 12,* 181–186.

Weathers, F., & Ford, J. (1996). Psychometric review of PTSD Checklist. In B. H. Stamm (Ed.), *Measurement of stress, trauma, and adaptation* (pp. 250–251). Lutherville, MD: Sidran Press.

Weathers, F. W., Keane, T. M., & Davidson, J. R. (2001). Clinician administered PTSD Scale: A review of the first ten years of research. *Depression & Anxiety, 13,* 132–156.

Weathers F., Litz, B. T., Huska J, & Keane T. (1991). *The PTSD Checklist* (PCL). Boston, MA: National Center for PTSD.

Weathers, F. W., Ruscio, A. M., & Keane, T. M. (1999). Psychometric properties of nine scoring rules for the Clinician-Administered Posttraumatic Stress Disorder Scale. *Psychological Assessment, 11,* 124–133.

Weaver, T. L. (1998). Method variance and sensitivity of screening for traumatic stressors. *Journal of Traumatic Stress, 11,* 181–185.

Webster, R. A., McDonald, R., Lewin, T. J., & Carr, V. J. (1995). Effects of a natural disaster on immigrants and host population. *Journal of Nervous & Mental Disease, 183,* 390–397.

Weinborn, M., Orr, T., Woods, S. P., Conover, E., & Feix, J. (2003). A validation of the test of memory malingering in a forensic psychiatric setting. *Journal of Clinical and Experimental Neuropsychology, 25,* 979–990.

Weinstein, D., Staffelbach, D., & Biaggio, M. (2000). Attention-deficit hyperactivity disorder and posttraumatic stress disorder: differential diagnosis in childhood sexual abuse. *Clinical Psychology Review, 20,* 359–378.

Weiss, D. S., & Marmar, C. R. (1997). The Impact of Event Scale—Revised. In J. P. Wilson & T. M. Keane (Eds.), *Assessing psychological trauma and PTSD* (pp. 399–411). New York: Guilford Press.

Weissman, H. N. (1990). Distortions and deceptions in self-presentation: Effects of protracted litigation on personal injury cases. *Behavioral Sciences and the Law, 8,* 670–674.

Wenzel, S. L., Leake, B. D., & Gelberg, L. (2001). Risk factors for major violence among homeless women. *Journal of Interpersonal Violence, 16,* 739–752.

West v. Zehir (unreported), Alta. J. 818, Action No. 9001–14124 (Alta. Ct. Q.B. August 11, 1997).

Wetter, M. W., Baer, R. A., Berry, D.T.R., & Reynolds, S. K. (1994). The effect of symptom information on faking on the MMPI-2. *Assessment, 1,* 199–207.

Wetter, M. W., Baer, R. A., Berry, D.T.R, Robison, L. H., & Sumpter, J. (1993). MMPI-2 profiles of motivated fakers given specific symptom information: A comparison to matched patients. *Psychological Assessment, 5,* 317–323.

Wetter, M. W., Baer, R. A., Berry, D. T., Smith, G. T., & Larson, L. (1992). Sensitivity of MMPI-2 validity scales to random responding and malingering. *Psychological Assessment, 4,* 369–374.

Wetter, M. W., & Deitsch, S. E. (1996). Faking specific disorders and temporal response consistency on the MMPI-2. *Psychological Assessment, 8,* 39–47.

What is PTSD? (1997). *The American Journal of Psychiatry, 154,* 143–145.

Widiger, T. A., Mangine, S., Corbitt, E. M., Ellis, C. G., & Thomas, G. V. (1995). *Personality Disorder Interview–IV: A Semistructured interview for the assessment of personality disorders.* Odessa, FL: Psychological Assessment Resources.

Wiener, D., & Harmon, L. (1946). *Subtle and obvious keys for the MMPI: Their development* (Advisement Bulletin No. 16). Minneapolis, MN: Regional Veterans Administration Office.

Wiener, D. N. (1948). Subtle and obvious keys for the MMPI. *Journal of Consulting Psychology, 12,* 164–170.

Williams, J.B.W., Gibbon, M., First, M. B., Spitzer, R. L., Davies, M., Borus, J., Howes, M. J., Kane, J., Pope, H. G., Rousaville, B., & Wittchen, H.-U. (1992). The structured clinical interview for DSM-III-R (SCID): II. Multisite test-retest reliability. *Archives of General Psychiatry, 49,* 630–636.

Wittchen, H.-U., Kessler, R. C., Zhao, S., & Abelson, J. (1995). Reliability and clinical validity of UM-CIDI DSM-III-R generalized anxiety disorder. *Journal of Psychiatric Research, 29,* 95–110.

Wittchen, H.-U., Lachner, G., Wunderlich, U., & Pfister, H. (1998). Test-retest reliability of the computerized DSM-IV version of the Munich-Composite International Diagnostic Interview (M-CIDI). *Social Psychiatry & Psychiatric Epidemiology, 33,* 568–578.

Wittchen, H.-U., Uestuen, T. B., & Kessler, R. C. (1999). Editorial. Diagnosing mental disorders in the community: A difference that matters. *Psychological Medicine, 29,* 1021–1027.

Wolfe, J., & Kimerling, R. (1997). Gender issues in the assessment of posttraumatic stress disorder. In J. P. Wilson & T. M. Keane (Eds.), *Assessing psychological trauma and PTSD* (pp. 192–238). New York: Guilford Press.

Wolfe, J., Schnurr, P. P., Brown, P. J., & Furey, J. (1994). Posttraumatic stress disorder and war-zone exposure as correlates of perceived health in female Vietnam War veterans. *Journal of Consulting and Clinical Psychology, 62,* 1235–1240.

Wong, C. M., & Yehuda, R. (2002). Sex differences in posttraumatic stress disorder. In F. Lewis-Hall & T. S. Williams (Eds.), *Psychiatric illness in women: Emerging treatments and research.* Washington, DC: American Psychiatric Publishing.

World Health Organization. (1990). *Composite international diagnostic interview (CIDI)— version 1.1.* Geneva: Author.

World Health Organization. (1992). *International statistical classification of diseases and related health problems, 1989 revision.* Geneva: Author.

World Health Organization. (1993). *Composite international diagnostic interview (CIDI).* Geneva: Author.

World Health Organization. (2002). Other risks to health. In *The world health report 2002: Reducing risk, promoting healthy life* (chap. 4). Retrieved from http://www.who .int/whr/2002/chapter4/en/index9.html.

Wright, J. C. & Telford, R. (1996). Psychological problems following minor head injury: A prospective study. *British Journal of Clinical Psychology, 35,* 399–412.

Wyatt, G. E. (1990). Sexual abuse of ethnic minority children: Identifying dimensions of victimization. *Professional Psychology: Research & Practice, 21,* 338–343.

Yehuda, R. (2002). Post-traumatic stress disorder. *New England Journal of Medicine, 346,* 108–114.

Yehuda, R., & McFarlane, A. C. (1995). Conflict between current knowledge about posttraumatic stress disorder and it original conceptual base. *American Journal of Psychiatry, 152,* 1705–1713.

Yehuda, R., McFarlane, A. C., & Shalev, A. Y. (1998). Predicting the development of posttraumatic stress disorder from the acute response to a traumatic event. *Biological Psychiatry, 44,* 1305–1313.

Zayfert, C., Becker, C. B., Unger, D. L., & Shearer, D. K. (2002). Comorbid anxiety disorders in civilians seeking treatment for posttraumatic stress disorder. *Journal of Traumatic Stress, 15,* 31–38.

Zhang, A. Y., Snowden, L. R., & Sue, S. (1998). Differences between Asian and White Americans' help seeking and utilization patterns in the Los Angeles area. *Journal of Community Psychology, 26,* 317–326.

Zlotnick, C., Franklin, C. L., & Zimmerman, M. (2002). Is comorbidity of posttraumatic stress disorder and borderline personality disorder related to greater pathology and impairment? *American Journal of Psychiatry, 159,* 1940–1943.

Zoellner, L. A., Feeny, N. C., Fitzgibbons, L. A., & Foa, E. B. (1999). Response of African American and Caucasian women to cognitive behavioral therapy for PTSD. *Behavior Therapy, 30,* 581–589.

Zoellner, L. A., Foa, E. B., & Bartholomew, D. B. (1999). Interpersonal friction and PTSD in female victims of sexual and nonsexual assault. *Journal of Traumatic Stress, 12,* 689–700.

Index